W9-CNV-282

AFRICAN ENVIRONMENT AND DEVELOPMENT

KING'S SOAS STUDIES IN DEVELOPMENT GEOGRAPHY

Series Editors:
Robert W. Bradnock and Kathy Baker-Smith

Both the School of Oriental and African Studies and King's College, whose geography departments have recently merged, have established international reputations for their research into these areas. This series publishes original research into all aspects of geography in the developing world, particularly linking environmental and development issues. It will be of critical interest to geographers and academics in the fields of development studies, political science, environmental studies and economics.

Also in the series

Environment, Knowledge and Gender
Local Development in India's Jharkhand
Sarah Jewitt

NGO Field Workers in Bangladesh
Mokbul Morshed Ahmad

Perspectives of the Silent Majority: Air Pollution, Livelihood
and Food Security
Indepth Studies through PRA Methods on Community Perspectives in Urban
and Peri-Urban Areas of Varanasi and Faridabad, India
Amitava Mukherjee

Wide Crossing
The West Africa Rice Development Association in Transition, 1985-2000
John R. Walsh

Water Stress: Some Symptoms and Causes
A Case Study of Ta'iz, Yemen
Chris D. Handley

Global Thinking and Local Action
Agriculture, Tropical Forest Loss and Conservation in Southeast Nigeria
Uwem E. Ite

A Clash of Paradigms: Intervention, Response
and Development in the South Pacific
Susan Maiava

African Environment and Development

Rhetoric, Programs, Realities

Edited by

WILLIAM G. MOSELEY
Macalester College, USA

B. IKUBOLAJEH LOGAN
The University of Georgia, USA

ASHGATE

Published by
Ashgate Publishing Limited
Gower House
Croft Road
Aldershot
Hants GU11 3HR
England

Ashgate Publishing Company
Suite 420
101 Cherry Street
Burlington, VT 05401-4405
USA

Ashgate website: http://www.ashgate.com

British Library Cataloguing in Publication Data
African environment and development : rhetoric, programs,
    realities. - (King's SOAS studies in development geography)
    1. Political ecology - Africa - Congresses 2. Sustainable
development - Africa - Congresses 3. Environmental policy -
Africa - Congresses 4. Environmental economics - Africa -
Congresses 5. Conservation - Africa - Congresses 6. Africa -
Economic policy - Congresses
    I. Moseley, William G. II. Logan, Bernard Ikubolajeh
III. University of London. School of Oriental and African
Studies
304.2'096

Library of Congress Cataloging-in-Publication Data
African environment and development : rhetoric, programs, realities / edited by William G.
Moseley and B. Ikubolajeh Logan.
    p. cm. -- (King's SOAS studies in development geography)
    Includes bibliographical references and index.
    ISBN 0-7546-3904-5
    1. Economic development--Environmental aspects--Africa. 2. Sustainable
development--Africa. 3. Political ecology--Africa. 4. Africa--Economic conditions--1960-
I. Moseley, William G. II. Logan, Bernard Ikubolajeh. III. Series.

HC800.Z9E528 2003
338.967'07--dc22

2003060040

ISBN 0 7546 3904 5

Printed and bound in Great Britain by Athenaeum Press Ltd., Gateshead

Contents

List of Figures and Tables

Figures

Tables

List of Contributors

Jim Bingen, Professor, Department of Resource Development, Michigan State University, USA

Jennifer E. Coffman, Assistant Professor, Department of Sociology and Anthropology, James Madison University, USA

Mirjam de Bruijn, Research Anthropologist, Africa Studies Centre, University of Leiden, The Netherlands

Rachel B. DeMotts, Ph.D. Candidate, Department of Political Science, University of Wisconsin at Madison, USA

Han van Dijk, Research Anthropologist, Africa Studies Centre, University of Leiden, The Netherlands

Emmanuel Kreike, Assistant Professor, Department of History, Princeton University, USA

Paul Laris, Assistant Professor, Department of Geography, California State University at Long Beach, USA

B. Ikubolajeh Logan, Professor, Department of Geography, University of Georgia, USA

William G. Moseley, Assistant Professor, Department of Geography, Macalester College, USA

Phia Steyn, Lecturer, Department of History, University of the Free State, South Africa

Stephen R. Wooten, Assistant Professor, Departments of Anthropology and International Studies, University of Oregon, USA

Preface and Acknowledgements

This book emanates from three organized paper sessions on 'African Rural Livelihoods in a Political Ecology Context' at the 2001 Annual Meeting of the African Studies Association (held November 15-18, 2001 in Houston, Texas, USA). Of the 15 papers presented in those sessions, ten are featured here. The book's contributing authors approach the study of environment and development in Africa from a variety of disciplinary backgrounds (anthropology, geography, history and political science) and are based at institutions located in Africa, Europe and North America. Topics range from those that have received considerable attention in recent years, such as community-based wildlife management in East and southern Africa or burning regimes in West Africa, to issues that are less frequently associated with environment and development studies, such as the environmental impacts of war or cash cropping.

As scholars and editors of this volume, we each approach the environment-development nexus in Africa from slightly different perspectives. The book's editor, William Moseley, is an American who began working in Africa as a United States Peace Corps Volunteer in Mali. This experience led to a ten year term as a development professional, followed by a second career in academia. As a development practitioner, he experienced first hand the often frictional connections between local initiatives and the broader political and economic environment (a primary theme of this book). Try as he might, some projects were destined to flounder if the incentive structure was not conducive to such activity. What he failed to recognize at the time was the influence of dominant environment and development narratives (or widely held truisms) on his conception and design of conservation and development initiatives (a second major theme of this volume). Notions of desertification, poverty-induced environmental degradation, deforestation, soil degradation, ecological equilibrium and inappropriate burning all held sway in the 1980s and 1990s when he was a practicing conservation and development professional.

Subsequent study and reflection have allowed Moseley to put his years of development praxis into perspective. He struggles with the tension that often exists between those who work on the front lines of environment and development and those who study and theorize about the process. He understands that those working to foster conservation and development do not have an easy task, and therefore commentators must be careful to understand the constraints in play before they criticize action. He also believes that conservation and development practitioners often appreciate meaningful criticism, and as such, academics have a useful role to play in the development process as applied critics and theoreticians.

The co-editor of this volume, Ikubolajeh Logan, is a native of Sierra Leone. His approach to environment and development in Africa is both theoretical and applied. He seeks in his work to theorize on an analytical framework within which the dynamics of African development can be properly contextualized and conceptualized. Towards this end, he has argued that the metanarratives of African development, whether mainstream (example, modernization and dualistic theories) or radical (example, dependency and world systems theories), do not provide many insights into the workings of socio-economic structures in Africa. He attributes this theoretical shortcoming to the focus of the metanarratives, first on the historical experiences of the West and second, on the dynamics of the Western capitalist system (to the exclusion of other systems). Every explanation of the development business in Africa proceeds from the assumption that African systems are undynamic and react primarily to the prompting of capital. Thus, for mainstream analysts, African development is a matter of 'capital penetration,' while for radical analysts, African underdevelopment is a matter of global capitalist cooptation of African resources. In neither framework is there an implication that African systems are proactive and adaptive – modifying capital as they are being modified by capital.

Logan adopts the same critical approach in his attempts to elucidate on human environment relationships in Africa. He argues that this relationship can be understood properly only by unbundling the straightforward two variable (population growth and carrying capacity) narrative of mainstream discourse and the one variable (power dynamics) of Wallersteinian structuralist discourse, and linking the two together into a broader ecological narrative. He believes that this reconstituted narrative might make it more possible for development analysts to explore the links between ecological limits, international resource exchange, poverty, overpopulation, etc. Some of these thoughts on human-environment relationships in Africa are reflected in his treatment of sustainable development in chapter two of this volume.

At the applied and policy levels, Logan takes the position that economic development is first and foremost about poverty-alleviation. This focus has necessitated increasingly more frequent jaunts out of the hollowed halls of academia to meet the people who practise policy and the people upon whom policy is practised. Straddling the interface between these two groups has provided him with a stronger sense of the human-environment nexus and further informs his theoretical analyses.

This volume would not have been possible without the help of colleagues and family. We are grateful to the African Studies Association for allowing us to organize the sessions that led to this book. We also express our appreciation to the contributing authors for their patience and tenacity in shepherding their studies through the transition from conference paper to book chapter. We thank Katie Ashton of Macalester College, Ben Prewitt of the University of Georgia and the Ashgate staff for their help with copy editing and formatting. Finally, we are grateful to our families for their support and tolerance while working on this volume.

William G. Moseley   *B. Ikubolajeh Logan*
St. Paul, Minnesota, USA   *Athens, Georgia, USA*

Chapter 1

African Environment and Development: An Introduction

B. Ikubolajeh Logan and William G. Moseley

Introduction

Over the past few decades, scholars, policy makers and other interested groups have shown increasing concern over the state of the global environment. This concern has often found expression in a number of high level, UN sponsored conferences on the topic, including, Stockholm in 1972, Rio in 1992, Kyoto in 1997, and Johannesburg in 2002. A recurring theme at these conferences has been the different emphases placed by the global North and South, respectively, on the importance of environmental conservation versus economic development. A voluminous literature, authored primarily by Northern environmentalists, expresses alarm over 'Southern' problems like biodiversity loss (for example, Tobey, 1993; Swanson, 1996), deforestation (see, for example, Fearnside, 2001) and human population growth (for example, Cleaver and Schreiber, 1994, Dasgupta, 1996). By contrast, the focus of Southern scholarship and policy prescriptions, especially from Sub-Saharan Africa (subsequently referred to as SSA), seems to be more directed at issues relating to poverty-alleviation and livelihood security (see, for example, Sen, 1981; Mamdani, 1990; Guha, 1997; Logan, 2002). SSA experts have tended to view Northern preoccupation with environmental matters with skepticism, charging that the global environmental movement is part of a post-colonial agenda, which is directed at circumscribing resource autonomy, constricting development alternatives, and undermining national sovereignty on the sub-continent (Moore, 1996; Brockington and Homewood, 1996; Neumann, 1998; Schroeder, 1999; Bassett and Zueli, 2000; Igoe, 2000).

It is not surprising, under these general circumstances, that the environment-development debate has become rather bifurcated along geopolitical and ideological lines, with each side outlining different frames of reference and, therefore, different sets of solutions. The SSA position appeals for equity in global resource distribution to tackle poverty alleviation, perceived (at least in this view) to be the central development problem. As a result, this position directs a great deal of attention to issues of international trade, elimination of debt and debt servicing obligations, relaxation of international conservation treaties like the Convention on International Trade in Endangered Species (CITES), and the socioeconomic burdens associated with World Bank/IMF stabilization and adjustment programs. The Northern position, on the other hand, is founded on three interlinked fundamental propositions: that population growth is at the root of most environmental problems, that poverty-alleviation is impossible without population control; and that poverty-alleviation is not an end, but the means to the greater end of environmental conservation. While the SSA position often offers only rhetoric, the Northern position is often legitimized by scientific models, which find their philosophical heredity in Malthusian logic. Prominent examples of such models include Hardin's Tragedy of the Commons, which engages property rights to explain environmental degradation, the Model of Demographic Transition, which links demographic change to economic change, and the Environmental Kuznets Curve, which links economic change to environmental conservation.

In terms of its far-reaching imprint on SSA policy, perhaps the most important model to emerge from Northern environmental discourse in the past two decades is Sustainable Development (SD). Among other things, this meta-narrative, introduced to the development lexicon by the Brundtland Report of 1987, seeks to assure SSA countries that economic development and environmental conservation are not mutually exclusive goals (for contrasting views on the subject, see, Lele, 1991; Costanza and Patten, 1995; de Graaf *et al.*, 1996; Sneddon, 2000; Fergusson, 2001; Hukkinen, 2001). The SD meta-model acts as a conceptual umbrella for a number of policy models and approaches, including those pertaining to poverty-environment interactions, community-based natural resources management, *gestion de terroir*,[1] range management, and fire suppression. The SD model is used also to make the case that democratic and legal change, which place African communities fully in charge of their resources, is the best way to facilitate marketization and the benefits of improved standards of living and enhanced environmentalism that should follow. Due to its emphases, both on local level democratic change and on market-led development, Logan (2002) has suggested that SD may be viewed as part of a larger globalization agenda in which, according to Peet (2002), models like SD are disseminated through an Academic-Institution-Media (AIM) complex. Peet suggests that the AIM complex constructs the paradigms, which are used by development practitioners to legitimize the financial, political, and environmental objectives of global capital.

In its ascendant role in development, SD has palpable implications for development in SSA on a number of fronts: (i) at the conceptual level, it is used to prescribe and legitimize a particular ideological view of the conservation-development linkage; (ii) at the policy level, it is used to frame an alliance among the activities of the global environmental movement, the global democracy movement, and the global free trade (neoliberal) movement; and (iii) at the level of praxis, it is used to identify and allocate funds for a particular type of development program labeled community-based, grass roots, and local, to use a few descriptive typologies. In all of these ways SD touches on the livelihoods of common individuals and households on the subcontinent.

The Ideological dominance of SD is often manifested in its legitimitation of a particular view of politics, economics and conservation in SSA development. A prominent attribute of SD ideology is its avoidance of political economy and political ecology, a criticism that is borne out by the discourse in leading environment-development journals like *Ecological Economics* and *World Development*. That SD is apolitical, except for its advocacy for local autonomy in community-based development programs is a serious paradox, at least for two reasons. First, poverty-alleviation, ostensibly a focus of SD, has its ideological roots in political economy (perhaps more so than in environmental conservation). Second, SD does stress local political economy (local resource autonomy, community and grass roots participation, community-based development). Yet, in both discourse and praxis, there is serious vacillation by its proponents on issues pertaining to meta-scale political economy. SD discourse skirts around political economy analyses by making an implicit assumption that devolution of political power (democratic change) and an open market regime at the national level are sufficient conditions for improving standards of living at the local level. Unfortunately, neither market-led development, nor the one-person one-vote franchise, has proved useful for eliminating the structures and institutions that marginalize local communities and leave them at the mercy of environmental vicissitudes. In fact, a strong case can be made that without proper theoretical attention to the local, national and international power structures that underpin poverty, it will be impossible to achieve SD. This inherent paradox between the role that SD has set for itself (environmental conservation through poverty-alleviation) and its theoretical avoidance of power politics, adds yet another dimension to the North-South divide in the conservation-development debate.

The dominance of SD in the development-conservation debate and practice in SSA makes it impossible to avoid frequent references to it in a volume of this nature, although the level of attention given to the paradigm varies among chapters (chapter 2 and 3 discuss it to the greatest length). What we have tried to achieve is the elegant balancing act of drawing out the weaknesses of SD, and use that as a launching pad for our focus on political ecology. Within this broad political ecology framework, a very important thrust in nearly all of the chapters is to explore poverty-alleviation through improvements in livelihood systems, defined here, following Ellis (2000, p.10) as, '...the assets (natural, physical, human, financial and social capital), the activities, and the access to these (mediated by institutions and social relations) that together determine the living gained by the individual or household.' Each chapter aims to make either a conceptual or empirical contribution to the general case that poverty, resulting from weak or unstable livelihood systems, often has its roots in power dynamics. Consequently, each chapter reflects on one or a combination of ways in which analyses of power and politics can enhance strategies for sustainable livelihood systems in which real stakeholder participation becomes central to the business of poverty-alleviation. In our view of sustainable livelihood systems, we move beyond Ellis' definition of livelihood to engage Chambers and Conway (1992, p.6) who suggest that '[a] livelihood is sustainable when it can cope with and recover from stresses and shocks and maintains or enhances its capabilities and assets both now and in the future, while not undermining the natural resource base.' Building on this view, many of the chapters attempt to demonstrate that the stresses and shocks that affect livelihood systems at several scales are basically of a political economy nature, and that local environmental issues in Africa are connected intimately to national, regional and global political economies. We do not mean to suggest by this that we are economic determinists (for a discussion of this see Turner, 1997) who believe that broader scale political economic forces drive all outcomes at the local level. Indeed, the case made in many of the chapters is that local politics, ethnic customs and behaviors, and regional ecological characteristics are important influences on local natural resources management.

Political Ecology

The frame of analyses that underlies much of our discussion is political ecology, or the political economy of human-environment interactions (Blaikie and Brookfield, 1987). Political ecology has close ties (and shared histories in some cases) with other interdisciplinary subdisciplines such as cultural ecology, human ecology, ecological anthropology, ecological economics, radical development geography and environmental history. At its best, political ecology analysis seeks to combine a thorough analysis of local level human-environment interactions with well documented connections to relevant (and equally well researched) broader scale phenomena. While political ecology is not without its critics (for example, Peet and Watts, 1996; Vayda and Walters, 1999), we believe its attention to class based differences, scale and historical context, make it a worthy analytical approach for this volume.

Political ecologists believe it is important to study human-environment interactions in their historical, political-economic and spatial context (Blaikie, 1985; Watts, 2000). The approaches adopted by political ecologists that are relevant to this volume include: 1) the examination of inter-linked political and ecological problems (such as soil erosion) in a specific geographic region, often called regional political ecology; 2) the study of a concept, such as deforestation or desertification, to understand how discourses are developed to facilitate or block the promotion of specific interests; 3) the exploration of political-ecological questions in light of gender, ethnicity and class; and 4) a focus on the interests, characteristics and actions of different types of actors in understanding political-ecological conflicts (Bassett, 1988; Bryant and Bailey, 1997). Of course, neither African political ecology scholarship in general, nor all the chapters in this book, fall neatly into these four categories (as there are a number of authors whose works cuts across these divisions).

In the African context, political ecological scholarship has addressed a wide variety of issues using all of the aforementioned approaches. Regional political ecology is probably the oldest approach, dating back to the pioneering work of Blaikie (1985) and Blaikie and Brookfield (1987). A number of studies have been undertaken in Africa using this approach, including, for example, Bassett's (1988) work on farmer-herder conflicts in northern Cote d'Ivoire, Watt's (1983) investigation of famine in northern Nigeria, Neumann's (1997, 1998) studies of human-wildlife conflict in East and southern Africa, and Peters' (1987) examination of the tragedy of the commons paradigm in Botswana. Working within the political ecology tradition, these scholars frequently have made a distinction between the proximate and ultimate causes of environmental degradation. While poverty or hunger, for example, may be the proximate cause of environmental unsustainability, structural inequalities at the global and local levels are often the ultimate driving force. This regional political ecology work clearly builds on the African cultural ecological tradition established by scholars like Mortimore (1989), Tiffen *et al.* (1994), Richards (1985), Adams (1993) and Baker (2000).

The second approach which seeks to interrogate key environmental discourses (and western ecological science more generally), increasingly is referred to as a literature on environmental narratives or orthodoxies. Here the most well known work in Africa probably has been done by Fairhead and Leach (1996) on forest cover trends in Guinea. Others include Swift (1996) on desertification in the Sahel, Behnke *et al.* (1993) on rangelands in southern Africa, and Bassett and Zueli (2000) on deforestation in Côte d'Ivoire. A key critique of the scholarship on environmental narratives, particularly that of Fairhead and Leach, has come from Bernstein and Woodhouse (2001), who suggest that the work does not adequately consider the global capitalist system and its transformative effect on African landscapes.

Related to this political ecology approach on environmental narratives is a broader body of geographical literature on scale analysis. Scale analysis seeks to provide insights into the ways particular agents construct and reconstruct space and the institutions controlling space to fit particular agendas (see, for example, Herod, 1997; Herod and Wright, 2001). We have noted earlier that SD avoids political analysis at the macro scale while focusing on it at the micro scale. This kind of space construction has been shown to be an effective tool used by those in power to maintain control over resources. Scale also can be used to obscure cause and effect in order to privilege a particular type of development program. For example, population growth at the local scale has often been used in conservation discourse to explain global scale environmental problems. In their work in northern Cote d'Ivoire, Bassett and Zueli (2000) explicitly linked scale analysis to the environmental narrative issue via what they referred to as the 'disjointed scale problem' wherein macro scale deforestation was falsely assumed to be indicative of local scale trends by outside development agents.

There are a number of authors who have explored political-ecological questions in light of gender, ethnicity, class and wealth. Among political ecologists working on these issues, gender probably has received the most attention in recent years, including, for example, work by Carney (1996) and Schroeder (1999) in the Gambia, Thomas-Slayter and Rocheleau (1995) in Kenya, and Hodgson (2001) in Tanzania. Attention to ethnicity is an older concern (for example, Bassett, 1988), whereas attention to wealth differences is an emerging issue (for example, Moseley, forthcoming).

Finally, some scholars have focused on different actors to understand resource conflicts. Igoe's (2000) work on conservation NGOs in Tanzania or Bryant and Bailey's (1997) attention to multilateral institutions are good examples of this. As suggested by Igoe's work (2000), an extremely important outcome of SD-led development is the rise to prominence of NGOs as implementers of community based programs (see also, Makoba, 2002; Jordan and Tuijl, 2002; Atack, 1999; Ashman, 2001). The role of NGOs in the SD framework has had implications in various areas, especially in terms of donor funding and the centrality of the African state in development efforts. The case for NGOs in development programming is often based on arguments that they provide a positive example to local communities in the areas of managerial transparency, participatory governance and administrative stability. This view repudiates the African state as a vehicle for development on grounds that it is often undemocratic, cleptocratic, opaque, and ineffective for addressing poverty-alleviation. We do not intend to engage in this debate as a vital thesis of the present volume, but it merits mention that there is not sufficient empirical evidence to support claims of NGO superiority over the state in addressing poverty, particularly as such claims often emanate from the NGO community itself (for example, Igoe, 2000; Glenzer, 2002). As far as the discussions in this volume are concerned, it is sufficient to point out that claims of their administrative virtues notwithstanding, international NGOS are notoriously undemocratic in their interactions with local NGOs and with local communities and that their paternalistic relationships with the African state often undermines their own effectiveness in poverty-alleviation (Glenzer, 2002). As a result, the SSA state whose stability has, at best, always been precarious, has become increasingly marginalized and further weakened by NGO activity. Some states, especially in the south of the sub-continent (for example, Zimbabwe, Botswana, Namibia and to some extent, even the Republic of South Africa), have responded to what they perceive to be an onslaught against state viability by appealing to nationalism. These tensions have added a further dimension of mistrust to the North-South debate over conservation and development.

Recent edited volumes that employ a political ecology approach in Africa tend to focus on a specific issue or sub-theme of political ecology. For example, Benjaminsen and Lund (2001) focused on land tenure, Broch-Due and Schroeder (2000) on poverty-environment interactions and Leach and Mearns (1996) on environmental narratives. Of those books that explore political ecology more broadly (for example, Peet and Watts, 1996; Bryant and Bailey, 1997; Stott and Sullivan, 2000), none exists that is devoted solely to the African continent. This volume employs the four different political ecology approaches described above to explore a broad range of environmental issues in Africa. The first section of this volume largely falls within the environmental narrative tradition, examining key discourses related to sustainable development, poverty-induced environmental degradation and fire suppression. The second and third sections of the book are more in line with the regional political ecology tradition. Certain individual chapters draw on the third and fourth approaches discussed previously, especially Chapter 3 dwelling on the importance of local level wealth differences and Chapter 9 addressing the place of NGOs in conservation efforts.

To summarize, the key ideas that hold the book together conceptually are an attention to global environmental discourses (particularly sustainable development as concept and practice), livelihood security and poverty alleviation, and political ecology. Using these conceptual pillars, the chapters may be grouped into three interrelated thematic categories: (i) the influence of certain global environmental narratives on African environmental policy and practice (chapters 2, 3, and 4); (ii) the interplay between regional political economy and rural livelihoods (chapters 5-8; and (iii) environmental management as a result of global environmental politics and local agency (chapters 9-11). These divisions are not self-contained or mutually exclusive. Quite to the contrary, many of the chapters deal with more than one of the three substantive themes. In this way, the chapters support each other conceptually and, sometimes, empirically.

Environmental Narratives and African Realities

In chapters 2-4, the authors address the links between mainstream environmental discourse, environmental policies and poverty alleviation in Africa. Logan (chapter 2), Moseley (chapter 3) and Laris (chapter 4), examine various attributes of the hegemony of mainstream environmental meta-narratives on policy formulation and program implementation in Africa. In critiquing conservation meta narratives, Logan focuses specifically on SD and frames three arguments: that SD is less about science and more about globalization (Western hegemony); that SD is integral to the globalization of environmental policy; and that SD is supported by a discourse, which claims that poverty and environmental degradation are mutually reinforcing. Both Logan and Laris explore the unfortunate impacts of conservation meta-narratives on environmental policy (fire protection in the case of Laris) and livelihood outcomes (the Lesotho Highland Water Project in the case of Logan). Laris argues that the perpetuation of grand environmental narratives in policy, from the colonial to the post-independence period, has to do more with maintaining the hegemony of global capital and the global environmental movement, than with fire-fighting. This process has been further facilitated in recent times by the activities of the World Bank and a host of NGOs.

To address what the authors perceive to be shortcomings in mainstream conservation narratives, Logan suggests that its poverty-alleviation goals can be better approached through environmental security (ES). According to him, ES approaches poverty-alleviation as a task in minimizing conflicts over resources through negotiation and compromise. For this to occur, grassroots political institutions must be central in resource management decisions, and grassroots institutions and the aspirations they express must be coordinated in national action plans. The ES approach is seen to be practical because it addresses resource problems where they occur – in the political realm.

All three chapters demonstrate that scale becomes a prominent factor in unbundling the links between ideology, politics, power and practice. The scale dimension is very relevant in Moseley's investigation of cotton production in Mali. Following political ecology tradition, he traces the historically changing dynamic in the roles of the major stakeholders in the industry: foreign donors, the state, the cotton company (CMDT), and local farmers. The state and donors have used mainstream environmental discourse to attribute meso-scale (regional) environmental degradation to the practices of poor, local-scale, peasant producers. Laris examines a similar indictment of local-scale activities in mainstream fire-fighting discourse. This mainstream environmental orthodoxy attributes regional (sahelian) environmental degradation to indigenous (local) practices. According to Laris, the conflation of cause-effect scalar relationships has given birth to terms like desertified, sahelized, and savanized. Moseley's research provides evidence to reject the mainstream cause-effect scale analysis. He uses empirical evidence to argue that the environmental impacts of cotton production is, indeed, a matter of scale but within a much broader context than identified in mainstream discourse. According to him, scale is important in terms of the agricultural practices of local producers, but scale is also important in terms of disaggregating producers on the basis of class. His findings indicate that rich local farmers, because they have access to certain types of agricultural inputs, are more likely to engage in environmentally deleterious practices to the same extent or more so than their poor counterparts. He goes on to suggest that international capital has formed an alliance with rich local farmers through agricultural extension programs, which are often environmentally destructive since they proliferate introduced crops and technologies that are unfriendly to the local environment. The alliance between the local rich, the state, and international capital has a particularly pernicious effect on the livelihoods of the local poor. Moseley's conclusions are echoed by Laris (and also by Bingen in chapter 6) who uses the 'chains of explanation' approach in political ecology to examine the impact on policy by the chain of controlling structures, from the local to the global, and shows how this structure has served to perpetuate the dominant narrative while ignoring local wisdom. The main findings in this section are that a global, mainstream environmental narrative is responsible for legitimizing certain policies and practices that contribute to injure the African environment and at the same time, undermine the stability of local livelihood systems.

Political Economy, Rural Livelihoods and the Environment

In the second section of the book (chapters 5,6,7 and 8), the authors invoke political ecology to provide a more direct exploration of the impacts of state and supra state policies and actions on local environments and livelihoods. This link is no more explicit than in chapter 5, in which Krieke places local environmental problems and population disruption within the framework of the apartheid wars in southern Africa. The South African forces adopted three strategies in their war against the freedom fighters: hearts and mind campaign in which the SA forces provided social welfare services for local communities; creation of 'killing zones'or scorched earth tactics to establish buffer zones from which local communities were barred; and terrorism of local communities to prevent them from rendering assistance to liberation forces. The first strategy, even though ostensibly benign, had a negative effect on livelihood systems by creating dependency. The second strategy worsened this dependency by destroying the environmental base of the livelihood system. Environmental degradation was exacerbated by the erection of wire fences and the destruction of vegetation to establish 'no-go' or 'killing zones', which according to Krieke, 'disrupted rural life and livelihood in the border zone, pushing forcibly removed households into already congested villages further south...[it] also effectively denied cattle holders from Namibia access to critical dry season and drought cattle grazing areas...aggravating pressure on scarce water and pasture resources.'

Krieke, Bingen (chapter 6), Wooten (chapter 7) and de Bruijn and van Dijk (chapter 8) all underscore the influence of power and power institutions (including technology) on environmental destruction in Africa. For this reason, Bingen advises that discourse must shift from a techno-centric to a holo-centric paradigm, which examines the use of power in the quest for poverty-alleviation in SSA. Krieke demonstrates quite clearly how power was used by the South African apartheid regime to destroy the livelihood of local communities and Bingen illustrates equally clearly that power is an important explanation of the role of pesticides in the 'pesticide treadmill' which acts through a chain of power and control (including organized science, policy control (funding and structural adjustment programs), and state regulations) to destroy the livelihoods of local farmers on the sub-continent.

The four chapters in this section address the issue of scale in different ways. Krieke and Bingen examine the power of mega-scale institutions (for Krieke the apartheid government and for Bingen international chemical companies) on local livelihoods – in essence, they both look from the top down. To some extent, Wooten adopts a similar orientation by examining the link between local agriculture and the regional market system. However, both Wooten and de Bruijn and van Dijk are more focused on local level adaptations to external stresses on the stability of livelihood systems (essentially looking from inside out). Wooten uses livelihood diversification discourse to study horticultural production (agricultural intensification) by a rural Bamanan community in Mali. He employs the plant technique of grafting as a metaphor to describe the process by which this local community has modified its livelihood options by adding specialized horticultural production to its traditional agricultural activities. The analysis of de Bruijn and van Dijk, a case study of the Fulbe of Central Mali, adopts a similar orientation in its examination of the influence of power on livelihoods at the very local level. The authors claim that local power determines the distribution of land, and, therefore, of ecological risks among the Fulbe. As the ecological risks have become more severe over the past hundred years or so, local power has become a more important factor in determining access to and control of resources.

In general, the chapters in this section provide empirical cases to support some of the broader conceptual arguments provided in the first section. The case study approach comes from two orientations (from outside looking in; and from inside, looking out). In this way, the case studies provide insights from several vantages on the importance of scale for understanding the impacts of political dynamics on environmental degradation, livelihood stress and livelihood adaptation.

Global Environmental Politics and Conservation in Africa

The third section (chapters 9, 10 and 11) gives explicit attention to the empirical manifestations in SSA of contemporary conservation and development narratives. As in the other two sections of the book, scale and power distribution are undercurrents in this section. In all three chapters, local, national, regional and international politics are embedded in each other and insinuate themselves into local livelihood systems. Coffman's account in chapter 9, of wildlife conservation and livelihood enhancement in Kenya is quite different from the Malian experience described by Wooten in chapter 7. Coffman argues that community-based wildlife management (CBWM) has not succeeded in overcoming poverty because the programs are based on a grand narrative that seeks to manage people, their natural resources as well as wildlife. This narrative seeks to construct nature, the environment and environmental resources in ways that do not accommodate local interpretations of these phenomena. The grand narrative assumes that the production of knowledge and the theorization of nature is unproblematic, thereby, contributing to contestation over these concepts by various stakeholders, including foreign scholars, foreign donors and NGOs, the state, local entrepreneurs and local communities. For this reason, Coffman starts her empirical survey by asking some pertinent conceptual questions. What is the meaning of conservation or preservation? What is the meaning of community based wildlife management?

Coffman's questions are answered to some extent by Demotts (chapter 10) who traces the evolution of community-based conservation policies in Namibia. According to her, the Namibian case is widely considered to be a model for the inclusion of local communities in conservation initiatives and the country's programs provide a lens through which to examine ways to integrate conservation in local contexts. Interestingly, DeMotts' positive assessment of the empirical case does not quite refute Coffman's concerns over the power of narrative and how this power is used to perpetuate hegemony not only of knowledge but how knowledge is transformed into policy and implemented on local communities and their livelihood systems. According to Coffman, since CBWM emanates from, and is guided by a mainstream narrative, it is essentially a foreign endeavor that is being implemented primarily by foreign experts. She concludes that CBWM has failed in Kenya as a result of two factors: the community is not a fixed and unchanging phenomenon – in particular, it is being constantly changed in its interactions with capital; secondly, the CBWM requires and will lead to more precise demarcations of land holdings – sometimes, the outcomes of this 'scientific process' is likely to be quite at odds with the estimates of local communities.

While Coffman concludes that policies guided by grand narratives emanating from academia have not always been in the best interest of the Masaai and their pastoral life, both DeMotts and Steyn (chapter 11) adopt a more practical approach to their analyses. DeMotts compares the conservation policies of two countries, Namibia and South Africa, on local livelihoods, while Steyn examines the impact of petroleum exploitation on the livelihoods of local communities in Nigeria. Implicit in the approach adopted by the two is the idea that impacts analyses are to be privileged over discourse analyses. The differences in approach by Coffman, on the one hand, and DeMotts and Steyn, on the other, rather than being disputive, tend to complement each other since the empirical cases provided by the latter lend justification to the conceptual arguments of the former.

DeMotts' research contrasts Namibia and South Africa in community-based natural resource management (CBNRM). While Namibia embarked on a policy of community inclusion at the very early stages of its programs, South Africa implemented a large scale or regional policy that did not explicitly incorporate local aspirations. Although both countries now pursue trans-frontier conservation initiatives, they continue to differ significantly in the degree to which they involve local communities in program planning and implementation: Namibian approaches are focused on the creation and extension of conservancies managed by local communities and South Africa's focus is on finding ways to connect local communities to larger protected areas through means such as contractual national parks. The result is that while Namibia appears to be trying to extend community-level projects into international conservation areas, South Africa is extending existing national parks into larger, mixed land use areas and creates roles for local communities around these international parks

In her chapter, Steyn explores the environmental impact of oil politics in Ogoniland. Her analyses focus on three main aspects of this issue: the environmental problems associated with oil production in Nigeria in general, and in Ogoniland in particular; the environmental and human rights struggle of Ken Saro-Wiwa and the Ogoni against Shell Nigeria in the 1990s; and the environment-related political impact of this struggle on Shell International. The main argument of the chapter is that the Ogoni struggle in Nigeria played a key role in bringing about radical changes in the way in which Shell International viewed the environment and the rights of ethnic minority groups in oil producing regions, which in turn has led to improved environmental management practices within this multinational oil company in the late 1990s.

This volume concerns itself with human use of the African environment, obviously a broad subject. For that reason, the chapters focus on specific themes which attempt to provide insights on the political ecology of development, the political institutions and power distributions that underpin resource allocation, and the impacts of both on livelihood systems. Threading though much of the discussions is the issue of scale and its influence on the tensions that often exist among stakeholders as they seek to maximize specific group utilities.

Note

1 *Gestion de Terroir*, roughly translated as territory management, is the approximate equivalent of community-based natural resources management (CBNRM) in many of the francophone African countries. In contrast to CBNRM, The *terroir* approach places a greater emphasis on land-based resources and the import of circumscribing village territories.

References

Adams, W.M. (1993), 'Indigenous use of wetlands and sustainable development in West Africa.' *Geographical Journal.* 159(2), pp. 209-218.
Ashman, D. (2001), 'Civil Society Collaboration with Business: Bringing Empowerment Back in.' *World Development* 29 (7), pp. 1097-1113.
Atack, I. (1999), 'Four criteria of development NGO legitimacy.' *World Development* 27 (5), pp. 855-864.
Baker, K. (2000), *Indigenous Land Management in West Africa: An Environmental Balancing Act.* New York: Oxford University Press.
Bassett, T.J. and Zueli, K.B. (2000), 'Environmental Discourses and the Ivorian Savanna.' *Annals of the Association of American Geographers.* 90(1), pp. 67-95.
Behnke, R.H., Scoones, I. and Kervan, C. (1993), *Range Ecology at Disequilibrium: New Models of Natural Variability and Pastoral Adaptation in African Savannas.* London: Overseas Development Institute.
Benjaminsen T. and Lund, C. (eds.) (2001), *Politics, Property and Production in the West African Sahel: Understanding Natural Resources Management.* Uppsala, Sweden: Nordiska Afrikainstitutet.
Bernstein H. and Woodhouse, P. (2001), 'Telling Environmental Change Like It Is? Reflections on a Study in Sub-Saharan Africa.' *Journal of Agrarian Change.* 1(2), pp. 283-324.
Blaikie, P.M. (1985), *The Political Economy of Soil Erosion in Developing Countries.* London: Longman.
Blaikie, P.M. and Brookfield, H. (1987), *Land Degradation and Society.* New York: Methuen & Co.
Broche-Due, V. and Schroeder, R. (eds.) (2000), *Producing Poverty and Nature in Africa.* Uppsala, Sweden: Nordiska Afrikainstitutet.
Brockington, D. and Homewood, K. (1996), 'Wildlife, Pastoralists & Science: Debates Concerning Mkomazi Game Reserve, Tanzania.' in: Leach, M. and Mearns, R. (eds). *The Lie of the Land.* Oxford: James Curry.
Bryant, R.L. and Bailey, S. (1997), *Third World Political Ecology.* New York: Routledge.
Carney, J.A. (1996), 'Converting the Wetlands, Engendering the Environment: The intersection of gender with agrarian change in Gambia.' In: Peet, R. and M. Watts (eds). *Liberation Ecologies: Environment, Development, Social Movements.* New York: Routledge.

Chambers, R. and Conway, G.R. (1992), 'Sustainable Rural Livelihoods: Practical Concepts for the 21st Century' *Institute of Development Studies Discussion Paper 296*. London: Institute of Development Studies.

Cleaver, K.M. and Schreiber, G.A. (1994), *Reversing the Spiral: The Population, Agriculture and Environment Nexus in Sub-Saharan Africa*. Washington, D.C.: The World Bank.

Costanza, R. and Patten, B. (1995), 'Defining and predicting sustainability.' Ecological Economics, 15, 193-196.

Dasgupta, P. (1995), 'Population, Poverty and the Local Environment.' *Scientific American*. February. pp. 40-45.

de Graaf, H., Musters, C. and ter Keurs, W. (1996), 'Sustainable development: looking for new strategies.' *Ecological Economics* 16, pp. 205-216.

Ellis, F. (2000), *Rural Livelihoods and Diversity in Developing Countries*. Oxford: OUP.

Escobar, A. (1995), *Encountering Development*. Princeton University Press, Princeton.

Fairhead, J. and Leach, M. (1996), *Misreading the African Landscape*. Cambridge: Cambridge University Press.

Fergusson, A. (2001), 'Comments on eco-footprinting.' *Ecological Economics* 37 (1), 1-2.

Glenzer, K. (2002), 'State, Donor and NGO Configurations in Malian Development 1960-1999: The Enactment and Contestation of Global Rationalized Myths in an Organizational Field.' In B. I. Logan (ed.) *Globalization, The Third World State and Poverty-Alleviation in the Twenty-First Century*. London: Ashgate, pp. 161-180.

Guha, R. (1997), 'The Authoritarian Biologist and the Arrogance of Anti-Humanism: Wildlife Conservation in the Third World.' *The Ecologist*. 27(1): 14-20.

Harpviken, K. (2002), Book Review of Katrina West 'Agents of Altruism: The Expansion of Humanitarian NGOs in Rwanda and Afghanistan.' *Journal of Peace Research* 39 (5), pp. 644.

Herod, A. (1997), 'Labor's Spatial Praxis and the Geography of Contract Bargaining in the US East Coast Longshore Industry.' *Political Geography* 16 (2), pp. 145-169.

Herod, A. and Wright, M. (2001), *Placing Scale*. Oxford: Blackwell.

Hodgson, D.L. (2001), *Once Intrepid Warriors: Gender, Ethnicity and the Cultural Politics of Maasai Development*. Bloomington, Indiana: Indiana University Press.

Hukkinen, J. (2001), 'Eco-efficiency as abandonment of nature.' *Ecological Economics* 38 (3), pp. 311-315.

Igoe, J. (2000), *Ethnicity, Civil Society, and the Tanzanian Pastoral NGO Movement: The Continuities and Discontinuities of Liberalized Development*. PhD Dissertation. Department of Anthropology. Boston University.

Jordan, L. and van Tuijl, P. (2000), 'Political Responsibility in Transnational NGO Advocacy.' *World Development* 28(12), pp. 2051-2065.

Leach, M. and Mearns, R. (1996), *The Lie of the Land: Challenging Received Wisdom on the African Environment*. Oxford: James Curry.

Lele, S. (1991), 'Sustainable Development: A Critical Review.' *World Development* 19 (6), pp. 607-621.

Logan, B.I. (2002), 'Globalization, the Third World State and Poverty-Alleviation in the Twenty-First Century.' In B. I. Logan (ed.) *Globalization, the Third World State and Poverty-Alleviation in the Twenty-First Century*. Aldershot: Ashgate.

Makoba, J. (2002), 'Nongovernmental organizations (NGOs) and third world development: An alternative approach to development.' *Journal of Third World Studies* 19(1), pp. 53-63.

Mamdani, M. (1990), 'Uganda: contradictions of the IMF programme and perspective.' *Development and Change*. 21(3), pp. 427-467.

Moore, D. (1996), 'Marxism, Culture and Political Ecology: Environmental Struggles in Zimbabwe's Eastern Highlands.' In Peet, R and M. Watts (eds). *Liberation Ecologies: Environment, Development, Social Movements*. London: Routledge.

Mortimore, M. (1989), *Adapting to Drought: Farmers, Famines and Desertification in West Africa*. New York: Cambridge University Press.

Moseley, W.G. (forthcoming), 'Global Cotton and Local Environmental Management: The Political Ecology of Rich and Poor Small-Hold Farmers in Southern Mali.' *Geographical Journal*.

Neumann, R. (1998), *Imposing Wilderness: Struggles Over Livelihood and Nature Preservation in Africa*. Berkeley: University of California Press.

Peet, R. (2002), 'Neoliberalism in South Africa.' In B. I. Logan (ed.) *Globalization, the Third World State and Poverty-Alleviation in the Twenty-First Century*. Aldershot: Ashgate, pp. 125-142.

Peet, R. and Watts, M. (eds). (1996), *Liberation Ecologies: Environment, Development, Social Movements*. New York: Routledge.

Peters, P. (1987), 'Embedded Systems and Rooted Models: The Grazing Systems of Botswana and the Commons Debate.' In: McCay, B. and J. Acheson (eds.). *The Question of the Commons*. Tucson: The University of Arizona Press.

Richards, P. (1985), *Indigenous Agricultural Revolution*. Boulder: Westview Press.

Schroeder, R.A. (1999), *Shady Practices: Agroforestry and Gender Politics in the Gambia*. Berkeley: University of California Press.

Sen, A. (1981), *Poverty and Famines*. Oxford: Clarendon.

Sneddon, C. (2000), '" Sustainability" in ecological economics, ecology and livelihoods: a review.' *Progress in Human Geography* 24(4), pp. 521-549.

Stott, P. and Sullivan, S. (2000), *Political Ecology: Science, Myth and Power*. London: Arnold.

Swanson, T. (1996), 'The reliance of northern economies on southern biodiversity: biodiversity as Information.' *Ecological Economics* 17, pp. 1-8.

Swift, J. (1996), Desertification: Narratives, Winners and Losers. In Leach, M. and Mearns, R. (eds.). *The Lie of the Land*. Oxford: James Curry.

Thomas-Slayter, B. and Rocheleau, D. (1995), *Gender, Environment, and Development in Kenya: A Grassroots Perspective*. Boulder: Lynne Rienner.

Tiffen, M., M. Mortimore and Gichuki, F. (1994), *More People, Less Erosion: Environmental Recovery in Kenya*. New York: J. Wiley.

Turner, B.L. (1997), 'Spirals, Bridges and Tunnels: Engaging Human-Environment Perspectives in Geography.' *Ecumene*. 4, pp. 196-217.

Vayda, A.P. and B.B. Walters. (1999), 'Against Political Ecology.' *Human Ecology*. 27(1), pp. 167-179.

Watts, M. (1983), *Silent Violence: Food, Famine and Peasantry in Northern Nigeria*. Berkeley: University of California Press.

Watts, M. (2000), 'Political Ecology.' In *The Dictionary of Human Geography, 4th Edition*. Malden, Massachusetts: Blackwell Publishers Ltd., pp. 590-592.

PART I
ENVIRONMENTAL NARRATIVES
AND AFRICAN REALITIES

Chapter 2

Ideology and Power in Resource Management: From Sustainable Development to Environmental Security in Africa

B. Ikubolajeh Logan

Introduction

Environmental management and resource autonomy are now recognized as central planks of the search for rural poverty-alleviation in Africa (Logan and Moseley, 2002; McManus, 1996; Behera and Erasmus, 1999). This chapter is used to take a serious look at the mainstream discourse, which shapes and guides environmental policy in Africa, with particular attention to sustainable development (SD). The discussion is constructed around the initial propositions that SD is first and foremost a mechanism of intellectual and policy domination in Africa, and only secondarily an instrument of poverty alleviation. This generalized proposition is elucidated through a set of hypotheses: (i) that SD is the environmental dimension of a broader globalization discourse, which also includes democratization and market liberalization; (ii) that at the practical, policy level, SD gains its power from its links to globalization, especially in the form of international treaties and bilateral and multilateral finance/aid for environmental projects; (iii) that at the conceptual level, SD, like its two complements, gains its power from language and discourse.

After examining these hypotheses, the discussion is directed at the thornier task of sketching out a potential alternative to or complement of SD. Ideally, this alternative framework should possess a minimum set of attributes, including the following: it should not be centrally located in the globalization agenda, it should be home-grown within Africa and have African development interests at its core, and it should be built around the concerns and aspirations of local African communities. Given that a conceptual framework with these attributes does not exist, a pragmatic approach to the task might be to opt for a model that, at a minimum, has the potential to address directly and seriously, issues of resource autonomy (and by extension, poverty-alleviation) in rural Africa. Environmental security (ES), which incorporates elements of political ecology, environmental management, local resource autonomy and national security and applies them at several spatial and social scales, is outlined in general terms as an approach that can be used to satisfy this urgent need.

The rest of the chapter is organized in three sections. Section two is used to provide a short background to SD as backdrop for exploring the three hypotheses elaborated earlier in section one. The discussion of SD is followed in section three by an overview of ES with some general comparisons with SD. Section 4 uses an empirical example, the Lesotho Highland Water Project, to illustrate the usefulness of ES compared to SD as a policy framework. The final section is used to make concluding comments that highlight ways by which ES might be used to improve on the status quo of resource management and poverty-alleviation in Africa.

Sustainable Development, Community Based Development and Poverty-Alleviation

SD, arguably the most influential environmental concept to emerge from globalization discourse, is archetypical of the colonization of environmental ideas and practice in Africa. In the West where it was developed and from where it has been propagated, SD is now primarily a matter of theoretical and intellectual curiosity. In Africa, by contrast, it remains firmly at the helm of development praxis where it has become a mantra used by a wide array of interests to legitimize resource adjudication under the broad aegis of globalization. In this role, SD has become the barometer by which most policy prescriptions in resource management, democratization, community enfranchisement, poverty-alleviation and human rights are judged. SD is also used as the yardstick around which development programs are designed and their financial, social and political feasibility are assessed.

To paraphrase the Brundtland Report, which is commonly credited for popularizing the concept, SD is development that maintains the living standards of the present generation without endangering the ability of future generations to obtain similar living standards (c.f. Lele, 1991; Munn, 1992; Redclift, 1992; Vierderinan, 1993). Implicit in this mainstream definition of SD is the idea that the present generation can aspire to higher standards of living only if it can do so without compromising the environmental base upon which future generations must rely for their own survival (Barrett, 1992; Ayres, 1993; Harte, 1995; Pasek, 1992). Two important thrusts of SD are environmental conservation (to protect the interests of future generations) and economic growth (to protect the well being of the present generation) (c.f. Beckerman, 1992; Costanza and Patten, 1995; Arrow et al., 1995; Azar, Holmberg, and Lindgren, 1996). Unfortunately, the fact that these goals are often at cross-purposes compounds the opaqueness of SD, especially in Africa where there is often no economic growth to sustain and where inter-generational concerns are likely to be secondary to existing north-south distributional inequities. Although the Brundtland Report does pay significant attention to southern poverty, development programs that have been implemented under the SD umbrella tend either implicitly or explicitly, to promote the neoliberal market agenda as the only avenue of escape from poverty (for commentaries on this issue, see, for example, van Pelt, 1993; McManus,

1996; Logan and Moseley, 2002).

The strong link between SD and neoliberal market economics creates significant problems for its useful application in African countries, which are often disenfranchised by international trade and in whose local economies market development is a nascent phenomenon. These limitations take on a practicality in development programs, which project SD as the cornerstone of efforts to merge conservation and economic growth.

Mainstream wisdom takes the position that SD, economic growth, environmental conservation and rural poverty-alleviation can all be obtained, in one fell swoop, through community-based development (CBD) projects in Africa and other Third World settings (Sundar, 2001; Agarwal, 2001; Ashman, 2001; Hackel, 1998). Unfortunately, CBD is fraught with difficulties at both the conceptual and practical levels, as manifested, for example, in lack of clarity over issues like the definition of community, differentiating between community and stakeholder, establishing and distinguishing between the geographical and cultural regions of a community; community empowerment relative to the role and authority of the central government, minimizing community loss and maximizing community benefits in conservation projects, and establishing suitable revenue-sharing mechanisms (see Logan and Moseley, 2002; Glenzer, 2002; Chatty, 1998). Thus, even though CBD has become an important element of SD praxis, its record on poverty-alleviation is not impressive (see for example Braidotti et al., 1994; Durbin and Ing, 1994; Hackel, 1998; Khasa, 1995; Matzkhe and Nabane, 1996; Songorwa, 1999; Marake et al., 1998).

Why do CBD programs prove to be so anemic even for the specific goals for which they have been designed? There is no correct set of answers to this question but CBD does contain some inherent problems. One is that because they are entrenched in neoliberalism and the globalization agenda, they do not attempt to overturn the national and international institutions that underlie and perpetuate resource mal-distribution and poverty in Africa (Boyce, 1994; Bryant, 1997; Gosselin, 1994). If CBD programs do not give proper attention to the power structures that underlie resource adjudication, their claims of resource empowerment are likely to remain foundless. Simply, since the power game is also a zero-sum game, the poor cannot be empowered without some loss of power by the rich and powerful. A key task for resource managers on the continent, therefore, is to elaborate a framework that will balance the needs of the market with those of political institutions, which traditionally have been the protector of the poor against the worst excesses of the market. This means that an important resource management endeavor in Africa is to develop meaningful institutional and policy formulae to bring all stakeholders, especially those at the community level, to the decision-making table. A second important mission is to locate poverty-alleviation at the center of all development efforts. Paradoxically, these are the goals of SD presented in the Brundtland Report. However, neither the market nor CBD seem to be properly equipped to deliver them because, as argued here, neither is willing to confront the vexing political economy issues surrounding resource control, resource exchange and poverty generation under the aegis of globalization.

Why does SD continue to be such a powerful policy instrument in Africa even though it demonizes institutions and policies that threaten the neoliberal agenda, and tends also to be antithetical to local poverty-alleviation? Why does it continue to be the clarion call of so many when it has proven to be of such limited utility in poverty-alleviation in the decade and a half since its rise to prominence? These questions are now explored in the context of the three hypotheses outlined in section one.

Hypothesis 1: Sustainable Development is less about science and more about globalization.

Three pillars - neoliberalism, democracy and SD, buttress the present form of globalization. The African experience shows that universal ideologies of this nature have questionable relevance for effective policy formulation towards poverty reduction, primarily because appropriate ideas, like appropriate technologies, have epistemological, cultural, geographical and historical specificity. Imported ideologies, when transferred from their specific ideological and philosophical settings, therefore, have sometimes taken quite unexpected and unsavory manifestations on the lives of African peoples.

SD has become an environmental orthodoxy (a meta narrative) that is often presented in scientific terms, which suggest that it is value-neutral and culturally benign. Nevertheless, its objective clarity has engendered a lot of debate (Pearce and Turner, 1996; de Graaf et al., 1996; Lusk and Hoff, 1994; Redclift, 1992; Suter, 1995). The voluminous outpouring of literature on SD has only underscored disciplinary contentiousness over its meaning(s), objectives and agendas. Lusk and Hoff (1994: 22) make the point that SD appeals to a broad cross-section of scientists and policy makers because it is '...internationalist, utilitarian, conservationist, and scientific.' Even if one is willing to put aside questions regarding its 'scientificness', it is difficult to ignore the more fundamental philosophical problem that because something is considered to be scientific does not mean that it is free from dogma. As Soderbaum (1999: 163) puts it, '[a] ccording to popular beliefs, science is about 'truth', 'objectivity' and 'value-neutrality,' but 'value-neutrality' is an illusion, which forbids mainstream discourse involving taboo subjects like ideology or political economy.' Myrdal (quoted in Soderbaum, 1999: 163) puts it even more cogently that 'there can be no view except from a viewpoint.' A major difficulty surrounding the appropriateness of SD for Africa is that its 'views,' 'viewpoints' and 'ideologies' are from a perspective that does not incorporate local ideations, even when attempts are made at community participation. Further, and perhaps more importantly, it is not even clear that SD has poverty-alleviation in Africa as a priority. Rather, a good case can be made that the priority of SD is to promote Western notions of biodiversity and conservation and Western hegemony over African interpretations of resource management and economic development. At the same time, SD might be construed to be a strategy to appease the poor while allowing neoliberalism to proceed uncontested. If the poor can be occupied with illusions of community empowerment it might be easier for the excesses of globalization through the World Bank, IMF and WTO, for example, to be overlooked by the poor. It may not be surprising, therefore, that after a decade and a half of service as the yardstick for development, there is neither empirical nor 'scientific' grounds to expect that SD can be achieved within its present neoliberal context. It is also little wonder that CBD efforts to clothe SD in humanitarian and economic respectability, still leave the emperor stark naked.

Hypothesis 2: Sustainable Development represents globalization of environmental policy

In addition to the power it derives from global environmental discourse, SD gains power from the legal policy frameworks that support globalization. The term itself emanates from the World Commission on Environment and Development, an international institution that is part of the global structure that legitimizes grand meta-policy frameworks (see, Moltke, 1992; Appiah-Opoku and Mulamootil, 1997; Babu et al, 2000, Sneddon, 2000). Consequently, it may not be coincidental that the international environmental movement and SD contributed mutually to each other's global status during the 1980s and 1990s. Haque (2000: 4) points out that;

> [t]he environmental discourse has gained increasing attention in almost all international forums on development, and the environment-development relationship is being seriously taken into account in practical policies and theoretical debates...Some of the most articulate advocates of this environment-development nexus have been the proponents of a more contemporary model of development known as 'sustainable development'...In the practical realm, there has emerged various national and international conferences, institutions, agreements, legal measures, and government agencies dealing with environmental issues...

In the past three decades or so, the SD model has been disseminated through a multiplicity of international meetings, including, forerunners like the 1968 UNESCO Biosphere Conference, the 1968 Washington Conference on the Ecological Aspects of International Development. Its rise to ascendancy may be traced back to the 1972 Stockholm Conference, which established the United Nations Environmental Programme (UNEP). However, SD really came into its own after the 1986 IUCN meeting, which laid the groundwork for the publication of the 1987 Brundtland Report that eventually made SD a development dogma. Since then, the quest for SD has continued in other arenas like the 1992 Rio Conference, the 1997 Kyoto Conference and the 2002 Johannesburg Conference.

As the SD model became increasingly popular during the 1990s, it was fully co-opted by many agendas, including that of the international environmental movement. Although this movement may not be monolithic in its aims, it presents a united front in efforts to link SD directly to financial assistance from the multilateral agencies (World Bank and IMF), to bilateral and multilateral overseas development assistance, and to foreign direct investment. Through links of this nature, financial resources have been provided to African and other Third World countries to establish governmental environment agencies as part of a global SD agenda. Haque (2000) points out that in 1972, only ten countries had an environment-related institution. By 1990, 130 countries, including 90 in the developing world, had an environmental ministry, agency or commission as part of their central governments. In addition, the IMF and World Bank have both 'greened' their conditionalities to include environmental impact assessment and national environmental action plans. Current Bank policy even seems to give implicit support to the concept of 'green' national accounts in which depletion of natural capital stocks and pollution would not reflect value towards GNP.

Action by international finance has been complemented by political and legal practice, which enshrines SD in international legislation and treaties around which African environmental policies, especially those pertaining to wildlife, are often designed. Perhaps the most well known of these treaties is the Convention on International Trade in Endangered Species of Wild Flora and Fauna (CITES). In general, policy makers in the Third World have viewed CITES with acceptance because of its flexibility (compared to previous global environmental treaties) and attention to Third World concerns. In particular, CITES embodies principles of biodiversity and resource autonomy, it supports species protection in the context of local needs for food, it accepts national authority over the management of biodiversity, it provides for regular meetings among signatories to review progress towards SD, and it also provides signatories with some autonomy over selective culling of wildlife.

Unfortunately, in its actual implementation, CITES has not turned out to be as progressive as it sounds on paper. The power to design environmental policy, oversight of such policies and monitoring of environmental programs has been largely wrested from the state and vested in civil society (INGOs and NGOs). The neoliberal view that the African state is a hindrance to development is very much in evidence in the environmental realm. The global environmental movement ensures that funds for environmental programs are channeled directly to INGOs, which use their financial power to decide policy orientation and program structure both for the state and for local civil society (see Glenzer, 2002). Thus, the treaty's concern for local community autonomy over resource management has remained hypothetical. In much of Southern Africa, CITES regulations are enforced by coercing the state, through the power of funding, to implement policies that seem to put the welfare of animals over that of people.

Hypothesis 3: Sustainable Development is Materially, Linguistically and Discursively Constituted in Neoliberalism.

SD is currently being promoted within globalization discourse as the goal of African development in the twenty-first century. The global environmental discourse projects the idea that SD is consistent with economic and ecological principles and, as such, the task at hand is simply to integrate the concept into the scientific parameters of the two disciplines (see, Lutz and Munasinghe, 1994; Amin, 1992). Among other things, this effort has resulted in a virtual explosion of literature on SD as part of economics and ecology, to the emergence of a new sub-discipline actually titled ecological economics and to the birth of a leading scholarly journal of the same name (see Sneddon, 2000).

Discursive attempts to enshroud SD in science also imbue it with the linguistic and ideological power of economics and ecology (paradoxically, this means that SD can 'view' only through the lenses of two disciplines that are notoriously short sighted to cultural nuances). The direct links between SD and economics/ecology, therefore, automatically limits its ideological potential to address non-mainstream activities, especially those that fall outside the realm of the neoliberal agenda. Ropke (1999, p.46) points out, '...we see what our theory allows us to see.' This may be true of SD proponents who often see only through the development lenses provided by the neoliberal ideology surrounding globalization. The power and authority of this ideology is maintained partly through 'scientific' discourse, partly through financial capital (grants and loans for specific projects) and partly through the threat of political isolation for countries, which fail to adopt the prevailing ideology.

The discursive process through which SD serves as an instrument of hegemony may be placed in the context of winners and losers (Boyce, 1994). Winners are able to impose their designs on losers under one of three conditions: the losers do not yet exist (example future generations), the losers exist but are unaware of their loss, the losers exist, are aware of their loss, but are powerless to address it (see also M'Gonigle, 1999; Baland and Platteau, 1999). The last two scenarios are relevant for SD-driven projects in Africa. Even when they are fully aware of their losses, losers both at the national and local levels lack the political and financial wherewithal to seek redress.

The power that SD brings to bear on losers derives from its direct links with global private, bilateral and multilateral capital; what Boyce (1994) describes as the ability of winners to bear greater transaction costs than losers. African governments and local communities can hardly compete financially with the international agents of SD; a problem exacerbated by the ability of the winners to use their legal and institutional power to change the rules constantly and make transaction costs prohibitive for the losers.

The linguistic and ideological case for SD is often built around a number of 'truisms' in globalization discourse (see, for example, Byrant, 1997*)*. One of these establishes a direct positive relationship between income and environmental protection. In this view, poor communities have high discount rates and high rates of time preference (both associated with present survival), which force them to degrade their environment (Broad, 1994; Reardon and Vosti, 1995; Arrow et al., 1995). As Lusk and Hoff (1994, p.23) put it, '...[p]overty accelerates resource depletion as the world's poor seek to meet immediate needs through short-run strategies which result in deforestation and overgrazing.' This principle is often depicted in the well-known environmental Kuznets curve (see Arrow et al, 1995), which shows that at the beginning of the development process, environmental degradation may increase, but as national incomes rise, environmental conservation/protection will also improve. Work by Moseley (2001) indicates that the poor do not necessarily have a predilection to overuse their physical resource base. Unfortunately, neither such reservations surrounding the Kuznet's U, nor empirical refutation of direct causality between poverty and environmental abuse, have reduced the popularity of the poverty-environmental degradation 'truism'.

A second 'truism', which follows directly from the first, indicates that since income and environmental protection increase in the same direction, the poor must be bad environmental stewards. Poverty and environmental degradation are seen to be mutually reinforcing in what Logan (1991, pp.42-43) critiques in the context of a 'vicious spiral of population-induced poverty'. In this mainstream scenario, malnutrition and poverty are caused by high rates of population growth, which force communities to adopt modes of production which exacerbate environmental disequilibria, especially through land use changes (shorter fallow). Soil erosion, deforestation and other forms of environmental degradation result in dwindling productivity, which, in turn, encourages producers to reassess their production possibilities. Since labor is the only production factor that can readily be manipulated in a precapitalist environment, producers resort to even higher rates of population growth, which becomes self-perpetuating. High population densities place even more pressure on the environment and the process continues inexorably. This view only grudgingly admits to the store of environment knowledge that African and other traditional societies may possess and use to conserve resources (for some examples see Durbin and Ing, 1994; Da Cunha et al., 2000).

A third 'truism' is that environmental degradation in Africa can be reversed primarily (if not only) through Western intervention, especially in the form of investment, knowledge and technology. Following the first two 'truisms', this philosophy sketches out a formula for environmental conservation that is predicated on improved standards of rural living. The path to high standards of living is to be paved with structural adjustment policies, which, when implemented properly, will attract direct foreign investment. Since investors are loathe to take capital to economies that are plagued by restraints on capital mobility, the first order of business in economic development is market liberalization and enforcement of the neoliberal order through the structural adjustment policies of the IMF and World Bank. Unfortunately, structural adjustment policies have had incontrovertibly deleterious effects on both the environment and poverty-alleviation in African and other Third World areas (see, for example, Abaza, 1995; Muradian and Martinez-Allier, 2001; Taylor, 1993; Logan and Tevera, 2001).

Mainstream 'truisms' regarding the links between poverty and environmental degradation are quite at odds with those of other viewpoints, for example, political ecology, which engage power differentials in society as the explanation for environmental degradation (Greenberg and Park, 1994; Merchant, 1992; M'Gonigle, 1999; Torras, 1999). One of the dominant principles in political ecology is that power is important in determining environmental use and management. Behera and Erasmus (1999, p.2) declare that '[e]nvironmental degradation, or ecological decline, usually arise due to ruthless exploitation of the biosphere by a small clique of greedy people, unmindful of the suffering of the vast majority of people...' Boyce (1994) argues further that as the power differential in a socio-economic system increases, environmental degradation is also likely to increase. The heart of the matter, therefore, is not whether a society is rich or poor but whether income (broadly defined), which underlies power, is distributed fairly equitably. It is also about the level of control that communities have over their immediate resources.

The political ecology line of analysis is pertinent for Africa, at least for two reasons. (i) The poor in Africa may degrade nature because they have been pushed to the economic and ecological margins of their environments (Bowyer-Bowyer, 1996; Logan and Moseley, 2002). (ii) African countries themselves may be pushed to over-tax nature because the income gap between rich and poor countries continues to push them to the margins of the global system. In fact, one might argue that the international trade system is anti the African environment in a number of operational ways: it forces the countries to rely increasingly on primary commodities, which are fetching increasingly less in the international market; these lower incomes force African producers to make increasingly greater demands on the environment by increasing the use of artificial inputs, which have serious environmental impacts. The World Bank, ostensibly a strong proponent of SD, continues to support these forms of unsustainable agricultural development as a possible solution to African poverty because they lack the courage to confront the more fundamental issue of trade inequities and political power imbalance.

If one accepts arguments that power institutions orchestrate the activities that degrade the environment, then one is also forced to accept that poverty is not an ultimate explanation of environmental degradation in Africa, but a symptom of pernicious structural irregularities in local and international resource transfers. These irregularities, marked by power differentials between rich and poor countries, are designed to maintain global hegemony not to solve the poverty dilemma in Africa. These political economy arguments are not new (Hackel, 1993; Songorwa, 1999). They are reiterated here only to set the stage for investigating resource problems in the context of political ecology and to argue for resolution in the same context. Unfortunately, while political ecology provides a good framework for analyzing these issues, it does not provide any explicit strategy for their resolution. It is in this regard that environmental security (ES) may potentially be used to broaden the conceptual and direct policy relevance of political ecology.

Broad Conceptual Configuration of Environmental Security

An attempt has been made in the previous two sections to establish a case that the shortcomings of SD with regard to resource and power distribution, resource autonomy and poverty-alleviation call for urgent attention. Environmental security (ES) has received some attention in this regard in recent years (Moyo and Tevera, 1993; Lonergan et al., 1999). The case for ES revolves most notably around its potential to draw attention to local level resource needs and, therefore, more directly to local resource control and poverty-alleviation. Even mainstream analysts like Lusk and Hoff (1994, p.26) agree that 'local governance' and local resource autonomy would enhance resource management and that local people have institutions and structures in place that may be consistent with environmental conservation. Behera and Erasmus (1999, p.1) make the following argument.

> Environment is primarily for the people. It is the human element that gives meaning to ecology, and the environmental question becomes relevant to society only to the extent that it is viewed in relation to the people who are affected by it. Hence, the main concern while studying the state of the environment has to be its relationship with the indigenous people who depend on it for survival.

ES has been defined in a variety of ways. In its most common usage, it provides a framework for examining how political conflicts emerge from resource scarcity. It is also used to examine how such conflicts can be avoided through negotiated distribution of resources among stakeholders. This second interpretation provides the conceptual guideline for the present discussion. In the broad sense of this interpretation, ES may be seen as a framework for improving resource availability at several geographic scales (local, national, regional) and at establishing legal and institutional frameworks for resource adjudication and conflict prevention/resolution at several political levels. These ES objectives are seen here to be centered on poverty-alleviation, community resource autonomy and environmental conservation as goals, which are to be obtained through political negotiation. In contrast to the implicit market orientation of SD, ES seeks to empower communities through political institutions, which would serve as mechanisms of conflict avoidance and conflict resolution. Moyo and Tevera (1999, p.3) note that environmental security examines '...the effects of the intertwined relationships between political institutions, economics and ecology...' as part of a multi-sector, multi-stake-holder approach to conflict avoidance in resource management. Resource problems are viewed in this perspective to be fundamentally political problems, whose fundamental solutions must be sought in the political realm. ES also seeks to give local stakeholders (as different from the national government or foreign interests) an important role in resource management. In the ES context, local communities and their institutions are to be linked to national and regional institutions and resource decisions at each institutional level are to be part of a broader national agenda that reflects the interests, aspirations and concerns of the whole society.

Shaw (1999) summarizes ES objectives into a tripartite level of activities - identifying the issues, determining the magnitude (spatial and temporal) of the issues, and identifying and implementing redress options. ES is marked by a number of key characteristics to achieve these goals. First, it indicates that most (if not all) conflicts arise out of contestation over resources. Second, these conflicts can be avoided or negotiated by focusing on resource redistribution. Third, conflict resolution requires the existence of strong political institutions at several scales to provide avenues for negotiated settlement. Fourth, conflict resolution requires full participation by all stakeholders, including local communities, which often bear the burden of resource exploitation without sharing in much of the benefits of the process. Real (as opposed to lip-service) community participation in these processes would involve mutual respect between institutions at all levels. This should mean that local institutions and national institutions together must design and implement resource management plans. In turn, this would mean that local communities must not merely be consulted or informed, they must be part and parcel of the decision-making process. If this dynamic can be obtained as part of the resource management process, it would, of necessity enhance community empowerment and lead to higher levels of poverty-alleviation.

The importance of consensus-building in resource management is now widely accepted by development practitioners. In their discussion of a new strategy towards sustainable development, de Graaf and ter Kleurs (1996, p.210) observe that it can only come about through negotiation and consensus. As they put it, '...consensus being a political item, should be reached by negotiation between the people involved. Of course, this can only be accomplished when these people feel involved...'

A second key characteristic of ES is that it is multi-faceted and dovetails conceptually and practically with a number of disciplines and approaches. For example, its emphasis on resource access and community empowerment, resonates with the United Nations' human security approach which covers basic needs attainment and issues surrounding political freedom, grass roots development, community advocacy and gender rights (UNDP, 1994). The prominence given in ES to political institutions over the market is an attribute shared with political ecology, and its attention to human-environment relationships creates links with disciplines like geography and ecology. As an important case in point, ES builds on political ecology's explanation that resource conflicts are caused by unequal access and power relations. While political ecology is quiet on the role of either the market or other institutions in correcting the causes of such conflicts, ES explicitly assigns this role to political and social institutions.

A third key characteristic is that the ES focus is directed at specific issues. Lonergan (1993) identify these to be avoidance or resolution of environmentally-induced conflicts (for example, the relationship between environmental change and security), avoidance or resolution of conflicts involving the environment (for example, environmental change, population movements and security), and conflicts over resource distribution. Thus, the ES approach (unlike SD) can be crystallized quite succinctly as dealing with issues pertaining to environmental stress and inaccessibility to resources as cause and outcome of conflict. Increasingly, the scope of ES is being broadened from these core concerns to address related issues, including the United Nations five basic needs - food, health, education, shelter, and clothing (see for example, Homer-Dixon, 1991; 1995; Lonergan, 1993); political freedom, grass roots development, community advocacy and gender rights (UNDP, 1994; Zarsky, 1999; Suhrke, 1991).

In summary, ES differs from SD in a number of ways, which may be important for resource management in Africa. (i) The ES frame of analysis makes it possible to incorporate into resource management, local value systems that may fall outside the direct purview of the market. This is hardly possible in SD, which borrows its value system directly from the neoliberalism. (ii) The focus of ES on the locality makes it possible to view resource and environmental issues in Africa outside the direct scope of the globalization agenda (including neoliberal economics and international political and economic institutions). (iii) ES does not find it necessary to establish a causal relationship between poverty and environmental degradation. Like political ecology, it views poverty as a problem of limited resource accessibility and equally limited political options for the poor.

Assessing the Drawbacks of Environmental Security

It must be admitted that that the ES reliance on political institutions to preempt or resolve resource conflicts certainly is not unproblematic. Political institutions, especially in Africa, cater to specific constituencies and political institutions at the global level are designed to perpetuate hegemony. However, the market possesses similar frailties. *Ipso facto*, the pot of market-driven resource allocation can hardly cast color aspersions on the kettle of politically driven resource allocation. Given this equal culpability the ES focus on the embeddedness of socio-economic and political arrangements within a society could provide some advantages for the pursuit of development. A search for environmentally-based solutions which are politically grounded, and which have resolution where policies are conceived, seems to be a pragmatic approach to resource management.

A second potential problem with ES is that its emphasis on political institutions might seem like a call for statist control over resources. In actual fact, environmental security cannot be obtained unless authority over resources devolves to the owners of such resources. This goal may be achieved by putting local governments in charge of local resources, using communal control over the commons as a strategy towards resource conservation and using the market to obtain revenues from resource exploitation. Thus, the search for ES must not be seen to be antithetical to market operations (anyway, this will not be feasible within the existing global order). However, rather than give the market pride of place in resource allocation, ES conceives of a market bridled by ecological and political concerns and guided by local aspirations. In this construction, the globalization agenda is not regarded as a sufficient condition for rural poverty-alleviation; rather local empowerment to control local resources is seen to be a necessary condition for poverty-alleviation. Although the superimposition of political and administrative boundaries on natural resource systems can, and has led to resource conflicts, political jurisdictions represent a more amenable framework for resource allocation than market boundaries. Indeed, the market is often incapable of establishing a reasonable structure for resource administration because its borders are temporary and highly unstable (more so than political boundaries). The immaturity of African markets may also make political institutions a more suitable vehicle for arbitrating and negotiating between different claimants.

Governments at several levels typically have the ability to move in and adjudicate between actual and potential disputants more swiftly and comprehensively than the market, which has yet to 'penetrate' many rural areas on the continent.

Governments typically have an incentive to engage in such activities because their own survival depends on ensuring political stability. Of course, this does not mean that governments in Africa are good stewards of human rights and political freedom. However, they have more of a stake in keeping the body politic happy than does the market, which often has no particular local allegiances.

Third, like SD, ES is also a cultural import. If SD is to be discarded because its ideas regarding resource management do not coincide with those of many African societies, why should not the same standards be applied to ES? It is possible to respond to this query by emphasizing the role of local communities in ES. CBD programming in SD approaches community empowerment by advocating community consultation. In reality, this is merely a method of telling communities what has been decided for and about their future. By contrast, ES approaches this problem by requiring community leadership in decision-making. It is the community, which determines its own constitution, its own collective short and long-term goals and the best strategies towards obtaining those goals. The role of national and international civil society in this scenario is to consult, advise and work with policy makers to coordinate community programs into a national program. ES, therefore, turns the traditional roles upside down: the community decides and civil society is consulted for input and coordination.

Reliance on communities to develop and strategize local problems is certainly not going to be problem-free. Perhaps, the greatest potential problem is that local communities are not monolithic wholes without gender, class, and political differences. For this reason, there are likely to be inequities in the types of programs chosen for development. Unfortunately, it is unrealistic to expect problems of this nature to be completely avoided; it may be better to encourage communities to put in place checks and balances to minimize their potential negative impacts.

ES program, like all other forms of development initiatives will rely on foreign financial assistance. However, a case can be made that the amount of foreign financial support that will be required for ES programs will far less in comparison say, with SD community-based programs. In SD programs, foreign and local experts write their proposal budgets for funding based on their own expectations and including their own needs. Often, these budgets include substantial amounts for overhead costs and the salaries and benefits for experts. If the decision-making concerning resource management is removed to the community, it is unlikely that community leaders will require as much funding. Communities are more likely to identify needs that are based on their local resources and the actual financial requirements are likely to be small when compared to those of local NGOs and INGOs.

Clearly, ES is not problem-free, but it is unlikely that a development approach can be devised that would satisfy all ideal conditions. A realistic goal in the search for a mechanism towards resource autonomy and poverty-alleviation in Africa should be to assess whether that mechanism has the potential to improve significantly on the status quo. In the brief overview that follows in the next subsection, I use the example of the Lesotho Highland Water Project to illustrate some practical differences between ES and SD and to comment on ways by which these differences make ES a potentially better mechanism than SD for delivering resource autonomy and poverty-alleviation benefits to local communities in Africa.

Contested Interest Over Water: The Lesotho Highland Water Project

The Lesotho Highlands Water Project (LHWP) represents contested interests over water in the semi arid regions of southern Africa. The LHWP is a transnational agreement signed in 1986 between the Republic of South Africa (RSA) and the Kingdom of Lesotho. The initial phase of the project started in 1990 and the whole project should be completed in 2017. The World Bank, a combination of European export credit agencies and South African banks, are expected to provide its total cost of US$8 billion.

The primary goal of the LHWP is to transfer water from Lesotho to the RSA. The project will draw water from the source of the Orange River and divert it away from the Atlantic to the Vaal River Basin and the heavy demand areas surrounding Johannesburg. Four dams, the Katse, Muela, Mohale, and Matsoku will be built, 200 kilometers of tunnels blasted through the mountains, and an underground hydroelectricity generating plant erected to provide electricity for Lesotho (Horta, 1996; Klunne, 2000).

As the program unfolds, it will have clear winners and losers. Benefits to the RSA will include two billion cubic meters of water per year for its agricultural, industrial and domestic sectors. Lesotho's central government will benefit from a significant infusion of foreign currency and some infrastructure development. In addition to the electricity plant mentioned above, Lesotho will enjoy other social and economic dividends including roads, electric transmission networks, communication networks and agricultural development. Lesotho is also expected to obtain export earnings estimated at US$80 million per year, in addition to the jobs the various projects are expected to generate.   On the other side of the equation, the heaviest environmental, economic and social costs are likely to be borne by local communities in Lesotho which realize that they are losers in the program but have very little political recourse for restitution. The losses to local communities (dealt with in more detail below) include loss of land and water, geographic and social displacement and loss of livelihood.

In the eyes of its many supporters, including the World Bank and policy makers in the two countries, the project's economic and social benefits far outweigh its environmental impacts, which are perceived to be quite benign. Feasibility studies conducted under the auspices of the World Bank covered, among other things, agriculture and land use, social structure and rural economy, conservation and cultural heritage, impacts on water quality and fishing, and health. These studies concluded that the project is well within the realms and major objectives of SD and the local communities in Lesotho will be uplifted from poverty. As a consequence, the LHWP is being hailed as a prototype of sustainable development – a win-win situation for all stakeholders. Yet, even the World Bank is reported to be uncertain about the project's true social impacts. The Bank has voiced concerns that the project might divert government funds from other pressing poverty-alleviation programs (Letsie, 1999). The Bank went further to admit in its 1995 report on poverty in Lesotho that the LHWP may not benefit the poor as much as simulation estimates may have indicated. Much of the concerns over the program's effects originate from a realization that its environmental effects may have been grossly underestimated. The program has been lauded by its proponents on claims that its ecological and environmental agendas were tailored to reflect the 1992 Earth Summit's call to '...to improve ...knowledge of mountain ecosystems, to foster integrated watershed development and to create alternative livelihood opportunities for mountain communities' (FAO Progress Report/Agenda 21/Chapter 13 - Sustainable Mountain Development, 1995). Despite this, the project was implemented without a comprehensive environmental impact statement. Rather, policy makers relied on feasibility studies, which concluded that the project had insignificant environmental impacts. Critics now claim that this casual approach to the environment ignored a number of important environmental questions. The TED Case Studies, 2000, p.5) observes that the Association for International Water and Forest Studies (an Oslo-based Think-Tank) disputes World Bank findings regarding the benign environmental impacts of the project by noting that the LHWP '...could seriously damage Lesotho's environment...the construction of the dam may endanger the survival of a certain number of species...' The project has also been linked to crustal instability in the highlands. Horta (1996, p.1) reports that;

[s]mall earthquakes have been rumbling in recent months through the Maluti Mountains in the small landlocked nation of Lesotho...Mountain villagers now live in fear of the ongoing earth tremors, such as one that left a crack through the middle of the village of Mapeleng, and damaged many traditional stone-built *rondvales* ...According to expert seismologists, the reason for the earthquakes is the filling of the Katse dam, which at a height of 182 meters is the highest dam ever built in Africa.

Another significant negative environmental impact of the program is increased soil erosion arising directly from construction activities and indirectly from flooding of arable land (for dams). Both sets of activities are expected to place even more stress on scarce land resources, in turn, forcing local communities to utilize marginal lands to farm and graze their cattle.

From a social perspective, the LHWP is a multidimensional and complex program with costs and benefits to stakeholders that are not easily convertible to market prices. Southern Africa is largely arid but Lesotho has been blessed with abundant water supply. Total water consumption in the country is estimated to be only 2% of the available natural supply (TED Case Studies, 2000). Water demand in Lesotho is not expected to increase significantly in the near future since the country's industrial base in infinitesimal, agricultural expansion is restricted by topography and growth in domestic consumption is constrained by low population (the country has one of Africa's lowest population growth rates). Fakir (2000) observes that southern Africa's general aridity, Lesotho's low water demand, and high water demand in RSA make water redistribution an attractive strategy, not only to meet regional water needs, but also to limit the potential for future conflict. It is the potential for conflict over water and the need for conflict resolution that locates the LHWP within ES. As Fakir (2000, p.1) puts it, '...[c]ountries in the region share many water ways and resources creating the potential for possible conflicts and tensions...if anything, crisis over water is the single most important factor likely to lead to political strife and possible war.' For example, the Senqu (Orange River, when it gets to RSA) originates in Lesotho, flows through the RSA and forms the boundary between the latter and Namibia which, therefore, has a vested interest in any decisions made in or treaties signed in Maseru concerning the disposition of the river's water.

The contestation over water is linked to a historical pattern of allocation based on race. Lesotho survived as a Basotho homeland largely because its mountainous landscape was not considered to be desirable agricultural land by the Dutch during the Boer Wars (1840-1869). In an ironic twist of fate, these same mountains now provide the water resources, which are so highly desired by the RSA. Current attempts to correct historical resource inequities (land reform is the most well documented example) mask the threat of serious crises, a fact that is reflected lucidly in the title of Fakir's (2000) assessment, 'Finding future water in Southern Africa: Avoiding Conflict and War.' It is not surprising, for example, that implementation of the LHWP has resulted in increased guerilla activity in northern Lesotho from groups, which wish to protect the water resources as a matter of national security. As Horta (1996, p.2) observes; 'South African engineers conceived the Lesotho Highlands Water Project in the 1950s, but many Basotho greeted the idea with skepticism, reflecting continuing Basotho resentment for having lost their land to white settlers in what is now the Orange Free State...' For many Basotho, the project represents a post-colonial mechanism of resource expropriation, not an attempt to alleviate their poverty. The sense that they are being exploited for the benefit of whites in the RSA is exacerbated by the fact that Lesotho has suffered from minor droughts since the mid-1990s.

Resettlement and compensation, two important aspects of the multi-faceted socio-economy of the LHWP, are also central to the contestation. The TED Case Study (2000, p.6) makes the following observation.

> More than 20,000 people are likely to lose their homes or part of their property when the dams are built. Farmers cannot be compensated with new fields because of the intense land pressures...The compensation scheme involves building homes for people whose property is destroyed and providing seedlings for lost trees. For each hectare of land lost, people receive 1,000 kg. of maize every year for 15 years. This is however insufficient for a year for a family of six, which is the average family size in Lesotho.

Rights to water and land resources are often inseparable in Africa and elsewhere. The LHWP, by granting the RSA rights to enormous amount of Lesotho water, automatically affects local water and land rights and tenure. Land in Lesotho belongs to the King and is administered in his name by regional and community leaders. Every married male resident of a community is entitled to arable land for farming. Traditionally, farmland is allocated in three plots to give each family access to soils of different fertility. In addition to arable land, residents have use-rights over rangeland, which is operated as a commons. Despite the 1979 Land Act, designed to give individuals ownership over land, traditional land rights predominate over much of the country (Marake *et al.*, 1998).

In the traditional tenure system, individuals can have right of farming and grazing only after they secure right of residence. Resettled communities, therefore, face a number of difficulties. To be allocated residential land, an applicant must show loyalty to the local ruler. Even though resettled communities may be granted land by direction of the King in Maseru, they are likely to remain new comers in the eyes of locals. In that case, existing chiefs and communities may make demands on their loyalty. To whom should resettled communities show their loyalties (the King in faraway Maseru)? Should the rulers of resettled communities have to pay homage to local rulers, if so how much and in what way(s) should this be manifested and what would this signify for the distribution of political power? To whom should the incoming settlers pay homage? Their chief? The local chief? To both? If so in what ways and in what proportion and would this also signify for the distribution of political (clan, lineage, ethnic group) power? These are important questions that would require serious negotiation and political settlement.

An important issue related to land access is the matter of compensation for land lost by local communities as a result of the program. Such compensation is designed to take the form of annual deliveries of corn, beans and animal feed. The compensation program should last for fifteen years, after which the projects Environmental Action Plan is expected to have provided alternative means of employment to make the communities food self-sufficient. Some of the problems that may be associated with the compensation program include the following: villagers will not be compensated for the various functions of land (building materials, small game, fruits); some of the functions of land, for example, spiritual attachment and sense of identity, do not have a simple market price; the alternative means of employment to which villagers must resort in fifteen years is not clear, especially as it might require them to change completely their lifestyles and systems of production; several of the infrastructure projects designed to benefit the poor, for example, road construction and rural training, have not been implemented.

What Insights Can Be Gained From Environmental Security?

The political and economic attributes of the LHWP are precisely those that SD is unwilling or unable to address. The project involves contestation between stakeholders at several political and social levels, all of which are associated with different levels of power. The political power dynamics in the LHWP cannot be addressed within SD (which is basically apolitical) even if it were being implemented as a CBD program. The political complexities associated with the program have led Hildyard (2000) to describe it as an exercise in corruption at the highest political and financial levels. Hildyard notes that the program was founded on 'rule-breaking' much of it of a political-ecology nature: the project did not adhere to World Bank administrative procedures; it was politicized at the highest levels of the global hierarchy to the extent that the loan was set up for Lesotho even though it was granted to and is to be repaid by the RSA (this subterfuge was designed to 'sanction-bust' UN isolation of apartheid South Africa); there was rampant illegal (corrupt) practices by several actors including international construction companies and members of the Lesotho government. In short, the SD goals outlined for the LHWP, including environmental protection and poverty-alleviation for local communities, have been subverted by shortcomings inherent to SD itself. These would include its unwillingness to confront vexing political questions, its unwillingness to place local community aspirations at the center of decision-making, and its relegation of local poverty-alleviation to a tangential objective when compared to larger global economic interests. Potential tensions between local chiefs, local resource autonomy, and national resource sovereignty are issues that cannot be miraculously transformed to economic costs and benefits and resolved in the market place.

The case for placing the LHWP in an ES framework can be supported by several considerations. First, as noted above, the program presently fails to meet even its own SD criteria: ecologically, an EIS statement was not prepared to safeguard environmental concerns; economically, its implementation, which has been plagued by corruption at all levels, fails to satisfy economic efficiency; and socially the concerns of local communities are not central to the program's cost-benefit equation (no attempt has even been made to approach it as CBD). Second and relatedly, SD mechanisms of resettlement and compensation fail to address the basic political ecology of the problem, including, land tenure rights and the true value of land, water and other resources to the rural communities (both those being resettled and those among whom they are being resettled). Third, given the historical-political context of colonialism in southern Africa, the market can hardly be expected to address properly the matter of transnational water rights. These difficulties and others of this nature can be addressed within the ES framework by bringing all stakeholders to the negotiating table and ensuring that voluntary and realistic compromise can be achieved for resource exchange. For this approach to succeed, a minimum number of things must be in place (the implementation of the program is presumed to be a given).

- Communities, which are to be resettled, must have input into the choice of a new location.
- Communities, which are to host resettlers, must communicate whether they desire this or not.
- The compensation scheme must be remodeled to reflect community valuation (include those for water and land).
- Local choices and decisions must be coordinated by the government through negotiations to reach compromises both on relocation and compensation.
- The government must facilitate local aspirations by enacting laws, which grant local communities autonomy to achieve their long-term land and water

resource goals and other environmental objectives.

- The amount of water to be sold to the RSA must be consistent with the needs, aspirations and valuation of local communities.
- The government must request local communities to select representatives who will voice their interests. If/when the need arises, these representatives will engage in negotiations with representatives of other communities and with the government to reach a compromise on resource allocation.
- Local aspirations must be central in future negotiations on the program between Lesotho and the RSA. This must be based on a government Action Plan that responds to and coordinates community goals.
- All representatives (local community and government, alike) will have the same vote on issues.
- All cost-benefit appraisals must be centered on local values of environmental resources and amenities.
- Local conservation strategies must be incorporated into any grand plan

This is a general list, not of ideals, but of concrete steps that must form the central core of an ES agenda. The list suggests, above all, that an ES community-based program must seek to redistribute power to the community and locate community representation, government representation and civil society representation as equals around the same negotiation table.

Conclusion

Most scholars and policy makers would agree that SD is a desirable goal. However, SD has remained elusive partly because it is not easily definable; it has inherent conceptual and theoretical problems which have evoked disciplinary rifts in the discourse between economics and ecology; and it is difficult to operationalize. At an even more fundamentally important level, the socioeconomic (even if not the environmental) goals of SD are impossible to obtain through the market, which is the model's catalyst of choice for poverty-alleviation. Despite these drawbacks, SD remains the foremost development paradigm within globalization discourse and is being increasingly used as the yardstick by which to judge policy and projects.

The discussion in this chapter has been used to point to the conceptual and practical limitations of the SD model for articulating a clear path towards local resource autonomy and poverty-alleviation in Africa. These limitations are attributed partly to the model's close links with globalization and partly, and relatedly, to its unwillingness to tackle serious political economy rigidities at several social and geographic scales. This unwillingness is often manifested in suspicion (if not outright rejection) of the state and other political institutions as instruments of resource allocation, and a correspondingly heavy reliance on market efficacy for resource distribution. Unfortunately, market-led approaches (for example, cost–benefit analyses), often used in CBD programming to achieve SD, do not incorporate important elements of the political economy of resource management. In particular, market-led approaches typically ignore power distribution and its impacts on resource access and resource autonomy. In trivializing political issues in this way, market-led approaches fail to address the fundamental structural props that create and perpetuate poverty. The ES framework provides a potentially more robust approach to the issues surrounding rural poverty. Within ES, poverty is viewed as a problem of power distribution, which, in turn, determines resource access. Redistribution of resources, therefore, becomes predicated on redistribution of power through negotiation and compromise to avoid conflicts. Successful conflict avoidance hinges on meaningful participation by all stakeholders, which means that each party must have respect for the representatives and institutions of the other party. This kind of mutual respect can come about only if local peoples have full political empowerment to voice their grievances, desires and aspirations. Local aspirations can then be consolidated into regional and national action plans, which reflect local needs as expressed by local peoples, instead of the perceptions of technocrats about rural needs.

One of the central messages of this chapter is that SD identifies community empowerment and poverty-alleviation as two of its broad goals. However, these goals cannot be obtained within the existing market-led SD framework advocated by SD practitioners. ES, with its insistence on political participation, negotiation and conflict avoidance, provides a potentially more reasonable pathway for obtaining these goals. Will central governments willingly devolve real authority to local institutions? Perhaps, not. However, governments have a self-preservationist incentive to try to appease local constituents and may, therefore, be willing to give local communities greater autonomy over their resources, especially if this will not only address poverty, but also avert conflict. In a conflict-ridden continent like Africa, even this potential makes ES a very attractive option compared to the status quo.

References

Abaza, H. (1995), 'UNEP/World Bank Workshop on the Environmental Impacts of Structural Adjustment Programmes' *Ecological Economics* 14, pp. 1-5.

Agarwal, B. (2001), 'Participatory Exclusions, Community forestry, and Gender: An Analysis for South Asia and a Conceptual Framework.' *World Development* 29 (12), pp. 2145-2179.

Amin, S. (1992), 'Can Environmental Problems Be Subject to Economic Calculations.' *World Development,* V.20 (4), pp. 523-530.

Appiah-Opoku, S. and Mulamoottil, G. (1997), 'Indigenous Institutions and Environmental Assessment: The Case of Ghana.' *Environmental Management,* 21 (2), pp. 159-171.

Arrow, K. et al. (1995), 'Economic growth, carrying capacity and the environment', *Ecological Economics* 15, pp. 93-95.

Ashman, D. (2001), 'Civil society Collaboration with Business: Bringing Empowerment Back in.' *World Development* 29 (7), pp. 1097-1113.

Ayres, R. (1993), 'Cowboys, cornucopians and long-run sustainability.' *Ecological Economics*, 8(3), pp. 189-207.

Azar, C., Holmberg, J. and Lindgren, K. (1996), 'Socio-ecological indicators for sustainability.' *Ecological Economics* 18, pp. 89-112.

Babu, S. Brown, L. and McClafferty, B. (2000), 'Systematic Client Consultation in Development: The Case of Food Policies in Ghana, India, Kenya and Mali.' *World Development* 28 (1), pp. 99-110.

Baland, J. and Platteau, J. (1999), 'The Ambiguous Impact of Inequality on Local Resource Management.' *World Development* 27 (5), pp. 773-788.

Barrett, C. (1996), 'Fairness, Stewardship and Sustainable Development.' *Ecological Economics* 19, pp. 11-17.

Beckerman, W. (1992), 'Economic Growth and the Environment: Whose Growth? Whose Environment?' *World Development* 20 (4), pp. 481-496.

Behera, D. K. and Erasmus, P. (1999), 'Sustainable Development of Indigenous Populations: Challenges Ahead.' *South African Journal of Ethnology* 22 (1), pp. 1-12.

Bowyer-Bowyer, T. (1996), 'Criticisms of environmental policy for land management in Zimbabwe.' *Global Ecology and Biogeography Letters* 5, pp. 7-17.

Boyce, J. (1994), 'Inequality as a cause of environmental degradation.' *Ecological Economics* 11, pp. 169-178.

Braidotti, R. et al. (1994), 'Responses to Crisis from Deep Ecology, social Ecology and Ecofemininsm.' In Braodotti, R. *et al.* (eds.) *Women, the Environment and Sustainable Development.* London: Zed Books, pp. 151-168.

Broad, R. (1994), 'The Poor and the Environment: Friends or Foes.' *World Development* 22 (6), pp. 811-822.

Bryant, R. (1997), 'Beyond the impasse: the power of political ecology in Third World environmental research.' *Area* 29, pp. 5-19.

Chatty, D. (1998), 'Enclosures and exclusions.' *Wildlife Conservation* 14 (4), pp. 2-9.

Costanza, R. and Patten, B. (1995), 'Defining and Predicting Sustainability.' *Ecological Economics* 15, pp. 193-196.

Da Cunha, M. and Almeida, M. (2000), 'Indigenous people, traditional people, and conservation in The Amazon.' *Daedalus* 129 (2), pp. 315-338.

de Graaf, H., Musters, C. and ter Keurs, W. (1996), 'Sustainable Development: Looking for New Strategies.' *Ecological Economics* 16, pp. 205-216.

Durbin, J and Ing, J. (1994), 'The Role of Local People in the Successful Maintenance of Protected Areas in Madagascar.' *Environmental Conservation* 21 (2), Summer, pp. 115-120.

Fakir, S. (2000), 'Finding future water in Southern Africa: Avoiding Conflict and War.' Southern Africa Water Crisis (SAWAC).

FAO Progress Report (1995), Agenda 21/Chapter 13 - Sustainable Mountain Development. Rome, Italy: FAO.

Glenzer, K. (2002), 'The Enactment and Contestation of Global Cultural Scripts in Malian Development.' In B. I. Logan (ed.) *Globalization, the Third World State and Poverty-Alleviation in the Twenty-First Century.* Aldershot: Ashgate, pp. 186-209.

Gosselin, P., Belenger, D., Bibeault, J., and Webster, A. (1993), 'Indicators for a Sustainable Society.' *Canadian Journal of Public Health* 84 (3), May-June, pp. 197-200.

Greenberg, J. and Park, T. (1994), 'Political Ecology.' *Journal of Political Ecology* 1, 1-11.

Hackel, J. (1993), 'Rural Change and Nature Conservation in Africa: A Case from Swaziland.' *Human Ecology* 21 (3), pp. 295-312.

Hackel, J. (1998) 'Community Conservation and the Future of Africa's Wildlife.' *Conservation Biology* 13 (4), pp. 726-734.

Harte, M. (1995), 'Ecology, Sustainability, and Environment as Capital.' *Ecological Economics* 15, pp. 157-164.

Hildyard, N. (2000) 'The Lesotho Highland Water Development Project - What Went Wrong?' Presentation to the Chatham House Conference: 'Corruption in Southern Africa– Sources and Solutions.' http://www.globalpolicy.org/nations/corrupt/lesotho.htm.

Homer-Dixon, T. (1991), 'On the Threshold: Environment Change as Causes of Acute Conflict.' *International Security* 16 (2), Fall, pp. 76-116.

Homer-Dixon, T. (1995), 'The Ingenuity Gap: Can Poor Countries Adapt to Resource Scarcity?' *Population and Development Review* 21 (3), September, pp. 587-612.

Horta, K. (1996), 'Making the Earth Rumble: The Lesotho-South African Water Connection.' *Multinational Monitor* 17 (5), pp. 1-8.

Khasa, P. et al. (1995), 'Utilization and management of forest resources in Zaire.' *The Forestry Chronicle* 71 (4), July-August, pp. 479-488.

Klunne, W. (2000), 'Lesotho Water Project.' http://www.geocities.com/wim_klunne/lesotho/

Lele, S. (1991), 'Sustainable Development: A Critical Review.' *World Development* 19 (6), pp. 607-621.

Letsie, D. (1999), 'Alexandra and the Lesotho Highlands Water Project: Poor Water Services And Rising Costs.' Paper presented at the conference on 'Water for all: Policy, Finance, and Institutions to Deliver our Basic Rights to Water.' Edenvael, South Africa, April.

Lintott, J. (1996), 'Environmental Accounting: Useful to Whom and For What?' *Ecological Economics* 16, pp. 179-190.

Logan, B. I. (1991), 'Overpopulation and Poverty in Africa: Rethinking The Traditional Relationship.' *Tijdschrift voor econ. en Soc. Geografie* 2 (1), pp. 40-56.

Logan, B. I. and Moseley, W. (2002), 'The political ecology of poverty alleviation in Zimbabwe's Communal Areas Management Programme for Indigenous Resources (CAMPFIRE).' *Geoforum* 33, pp. 1-14.

Logan, B. I. and Tevera, D. (2001), 'Economic Structural Adjustment, Agricultural Production and Urban Food Security.' *Canadian Journal of African Studies*.

Lonergan, S. (1993), 'Impoverishment, population and environmental degradation.' *Environmental Conservation*, 20 (4), pp. 328-334.

Lonergan, S., Bakary, T., Carlson, S., and Chernushenko, D (1999), *Environment and Security: An Overview of Issues and Resource Priorities for Canada.* University of Alberta.

Lusk, M. and Hoff, M. (1994) 'Sustainable Social Development.' *Social Development Issues* 16 (3), pp. 20-30.

Lutz, E. and Munasinghe, M. (1994), 'Integration of Environmental Concerns into Economic Analysis of Projects and Policies in an Operational Context.' *Ecological Economics* 10, pp. 37-46.

Marake, M., Mokuku, C., Majoro, M., and Mokitimi, N. (1998), *Global Change and Subsistence Rangelands in Southern Africa: Resource Variability, Access and Use Relation to Rural Livelihoods and Welfare.* Task O Project Document, National University of Lesotho.

Matzke, G and Nabane, N. (1996), 'Outcomes of a Community Controlled Wildlife Utilization Program In a Zambezi Valley Community.' *Human Ecology* 24 (1), pp. 65-85.

McManus, P. (1996), 'Contested Terrains: Politics, Stories and Discourses of Sustainability.' *Environmental Politics* 5 (1), pp. 48-73.

Merchant, C. (1992), 'Environmental Ethics and Political Conflict.' *Radical Ecology: The Search for a Livable World.* NY: Routledge, pp. 61-81.

M'Gonigle, M. (1999), 'Ecological economics and political ecology: towards a necessary synthesis.' *Ecological Economics* 28 (1), pp. 11-26.

Moltke, K. (1992), 'The United Nations Development System and Environmental Management.' *World Development* 20 (4), pp. 619-626.

Moseley, W. (2001), 'African evidence on the relation of poverty, time preference and the Environment.' *Ecological Economics* 38 (3), pp. 317-326.

Moyo, S. and Tevera, D. (1999), 'Regional Environmental Security in Southern Africa: Some Conceptual Issues.' Paper presented at SARIPS Methodology Workshop, Harare, Zimbabwe.

Myers, N. (1995), 'Economics of the Environment: a Seismic Shift in Thinking.' *Ecological Economics*, 15, pp. 125-128.

Munn, R. (1992), 'Towards Sustainable Development.' *Atmospheric Environment* 26A (15), pp. 2725-2731.

Muradian, R. and Martinez-Alier (2001), 'Trade and the environment: from a 'Southern' Perspective.' *Ecological Economics* 36 (2), pp. 281-297.

Pasek, J. (1992), 'Obligations to Future Generations: A Philosophical Note.' *World Development.* 20 (4), pp. 513-521.

Pearce W. and Turner, K. (1996), *Economics of Natural Resources and the Environment.* Baltimore: JHU Press, Chapter 17.

Reardon, T. and Vosti, S.(1995), 'Links Between Rural Poverty and the environment in Developing Countries: Asset Categories and Investment Poverty.' *World Development* 23 (9), pp. 1495-1506.

Redclift, M. (1992), 'The Meaning of Sustainable development.' *Geoforum* 23 (3), 395-403.

Ropke, I. (1999) 'Prices are not worth much.' *Ecological Economics* 29 (10), 45-46.

Shaw, B. (1999) *Defining Environmental Security.* Washington D.C.: Center for Environmental Security.

Sneddon, C. (2000), '"Sustainablity" in ecological economics, ecology and livelihoods: a Review.' *Progress in Human Geography* 24 (4), pp. 521-549.

Soderbaum, P. (1999), 'Values, Ideology and politics in ecological economics.' *Ecological Economics* 28 (2), pp. 161-170.

Songorwa, A. (1999), 'Community-Based Wildlife Management (CWM) in Tanzania: Are the Communities Interested?' *World Development* 27 (12), pp. 2061-2079.

Suhrke, A. (1991), *Environmental change, population displacement and acute conflict.* The American University.

Sundar, N. (2001), 'Is Devolution Democratization?' *World Development* 29 (12), pp. 2007-2023.

Suter, G. (1995), 'Adapting Ecological Risk Assessment for Ecosystem Valuation' *Ecological Economics* 14, pp. 137-141.

Taylor, L. (1993), 'The World Bank and the Environment: The World Development Report 1992.' *World Development* 21 (5), pp. 869-881.

TED Case Studies (2000) 'Lesotho Water Exports.' Http://www.american.edu/TED/LESOTHO.HTM.

Torras, M. (1999), 'Inequality, Resource Depletion, Welfare Accounting: Applications to Indonesia and Costa Rica.' *World Development* 27 (7), pp. 1191-1202.

United Nations Development Programme (UNDP) (1994), 'Redefining Security: The Human Dimension.' *World Development Report.* New York: UNDP.

van Pelt, M. (1993), 'Ecologically sustainable development and project appraisal in developing countries.' *Ecological Economics* 7, pp. 19-42.

Viederinan, S. (1993), 'Sustainability Development: What is it and how do we get there?' *Current History,* April, pp. 180-185.

Zarsky, L. (1999), 'Civil Society and Clean Shared Growth in Asia: Toward a Stakeholder Model of Environmental Governance.' Paper presented at the Outlook for Environmentally Sound Development Policies Workshop. Manila, Philippines.

Chapter 3

Environmental Degradation and 'Poor' Smallholders in the West African Sudano-Sahel: Global Discourses and Local Realities

William G. Moseley

Introduction[1]

The belief that the poor and hungry will often destroy their immediate environment in order to survive has been a prominent component of international discourse on environment and development since the late 1980s (for example, WCED, 1987; UNCED, 1993; World Bank, 1996). Rather than an obscure theoretical discussion, assumptions regarding poverty and environment interactions have been enormously influential in policy and program design. The notion that poverty is a cause of environmental degradation has been a central theme of the literature on sustainable development (Lele, 1991; Bryant, 1997), a concept that became widely known after publication of the 1987 Brundtland Commission Report (WCED), *Our Common Future*. A number of major conferences convened by the United Nations built upon the work of the Brundtland Commission regarding poverty and the environment: the Rio Conference on Environment and Development (1992), the Cairo Conference on Population and Development (1994), the Copenhagen World Summit on Social Development (1995), the Beijing Fourth World Conference on Women (1995), and the Istanbul Habitat II Conference (1996). Agenda 21, the action plan adopted at the Rio Conference, devoted a chapter to the relationship between poverty and environment (UNCED, 1993). The conferences in Cairo, Beijing and Istanbul each tackled questions of poverty and environment from their respective vantage points of population, the advancement of women, and human settlements. (UNDP, 2000). Poverty and environment again were a focus of discussion at the Earth Summit+10 in South Africa (September 2002).

While numerous conceptual papers have been written both in support of and against the notion that poverty is a cause of environmental degradation (for example, Logan, 1991; Lele, 1991; Reardon and Vosti, 1995; Vosti and Reardon, 1997; Dasgupta, 1997; Duraiappah, 1998; Malik, 1999; Scherr, 2000; Moseley, 2001a), this theoretical assumption has undergone amazingly little empirical assessment at the local level. Most quantitative research in this domain has been based on cross national comparisons (for example, World Bank, 1992; DeBruyn *et al.*, 1998; Kaufmann *et al.*, 1998; List and Gallet, 1999; Stern *et al.*, 1999; Dinda, 2000). Research at local scales, while it increased in the 1990s, was more limited (for example, Broad 1994; Forsyth *et al.*, 1998) and often focused on population-environment rather than poverty-environment interactions (for example, Mink, 1993; Grepperud, 1996; Templeton and Scherr, 1999).

Widely held, yet inadequately tested theories in the environmental realm are often referred to as environmental narratives, received wisdoms or orthodoxies (Fairhead and Leach, 1995; Leach and Mearns, 1996; Batterbury *et al.*, 1997). Political ecologists have increasingly examined key environment-development narratives in order to understand how these ideas are developed and understood by different actors. An understanding of national level environment-development narratives is important because such discourses can block or promote specific actor interests. Environmental narratives may influence the prioritization of development problems, the level of funding to projects, and the development of policies in the realm of taxation, agriculture and the environment. For example, Fairhead and Leach (1996) outline outsider conceptions of deforestation in Guinea and how this is contradicted by historical landscape analysis depicting a pattern of afforestation. Similarly, Bassett and Zueli (2000) describe how notions of declining tree cover are unfounded in northern Ivory Coast, yet these false conceptions heavily influenced the development of that country's national Environmental Action Plan. In the case of Mali, Glenzer (1999) and Van Beusekom (1999) discuss how dominant descriptions of the 'environmental problem' in the Sahel shifted radically throughout the 20th Century, yet these changes had little to do with hard data on the state of the environment. Finally, Logan (chapter 2 in this volume) examines the problematic application of the sustainable development concept in Africa and Laris (chapter 4 in this volume) outlines dominant misconceptions regarding fire policy in West Africa.

The broad objective of this chapter is to explore the development, influence and voracity of the poverty induced environmental degradation thesis in the West African Sudano-Sahel and the extent to which it may be considered an environment-development narrative. This goal is pursued through four interrelated research questions. 1) What are the key elements of the poverty induced environmental degradation discourse? 2) To what degree has the poverty induced environmental degradation thesis been internalized by policy makers in Mali? 3) Is there empirical evidence to support the notion of poverty induced environmental degradation in southern Mali? 4) What alternative explanations exist for environmental degradation in southern Mali and why have these causal factors been less prominent in environment-development discourse?

Mainstream Views Regarding Poverty Induced Environmental Degradation

This section briefly examines the key elements of the poverty induced environmental degradation narrative. I present the dominant perspective, rather than alternative interpretations, on poverty-environment interactions as this is the view that has been most influential in policy circles and in practice.

The notion of poverty-induced environmental degradation has become quite fashionable among mainstream policymakers in recent years (for example, WCED, 1987; UNCED, 1993; World Bank, 1996). As Bryant (1997, p.6) notes '[t]he vision of "poverty-stricken masses" caught up in a vicious cycle of poverty and environmental degradation has come to dominate the mainstream literature, and rapidly become an article of faith among key development agencies such as the World Bank and the International Monetary Fund.' Current, mainstream notions of poverty as a major cause of environmental degradation are deeply imbedded in the discourse on sustainable development, a concept that has been popular in the literature since the late 1980s.

The term sustainable development was first used in 1980 in the International Union for the Conservation of Nature's World Conservation Strategy (IUCN, 1980; Wilbanks, 1994; McManus, 2000). The term became much more prominent after it was used by the World Commission on Environment and Development (WCED) in *Our Common Future* (1987) and has been seriously debated since then (for example, Lele, 1991; Redclift, 1992; Wilbanks, 1994; Turner, 1997; Liverman, 1999; Logan, 1999; National Research Council, 1999; Sneddon, 2000). The most widely known articulation of the concept stems from this report (WCED, 1987, p.8), which defined the term vaguely as 'development that meets the needs of the present without compromising the ability of future generations to meet their own needs.' Linking poverty and environment was critical for the framers of sustainable development as it allowed them to make the conceptual breakthrough of joining development and environmental conservation. Formerly, these two processes were perceived as antagonistic. 'The major impact of the sustainable development movement is the rejection of the notion that environmental conservation necessarily constrains development and that development necessarily means environmental pollution . . .' (Lele, 1991, p.613)

The Brundtland Report (WCED, 1987, p.28) stated that '[t]hose who are poor and hungry will often destroy their immediate environment in order to survive: they will cut down forests; their livestock will overgraze grasslands; they will overuse marginal lands; and in growing numbers they will crowd into congested cities. The cumulative effect of these changes is so far reaching as to make poverty itself a major global scourge.' Tobey (1989) has referred to the phenomenon of poverty leading to environmental degradation as 'poverty related pollution.' Similarly, the World Bank (1996, p.13) has asserted that '[p]overty is also a factor in accelerating environmental degradation, since the poor, with shorter time horizons . . . are unable and often unwilling to invest in natural resource management . . .' Other institutions and authors have arrived at similar conclusions (e.g, Mellor, 1988; Beckerman, 1992; Mink, 1993;

UNCED, 1993; Cleaver and Schreiber, 1994; Ahmed and Doelemen, 1995; World Bank, 1996; Barret, 1996; Forsyth *et al.*, 1998).

The current mainstream argument regarding poverty and environmental degradation is amazingly similar to the Malthusian and neo-Malthusian conceptions of population induced environmental degradation (Ehrlich, 1968; Malthus, 1970; Dasgupta, 1995; Madulu, 1995). The Malthusian concept of a vicious cycle of population-induced poverty suggests that poverty leads to environmental degradation, leading to decreased land productivity, increasing labor needs, larger families, accelerating population growth, and greater poverty which causes the cycle to repeat itself (as described in Logan, 1991). In Africa, colonial administrators frequently blamed population induced poverty for soil degradation (Baker, 1983). While the Malthusians focused on the links between population and poverty, the sustainable development enthusiasts have largely adopted the same causal chain, yet chosen to emphasize (and more clearly articulate) poverty-environment links. Current conceptualizations of poverty induced environmental degradation have argued that poorer households are more likely to degrade the environment for at least two reasons: 1) a lack of resources to invest in environmental conservation, and 2) shorter time horizons. These two reasons are often inter-linked in the literature.

The notion that the poor do not have enough resources to invest in environmental conservation is fairly straightforward. The basic idea is that there is a cost to preserving natural resources or restoring a degraded environment and the poor are less able to do this. In a rural, developing country context, Reardon and Vosti (1995, p.1496) point out that 'the poor may 'mine' the soil through intensive cropping without accompanying investments in soil conservation . . .' Similar assertions have been made by van der Pol (1992) and Bremin *et al.* (2001) regarding grain farmers in the West African Sahel.

If a lack of resources to invest in environmental conservation is a major cause of environmental degradation, then a number of scholars have argued that economic growth is a prerequisite for sustainable natural resource use (see, for example, Beckerman, 1992; Pearce and Atkinson, 1993; Barret, 1996; Lomberg, 2001). In its 1992 development report (devoted to the environment and development), the World Bank (1992, p.25) stated that '[e]conomic development and sound environmental management are complementary aspects of the same agenda . . . income growth will provide the resources for improved environmental management.' Similarly, Beckerman (1992, p.482) notes that 'in the end the best – and perhaps only – way to attain a decent environment in most countries is to become rich.' In commenting on Africa specifically, the World Bank (1996, p.17) asserts that '[t]he prospect of strengthened economic growth in Africa presents a promise of greater resources available for environmental management . . . it is vital that sufficient resources are channeled to support the emergence of new environmental institutions, saddled with the task of shaping environmental legislation, regulation and policies...' Examples of soil conservation investments that household wealth might facilitate at the farm scale in the West African Sudano-Sahel include the application of manure and compost to fields or the construction of anti-erosion barriers such as contoured rock lines or gully plugs.

The second explanation given in the mainstream literature for why the poor are more prone to degrade the environment is that they have shorter time horizons, or they are more preoccupied with surviving in the present than thinking of long-term needs. Shorter time horizons translate to both a lack of willingness to invest in conservation and a greater tendency degrade in the short term because of little concern for the future. In its most extreme version, the idea is that poverty and hunger leave households with no choice but to abuse the immediate environment in order to meet their most basic needs.

The notion that the poor are more prone to degrade the environment is consistent with a body of theory in neo-classical economics regarding time preference and discount rates. A person or group's rate of time preference reflects the value they place on present versus future consumption. A person who places a high value on present consumption is said to have a high rate of time preference whereas a person who prefers to limit current consumption in favor of the future is said to have a low rate of time preference. Discount rates, for which time preference rates are a theoretical determinant, are used by economists to weight current versus future streams of income and expenditures. The higher the discount rate, the more highly current income and expenditures are valued relative to those in the future (Krutilla and Fisher, 1975; Pearce and Turner, 1990; Field, 1997).

It is typically argued that poorer people, particularly those facing food shortages, have a higher rate of time preference than their wealthier counterparts because they are more concerned about their basic needs (assumed to be universal or absolute) than they are about saving for the future (Murphree, 1993; Bardhan, 1996; Lumley, 1997). It is assumed, likewise, that wealthier people have lower personal rates of time preference as, with their most basic needs satisfied in the present, they are able to consider and save for the future.

> It is generally accepted that an individual's discount rate is influenced by a number of personal factors such as wealth and income profile...Wealthier, healthier, younger and better educated individuals are likely to have lower discount rates than their poorer, older, sicker and less well educated counterparts...if you are rich, you can afford to defer consumption of goods because you are already likely to have more of everything you want or need. (Lumley, 1997, pp.76-77)

Within the context of natural resource use, it is similarly assumed that the poor have very high rates of time preference in that they tend to over-exploit local resources so that they may feed their families in the short term. Dasgupta (1997, p.13) notes that '[a] recent intellectual tradition argues that the reason the poor today degrade their environmental resource base is that their poverty forces them to discount future incomes at unusually high rates.' For example, Murphree asserts that the behavior of lower income households in Zimbabwe towards the environment is indicative of a high rate of time preference.

A culture of poverty [exists] in which the individual is preoccupied with survival in the present and where any effective concern for the future is missing. A culture of poverty is one in which the future is discounted at a very high rate. This is a recipe for accelerated degradation because poverty is both the cause and effect of environmental degradation. (Murphree, 1993, pp.1-2)

Having briefly elaborated on the nature of the poverty-induced environmental degradation thesis, the next section examines the degree to which this thinking has been internalized by policymakers in Mali.

Localized Poverty-Environment Discourse: The Case of Mali

Policymakers in the West African nation of Mali have not been immune to the global discourse regarding poverty-induced environmental degradation. Mali's high rates of poverty and significant levels of natural resource degradation (World Bank, 1996)[2] have led many scholars to problematize Mali's development in terms of poverty-induced environmental degradation. For example, the belief that food insecure households and the environment are engaged in a mutually reinforcing, downward spiral is dominant in much of the literature regarding north and central Mali (for example, Leisinger and Schmitt, 1995; Davies, 1996; FEWS, 1997).

A review of Malian government and donor publications suggests that the notion of poverty as a cause of environmental degradation has influenced the formulation of policy and programs. For example, text in Mali's National Environment Action Plan or NEAP (GoM, 1998) asserts that environmental degradation in Mali is linked to climatic and anthropomorphic factors. For the Sikasso Province (in southern Mali), the NEAP identified the encroachment onto marginal lands and the over-exploitation of soil and forest resources as top environmental problems. The NEAP focuses on poverty and population growth as the drivers of this phenomenon. 'Agriculture pressure translates more broadly to a significant degradation of natural resources (soil and vegetative cover), which is highlighted, among other things, by an increase in cleared land in several regions where population pressure on marginal lands and forests is strong, combined with a decline in fallow periods and soil fertility as well as increasing erosion.' (author's translation from French) (GoM, 1998, pp.23) Given the assumption that poverty and population growth (two processes that Malian policy documents often link together) push farmers to degrade marginal lands, the NEAP calls for efforts to increase revenues and diversify income generation activities to address this issue (GoM, 1998). In another example, the World Bank sponsored *Lutte contra la Pauvreté* (or War on Poverty) in Mali has been started, among many reasons, to preserve the 'natural equilibrium' (GoM, 1998, GoM and World Bank, 2000). In both of the above cases, a connection has been made between environmental integrity and economic prosperity.

In interviews with government and donor representatives in 1999 and 2000, a number of officials articulated a belief that poorer farmers were largely responsible for the environmental degradation in southern Mali.[3] For example, a Bamako-based World Bank official said that 'the poor are preoccupied with feeding the family today. They cannot think about the environment. They do not have the resources for [agricultural] intensification.' A representative of the NGO consortium noted that 'drought, ignorance, poverty and population growth are the cause of environmental degradation.' Finally, an official at the Ministry of Environment stated that 'poverty pushes people to exploit natural resources.'

The Malian cotton company, or *Compagnie Malienne pour le Développement des Textiles* (CMDT), suggested that general economic development and a wealthier farming community will lead to more sustainable agricultural production (as they believe wealthier farmers are more likely to invest in soil conservation and intensify production than poorer farmers). A high ranking CMDT official explained that 'one needs economic sustainability for agricultural sustainability.' Supporting this statement was a comment by a United States Agency for International Development (USAID) official pointing out that 'we notice more development in areas where cotton is farmed.' The same individual noted that environmental degradation was more of a problem for the poor because 'poor people depend more on the natural resource base.'

The above comments suggest that the poverty-induced environmental degradation thesis has been internalized by many policymakers in Mali. It is difficult to know if governmental, non-governmental, and donor officials really believe that poverty is a primary cause of environmental degradation or if it is a causal framework that conveniently preserves the policy and programmatic status quo. After exploring the validity of the poverty-induced environmental degradation thesis in Mali, the paper will conclude by further exploring the political economy of environment-development discourse in this context.

Environmental Degradation and 'Poor' Smallholders in Mali's Cotton Zone

While poverty is increasingly viewed as a major cause of environmental degradation in Mali, there is very little empirical evidence to support this assertion. This section summarizes the results of fieldwork undertaken in 2000 (Moseley, 2001b) to examine, among other issues, the validity of the poverty-induced environmental degradation thesis in southern Mali.

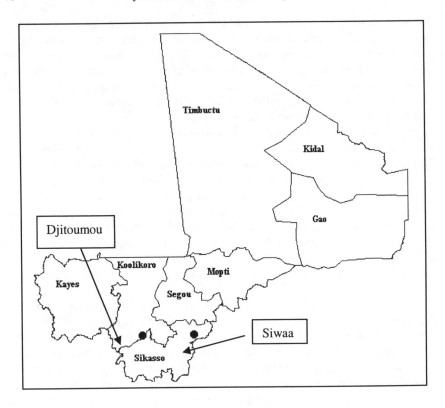

Figure 3.1 Map of Research Locations in Mali

The basic experimental design was to take a random sample of households (133 in total), stratified by wealth, and examine associated environmental indicators and management practices. While I could have examined a variety of environmental variables in this context, I chose to focus on farm field soil quality (infiltration, bulk density, pH and aggregate stability) as this was frequently mentioned as a major environmental concern in southern Mali and such variables were easier to relate to specific households with known wealth levels. The study's random sample of households was taken from four villages in the Siwaa area and from four villages in the Djitoumou area of southern Mali (see figure 3.1). Wealth levels were determined for each household based on an inventory of savings and assets (for example, livestock, ploughs, bicycles), with households subsequently classified as rich, intermediate or poor using local conceptions of these terms. Data on agricultural management practices was collected for all households while soil analysis was undertaken on a subset of farms.

While Mali is known for being one of the poorest countries in the world, farmers in the southern part of the country are among the nation's wealthiest (five times wealthier than rural households in other parts of the country) due to more favorable agricultural conditions (800-1000 mm of annual rainfall) and revenue from the cash cropping of cotton. The cash cropping of cotton in southern Mali is undertaken by individual smallholders (rather than on larger estates or plantations) and is one component of rural household economies that typically emphasize food crop production (mainly sorghum, millet and maize). Rural households in the southern part of the country have become differentiated over time in terms of size, wealth, assets and farming practices. In Djitoumou, for example, I found that the wealthier households in my sample (7 out of 65 households) had an average of 35 members and possessed, among many types of assets, 53 head of cattle, 5 plows and 4 bicycles. This compares with poorer households (40 out of 65 households) who had an average of 14 members and possessed 1 head of cattle, 1.7 plows and 1.6 bicycles. These differences in wealth, with for example, the richest 10 per cent of households being 59 times wealthier than the poorest tenth in Djitoumou, allowed me to examine if wealthier farmers took better care of the environment than their poorer counterparts.

Tables 3.1 and 3.2 present data on soil quality for poor, intermediate and wealthy farmers in the two study areas, Siwaa and Djitoumou. Using a dummy regression model to analyze the soils data for Siwaa, no significant relationship was found between the wealth group variable and any of the soil quality measures. Given the small sample sizes in Djitoumou, a non-parametric statistical test (Mann-Whitney) was run on the data to determine potential differences of mean rank in soil quality measures. This analysis suggested that the mean rank of infiltration measures was significantly better for the intermediate group than the rich; aggregate stability was worse for the poor than the rich; and bulk density was better for the poor and intermediate than the rich. This mixed result suggested that there was no clear difference between the rich and poor in Djitoumou, although it could be argued that the intermediate group was doing better than the rich (as the mean rank for two of the four measures was significantly better than that of the rich). It is difficult to make a convincing case that soil measures are significantly better or worse for the rich or the poor in either Siwaa or Djitoumou. This finding alone raises questions about the notion that the poor are a proximate cause of soil degradation.

African Environment and Development

Table 3.1 Mean (and Standard Deviation) of Integrity Measures by Wealth Strata in the Siwaa Area for Loamy Sand Soils

Group	Statistic	Final Infiltration (cm/hr)	PH-KCL[4]	Bulk Density (g/cm3)	% Water Stable Aggregates
	Mean	20.46	5.55	2.20	12.7%
Poor	St Dev	15.91	0.54	0.18	8.3%
	CV	.778	.097	.082	.654
	N/farms	41/6	43/6	43/6	43/6
	Mean	15.24	5.49	2.12	14.1%
Intermediate	St Dev	11.94	0.58	0.22	7.7%
	CV	.783	.106	.104	.546
	N/farms	30/4	32/4	32/4	29/4
	Mean	16.52	5.53	2.13	9.8%
Rich	St Dev	11.35	0.54	0.14	5.3%
	CV	.687	.098	.066	.541
	N/farms	31/4	32/4	32/4	32/4
	Mean	17.73	5.52	2.15	12.2%
Average	St Dev	13.59	0.55	0.19	7.4%
	CV	.766	.100	.088	.607
	N/farms	102/14	107/14	107/14	104/14
	Mean	30.68	5.74	1.84	21.9%
Control	St Dev	22.50	0.38	0.16	10.8%
	CV	.733	.066	.087	.493
	N	9	5	8	5

Note: Using a dummy regression model, no significant relationship was found between the wealth group variable and any of the soil quality measures.
CV = Coefficient of variation

Table 3.2 Mean (and Standard Deviation) of Integrity Measures by Wealth Strata in the Djitoumou Area for Sandy Clay Loam Soils

Group	Statistic	Final Infiltration (cm/hr)	pH-KCL	Bulk Density (g/cm3)	% Water Stable Aggregates
Poor	Mean	7.48	6.23	1.56*	34.5%*
	St Dev	6.38	0.45	0.17	16.3%
	CV	.853	.072	.109	.472
	N/farms	23/4	16/4	24/4	24/4
Intermediate	Mean	9.25**	5.93	1.55*	43.4%
	St Dev	6.81	0.40	0.16	12.6%
	CV	.736	.067	.103	.290
	N/farms	17/2	8/2	18/2	14/2
Rich	Mean	3.72	6.32	1.70	48.9%
	St Dev	2.10	0.41	0.16	18.5%
	CV	.565	.065	.094	.378
	N/farms	9/2	5/2	9/2	9/2
Average	Mean	7.41	6.16	1.58	39.9%
	St Dev	6.21	0.45	0.17	16.5%
	CV	.838	.073	.108	.414
	N/farms	49/8	29/8	51/8	47/8
Control	Mean	33.00	6.52	1.53	48.4%
	St Dev	38.13	0.39	0.31	13.9%
	CV	1.155	.060	.203	.287
	N	8	6	9	9

Note: CV = Coefficient of variation
* = Significantly different than the rich using Mann Whitney mean rank test (p<.05)
** = Significantly different than the rich using Mann Whitney mean rank test (p<.01)

I also sought to understand if there were any differences in soil and environmental management practices between rich and poor households. An examination of soil management practices from the household survey as well as individual case studies suggested that agricultural management practices did appear to be influenced by wealth levels as well as other factors such as labor availability, involvement with cotton farming, and soil characteristics. Data on farm management practices for the Siwaa area are presented in Tables 3.3a and 3.3b.

Table 3.3a Selected Farming Practices by Wealth Group for Larger Household Sample (n=68) in the Siwaa Zone, 1997-99

Group (n)	Stat	Total Ha	% Ha in No Till	% Ha Intercrop	%Ha w/ Insecticide
	Mean	7.2	30.1%	12.9%	23.8%
Poor	St. Dev.	3.1	23.4%	18.2%	11.2%
(31)	CV	.431	.777	1.411	.471
	Mean	13.2	18.8%	*29.8%	#32.7%
Inter	St. Dev.	6.1	18.0%	18.6%	15.8%
(23)	CV	.462	.957	.624	.483
	Mean	18.9	24.1%	11.7%	#32.2%
Rich	St. Dev.	8.1	21.6%	15.0%	8.3%
(14)	CV	.429	.896	1.282	.258
	Mean	11.7	25%	18.4%	28.5%
Mean	St. Dev.	7.1	21.6%	19.3%	13.0%
(68)	CV	.607	.864	1.049	.456

Note: CV = Coefficient of variance
* Significantly different (p<.01) than poor and rich using Mann-Whitney mean rank test.
# Significantly different (p<.05) than poor using Mann-Whitney mean rank test.

Table 3.3b Fertilizer Usage by Wealth Group for Larger Household Sample (n=68) in the Siwaa Zone, 1997-99

Group (n)	Stat	Total Ha	%Ha w/ Org Fert	Carts Org Fert per Ha	Kgs /Ha Inorg Fert	%Ha w/ Inorg Fert
	Mean	7.2	20.9%	8.2	77.4	48.1%
Poor	St. Dev.	3.1	17.8%	10.5	37.6	21.5%
(31)	CV	.431	.852	1.280	.486	.447
	Mean	13.2	28.4%	12.7	95.7	58.2%
Inter	St. Dev.	6.1	18.8%	15.8	21.1	16.7%
(23)	CV	.462	.662	1.244	.220	.287
	Mean	18.9	19.2%	5.8	#147.2	53.3%
Rich	St. Dev.	8.1	16.5%	7.2	150.8	18.9%
(14)	CV	.429	.859	1.241	1.024	.355
	Mean	11.7	23.1%	9.2	98.0	52.6%
Mean	St. Dev.	7.1	18.1%	12.2	76.8	19.7%
(68)	CV	.607	.784	1.326	.784	.375

Note: CV = Coefficient of variance

It was found that wealth encouraged some practices that were environmentally beneficial (such as fertilizer use up to a point) as well as other practices that were environmentally detrimental (such as pesticide use). This mixed wealth effect (rather than no effect at all) may be why soil quality measures were not clearly better for one group than another.

I concluded that the proper balance of techniques was more important than any specific mix of practices. In other words, the research revealed 'poor' and 'rich' paths to sustainability that included a number of 'either/or' combinations for arriving at relatively better soil quality measures (for example, if not organic inputs then practices that preserve soil organic matter). These more sustainable paths may be juxtaposed with a number of unsustainble combinations. These included those rich and poor households that neither applied sufficient organic inputs nor a mix of measures to maintain or restore soil organic matter.

In addition to wealth, another variable that correlated with more problematic environmental practices (for example, overuse of inorganic fertilizers, heavy pesticide use) was the degree to which a household was involved with cotton farming. As Table 3.4 indicates, wealthier households farm more cotton than the poor (and have a greater proportion of their farms in cotton). In the absence of the proper mix of inputs, cotton cultivation negatively impacts soil fertility. Furthermore, semi-structured interviews revealed that wealthier households often called upon the land and labor resources of poorer households, thereby constraining the production systems of the poor, in order to meet the demands of cotton production. The level of cotton farming also correlated with ownership of ploughs and draft animals. Animal and motorized traction negatively influenced the economics of extensive versus intensive farming as well as the distribution of land due to local land tenure practices. These processes often resulted in more extensive agriculture by the rich and less land for the poor. Finally, cotton farming generated wealth that impacted the landscape through higher levels of livestock ownership. In sum, the direct effect of cotton on the land, as well as the multiple indirect effects, made it, rather than poverty, the major contributor to land degradation in southern Mali.

Table 3.4 Cotton by Wealth Group in Siwaa and Djitoumou Zones in 1997-99

Zone	Wealth Group	% Cotton	Farming Ha in Cotton	% Total Ha in Cotton
Siwaa	Poor	93.5%	2.0	23.8%
	Intermediate	100%	4.4	33.1%
	Rich	100%	6.2	32.2%
	Average	97.1%	3.7	28.7%
Djitoumou	Poor	82.5%	1.9	22.4%
	Intermediate	100%	3.8	29.4%
	Rich	100%	8.5	39.1%
	Average	89.2%	3.1	26.1%

Alternative Explanations for Environmental Degradation in Southern Mali: The Political Economy of Environment-Development Discourse

This section explores alternative understandings of environmental degradation in southern Mali and why such explanations have been less prominent in environment-development discourse. Among other issues, I will elaborate on unsustainable cotton production as an under recognized cause of environmental degradation in southern Mali.

While Mali historically had a lively market for indigenous cotton varieties, the French undertook a number of steps in the mid-20th century to facilitate the production of hybrid varieties in southern Mali for export (Roberts, 1995, 1996). This production has been maintained in the post-colonial era through the work of a quasi-privatized parastatal, the *Compagnie Malienne pour le Développement des Textiles* (CMDT), that has monopoly control over the local cotton market. In light of the erratic world market for cotton, including long (several year) stretches when world cotton prices remained low, steady increases in production over the past 50 years were maintained through guaranteed purchase, a minimum floor price and credit for inputs (support that is not available for any other crop in Mali).

Malian cotton production peaked in the 1998-99 season when it produced over 500,000 metric tonnes, making Mali the leading producer of the crop in Sub-Saharan Africa (EIU, 1998; Bah, 2000). More recent reports suggest that production for the 2001-2002 season has been even higher (USDA, 2001). Total output from the Africa Franc Zone (of which Mali accounted for 22.5%) in 1998-99 totaled 2.1 million metric tonnes and made the region the world's third largest exporter after the United States and Uzbekistan (Manley, 1999; Levin, 1999). Dramatic production increases through the late 1990s tended to confirm that the cotton growing areas were the 'success story of agricultural and rural development in Mali.' (Bingen, 1998, p.271). This cotton success story has been touted by donors and the Malian government. Cotton is frequently referred to as the 'motor of development.' (GoM, 1998, p.16) This notion has been reinforced by a number of authors who have written on the positive aspects of cotton production in southern Mali, highlighting the benefits of this activity for household food security and the modernization of agricultural practices (for example, World Bank, 1990; Fok et al., 2000).

The Government of Mali has been very reluctant to recognize ecological problems associated with cotton cultivation. In general, the environment has been less of a priority for the government than economic development. In a recent interview (Lange, 2001, p.116), Askia Muhamed, press secretary for now former Malian President Alpha Konare, said, in relation to an environmental issue, 'the national interest must override the local. "Mali cannot feed itself . . . The Priority is development. One cannot stop development, even to save the country's heritage."' Perhaps more importantly, part of Government's reluctance may be explained by the fact that it depends on cotton for nearly 50% of its revenues (the actual figure varies between 43% to 48%). One Malian Government official referred to cotton production as the country's *vache laitière* or cash cow. As such, tempering cotton production for environmental reasons would entail considerable fiscal hardship. Rather than seeking to temper production while searching for more sustainable alternatives, the Government is hoping to increase cotton production to between 700 and 800 million metric tonnes over the next few years (Berthe, pers. comm., 2000).

While cotton has long been an important source of revenue for the Government, this source of income is increasingly important in light of agreements with multilateral donors to implement policies of structural adjustment that put added pressure on the government to balance the budget (World Bank, 1997; IMF, 1999). Somewhat ironically, democratization has also created new financial constraints as some highly unpopular forms of taxation, for example, the head tax, were eliminated with the transition to a popularly elected government in 1992.

In general, the Government and the CMDT have preferred to expand production in new areas rather than seek sustainable alternatives in older production zones. This has led to a situation of declining yields in the old cotton basin (Koutiala and Sikasso Districts) and expansion into the new cotton basin (Bougouni, Kati and Dioila or Fana Districts) and cotton frontier (Kita District) (Bingen, 1998). Interestingly enough, there is a growing awareness among farmers in the old cotton basin that the current production system is unsustainable. This includes increasing calls from the farmers' union (SYCOV)[5] for improved extension and government support for alternatives to cotton (Sanogo, personal communication, 2000-2001). The CMDT has tried to introduce specific techniques that would lead to greater sustainability (for example, composting, rock lines). The problem is that the CMDT has been reluctant to explore more fundamental changes that may jeopardize short or medium term production levels of cotton as it is dependent on these revenues for it own operating budget.

There is now some debate about whether production declines in the old cotton basin represent a short term economic problem (related to prices) or a longer term crisis related to ecological deterioration. While an awareness of the latter possibility is most palpable in the old cotton basin, the CMDT can avoid serious national debate on the issue by maintaining high levels of production at the national level by continuing to push for production increases in the new cotton basin (which includes Djitoumou) and further west on the cotton frontier. The way in which Mali (with some of the oldest cotton producing zones in the region) chooses to deal with the problem of cotton induced environmental degradation may set a precedent for the rest of the African Franc Zone, a region in which the French owned *Développement des Agro-Industries du Sud* (DAGRIS)[6] is a stake holder in most of the national cotton companies.

A convenient development at the level of international environment-development discourse has been the notion that poverty is the cause of environmental degradation. The World Bank has been especially fond of the poverty-induced environmental degradation thesis (for example, World Bank, 1992, 1996) and one wonders if this is because it allows the Bank to push on with its structural adjustment package focusing on increased export earnings and leaner government services. As described earlier, this international discourse has now pervaded the national policy-making apparatus in Mali. Donors, government officials and NGO representatives routinely suggest that poverty is at the root of many of Mali's environmental problems.

This focus on poverty in environmental discussions has allowed the government to avoid a serious debate on the sustainability of cotton production. If poverty is the source of environmental degradation in southern Mali, then the government, the cotton company and donors can feel comfortable pushing for further increases in cotton production. Such increases will enrich all parties concerned (including the donors who want to see debts repaid), while allowing them to assert that this is a key step in the process of poverty reduction and improved environmental management.

Conclusion and Policy Considerations

Despite the prevalence of the poverty-induced environmental degradation thesis in global and national policy circles, this notion is not substantiated by evidence on the ground in southern Mali. Rather than poverty driving environmental degradation, this change seems to be more clearly linked to the technological package of export oriented cotton production as well as the wealth spin-offs of this production. In other words, it is the use of chemical inputs and animal traction, the high nutrient demands of the cotton crop itself, the decline in intercropping and no-till, and cattle investments that all seem to have interacted to cause soil degradation.

Although there are growing ecological concerns related to cotton production in southern Mali, poverty remains the favored causal explanation for environmental degradation in this region of Africa. The prevalence and continued 'rength of this narrative at the national level is linked to a constellation of actors (donors, the Government of Mali, the Malian cotton company and its French-owned parent corporation) who would all prefer to expand cotton production and ignore associated environmental issues. While governments turning a blind eye to the environmental costs of economic development is nothing new, the poverty-induced environmental degradation narrative allows the Government of Mali to do so with the full support of the development community. Furthermore, blaming poverty for environmental degradation suggests that cotton production, as the engine of economic growth in southern Mali, should not only be maintained but expand.

The alternative is to recognize that the West African cotton-based production system is not ecologically sustainable in its current state. At the most basic level, greater efforts are required to sustain agricultural soils in southern Mali. Government, NGOs, and local farmers should work together to assure increased technical support for no-till agriculture and the production and application of organic inputs (for example, compost, animal manure and green manure) as well as subsidies for donkey carts to transport these inputs. More serious experimentation with organic cotton should also be contemplated by the agricultural extension service as it offers a higher world price with a lower environmental impact. There is also a need to diversify rural livelihoods by introducing new crops and income generating possibilities.

Unfortunately, such a shift in production strategies is unpalatable to donors, the government and the cotton company because it may mean short-term losses in production and revenues, and a lack of progress in balancing the state budget. An, as of yet, unthinkable alternative for the donors would be to provide loans to make the transition to sustainability.

The findings of this study support a view held by many political ecologists that international capitalism is the ultimate cause of local land degradation (for example, Blaikie, 1985; Blaikie and Brookfield, 1987). However, the on-the-ground specifics of how this degradation unfolds is different than that described by many scholars. For many political ecologists, capitalism creates poverty, which in turn leads to environmentally destructive behavior. For example, Blaikie notes that poor households from whom surpluses are extracted 'then in turn are forced to extract 'surpluses' from the environment . . . [leading] to degradation'(1985, p.124). Furthermore, '[p]easants destroy their own environment in attempts to delay their own destruction' (Blaikie, 1985, p.29). Similarly, Watts (2000, p.591) suggests that a central tenet of political ecology is that 'society and land-based resources are mutually causal in such a way that poverty, via poor management, can induce environmental degradation which itself deepens poverty.'

In contrast, this research suggests that the relatively rich, rather than the relatively poor, are the proximate cause of environmental degradation in southern Mali. Due to their favorable position in terms of production and access to the natural resource base, international capital sought out the local wealthy through agricultural extension programs in order to proliferate and intensify cotton cash cropping and its associated technologies. It is these introduced crops, technologies, and their indirect effects (for example, investment in livestock) that have been detrimental to the environment. While poorer members of rural communities sought to emulate the rich when they saw the short-term profits generated by cash cropping, they never had the means to practice resource exploitation on the same scale.

In conclusion, the empirical evidence in southern Mali supports the notion of cotton (and related wealth) induced environmental degradation, yet a global discourse linking poverty to environmental degradation dominates national level policy discussions because it aids and abets the persistence of a cotton production system that benefits local and national elites, global capital, and bilateral and multilateral donors. Many political ecologist tolerated certain aspects of this poverty-environment linkage (i.e., poverty as a proximate but not ultimate cause of environmental degradation) in the global discourse because it fit their own causal chain of capitalism leading to poverty leading to environmental degradation.

Notes

1 I am grateful to Ikubolajeh Logan for feedback on an earlier version of this manuscript, and to those who participated in this study, especially households and village councils in the communities of Falan, Nianzana, Sanankoro-Djitoumou, Zambougou, Kaniko, Try, Mperesso and Ngoukan. I also would like to thank the Institut d'Economie Rurale (IER) who acted as my host institution while in Mali. Financial support for this study was provided by a Fulbright-Hays Doctoral Dissertation Research Abroad Program Grant from the U.S. Department of Education, a finishing dissertation award from the Graduate School of the University of Georgia (UGA), travel assistance from the UGA Office of International Agriculture's Sustainable Agriculture and Natural Resources Management Collaborative Research Support Program (SANREM CRSP), and a field study award from the Cultural Ecology Specialty Group of the Association of American Geographers.
2 However, the dominant perspectives on ecological degradation have been vigorously questioned in recent years (Behnke et al. 1993; Lambin and Ehrlich 1997).
3 All of the comments presented here were made by Malians, as opposed to expatriate advisors, within and outside of the government.
4 The figures for pH-KCL are roughly comparable to those found by de Vos (1991) for the village of Try (one of the Siwaa study villages). De Vos (1991) found pH-KCL values of 6.0 under natural vegetation and 4.8-5.6 in farm fields. These are averages for all soil texture classes.
5 The farmers' union has become increasingly sophisticated in recent years and has a sound knowledge of the world cotton market due to its contacts with the international labor and farmer movements (Docking, 1998).
6 Until very recently, this entity was known as the *Compagnie Française pour le Développement des Textiles* (CFDT).

References

Ahmed, I. and Doeleman, J.A. (1995), *Beyond Rio: The Environmental Crisis and Sustainable Livelihoods in the Third World*. New York: St. Martin's Press.

Bah, B. (2000), 'Analyse des politiques de la filiere engrais. Rapport provisoire.' Institut d'Economie Rurale. Bamako.

Baker, R. (1983), 'Protecting the Environment Against the Poor: The Historical Roots of Soil Erosion Orthodoxy in the Third World.' *The Ecologist*. 14(2), pp. 53-60.

Bardhan, P. (1996), Research on Poverty and Development Twenty Years after Redistribution with Growth. Proceeding of the Annual World Bank Conference on Development Economics 1995. Supplement to the World Bank Economic Review and the World Bank Research Observer, pp. 59-72.

Barrett, C. (1996), 'Fairness, Stewardship and Sustainable Development.' *Ecological Economics*, 19, pp.11-17.

Bassett, T.J. and Zueli, K.B. (2000), 'Environmental Discourses and the Ivorian Savanna.' *Annals of the Association of American Geographers*. 90(1), pp. 67-95.

Batterbury, S., Forsyth, T., and Thomson, K. (1997), Environmental transformations in developing countries: hybrid research and democratic policy. *The Geographical Journal*, 163(2), pp. 126-132.

Beckerman, W. (1992), 'Economic Growth and the Environment: Whose Growth? Whose

Environment?' *World Development.* 20(4), pp. 481-496.

Behnke, R.H., Scoones, I. and Kervan, C. (1993), *Range Ecology at Disequilibrium: New Models of Natural Variability and Pastoral Adaptation in African Savannas.* London: Overseas Development Institute.

Bingen, R.J. (1998), 'Cotton, Democracy and Development in Mali.' *The Journal Modern African Studies.* 36(2), pp. 265-285.

Blaikie, P.M. (1985), *The Political Economy of Soil Erosion in Developing Countries.* London: Longman.

Blaikie, P.M. and Brookfield, H. (1987), *Land Degradation and Society.* New York: Methuen & Co.

Bremin, H., J.J.R. Groot and van Keulen, H. (2001), 'Resource limitations in Sahelian agriculture.' *Global Environmental Change.* 11(1), pp. 59-68.

Broad, R. (1994), 'The Poor and the Environment: Friend or Foes?' *World Development.* 22(6), pp. 811-812.

Bryant, R.L. (1997), 'Beyond the impasse: the power of political ecology in Third World environmental research.' *Area.* 29(1), pp. 5-19.

Cleaver, K.M. and Schreiber, G.A. (1994), *Reversing the Spiral: The Population, Agriculture and Environment Nexus in Sub-Saharan Africa.* Washington, D.C.: The World Bank.

Dasgupta, P. (1995), 'Population, Poverty and the Local Environment.' *Scientific American.* February. pp. 40-45.

Dasgupta. P. (1997), *Environmental and Resource Economics in the World of the Poor.* Resources for the Future, Washington, D.C.

Davies, S. (1996), *Adaptable Livelihoods: Coping With Food Insecurity in the Malian Sahel.* New York: St. Martin's Press, Inc.

De Bruyn, S.M., van den Bergh, J.C., and Opschoor, J.B. (1998), 'Economic Growth and Emissions: Reconsidering the Empirical Basis of Environmental Kuznet's Curves. *Ecological Economics.* 25(2), pp. 161-175.'

De Vos, H. (1991), 'L'Erosion et La Dégradation des Sols dans La Zone CMDT. Les Cas des Villages des Try.' Institut Royal des Tropiques (KIT). Amsterdam, Holland.

Dinda, S. (2000), 'Air Quality and Economic Growth: An Empirical Study.' *Ecological Economics.* 34(3), pp. 409-423.

Docking, T. (1998), *International Influence on Civil Society in Mali: The Case of the Cotton Farmers' Union, SYCOV.* Ph.D. Dissertation. Boston University.

Duraiappah, A.K. (1998), 'Poverty and Environmental Degradation: A Review and Analysis of the Nexus.' *World Development.* 26(12), pp. 2169-2179.

(EIU) Economist Intelligence Unit. (1998), *Mali Country Report 1998-99.* London: Business International.

Ehrlich, P.A. (1968), *The Population Bomb.* New York: Simon and Schuster.

Fairhead, J. and Leach, M. (1995), 'False Forest History, Complicit Social Analysis – Rethinking Some West African Environmental Narratives.' *World Development.* 23(6), pp. 1023-1035.

Fairhead, J. and Leach, M. (1996), *Misreading the African Landscape: Society and Ecology in a Forest-Savanna Mosaic.* Cambridge: Cambridge University Press.

FEWS. (1997), *Living on the Edge.* FEWS in Depth Report No. 2. Washington, DC: Famine Early Warning System, United States Agency for International Development.

Field, B.C. (1997), *Environmental Economics: An Introduction, 2nd Edition.* New York: Irwin/McGraw-Hill.

Fok, A.C.M., Djouara, H. and Ballo, B. (2000), 'Farmers' Response to the Evolution Towards

Globalization: The Case of Cotton Production in Mali.' Paper presented at the *International Farming Systems Association Symposia*. November. Saniago, Chile.

Forsyth T., Leach, M. and Scoones, I. (1998), 'Poverty and Environment: Priorities for Research and Policy.' Prepared for the UNDP and the European Commission. Institute for Development Studies, Sussex, U.K.

Glenzer, K. (1999), 'La Secheresse: The Social and Institutional Construction of a Development Problem in the Malian (Soudanese) Sahel, c. 1900-1982.' Presentation at the *Annual Meeting of the African Studies Association*. Philadelphia, PA. November 11-14.

(GoM) Government of Mali. (1998), *Plan National d'Action Environnementale*. Bamako: Ministry of Environment.

Grepperud, S. (1996), 'Population pressure and land degradation: the case of Ethiopia.' *Journal of Environmental Economics and Management*. 30(1), pp. 18-33.

(IUCN) International Union for the Conservation of Nature and Natural Resources. (1980), *World Conservation Strategy: Living Resource Conservation for Sustainable Development*. Gland, Switzerland: IUCN, UNEP and WWF.

Kaufmann, R.K., Davidsdottir, B., Garnham, S. and Pauly, P. (1998), 'The Determinants of Atmosheric SO2 Concentrations: Reconsidering the Environmental Kuznet's Curve.' *Ecological Economics*. 25(2), pp. 209-220.

Krutilla, J.V. and Fisher, A.C. (1976), *The Economics of Natural Resources: Studies in the Valuation of Commodity and Amenity Resources*. Washington, D.C.: Resources for the Future, Inc.

Lamden, E. and Ehrlich, D. (1997), 'Land-Cover Changes in Sub-Saharan Africa (1982-1991): Application of a Change Index Based on Remotely Sensed Surface Temperature and Vegetation Indices at a Continental Scale.' *Remote Sensing of Environment*. 16(2), pp. 181-200.

Lange, K.E. (2001), 'Djénné: West Africa's Eternal City.' *National Geographic*. 199(6), pp. 100-117.

Leach, M. and Mearns, R. (eds.). (1996), *The Lie of the Land: Challenging Received Wisdom of the African Environment*. Oxford: James Curry.

Leisinger, K. and Schmitt, K. (1995), *Survival in the Sahel: An Ecological and Developmental Challenge*. The Hague: International Service for National Agricultural Research (ISNAR).

Lele, S.M. (1991), 'Sustainable Development: A Critical Review.' *World Development*. 19(6), pp. 607-621.

Levin, A. (1999), 'Developments and Outlook for Cotton in Francophone West Africa.' Paper presented at the *Beltwide Cotton Conference*. January. Orlando, FL.

List, J.A. and Gallet, C.A. (1999), 'The Environmental Kuznet's Curve: Does One Size Fit All?' *Ecological Economics*. 31(3), pp. 409-423.

Liverman, D. (1999), 'Geography and the Global Environment.' *Annals of the Association of American Geographers*. 89(1), pp.107-120.

Lomborg, B. (2001), *The Skeptical Environmentalist: Measuring the Real State of the World*. New York: Cambridge University Press.

Lumley, S. (1997), 'The environment and the ethics of discounting: An empirical analysis.' *Ecological Economics* 20, pp. 71-82.

Logan, B.I. (1991), 'Overpopulation and Poverty in Africa: Rethinking the Traditional Relationships.' *Tijdschrift Voor Economische en Sociale Geografie*. 82(1), pp. 40-57.

Logan, B.I. (1999), 'Environmental Security, Sustainable Development and Resource

Management in Africa: Some Conceptual Considerations.' Paper presented at the *Methodology Workshop, Southern African Political Economy Series Trust*, Harare, Zimbabwe, July.

Madulu, N.F. (1995), 'Population-growth, Agrarian Peasant-Economy and Environmental Degradation in Tanzania.' *International Sociology.* 10(1), pp. 35-50.

Malik, S.J. (1999), 'Rural poverty and land degradation: what does the available literature suggest for priority setting for the Consultative Group on International Agricultural research?' report prepared for the Technical Advisory Committee of the CGIAR, Vienna, VA.

Malthus, T.R. (1970), *An Essay on the Principle of Population and a Summary View of the Principle of Population.* Flew, A. (ed.) London, Pelican.

McManus, P. (2000), 'Sustainable Development.' In *The Dictionary of Human Geography, 4th Edition.* Malden, MA: Blackwell Publishers Ltd., pp. 812-816.

Mellor, J.W. (1988), 'The Intertwining of Environmental Problems and Poverty.' *Environment.* 30(9), pp. 8-13.

Mink, S.D. (1993), 'Poverty, Population and Environment.' *World Bank Discussion Paper #189.* The World Bank, Washington.

Moseley, W.G. (2001a), 'African Evidence on the Relation of Poverty, Time Preference and the Environment.' *Ecological Economics.* 38(3), pp. 317-326.

Moseley, W.G. (2001b), 'Sahelian "White Gold" and Rural Poverty-Environment Interactions: The Political Ecology of Cotton Production, Environmental Change, and Household Food Economy in Mali.' Ph.D. Dissertation. Department of Geography. Athens: University of Georgia.

Murphree, M. (1993), 'Communal Land Wildlife Resources and Rural District Council Revenues.' CASS, University of Zimbabwe, Harare.

National Research Council. (1999), *Our Common Journey: A Transition Toward Sustainability.* Washington, D.C.: National Academy Press.

Pearce, D. and Atkinson, G. (1993), 'Capital theory and the measurement of sustainable development: an indicator of "weak" sustainability.' *Ecological Economics*, 8, pp. 103-108.

Pearce, D. and Turner, R.K., 1990. *Economics of Nautral Resources and the Environment.* Baltimore: Johns Hopkins University Press.

Reardon, T. and Vosti, S.A. (1995). 'Links between rural poverty and the environment in developing countries: asset categories and investment poverty.' *World Development.* 23(9), pp. 1495-1506.

Redclift,M. (1992), 'The Meaning of Sustainable Development.' *Geoforum.* 23(3), pp. 395-403.

Roberts, R.L. (1995), 'The Coercion of Free Markets: Cotton, Peasants, and the Colonial State in the French Soudan, 1924-32.' In Isaacman, A. and Roberts, R. (eds), *Cotton, Colonialism, and Social History in Sub-Saharan Africa.* London: James Currey, Ltd.

Roberts, R.L. (1996), *Two Worlds of Cotton: Colonialism and the Regional Economy in the French Soudan,* 1800-1946. Stanford University Press.

Scherr, S. (2000), 'A downward spiral? Research evidence on the relatioship between poverty and natural resource degradation.' *Food Policy.* 25: 479-498.

Sneddon, C. (2000), ' "Sustainability" in ecological economics, ecology and livelihoods: a review.' *Progress in Human Geography* 24(4), pp. 521-549.

Stern, D.I., Common, M.S., and Barnier, E.B. (1999), 'Economic Growth and Environmental Degradation: The Environmental Kuznet's Curve and Sustainable Development.' *World Development.* 24(7), pp. 1151-1160.

Templeton, S. and Scherr, S. (1999), 'Effects of demographic and related microeconomic change on land quality in hills and mountains of developing countries.' *World Development.* 27(6), pp. 903-918.

Tobey, J.A. (1989), 'Economic Development and Environmental Management in the Third World: Trading-off Industrial Pollution with the Pollution of Poverty.' *Habitat International.* 13(4), pp. 125-135.

Turner, B.L. (1997), 'The Sustainability Principle in Global Agendas: Implications for Understanding Land-Use/Cover Change,' *Geographical Journal*, Vol. 163, pp. 133-140.

(UNCED) United Nations Conference on Environment and Development. (1993), *Agenda 21: The Earth Summit Strategy to Save Our Planet.* Boulder, Colorado: EarthPress.

(UNDP) United Nations Development Programme. (2000), 'Attacking Poverty While Improving the Environment: Towards Win-Win Policy Options.' Poverty & Environment Initiative. URL: http://www.undp.org/seed/pei/.

(USDA) United States Department of Agriculture Foreign Agricultural Service. (2001), 'Mali's Cotton Production Doubles and Nears Record Levels.' October 18. http://www.fas.usda.gov/pecad/highlights/2001/10/mali/mali_cotton_01.htm.

Van Beusekom, M.M. (1999), 'From underpopulation to overpopulation: French perceptions of population, environment and agricultural development in French Soudan (Mali), 1900-1960.' *Environmental History.* 4(2), pp. 198-219.

Van der Pol, F. (1992), *Soil Mining: An Unseen Contributor to Farm Income in Southern Mali.* Bulletin 325. Amsterdam: Royal Tropical Institute.

Vosti, S. and Reardon, T. (eds). (1997), *Sustainability, Growth and Poverty Alleviation: A Policy and Agroecological Perspective.* Johns Hopkins University Press, Baltimore, Maryland.

Watts, M. (2000), 'Political Ecology.' In *The Dictionary of Human Geography, 4th Edition.* Malden, Massachusetts: Blackwell Publishers Ltd., pp. 590-592.

Wilbanks, T. (1994), ' "Sustainable Development" in Geographic Perspective.' *Annals of the Association of American Geographers.* 84(4), pp. 541-546.

World Bank. (1990), *Sub-Saharan Africa: From Crisis to Sustainable Growth: A Long-Term Perspective Study.* Washington, D.C.: World Bank.

World Bank, (1992), *World Development Report 1992. Development and the Environment.* Oxford University Press, New York.

World Bank. (1996), *Toward Environmentally Sustainable in Sub-Saharan Africa: A World Bank Agenda.* Development in Practice Series. Washington, DC: The World Bank.

(WCED) World Council on Environment and Development. (1987), *Our Common Future.* New York: Oxford University Press.

Chapter 4

Grounding Environmental Narratives: The Impact of a Century of Fighting Against Fire in Mali

Paul Laris

Man has already created deserts by destroying natural richness. Among the destructive factors, fire is the most efficient, then it is against it that the fight must be intensified. (Ortoli, Governor of French Sudan, 1955, p.15).

I invite hunters, fisherman, herders, car drivers, travelers, wanderers, and tourists, to abstain from setting fire to the bush and to participate in the fight against any type of fire (Traoré, President of Mali, 1980, p.2).

No matter the reason, fire is nothing other than a means to fight – man fighting against nature (Nasi and Sabatier, 1988, p.36).

Introduction

In November of 1980, during the height of fears that destructive indigenous land management practices were contributing to widespread degradation of the savanna in Mali, President Moussa Traoré addressed his nation and issued a decree banning the use of fire in rural areas. In his address, Traoré (1980, p.1) linked savanna fires to a number of processes of degradation commonly associated with desertification and savannization in the zone (see figure 4.1):

Fires are very dangerous in the middle of the dry season; they burn our pastures and starve our animals, they burn to cinder the organic material of the soil and transform its vegetation into ashes that blow away. The soil structure deteriorates, its water retention ability diminishes and the action of erosion is fully favorable and the water table progressively lowers every year...Bush fires, no matter their nature and the reason for them, are harmful. In the present state of our rural economy, these fires go through the fallow lands considerably reducing the advantage the lands should get from a period of rest following that of cultivation. No one can question the enrichment of a soil subtracted for some years from exposure to fires.

Figure 4.1 'Bush Fire Causes Desertification'
Numerous roadside placards linking fire with desertification were posted during the *Fight Against Fire* in Mali.

Traorés view of the damaging effects of fire on savanna vegetation was not new. He drew upon a long lineage of thinking on savanna fire. Fire has been viewed as a major cause of regional-scale environmental degradation by influential foresters, botanists, and governmental officials from early on in the colonial era. The French and British colonial governments were obsessed with eliminating fire from the West African landscape. They persistently implemented anti-fire policies aimed at suppressing fire in order to encourage the growth of trees and woody vegetation to counter what they perceived to be the problem of savannization (de-wooding) of the landscape. Although these anti-fire policies rarely had a significant impact on the burning practices of Africans, many of them remain in place in the post-colonial era where it is has been argued that they remain ineffective (Fairhead and Leach, 1995; Pyne, 1999; Schmitz, 1996).

The anti-fire view is part of a narrative of environmental degradation that has dominated thinking on the West African savanna and dry woodlands for most of the twentieth century. The narrative is built upon the view that the West African landscape has been undergoing a process of environmental degradation whereby vegetation cover has become increasingly less wooded and sparse as a result of the destructive land-use practices of Africans.[1] The degradation processes involved may include soil erosion, soil nutrient depletion, savannization, deforestation, and the disappearance of useful species. Desertification[2] is the term most often used as a heading under which these processes are organized (Mortimore, 1998; Rasmussen *et al.*, 2001).

During the past decade there has been a growing academic effort to evaluate the common wisdoms or narratives about the human role in environmental change and to analyze how these persistent views shape or justify environmental policy (Bassett and Zueli, 2000; Fairhead and Leach 1996, 1998; Grove and Anderson, 1987; Kull, 2000; Leach and Mearns, 1996; Mc Cann, 1997; Showers, 1989; Swift, 1996). To date the emphasis of much of this body of work has been on demonstrating the enduring influence of a set of dominant environmental views in the policy arena. By tracing the lineage of such views back to their origins, often found in the colonial era, much of this work seeks to explain why particular views persist in spite of a lack of supporting evidence (for example, Leach and Mearns 1996). In general these studies have not sought to explore the linkages between the dominant environmental view in question and tangible environmental and social changes on the ground (see Rocheleau *et al.*, 1995 and Showers, 1989 for notable exceptions).

This chapter explores the impact the West African degradation narrative has had on fire in Mali by tracing the linkages between narrative and specific changes in rural burning practices during different environment/development eras. It is argued here that while there is no evidence to suggest that fire policy resulted in fire *suppression* during the twentieth century, anti-fire policies nevertheless have had enduring impacts on society and the environment in Mali. Throughout the twentieth century anti-fire rhetoric perpetuated through policy documents, governmental addresses and memos, and forestry literature stifled the development of effective fire management practices by ignoring the benefits of local knowledge and practice. Yet, during the colonial era there was never a period when sufficient resources were allocated to fire suppression and environmental policing efforts to have more than a minimal impact on local burning.

What was unique about the Traoré era was that for a brief period fire suppression policy was implemented and enforced with sufficient rigor to alter rural burning practices and to bring about changes in fire regimes with implications for savanna vegetation on a national scale. According to my interviews and survey results, Traoré's *Fight Against Fire* campaign produced the largest and most intense fires in human memory (Laris, 2002b). In addition to these immediate effects of the fires, Traoré's campaign has had an enduring and negative impact on fire management efforts in Mali. The oppression and corruption associated with the *Fight Against Fire* served to intensify a pre-existing rift between the rural population and the forest service. This rift persists to this day where it serves as a barrier to the useful exchange of indigenous and technical knowledge on fire management. To understand the reasons why the *Fight Against Fire* had such a powerful impact this chapter draws on a 'chain of explanation' approach from political ecology to examine the inter-connections between an environmental narrative, environment-development context, anti-fire policy, and the burning practices of rural Malians.

The Chain of Explanation Approach in Political Ecology

One important focus of research in political ecology is to link specific kinds of resource degradation to their socio-political causes, most of which are linked in 'chains' of controlling structures (i.e., rules or controlling power) from the local to the global levels (for example, Blaikie and Brookfield, 1987; Blaikie, 1985; Grossman, 1984). A second focus is to examine how these structures and their outcomes are captured by global environment/development discourses (for example, Leach and Mearns, 1996; Stott and Sullivan, 2000; Bryant, 1996). Studies in political ecology have examined the dynamics surrounding material and discursive struggles over the environment (for example, Peet and Watts, 1996); and they have analyzed how individuals and groups negotiate, cooperate, and fight over the control over, use of, and character of natural resources (for example, Rocheleau *et al.*, 1996; Carney, 1993; Schroeder, 1993). In general, particular attention is given to the ways in which these struggles are linked to systems of political and economic control first elaborated during the colonial era.

The approach using a chain of explanation facilitates researchers in examining and explaining the ambiguities and complexities associated with the links between social and environmental processes. An important advantage of this approach is that researchers are able to ground their social theory (both literally and figuratively) to explain the causes of environmental degradation in specific locales. Grounding high-level or abstract concepts in local events was a defining characteristic of early political ecological studies (for example, Basset, 1988; Blaikie and Brookfield, 1987; Grossman, 1984).

Recently, as the field of political ecology has expanded to incorporate numerous emerging social theories linking society and environment, some authors have placed the emphasis on theory development and have lessened or eliminated the focus on local level resource degradation or environmental change analysis. Thus influential works on environment/ development discourse (for example, Bryant, 1996; Escobar, 1996; Peet and Watts, 1996) or on environmental narratives (for example, Leach and Mearns, 1996), which seek to explain the origins and persistence of dominant views, do not necessarily address the causes of physical environmental change. In some cases these approaches are concerned with explaining social change, albeit social change related to environmental visions, imaginaries, or social movements (Peet and Watts, 1996; Bryant and Bailey, 1997). Others emphasize the social construction of nature and/or environmental problems (Bryant, 1996; Robbins, 1998). One aim of this work is to return the focus to the physical environment by using the 'chain of explanation' to disclose the key factors that determine the conditions necessary for a regional environmental narrative to have tangible environmental effects.

This chapter examines how the West African degradation narrative dominated official discourse and shaped regulations and enforcement of fire use during the past century. It seeks to explain how and why the impact of the dominant view varied during different governmental regimes, and it explores the way by which an environmental narrative becomes grounded in particular locales.

Using the chain of explanation approach it examines linkages through four discrete periods: the early colonial (1900-1949), late colonial (1950-1959), first independent government (1960-1967), and second independent government (1968-1991). For each period three factors are examined: (i) the environment/development context, (ii) changes in fire policy and practice, and (iii) changes in local institutions, burning practices, and environmental impacts in southern Mali.

The Enduring Narrative of Desertification and Savannization

Numerous scholars have documented the historical development of the West African degradation narrative while noting its enduring impact in the policy arena. They argue that the narrative, which can be traced back to the views of colonial foresters and botanists, has persisted for nearly a century, and remains highly influential in policy circles (Bassett and Zueli, 2000; Benjaminsen, 2000; Fairhead and Leach, 1996; Mortimore, 1998; Ribot, 1999; Swift, 1996). Although there have been dissenting views, particularly concerning the degree to which the origins of present vegetation cover are natural as opposed to anthropogenic (for example, Fairhead and Leach, 1996; Nicholson *et al.*, 1998; Tucker *et al.*, 1991), the degradation narrative is so central to environmental discourse of the region that it is considered by many to be the dominant view (for example, Bassett and Zueli, 2000; Fairhead and Leach, 1996).

Dominant environmental views, variously referred to as 'received wisdoms' (Leach and Mearns, 1996), 'environmental orthodoxies' (Batterbury *et al.*, 1997), or 'dominant narratives' (Roe, 1991), are ideas which are held as correct and perpetuated by powerful political establishments despite their potential weaknesses and/or lack of supporting data. These views often take the form of narratives in that they at once describe a problem, articulate the main cause of it, and propose a solution. Environmental narratives, thus, tell a story about what will happen if corrective action is not taken to curb destructive behavior (Roe, 1991). Environmental narratives persist despite limited evidence in part because they are compelling stories with clear and simple explanations (Roe, 1991), but also because they serve the purposes of powerful groups (Leach and Mearns, 1996; Batterbury *et al.*, 1997).

Scholars have also pointed out how narratives of environmental degradation often form part of a systematic discourse used by the state to claim control over natural resources. By placing the blame for perceived degradation on the 'careless natives,' many colonial governments restricted the access of indigenous populations to natural resources such as woodlands and forests (Becker, 2001; Fairhead and Leach, 1996; Kull, 2000). Still others have argued that dominant narratives pose a serious threat to sustainable environmental practices because they frequently serve to obscure or transform alternative views such as those of the common peasant, herder, or hunter since the narratives frame problems in a way such that the solutions justify the desires of the interested parties. The

West Africa degradation narrative, for example, has paid little heed to the perceptions of the indigenous population and has persistently stood in the way of effective approaches for addressing environmental issues by focusing attention on poorly defined problems and misguided solutions (Mortimore, 1998; Swift, 1996).

It is well documented that during the colonial era, ideas of desertification and savannization became established features of ecological thinking that heavily influenced the policies created by the French and British forestry departments (Benjaminsen, 1997; Bassett and Zueli, 2000; Fairhead and Leach, 1995, 1996, 2000; Ribot, 1999; Swift, 1996). Colonial scientists such as the botanists Chevalier, Adam, and Aubréville, who also worked as civil servants in the Forest Service, supported a vision of severe deforestation and land degradation caused by the destructive land uses of the indigenous population. The image presented by these scientists was of a general process of environmental degradation; the linking of this image to local resource management was gradually institutionalized within the French West African Forest Service (Benjaminsen, 1997).

The notion that forests and woodlands were being degraded and transformed into grass-dominated savannas as a result of the destructive land-use practices dates from early in the twentieth century. Stebbing (1935) advanced the idea that humans were responsible for wide-scale degradation in West Africa. In his view the term 'savanna' was a misnomer since savanna conveys the idea of open grassy areas of little value. Stebbing argued that the wooded-savanna of West Africa could be reclassified as forest following 'the simple procedure of closure and fire protection' (Stebbing, 1935, p.507).

The work of Aubréville, who popularized the term 'desertification,' is thought to have been particularly influential in developing this dominant environmental view (Bassett and Zueli, 2000; Mortimore, 1998; Fairhead and Leach, 1996). According to Aubréville, desertification is a regional-scale phenomenon for it involves an environmental transformation on two fronts. On the southern front, forests and dense woodlands are subject to savannization as woodlands are cleared for farming and then repeatedly burned until replaced by grasses. On the northern front, the savanna and deciduous forests are being degraded into more grass dominated savannas as a result of shifting cultivation and persistent annual burning (Aubréville, 1949; Bassett and Zueli, 2000).

No force is thought to have a more widespread and negative impact on the wooded savanna and forest in West Africa than the annual burning practices of the rural population. As Aubréville (1949, p.341, cited in Mortimore, 1998, p.21) has argued, annual fires were a major cause of degradation in the region:

> The closed forests are shrinking and disappearing, like evaporating spots. The trees of the open forests and savannas are more and more spaced out. On all sides the bare skin of Africa appears as its thin veil of savanna burns releasing a gray fog of dust into the atmosphere... During the dry season, the whole of Africa burns, lines of fire running everywhere, chased by the dry winds, no portion left undamaged... Thus we see how tropical Africa would be transformed if the 'savannization' towards which she is fast proceeding were some day to be accomplished.

Indeed the official view of the Traoré regime closely resembled Aubréville's early view.[3] In Mali during the 1980s the term desertification was used to describe the process by which adjacent vegetation zones are steadily degraded as each zone (the desert, the Sahel, and the savanna) is perceived to be moving progressively southward. As such the Sahel has become desertified, the savanna 'Sahelized' and the forest and woodlands 'savannized' (Doumbia, 1991). These view of anthropogenic fire regimes as a degrading force in savanna environments is at odds with emerging theories on savanna dynamics.

An Emerging Counter View of Savanna Dynamics

There is little evidence to support the argument that savanna fires are causing wide-scale savannization in West Africa (Laris, 2002b). Although in many areas savanna fires annually burn as much as half the landscape (Barbosa *et al.*, 1999; Eva and Lambin, 1998, Menault *et al.*, 1991), the impact of a fire on savanna vegetation is largely dependent upon the timing of the burn. Numerous studies have documented that 'early' dry-season fires cause little damage to trees, while 'late' dry-season fires, which occur when savanna vegetation is sapped of moisture, kill small trees and may damage larger, mature ones (Louppe *et al.*, 1995; Brookman-Amissah *et al.*, 1980; Menault *et al.*, 1995; Rose-Innes, 1971).

A number of recent studies have documented that the majority of the fires in the savanna are set early in the dry season and not late (Deshler, 1974; Dwyer *et al.*, 2000; Laris, 2002b, Menault *et al.*, 1991; Neilsen and Rassmussen, 1997). Thus, based on the fire evidence alone, it is unlikely that savannization is occurring on a regional scale as a result of indigenous burning. Moreover, several recent studies find that the density of trees is increasing in parts of the West African savanna despite annual burning.[4]

Recent studies of indigenous burning practices in Senegal and Mali find rural populations have a number of reasons for setting fires early in the dry season. For example, early fires encourage new growth of perennial grass shoots that create ideal grazing and hunting conditions, eliminate pests, and prevent damaging late dry-season fires (Laris, 2002a; Mbow *et al.*, 2000). My research suggests that the rural population in Mali has a deep understanding of the effects of late dry-season fires and have traditionally taken action to prevent damages from these fires by setting numerous early fires across the landscape. By fragmenting the landscape into burned and unburned patches – by setting numerous fires early in the dry season – the indigenous population has historically prevented the most damaging kinds of hot, late season wildfires from racing through the desiccated savanna while simultaneously rendering the landscape useful for a number of productive activities (Laris, 2002a).

Recent research in savannas and other wet/dry and savanna environments suggests that numerous indigenous groups practiced similar regimes of mosaic burning (Boyd, 1999; Lewis and Ferguson, 1988; Parr and Brockett, 1999; Russell-Smith *et al.*, 1997). It has been demonstrated that efforts to suppress fire in these environments results in an increase in the intensity and environmental damage caused by fires because once the early fires are eliminated, more intense, late season fires can quickly spread across an un-fragmented and uniformly dry landscape. Indeed, in the savanna of Northern Australia and Southern Africa, environmental managers now argue that the indigenous burning practices of past groups served to prevent environmental degradation and land managers are now attempting to reintroduce fire regimes that mimic past indigenous practices (Parr and Brockett, 1999; Russell-Smith *et al.*, 1997). These recent developments have been over-looked by West African forest services.

Historical Account of Shifts in Fire Policy and Enforcement in Mali

According to Pyne (1997) the view that burning causes environmental degradation is rooted in the ecological ideas of the colonial period, which typically viewed fire as damaging. Fire suppression, like the exclusionary practices of creating national parks and establishing forestry codes was an expression of colonial rule and one of the most powerful means of controlling indigenes. As Pyne (1990, 1997) has noted, whether indigenous populations retained political access to reserve sites or not, they lacked biological access to the potential resources unless they could employ fire because proper burning renders vegetation useful for a wide variety of uses including hunting, herding, farming, and gathering of wild products.

My interviews with rural Malians found that prior to the colonial era and the establishment of a national forest service in Mali, the indigenous Hunter Society played a critical role in managing the natural environment (Laris 2002b). Two important activities of the Society were to insure that the vast areas of uninhabited savanna were burned on a regular and timely basis and to police the environment thereby preventing people from setting untimely, or late, and damaging fires. As the forest service became more powerful and as forest agents were placed deeper into the hinterland, regulation of fire gradually shifted from the Hunter Society to the forest service.

The Early Colonial Period in West Africa (1900-1949): The Seeds of Fire Suppression

The Environment/Development Context

From the beginning French colonial forestry and anti-fire legislation in West Africa combined elements of conservation and exclusion. Conservationist policy predominated on lands settled and controlled by villages. A policy of exclusion was implemented in unpopulated areas, and/or those areas designated as national forest and reserves. The two were inter-linked as the enforcement of conservation policy on occupied lands was driven by the government's fear that without conservation measures peasants would soon expand agriculture onto lands designated as forest. It was thought that peasants preferred to clear and burn woodlands for their farms and was feared that the indigenous system of rotational agriculture combined with annual fires on fallow lands was reducing the agricultural potential of the region.

Legislation, Goals and Enforcement

To a large degree, the legislation passed during the early colonial period remained the basis for forestry management and environmental policing in Francophone countries for most of the 20th century. The first law relating to the use of forest and forest products was the decree of 20 July 1900 that allocated limited use rights to indigenous populations to collect nuts and wood, hunt, and use the forest areas as pastures. In addition to these restricted use rights, the decree also introduced permits for commercial extraction of forest products and fines for infractions of the rules (Benjaminsen, 2000).

In 1935, the government passed a second piece of legislation that refined the forestry codes and created a forest service (*Le Service des Eaux et Forêts*). A key aspect of the law was its distinction between classified and protected forests. Classified forests were managed directly by the state. All other forests not classed as privately owned were classed as protected. The law imposed restrictions on access to and use of natural resources depending upon the category of forest, and established a system of permits and fines to enforce restrictions.

The forest service was charged with the responsibility of protecting the county's resources from overexploitation or destruction and the regulation specified the police powers necessary to carry out the rules enumerated in the decree (Brinkerhoff, 1995). Perhaps the most potent and controversial element of the forestry code was the collective penalty. Adopted from French law, the collective penalty allowed the forest service to hold villages collectively responsible for violations of the forestry code (Steiber and du Saussay, 1987).

The Impacts on Local Institutions, Burning Practices and the Environment

The legislation laid the foundation for a struggle of authority between the Hunter Society and the forest service. Due to the sparse presence of field officers during the early decades, however, there were few confrontations and the policy had little impact. While the laws gave the government broad powers over land and land-based natural resources, the French did not grant the government the personnel and equipment necessary for widespread application of the laws. At the time of its creation forest agents were primarily recruited from the military and police. In keeping with its paramilitary roots, the forest service's approach to fulfilling its protective mission was to pursue policing and enforcement of regulations as vigorously as its staffing levels and operating resources allowed. The forest service focused on protecting reserves, thus the impact of the policy was probably most heavily experienced by villagers living in areas adjacent to the protected forests (for example, Becker, 2001). Outside of these areas the Hunter Society and other traditional institutions remained the dominant force on the landscape.

The Late Colonial Period (1950-1960): Fire as a 'Necessary Evil'[5]

The Environment/Development Context

The late 1940s and early 1950s were characterized by an increasing confluence of concerns about environmental policy, development, and desertification. The predominant scientific ideas of the era remained unchanged as the desertification arguments were reiterated and strengthened during the 1950s (Fairhead and Leach, 2000). The dustbowl in the United States captured the attention of colonial governments and there was an increase in the level of anxiety that the indigenous practices caused degradation (Grove and Anderson, 1987). This translated into growing concern that savanna burning was ruining the potential of African soils for agricultural production by increasing erosion and causing savannization. It was feared that soil and vegetation degradation forced farmers to constantly seek out virgin woodlands to farm. Fire was, thus, perceived not only a threat to nature, but also as a threat to the agricultural and forestry production in the region.

Legislation, Goals and Enforcement

During the 1950s colonial policy gradually moved toward one of increased regulation of burning, but there was never an extensive effort to ban fire altogether. The defining article of the period was a 1955 memo from the governor of French Sudan (Mali) (Ortoli, 1955). The general approach the government adopted to solve the fire problem was pragmatic and participatory rather than top down as is evident in three key elements of the plan. First, the policy did not ban savanna burning or rotational agriculture; on the contrary it recognized the importance of these activities for the rural population. Second, the forest service incorporated some indigenous practices into its fire management plan and sought the involvement of the rural population in an early burning campaign. And third, the governor requested feedback from field agents at all levels so as to gain from their experiences.

The French colonials saw 'millions of Africans' contributing to the fire problem, it was thus not a technical problem but a human one requiring an educational campaign. Governor Ortoli's words suggest that forestry agents learned from their earlier experiences that rural people would not quickly and easily give up their right to burn. Rather than attempt to ban burning, the government chose a policy based on a combination of education, participation, and policing. In his memo, Ortoli (1955, p.7) argues for shifting away from previous fire suppression strategies:

The first idea was an authoritarian solution to ban all fires, obliging people to fight them and in case of failure to find the guilty people, proceed to collective penalties. This formula can give nothing as a result and they do not fit our regime.

The new policies of 1950s reflected the governments mixed feelings about fire: on the one hand it was recognized that fire had a degrading impact on the environment; on the other it was gradually understood that some forms of fire were better, or at least less damaging, than others. Fire was thus perceived as a 'necessary evil' the effects of which needed to be minimized, rather than eliminated:

> Early fires are a goal in themselves when it comes to assure a minor damage to the forest... Early fires are primarily a means to protect agriculture lands and fallow against big blazes by constitution of a barrier distant from combustible materials (Ortoli, 1955, p.11).

The forest service thus instituted a widespread campaign to ring important areas, including young fallow lands, with a band of early burning. In so doing it drew upon the participation and knowledge of the rural population in this effort:

> When early fires were set in the past, teams of guards [foresters], and sometimes laborers, were in charge of setting the fires following itineraries. That is no longer possible. The choice of lands, their burning or their protection is the responsibility of the inhabitants (Ortoli, 1955, p.13).

According to my interviews, during the 1950s, forest agents began distributing matches to village chiefs who passed them on to the leaders of the hunter society. Elder hunters and village leaders claim that this practice reinforced rather than altered traditional early burning practices.

On village lands conservation measures such as early burning were the norm, while in designated forest zones foresters strengthened their efforts to eliminate all fires by cutting firebreaks and/or ringing areas with early fires (Ortoli, 1955). Here too, the forest service drew upon indigenous techniques such as setting fires to the short grasses on thin soils early in the dry season in order to protect woodlands:

> The limits of the zones to protect are chosen in a way in which they are identified with the dividing lines between two types of herbaceous vegetation in relation to a difference in the nature of the soils. The limits are transformed into a simple firebreak...outside which starting early fires is facilitated by the very quick drying up of the herbaceous carpet (Republic du Mali, 1957, p.20).

The shifts in forestry practice and policy in Mali during this era reflected a wider debate that had emerged within the scientific and forestry communities over the appropriate role of fire in African savannas (Dungan, J., 1944; Fairhead and Leach, 1995; Guilloteau, 1957; Jeffreys, 1945). In spite of these debates the over-arching degradation narrative persisted and was never seriously challenged during the colonial period (Fairhead and Leach, 2000).

The Impacts on Local Institutions, Burning Practices and the Environment

The impacts of the policy on local institutions, burning practices, and the environment were again minimal. In areas controlled by villages the policy tended to support the indigenous system of burning. Except for areas in close proximity to the classified forests, there was little change in burning patterns during the colonial era.

Following independence, many West African countries including Mali and Guinea adopted the colonial forestry and fire codes with little modification. The vigor with which they were implemented and the level of enforcement varied by country and over time (for example, Brinkerhoff, 1995; Fairhead and Leach, 1995). By 1980 the new Malian administration's view of fire had completely transformed, burning came to be viewed as a crime against nature and was treated as a crime against the state.

The First Independent Regime (1960-1967): A Green Vision of Mali

The Environment/Development Context

The first two leaders of independent Mali drew heavily on the degradation narrative in establishing anti-fire campaigns, although their motives, methods, and even the environmental imagery they adopted differed greatly. Moreover, the contrast in the environmental context of the two periods could not have been greater. Modibo Keita ruled Mali from 1960 through early 1967 the tail end of an unusually long wet period in the region, while Moussa Traore's rule carried Mali through the longest and deepest drought of this century.

Legislation and Goals

During the 1960s Keita, Mali's first independent leader, called on his citizens to refrain from burning the savanna so that Mali would become more forested. Elder farmers and hunters recall that Keita's vision was of a greener, more wooded Mali that would transform the local climate, allowing Malian farmers to grow some of the forest region's cash crops that were bringing wealth to its southern, wetter neighbor, the Ivory Coast. Thus, Keita, a socialist, appealed to a sense of nationalism for economic development in his effort to suppress fire. He drew on desertification ideas in his fire prevention position but embodied them in an environmental vision of a greener, more economically prosperous Mali. According to the accounts of rural elders, Keita argued that by preventing burning Mali could become more forested.

The Impacts on Local Institutions, Burning Practices and the Environment

According to my interviews, Keita's plan was a complete failure. People followed his call to reduce burning, and perhaps initially they approved of his goals. After a year or two of reduced burning, large, hot dry season fires engulfed the countryside. Local inhabitants quickly realized the impossibility of preventing fire and resorted to their time-tested ways of using it to burn the bush gradually in a more controlled fashion. In the minds of rural farmers, hunters and herders I interviewed, the Keita era, and not the French colonial period, marked the first time fire suppression was ever widely applied in Mali.[6] The large conflagrations that occurred during this era forever marked the minds of those who witnessed them as an example of the damaging power of fire. Apparently, the government relaxed its restrictions on burning after the conflagrations.

The Traoré Regime (1968-1991): The *Fight Against Fire*

The regime of Traoré marked a radical shift in the enforcement of anti-fire policy. Following a period when at least some forms of fire were tolerated by the forest service, burning was banned outright by president Traoré in 1980.[7] In his address to the nation, Traoré drew heavily on the environmental narrative (see quotation at beginning of chapter). Although the use of the narrative in his address differed little from the rhetoric of his colonial predecessors, the extreme droughts of the period provided the apparent physical evidence that desertification was indeed occurring; moreover, by 1980 the international environment/development context had dramatically shifted.

The Environment/Development Context

Key shifts in fire policy and enforcement needs to be understood in the context of the Sahelian droughts of the 1970s and 80s and the growing role international development agencies played in funding environmental projects. The droughts, coupled with a more fervent and vocal international environmentalism, served to revitalize a somewhat dormant desertification narrative (Swift 1996). International concern over desertification was mobilized on a large scale after a United Nations conference on desertification produced a master 'Plan of Action to Halt Desertification.' The UN Plan became the basis for the Malian *Campaign Against Desertification* which was the major focus of the Forestry Service and donor organizations during the 1980s (Republic du Mali, 1987). A key element of this new agenda was the *Fight Against Fire* campaign.

With the rise of international environmentalism in the 1980s the influence of environmental narratives materialized in unexpected ways. For example, Ribot (1995) has argued that the President Traoré tailored his environmental policies so as to appeal to the environmental concerns of the major donor agencies. According to this view Traoré instituted oppressive legislation, including high fines on cutting branches and setting fires, to appear to be a staunch environmentalist in order to attract foreign aid (Ribot, 1995; Benjaminsen, 2000). More generally, Leach and Mearns (1996) argue that the late 1980s saw the onset of 'green conditionality' (Davies, 1992) as donor agencies began to use environmental goals as a form of leverage over national governments in dialogue about policy. National Environmental Action Plans (NEAPs), which were developed with assistance from powerful institutions such as the World Bank and other international funders, incorporated the view that fires were causing savannization. In this manner the dominant environmental view was worked into national- and even local-level environmental management plans and programs (Basset and Zueli, 2000; Schroeder, 1999).

In Mali, reassessment of natural resource policies by the major donor agencies began in response to the drought in the 1970s and continued into the 80s. The effectiveness and appropriateness of the Traoré administration's approach to forestry policy came to be increasingly questioned, as was the forest services capacity to implement it. This resulted in policy shifts and the functions of service were expanded to include more education and management oriented goals to combat desertification (Brinkerhoff, 1995).

Much of the change in policy was given impetus by donor-supported initiatives such as those designed to build the service's institutional capacity to become an extension service with core social forestry techniques and expertise. Until this point a large percentage of the forest guard was composed of former military agents with little forestry training, but during the late 1970s and early 1980s their was a increase in the number of new agents with formal training in forestry. The changes in policy and personnel brought on a kind of schizophrenia in the forest service between old guard and new social foresters whereby the Forest Service leaders espoused a participatory extension message while the field agents engaged in increasingly abusive policing practices (Brinkerhoff, 1995).

Legislation, Goals and Enforcement

During the Traoré regime the effort to couple environmental police work with social forestry proved difficult to put into operation and in the end it was policing and fining and not education that came to define the period. According to Brinkerhoff (1995) this was primarily due to the financial constraints of the forest service. The forest service, as part of Mali's governmental apparatus, shared many of the operating constraints that characterize developing country public sector agencies: limited operating budgets, low salaries, cumbersome civil service personnel policies and practices, and few rewards for good performance.

Indeed, by the late 1970s the forest service was struggling to find a way to improve its financial situation. It eventually found it in the permit and fines system established during the colonial era. The system provided a key revenue source supplementing the agencies operating budget as well as the salaries of individual agents. These revenues fed the forestry fund established in 1967 over which the forest service had discretionary authority. For individuals there was a formula that distributed a percentage of the fines among the agent administering the infraction, his superiors, and national-level staff. The administration recognized that the educational goal would jeopardize an increasingly important funding source, revenues from fines, because increased efforts in education would result in an immediate drop in receipts. To compensate for a possible loss in revenue, the service envisioned a major anti-fire campaign that could be quickly mobilized generating its own income through new revenues from fines (Republic du Mali, 1980). Indeed by the mid-1980s a significant portion of the forest service budget was coming from fines collected in rural areas (Steiber and du Saussay, 1987).

The impact of the new policy on forest service revenue and personnel numbers was immediate. The number of field agents rose five-fold between 1975 and 1990 (Republic du Mali, 1994). By the mid-1980s receipts from penalties for fires covered 37 per cent of the total forest service budget according to forest service records (Doumbia, 1991, Steiber and du Saussay, 1987). In terms of finances the ratio of permits to fines went from 41/59 per cent in 1971 to 32/68 per cent in 1986. This was accompanied by a whopping seven-fold increase in overall receipts (74.6 million CFA to 504 million CFA) (Republic du Mali, 1994, p.25).

By the late 1980s the conflict between the educational and policing missions of the forest service was apparent. In additional to the financial constraints, a number of other factors served to hamper social forestry efforts: field agents operated with minimal support for the technical programs; Malian peasants perceived forest agents as policemen, not rural extension agents; and finally, the Forest Service's paramilitary ethos, which had been built-up over many years, meant that the profile of the average agent was more conducive to policing, in terms of mentality and training, rather than assisting the rural populous (Brinkerhoff, 1995).

In 1987 a report by a Swiss NGO raised concern about the fire policy. The Swiss report recognized the difficult position of the forestry agents, many of whom were forced to rely on fines and bribes because the government failed to pay their salaries.

> The mission [forest service] was aware of the necessarily urgent situation of the forestry agents who require additional financial means to supplement their salaries in order to meet minimum economic needs and perform their numerous tasks in application of the new forestry policy... [s]ome agents play the role of informers and cash the fines rather than trying to stimulate collaboration of villagers in fighting the offenders, fire starters. Individual agents themselves point out the insufficient regularity in paying their salaries (Steiber and du Saussay, 1987, pp.22-26).

The Impacts on Local Institutions, Burning Practices and the Environment

The *Fight Against Fire* campaign was a complete failure in terms of its environmental and social impacts. The forest services' own records show the number of fires increasing during this era (Doumbia, 1991). Whether this represents an increase in the number of burning violations cited by agents or a true increase in fire is unknown since no measurements of burned areas were taken. Results from a survey of rural farmers in southern Mali find that the majority of the population believes that fires were worse during the Traoré regime than during any prior period (Laris, 2002b). According to local accounts of hunters, farmers, and herders the policy caused an increase in unusually large and damaging fires. These large fires, which were uncommon before the anti-fire policy was implemented, swept through the landscape scorching trees, killing animals, and occasionally burning small villages.   As noted above, the indigenous practice of setting numerous fires early in the dry season created a mosaic of burned and unburned patches that tended to prevent more intense late season fires from spreading. By forcibly removing the early fire regime, the forest service created exactly the kinds of fires it had intended to suppress large, intense, late dry-season fires that are most damaging to trees and can cause savannization.

The costs to rural areas were social and economic as well as ecological. A typical fine for a single fire was nearly the equivalent of the annual per capita income of a Malian citizen.   During the campaign the level of animosity in relations between forestry agents and rural inhabitants reached an all time high. Corruption, which was rampant in the countryside, tended to increase environmentally degrading behavior. Forest agents lit fires themselves so that they could return later and collect fines.   Villagers elected to risk illegal behavior knowing that they could bargain the agents down to a lesser fine if and when they were caught. Because the negotiated fines bore no relationship to the magnitude of the infraction, peasants burned as much as they wanted, recognizing that the fine would be the same for a small infraction as for a large one.   Residents came to view fines as the price of access to forest resources or, in the case of fire, as the price of protection from damaging fire.

Ultimately people in the countryside resisted the intrusive behavior of the forest service. Members of the Hunter Society were especially resentful and there were numerous accounts of forest agents being captured in the bush and tortured by hunters.[8] Animosity peaked during the late years of the Traoré regime when villagers set fire to the bush during Traoré's visits in a kind of formal protest against the policy. Forest agents who had earned a reputation for abuse and repression were singled out for reprisals at the hand of the rural population at the time of Mali's coup d'etat in 1991 (Brinkerhoff, 1995; Benjaminsen, 2000; Ribot 1995, 1996).

Links in the Chain: Narrative to Human-Environment Impacts

An examination of the historical record finds that the anti-fire policies of the 20th century in Mali were heavily influenced by a persistent and dominant environmental narrative which viewed fire as a major cause of degradation. The linkages between this dominant environmental view, the enforcement of anti-fire policy, and the burning regimes of rural Malians are complex and they shifted over time. This study finds that the impacts of the policies were most often mediated by pressing colonial or national economic concerns and by international development agendas. Thus although the degradation narrative endured as the predominant view through the century, the environment/development context of each period influenced how the fire problem was perceived by government agencies and dictated how scarce human resources, such as forest agents, were deployed. For most of the century, fire suppression efforts had little if any tangible impact on the burning practices of Mali's rural population because while the governments viewed fire as a major problem, it was not worthy of heavy investment. Only during the 1980s, when a confluence of factors at different levels along the chain of explanation came into play, did the number of forestry agents increase to the point to modify local burning practices with impacts on the environment on a wide-scale. Thus the study illustrates the usefulness of the chain of explanation approach for explaining not only why environmental change occurs, but also, why it does not.

Several scholars have argued that the West African degradation narrative has remained influential, if not hegemonic, in spite of accumulating evidence to the contrary (Fairhead and Leach, 1996; Mortimore, 1998; Swift, 1996). To understand the longevity of an environmental narrative, Leach and Mearns (1996) argue it is necessary to ask whom the narrative has benefited the most. During the colonial period the West African narrative served to justify the formation and funding of national level executive agencies such as the forest service to be responsible for environmental management (Fairhead and Leach, 1996, 2000). More recently as Non-Governmental Organizations (NGOs) and international institutions such as the World Bank have gained power and become deeply involved in funding and managing environmental projects, these groups have also served to perpetuate the environmental narrative in their policy documents and reports (for example, Bassett and Zueli, 2000; Schroeder, 1999; Ribot, 1999).

Environmental events, such as long term droughts, also influenced anti-degradation policy, but has Swift (1996) argues these are not sufficient to perpetuate a dominant view. Swift notes that it was no accident that the first crisis narratives of desertification appeared shortly after the severe droughts of the early twentieth century. Nor was it surprising that the surge in international interest and intense UN and donor activity in the 1970s and 80s began during the driest decade this century. Swift (1996, p.87) argues, however, that: '...a misreading of climatic variability is not enough to explain the tenacious hold of the received desertification narrative on the minds of politicians, civil servants, aid administrators and some scientists.' In Swift's view, these groups were the big winners during the revitalization of the degradation narrative of the 1980s. The national governments used the desertification 'crisis' to claim rights to stewardship over resources previously outside of their control; the Aid Bureaucracies used the narrative to call for increased aid flows; and, some scientists used the crisis for personal benefit by becoming involved in policy making.

The Mali case demonstrates, however, that the 'winners' of the anti-fire campaign were not only the powerful and the few but also forestry agents at every level of the forestry service. Field agents as well as their superiors earned substantial bonuses to their salaries through fines and bribes as the benefits trickled up from the monies collected by common agents. The revenues collected from fines were a major reason the service was able to expand during the 1980s. The expansion, in turn, generated additional revenue the forestry service. It was only through this expansion of the forest service's field force that the degradation narrative was finally able to have an impact on the burning practices of individuals and on the landscape. Thus the case also illustrates how an environmental narrative can persist for decades in spite of a lack of supporting evidence, have few tangible impacts, and then suddenly emerge from a slumber during a unique environment/development context to have a dramatic impact on nature and society.

The big losers of the *Fight Against Fire* campaign were the rural population and the environment. The political ecological context of the 1980s was such that foresters in Mali were police first and educators last. The practice of fining villages for setting fires persisted for over a decade despite protests from the rural population and documented failure of the policy to suppress fire. The real tragedy of the *Fight Against Fire* is that the 1980s was a period when the rural population needed the kinds of educational and extension services the forest service could have provided. Many villages were learning to cope with drought and were seeking new information and techniques to deal with a changing environment, the forest service could have put the indigenous strategy of early burning to work to reduce fire damage during the drought, but the level of mistrust generated by a system of fining and bribery shattered the possibility of a collaborative effort.

Epilogue

Following the overthrow of the Traoré regime in 1991 a national debate was held to determine a new fire code. The 'National Debate for a New Strategy to Combat Bush Fire,' which included town meetings that allowed villagers to voice their grievances and offer policy suggestions, resulted in a new fire code that legitimized and legalized the indigenous practices of early burning (Doumbia 1991). The new legislation established specific dates for early burning and removed the controversial 'collective penalty' clause (Republic du Mali n.d.). Late burning continues to be illegal in Mali, however, and according to the fire code, permits are required for early preventative fires, although in practice foresters have refrained from issuing fire citations. There remains a great deal of mistrust between villagers and forest extension agents.

Notes

1 Numerous scholars have argued that the popular view of the dynamics of vegetation change in the West African savanna are based more on myth than on rigorous scientific study (for example, Bassett and Zueli, 2000; Fairhead and Leach, 1996; Mortimore, 1998; Ribot, 1999; Swift, 1996).

2 The term desertification has been widely used to describe land degradation processes in Africa. To avoid confusion, I use a convention adopted by Swift (1996) who defines desertification as the most general term that encompasses a number of distinct phenomena including desiccation and dry-land degradation. I use the term savannization to refer to the process of the replacement of trees by grasses.

3 In his later works Aubréville shifted his stance and argued that the savanna's origin was at least partly natural (climatic) (Chris Duvall, personal communication).

4 The works of Fairhead and Leach (1996) and Bassett and Zueli (2000) find that woody vegetation cover has increased in recent decades in the savanna of Guinea and the northern Ivory Coast respectively. Dauget and Menault (1992, p.621) document a 'strong increase' in woody vegetation cover during the past 20 years in central Ivory Coast in spite of annual burning.

5 Thanks to Christian Kull for this term.

6 My accounts of Keita's discourse are based solely on the recollections of rural inhabitants. I did not find written records of his statements.

7 Traoré's policy, which had already been widely applied in the field, officially became law in 1986 (Republic du Mali, 1986).

8 In one particularly brutal account, a hunter 'captured' a forest agent in the bush, stripped him and left him to die tied to a tree. The agent was later rescued and transferred to another region.

References

Aubréville, A. (1949), *Climats, Fôrets et Désertification de l'Afrique Tropicale*. Société d'Edition Géographie Maritime et Coloniale, Paris.

Barbosa, P.M., Grégoire, J. M., Pereira, J.M.C. (1999), 'An algorithm for extracting burned areas from time series of AVHRR GAC data applied at continental scale.' *Remote Sensing and Environment*, 69, pp. 253-263.

Basset, T. (1988), 'The Political Ecology of Peasant-Herder Conflicts in Northern Ivory Coast.' *Annals of the Association of American Geographers*. 78(3), pp. 453-72.

Bassett, T.J. and Zuéli, K.B. (2000), 'Environmental Discourses and the Ivorian Savanna.' *Annals of the Association of American Geographers* 90(1), pp. 67-95.

Batterbury, S., Forsyth, T., and Thomson, K. (1997), 'Environmental transformations in developing countries: hybrid research and democratic policy.' *The Geographical Journal*, 163(2), pp. 126-132.

Bebbington, A. (2000), 'Reencountering Development: Livelihood Transitions and Place Transformations in the Andes.' *Annals of the American Association of Geographers* 90(3), pp. 495-520.

Becker, L.C. (2001), 'Seeing green in Mali's Woods: Colonial Legacy, Forest use, and Local Control.' *Annals of the Association of American Geographers* 91(3), pp. 504-526.

Benjaminsen, T.A. (1997), 'Natural Resource Management, Paradigm Shifts, and the Decentralization Reform in Mali.' *Human Ecology* 25 (1), pp. 121-143.

Benjaminsen, T.A. (2000), 'Conservation in the Sahel: Policies and People in Mali, 1900-1998.' In V. Broch-Due and R. Schroeder (eds). *Producing Nature and Poverty in Africa.*Stockholm: Nordiska Afrikainstitutet, pp. 94-108.

Blaikie, P. (1985), *The Political Economy of Soil Erosion in Developing Countries.* Development Series. London: Longman.

Blaikie, P. and Brookfield, H. (1987), *Land Degradation and Society.* London: Methuen.

Boyd, R. (ed.). (1999), *Indians Fire and the Land in the Pacific Northwest.* Corvaillis: Oregon State University Press,

Brinkerhoff, D.W. (1995), 'African State-Society Linkages in Transition: The Case of Forestry Policy in Mali.' *Canadian Journal of Development Studies* 16(2), pp. 201-228.

Broch-Due, V. and R. Schroeder (eds.) (2000), *Producing Nature and Poverty in Africa.* Stockholm: Nordiska Afrikainstitutet.

Brookman-Amissah, J., Hall, J.B., Swaine, M.D. and Attakorah, J.Y. (1980), 'A re-assessment of a fire protection experiment in North-Eastern Ghana savanna.' *Journal of Applied Ecology* 17, pp. 85-99.

Bryant, R. (1996), 'Romancing Colonial Forestry: The Discourse of "Forestry as Progress" in British Burma.' *The Geographical Journal* 162 (2), pp. 169-178.

Bryant, R.L. and Bailey, S. (1997), *Third World Political Ecology.* New York: Routledge.

Bucini, G. and Lambin, E. (2002), 'Fire impacts on vegetation in Central Africa: A remote sensing-based statistical analysis.' *Applied Geography,* 22(1): pp. 27-48.

Carney, J. (1993), 'Converting the Wetlands, Engendering the Environment: The Intersection of gender with Agrarian Change in The Gambia.' *Economic Geography* 69 (4), pp. 329-348.

Dauget, J.-M. and J.-C., Menault. (1992), 'Evolution sur 20 ans d'une parcelle de savane boisée non protégé du feu dans la réserve de Lampto (Côte-d'Ivoire).' *Canondellea,* 47 (2), pp. 621-630.

Davies, S. (1992), 'Green Conditionality and Food Security: Winners and Losers from the greening of Aid.' *Journal of International Development.* 4 (2), pp. 151-165.

Deshler, W. (1975), 'An Examination of the Extent of Fire in Grasslands and Savanna of Africa Along the Southern Side of the Sahara.' Proc. 9th International Symposium on Remote Sensing of the Environment. ERIM, Ann Arbor, Michigan.

Doumbia, Y. (1991), 'Problematic des Feux de Brousse au Mali.' *Debat Nationale sur les feux de brousse.* Unpublished report. Direction Nationale des Eaux et Fôret, Bamako.

Dungan, J. (1944), 'The burning question.' *Farm and Forest* June, pp. 8-10.

Dwyer, E., Pinnock, S. and Gregoire, J.-M. (2000), 'Global Spatial and Temporal Distribution of Vegetation Fire as Determined from Satellite Observations.' *International Journal or Remote Sensing.* 21 (6), pp. 1289-1302.

Escobar, A. (1996), 'Constructing Nature: elements for a Poststructural Political Ecology.' In R. Peet, and M. Watts (eds) *Liberation Ecologies.* New York: Routledge.

Eva, H. and Lambin, E.F. (1998b), 'Burnt area mapping in Central Africa using ATSR data.' *International Journal of Remote Sensing,* 19, pp. 3473-3497.

Fairhead, J. and Leach, M. (1995), 'Reading Forest History Backwards: The interaction of Policy and Local Land Use in Guinea's Forest Savanna Mosaic, 1893-1993.' *Environment and History* 1, pp. 55-91.

Fairhead, J. and Leach, M. (1996), *Misreading the African Landscape.* Cambridge: Cambridge University Press.

Fairhead, J. and Leach, M. (2000), 'Dessication and domination: science and struggles over environment and development in colonial Guinea.' *Journal of African History* 41, pp. 35-54.

Grossman, L. (1984), *Peasants, Subsistence Ecology and Development in the Highlands of Papua New Guinea*. Princeton, New Jersey: Princeton University Press.

Grove, R. and Anderson, D. (eds). (1987), *Conservation in Africa: People, Policies and Practice*. Cambridge: Cambridge University Press.

Guilloteau, J. (1957), 'The problem of bush fires in land development and soil conservation in Africa south of the Sahara.' *African Soils* 4, pp. 64-102.

Jeffreys, M.D.W. (1945), 'The burning question.' *Farm and Forest* July, pp. 115-124.

Kull, C.A. (2000), 'Deforestation, Erosion, and Fire: Degradation Myths in the Environmental History of Madagascar.' *Environment and History*, 6, pp. 423-450.

Laris, P. (2002a), 'Burning the Seasonal Mosaic: Preventative Burning Strategies in the West African Savanna.' *Human Ecology*. 30(2), pp. 155-186.

Laris, P. (2002b), *Burning the Savanna Mosaic: Fire Patterns, Indigenous Burning Regimes, and Ecology in the Savanna of Mali*. Unpublished Dissertation. Clark University, Worcester, Massachusetts.

Leach, M. and Mearns, R. (eds.). (1996), *The Lie of the Land*. Oxford: James Curry.

Lewis, H. T. and Ferguson, T.A. (1988), 'Yards, corridors, and mosaics: how to burn a Boreal Forest.' *Human Ecology* 16, pp. 57-77.

Louppe, D., N. Oattara, and Coulibaly, A. (1995), 'The effects of brush fires on vegetation: the Aubréville Fire Plots after 60 years.' *Commonwealth Forestry Review* 74 (4), pp. 288-291.

Mbow, C., T.T. Nielson, and Rasmussen, K. (2000), 'Savanna Fires in East-Central Senegal: Distribution Patterns, Resource Management and Perceptions.' *Human Ecology*, 28(4), pp. 561-583.

McCann, J.C. (1999), *Greenland, Brownland, Blackland*. Portsmouth, New Hampshire: Heinemann.

Menault, J.C., Abbadie, L., Lavenu, F., Loudjani, P. and Podaire, A. (1991), 'Biomass Burning in West African Savannas.' In Levine, J.S. (ed.). *Global Biomass Burning*. Cambridge, Massachusetts: The MIT Press, pp. 133-142.

Menault, J.C., Lepage, M. and Abbadie, L. (1995), 'Savannas, Woodlands, and Dry Forests in Africa.' In S.H. Bullock, H.A. Mooney and E. Medina. (eds.) *Seasonally Dry Tropical Forests*, pp. 64-92. Cambridge: Cambridge University Press.

Mortimore, M. (1998), *Roots in the African Dust*. Cambridge: Cambridge University Press.

Ortoli, P.I. (1955), *Lutte Contre Les Feux*. Direction Locale des Affaires Economiques. Soudan Francais, Koulouba, Mali.

Nasi, R. and Sabatier, M. (1988), 'Projet Inventaire des ressources Ligneuses au Mali.' DNEF, Bamako.

Nicholson, S.E., Tucker, C.J., Ba, M.B. (1998), 'Desertification, drought and surface vegetation: an example from the West African Sahel.' *Bulletin of the American Meteorological Society* 79, pp. 815-830.

Nielsen, T.T. and Rassmussen, K. (1997), 'The distribution in time and space of savanna fires in Burkina Faso as determined from NOAA AVHRR data.' *Geografisk Tidsskrift* 97, pp. 86-97.

Parr, C.L. and Brockett, B.H. (1999), 'Patch-Mosaic Burning: A new Paradigm for Savanna Fire Management in Protected Areas?' *Koedoe* (42), pp. 117-130.

Peet, R. and Watts, M. (eds) (1996), *Liberation Ecologies: Environment, Development and Social Movements*. London and New York: Routledge.

Pyne, S.J. (1982), *Fire in America*. University of Washington Press, Seattle.

Pyne, S.J. (1990), 'Fire Conservancy: The origins of Wildland Fire Protection in British India, America, and Australia.' In J.G. Goldammer (ed). *Fire in the Tropical Biota: Ecosystem Processes and Global Challenges*. New York: Springer-Verlag.

Pyne, S.J. (1997), *Vestal Fire*. Seattle: University of Washington Press.

Pyne, S.J. (1999), Ghana with the Wind. *International Forest Fire News*, 21, pp. 2-11.

Rasmussen, K., Fog, B., and Madsen, J.E. (2001), 'Desertification in Reverse? Observations from Northern Burkina Faso.' *Global Environmental Change*. 11, pp. 271-282.

Republic du Mali (1957), *Rapport Annuel des Eaux et Forêts*. Republic du Mali, Bamako.

Republic du Mali (1979), *Synthése des Rapports Annuels des Eaux et Forêts*. Republic du Mali, Bamako.

Republic du Mali (1980), *Rapport Annuel des Eaux et Forêts*. Republic du Mali, Bamako.

Republic du Mali (1986), 'Loi #86-42/AN-RM. Portant Code de Gestion de Feu.' Assemblee Nationale, Republic du Mali, Bamako.

Republic du Mali (1987), *Program National de Lutte Contre la Désertification: Synthese*. Republique du Mali, Bamako.

Republic du Mali (1994), *Diagnostic de la Formation Forestiere au Mali*. Republique du Mali, Bamako.

Republic du Mali (Undated), 'Projet de loi #___/AN-RM. Portant Code des Feux de Brousse.' President de la Republique, Republique de Mali, Bamako.

Ribot, J. (1995), *Local Forest Control in Mali: An Institutional Analysis of Participatory Policies*. Washington, DC: The World Bank.

Ribot, J. (1996), 'Participation without representation.' *Cultural Survival Quarterly*. Fall, pp. 40-44.

Ribot, J.C. (1999), 'A History of Fear: Imagining Deforestation in the West African Dryland Forests.' *Global Ecology and Biogeography*. 8, pp. 291-300.

Robbins, P. (1998), 'Paper Forests: Imagining and Developing Exogenous Ecologies in Arid India.' *Geoforum*. 29(1), pp. 69-86.

Rocheleau, D.R., Steinberg, P.E., and Benjamin, P.A. (1995), 'Environment, Development, Crisis, and Crusade: Ukambani, Kenya, 1890-1990.' *World Development*, 23(6), pp. 1037-1051.

Rocheleau, D., Thomas-Slayter, B. and Wangari, E. (eds) (1996), *Feminist Political Ecology: Global Issues and Local Experiences*. London: Routledge.

Roe, E. (1991), 'Development Narratives or Making the Best of Blueprint Development.' *World Development* 15 (4), pp. 287-300.

Rose-Innes, R. (1971), 'Fire in West African Vegetation.' *Proceedings Tall Timbers Fire Ecology Conference* 11, pp. 175-200.

Russell-Smith, J. et al. (1997), 'Aboriginal resource utilization and fire management practice in western Arhem Land, monsoonal northern Australia: notes for prehistory, lessons for the future.' *Human Ecology* 25(2), pp. 159-195.

Schmitz, A. (1996), 'Contrôle et utilization du feu en zones arides et subhumides africaines.' Rome: FAO.

Schroeder, R. (1993), 'Shady Practice: Gender and the Political Ecology of Resource Stabilization in Gambian Gardens/Orchards.' *Economic Geography* 69(4), pp. 349-365.

Schroeder, R. (1999), 'Community, Forestry, and Conditionality in The Gambia.' *Africa* 69(1), pp. 23-65.

Showers, K.B. (1989), 'Soil Erosion in the Kingdom of Lesotho: Origins and Colonial Response.' *Journal of Southern African Studies*, 15(2), pp. 263-268.

Sivaramakrishnan, K. (2000), 'State Sciences and Development Histories: Encoding Local Forestry Knowledge in Bengal.' *Development and Change*. 31, pp. 61-89.

Stebbing, E. P. (1935), 'The Encroaching Sahara: The Threat to the West African Colonies.' *Geographic Journal.* 88, pp. 506-24.

Steiber, J and du Saussay, C. (1987), 'Probelmatique de la Police Forestiere au Mali.' *Seminar National sur la Police Forestiere au Mali.* Chapter 2. pp. 11-53.

Stott, P. and Sullivan, S. (2000), *Political Ecology: Science, Myth and Power.* London: Arnold.

Swift, J. (1996), 'Desertification: Narratives, Winners and Losers.' In Leach, M. and Mearns, R. (eds.). *The Lie of the Land.* Oxford: James Curry.

Traoré, M. (1980), 'Circular Bamako, le 24 November 1980.' Unpublished Memo. Union Democratique du Peuple Malien. Bureau Executif Central. Republic du Mali.

Tucker, C.J., Dregne, H.E., Newcomb, W.W. (1991), 'Expansion and Contraction of the Sahara Desert from 1980-1990.' *Science,* 253, pp. 299-301.

PART II
POLITICAL ECONOMY, RURAL LIVELIHOODS AND THE ENVIRONMENT

Chapter 5

War and the Environmental Effects of Displacement in Southern Africa (1970s-1990s)

Emmanuel Kreike

People came in helicopters and fired on us from them. They killed people. Everything was on fire. Our houses and everything we owned was burned. Our village [Ohauwanga munene] was destroyed. We fled. I fled to Oshuli where one of my children lived. But Oshuli was also attacked and all the homes were burned down. We moved to Small Omukukutu next where we lived with my daughter until this village too, was destroyed. We fled to Ohaujave where my husband fell ill. We moved him to Ondangwa where he died at Onandjokwe hospital. We remained at Ondangwa for a long time because the war continued in our home area. The people who burned our homes came from Ondangwa (Shangeshapwako Rachela Hauladi, interview, 14 July 1993).

Introduction[1]

Shangeshapwako Rachela Hauladi's recollections about the war in the early 1980s in northern Namibia are representative of the experience of many inhabitants on the 'frontlines' of the Apartheid Wars: rural lives and livelihoods were destroyed. Many fled the terror of war. The bush quickly claimed deserted villages with only a scorched pole or fruit tree remaining as a silent testimony to what had been landscapes filled with people, livestock, homesteads, fields, and fruit trees. Shangeshapwako Rachela Hauladi fled the war, joining her daughter, who lived in a neighboring village near the Angolan border. When her daughter's village was also attacked, mother and daughter abandoned the border zone altogether and sought sanctuary at Ondangwa, where they remained for the duration of the war, until the late 1980s. Ondangwa, one of Ovamboland's two towns, was not only the administrative center of South African-occupied north central Namibia but also, ironically, home to a huge South African Defense Force (SADF) base for the helicopters that had brought the apocalypse to her village.

Namibia's Ovamboland, Angola's adjacent Cunene Province and Mozambique's Gaza Province were in the 'frontlines' of three decades of warfare that ravaged southern Africa from the 1960s to 1990s. Frontlines were not only ill-defined, but also constantly shifted because each border region was subjected to both conventional and unconventional warfare. The rural populations on both sides of each border constituting the 'Western Front' (Angola's Cunene Province and Namibia's adjacent Ovamboland) and the 'Eastern Front' (Mozambique's Gaza Province and South Africa's Gazankulu) shared linguistic and cultural traits. The inhabitants of Cunene and Ovamboland speak Ovambo dialects, while the inhabitants of Gaza Province and Gazankulu (a 'Homeland' that was scattered over much of the Lowveld) speak the Tsonga-Shangaan language. Clan affiliations in each border region facilitated both the 'hosting' and integration of refugees in the 'safe havens.'

Refugees from southern Angola and the Namibian border fled further southwards, deeper into Ovamboland. The South African Lowveld region, especially the former Gazankulu homeland, was a major safe haven for refugees from Mozambique's Gaza Province. While the places of refuge were not directly affected by violence, the influx of refugees frequently had a significant impact not only upon the lives and livelihoods of the local populations, but also on the local environment. The villages in Ovamboland and Gazankulu that served as safe havens were already short of land and food before the war, and the influx of refugees further exacerbated pressures on the local natural resource base. Meanwhile, the environment in deserted areas changed dramatically, not only because of, for example, mines and other war-related hazards, but also because the investment of human-made infrastructure was effectively undermined.

The chapter emphasizes the violence and dislocation in the war zones and resulting environmental impacts as human management and uses of natural resources ∙were forcibly conscribed. The chapter focuses primarily on environmental changes caused by forced population movements and the terror-inspired disinvestment of human labor from the creation and maintenance of rural infrastructure (wells, water holes, farms, fields, fences, fruit trees) and food production as reflected in the memories of survivors. Survivors' memories suggest how critically 'environment' is socially defined: interviewees unambiguously identify humans as central actors in describing and explaining processes of environmental change, which is triggered by intensification, dis-intensification, or absence of human management and use of a particular environment. Confronted with human-caused terror and destruction, inhabitants of war-affected areas were forced to choose amongst several options: to fight to defend their homesteads; to hide nearby until the immediate threat subsided; or to flee either to neighboring safe havens, or further afield, for the duration of the war. Most survivors resorted to more than one of the above strategies as new challenges arose.

While studies on the Apartheid Wars traditionally have concentrated on its military, political, and economic causes and consequences, less, but increasing attention has been paid to the social price of the resulting devastation and dislocations (see, for example, Minter, 1994; Leys and Saul, 1995; Urdang, 1989; Cleaver and Wallace, 1990; Allen and Morsink, 1994; Nordstrom, 1997). The environmental dimensions of three decades of warfare have as yet received little attention, although some studies have identified a link between the war and famine, while others have documented the widespread poaching that financed covert operations (Africa Watch, 1992, 1993; Ellis, 1990; Potgieter, 1995). A 1993 environmental profile of the southern African region identified war as a factor in environmental degradation only in the case of Mozambique (Moyo, O'Keefe, and Sill, 1993). Yet, in northern Namibia, southern Angola, and southern Mozambique, population dislocations and the terror of war turned cultural landscapes of farms and villages into deserted bush-encroached 'wilderness' while the villages, towns, and cities that – especially in northern South Africa – became 'safe havens' saw their natural and other resources burdened to the limit by the influx of war refugees. The Apartheid Wars' destruction and displacement in the rural environments not only caused a regional crisis in food security in the 1980s, but also severely handicaps post-war agro-ecological recovery.

The 1960s marked the transition to armed resistance for the nationalist movements throughout southern Africa. Armed insurrection in Angola in 1961 was brutally suppressed, but guerilla warfare organized by the *Movimento Popular de Libertação de Angola* (the Popular Movement for the Liberation of Angola, known by its Portuguese acronym as MPLA) and the *Frente Nacional de Libertação de Angola* (the Front for the National Liberation of Angola, known by its Portuguese acronym as FNLA) spread throughout Angola in the mid to late 1960s. The *União Nacional da Independencia Total de Angola* (the National Union for the Total Liberation of Angola, known as UNITA) joined the insurrection in Angola in the late 1960s. It was based mainly in central Angola but also had support amongst Ovambo speakers in southern Angola's Cunene Province. UNITA initially had strong ties with the South West African People's Organization (SWAPO), which launched its armed struggle for the liberation of Namibia in 1966. SWAPO found its main support in Ovamboland, where most of its leadership and membership originated. The *Frente da Libertação de Mozambique* (the Liberation Front for Mozambique, known as FRELIMO) that had strong support in southern Mozambique (including Gaza Province) resorted to armed resistance against Portuguese colonial rule in 1963. After the white minority in the British colony of (Southern) Rhodesia unilaterally declared its independence from Great Britain in 1966, black nationalists quickly organized an armed resistance (Marcum, 1978, vol. 2; Isaacman and Isaacman, 1983; Ranger, 1985; Katjavivi, 1988; Birmingham, 1992).

The war escalated rapidly during the second half of the 1970s, after the burden of fighting a colonial war on three fronts led to a coup in Portugal and the hasty granting of independence to Angola, Mozambique, and Guinea-Bissau in 1974 and 1975. Independent Angola and Mozambique allowed nationalist liberation movements from neighboring territories to establish bases on their soil to launch attacks against the remaining colonial regimes. In the late 1970s, SWAPO bases in southern Angola and Zimbabwe African National Union (ZANU) bases in southern and central Mozambique (including Gaza Province) became targets of cross-border attacks by conventional forces of, respectively the SADF and the Rhodesian security forces. Even more nefarious, and more widespread in its impact, however, was the South African security forces' shift to unconventional counterinsurgency warfare in 1977-1978, with an experimental stage confined largely to the 'Western Front.' The strategy was institutionalized both at the policy and military operational levels in 1980 and by the early 1980s had spread to the 'Eastern Front.'

During the late 1970s and 1980s, the South African security forces and their allies used various counterinsurgency strategies that targeted the rural populations and their home environment. One important strategy, which aimed to thwart guerilla infiltrations, combined 'killing' zones and scorched earth tactics to create buffer zones that were cleared of populations and their resource base. The buffer zones were heavily patrolled and any human presence in them was considered 'hostile.' A second strategy sought to terrorize the inhabitants of areas that could not be cleared to prevent them from lending guerillas any support of any kind.

The spread of various strategies and tactics from one war zone in the Apartheid Wars to another was facilitated by the movements of 'operators' from one front to another. South Africa's Special Forces, the *Recces* or Reconnaissance Commandos/Regiments, for example, absorbed elements of the Rhodesian Selous Scouts, Special Air Services, and Rhodesian Light Infantry (Stiff, 1999). General Geldenhuys was first the SADF commander in Namibia, and subsequently became the commander of the 'Eastern Front' (within South Africa). Colonel Eugene de Kock, one of the founding members of the infamous Koevoet counterinsurgency unit that operated on the 'Western Front' in the mid-1980s played a prominent role in expanding 'dirty trick' operations on the 'Eastern Front,' eliminating suspected ANC members both within and outside of South Africa (Geldenhuys, 1995; de Kock, 1998).

Killing Zones and Terror on the 'Western Front'

The Angolan civil war that erupted after the 1974 collapse of Portuguese rule caused relatively minor dislocation in the rural areas of Cunene Province, as fighting was mainly limited to the towns. Djami Hifihambo, who regularly visited relatives across the border from her Namibian home village, recalled:

> During my youth I visited my relatives in Ombondola [in Angola].... There were different types of armies there: you had the MPLA, UNITA, and FNLA. Here the war was not yet intense – it was limited to small movements, with the breaking of houses and things. But it became difficult to visit our relatives and we stopped going there (interview, 13 December 2000).

The confusion in the aftermath of the Portuguese collapse and SWAPO's good relations with both the MPLA – which gained the upper hand in the civil war– and with UNITA, allowed Namibia's liberation movement to establish bases in Cunene Province. The bases dramatically improved SWAPO's ability to infiltrate guerillas into Namibia: before 1975, SWAPO combatants had had to walk hundreds of miles from Zambia carrying all their supplies on their backs. By 1976, South African officials could no longer enter Eastern Ovamboland without a military escort (Secretary Agriculture, 13 April 1976 and 22 June 1976).

South Africa's security forces responded to the SWAPO threat in three ways. First, they launched cross-border strikes with conventional forces (mobile columns of armor and mechanized infantry, paratroopers, helicopters, and planes) against suspected SWAPO bases in Angola. The 1978 attack of the suspected SWAPO basis at Cassinga, deep within Angola, is perhaps the most infamous example. Most of the alleged guerilas killed at Cassinga were actually unarmed refugees. Although attacks on suspected SWAPO bases continued throughout the war, it soon became clear that this strategy alone would not destroy SWAPO, which responded by redistributing its troops and resources over a large number of widely dispersed smaller bases; frequently rotating guerilas from one base to another, and moving its larger rear-echelon bases deeper into Angola. South African strikes into Angola also resulted in confrontations with the Angolan army, which was increasingly better armed and trained. By the mid-to-late 1980s, the South African Air Force had lost its previous uncontested air superiority as Russian allies armed Angola with advanced Mig-23 fighters and sophisticated SAM air-defense systems. South Africa acutely felt the loss of several of its advanced fighter planes; given the economic sanctions in place, the planes were virtually irreplaceable (Grest, 1989, 124-131; Holness, 1989, 126-127).

A second counter-SWAPO strategy was the creation of 'killing zones.' In 1976, the SADF created a narrow cut-line running parallel and just south of the border, demarcating the southern edge of a no-go zone. Since some of the best land for settlement and crop cultivation was located along the border, numerous farms were razed to implement the new 'no-go' zone. Bulldozers removed all vegetation from the cut-line, exposing the sandy soil, and thus facilitating patrols to identify tracks of trespassers. The SADF made no exceptions: even the senior headman of Oshikango, who was loyal to South Africa, was forced to abandon his farm (Gabriel Katomba, interview, 9 March 1993; Mukwaluvala Amalia Mwetupunga, interview, 12 December 2000; Haikela Halwoodi, interview, 12 December 2000; Kreike, 1996). Displaced households more often than not had to settle for more marginal lands and had to invest a great deal of labor and other resources into rebuilding farm infrastructure: clearing bushland for a farm and fields, building huts and fences, and digging a waterhole. Displaced households also often lost access to fruit trees; it took up to ten years for a newly planted seedling of, for example, the marula tree, to produce fruit. Marula and other tree fruits were critical sources of nutrition during the annual 'hunger' season preceding the harvest of the staple grain crops and during famines (Kreike, forthcoming). The no-go zone thus not only radically altered the environment along the border but also threatened food security.

Although the SADF offered some compensation for the loss of homesteads and fields, good land was in very short supply. Dislocated households found it difficult to acquire new lands, especially in the floodplain in the western half of Ovamboland, because the area was already very densely populated.

Philippus Haidima had invested all his hard-earned savings from his labor contracts in the purchase of a farm in Okatale village on the border just east of Oshikango in 1972. Only four years later, 'the SADF ordered us to leave. Before I could buy this farm [where he lived in 1992] I stayed with village headman Johannes in his house...I received some compensation (interview, 9 December 1992).' Abusai Dula, who grew up in the border village of Oikokola and lost the farm he had lived on for thirty years, recounted that: 'I was told to leave that place in 1976. Joba's [Job, the homeland leader] government told us to leave because they wanted to deploy soldiers there and make a no-man's zone.... I also dug a waterhole [at my old farm] in the past and I hope it is still there (interview, 25 June 1993).' Israel Heendyala was also affected by the forced removals:

> The only reason I came here [Oshalembe] is the creation of the no-man's line during the independence war. I had my own garden in Okadweyo but we were removed during the war. This house [at Oshalembe] was a old farm which I only received after the former owner passed away. I had relatives here who advised me to come and look at this farm after the owner passed away. I paid a fee of 100 Rands to the village headman. It does not have good soil but I had little choice because we were told to leave the no-man's land and our homes were burned down. We received some compensation that we used to pay the fee for this farm (interview, 3 June 1993).

Anyone and anything approaching the cut line from the south was subject to brutal treatment by the security force patrols. Erastus Shilongo recounted:

> The 'Line' was very difficult. It was patrolled by armed men and if they found you with your animals at the line they could take one of your cattle and beat you so badly that you would never go near it again.... nobody could go across the line with cattle. People were very afraid because some lost their cattle, others were taken with their cattle, and others were killed (interview, 21 June 1993).

Emilia Nusiku Nangolo similarly recalled that the security forces' personnel routinely impounded cattle and beat people: ''*Omakakunja*' would take people's livestock, kill the animals, and beat people. *Omakakunja* are the soldiers (interview, 22 June 1993).' The unfortunate who were found north of the cut-line in Angola, however, often paid with their lives. According to village headman Haikela Halwoodi:

> [a]fter the line was cleared South African soldiers moved in to guard this border. Some of them were inside it and others were just outside it. They were on the lookout for anything that crossed – people, cattle – and shot it; they shot everything. If they killed your cattle you could not even get the meat (interview, 12 December 2000).

The 'killing zone' disrupted rural life and livelihoods in the border zone, pushing forcibly removed households into already congested villages further south. Moreover, the institution of the killing zone also effectively denied cattle-holders from Namibia access to critical dry season and drought cattle grazing areas on the Angolan side of the border, aggravating local pressures on scarce water and pasture resources. Abusai Dula explained that: '[b]efore the no-man's zone was created people from this side could go to Angola with their cattle wherever they wanted. During the dry season we could go to the other side with our cattle and stay there for a long time (interview, 25 June 1993; Director Agriculture, 1 November 1968; Kreike 1996).'

The 'killing zone,' however, proved unable to check SWAPO infiltrations. As a result, during the early 1980s, Koevoet's counterinsurgency tactics became a major weapon. The founder and commander of Koevoet, Hans Dreyer, had served in the Rhodesian security forces, and another infamous Koevoet operator, Eugene de Kock, received counterinsurgency training in Rhodesia. Initially, Koevoet took the Rhodesian Selous Scouts as their model, but it soon worked out a modified *modus operandi*. Koevoet recruited its Special Constables from among Ovambo 'Home Guards' who had served in the 1970s as border fence patrols and bodyguards for Ovambo chiefs threatened by SWAPO and Angolan refugees, and quickly developed into a proactive 'reaction force.' Mobile Koevoet units, in the early 1980s typically consisting of four heavily armed, armored and mine-proof Casspir or Wolf Turbo vehicles and an armored and mine-proof supply vehicle, moved from homestead to homestead until the Ovambo Koevoet soldiers, who were indispensable for the interrogations (very few white members of South Africa's security forces spoke the Ovambo language) and for tracking, either picked up information about guerilla presence or found suspicious tracks. If tracks were promising and recent, other Koevoet patrols were called in as reinforcements. When patrols made contact with the guerillas, the armored vehicles, supported by helicopter gun-ships, would bring their massive firepower to bear on the guerillas. Similar tactics were also adopted by 101 Battalion (an 'ethnic' Ovambo unit of the South West African Territorial Forces), 32 Battalion, the Bushman Battalion, and 54 Battalion (which also employed motorcycle mounted trackers). All these units operated in Ovamboland, although 32 Batallion and the Bushman Batallion also operated frequently in Kavango (to the east of Ovamboland) and Angola. The areas most affected by these types of operations were the border zone with Angola – and Angola itself – and Eastern Ovamboland east of Etosha Park, including the Mangetti area (Herbstein and Evenson, 1989; Hooper, 1990).

Key to the success of these patrols was 'intelligence' obtained from the local population through intimidation and physical violence. The border zone where both Koevoet and Battalion 101 operated was very densely settled, especially in the floodplain. Village headman Haikela Halwoodi recalled:

> At that time they would come to your house when you were sleeping. When the dogs barked they would ask 'what side are your dogs barking on?' But you would not know because you were sleeping. The army then would beat you saying that it would indicate where the PLAN [the People's Liberation Army of Namibia, SWAPO's armed wing] fighters where (interview, 12 December 2000).

Mukwaluvala Amalia Mwetupunga similarly recounted that: '[w]hen PLAN was spotted here the army would interrogate and beat people, and sometimes kill people (interview, 12 December 2000).'

In the densely settled Ovambo floodplain, army bases were inevitably surrounded by villages, farms, and fields, and the number of army bases in only increased as the war intensified. Julius Abraham witnessed the war's escalation in Okalongo:

> SWAPO guerillas pinpointed the positions of the guards in the no-man's zone nearby, slipped across the cut-line and attacked them during the night, killing them to the man. The border guards were then pulled back and the SADF established a base near the homestead of the headman of Okalongo, Mathias. The base was even larger than the SADF base at Ogongo. The base was repeatedly subjected to night attacks and we abandoned our home every time that happened (interviews, 16 and 18 June 1993).

Gunfire between security forces and guerillas caught villagers at their homes or in their fields in the crossfire. Mukwaluvala Amalia Mwetupunga stressed: '[i]n those days you could be sitting like we are and one of us could suddenly be shot – man or woman (interview, 12 December 2000).' Moreover, in the aftermath of fire fights, villagers frequently were exposed to the wrath of soldiers, especially if the soldiers had lost comrades. When security forces were ambushed near villages, the local population was often suspected of having been in collusion with guerillas. For example, the security forces suspected that the inhabitants of Epinga were active supporters of SWAPO. When the village headman of Epinga was murdered in 1975 – village headmen were responsible for the enforcement of Apartheid policies at the local levels – the police attributed the killing to SWAPO. The police arrested Epinga's village pastor, Stefanus Shimbodi, and the village nurse, holding them at Oshikango for two weeks for constant interrogations about the headman's murder and the killing of six policemen in the area. Consequently, when SWAPO fighters ambushed a SADF patrol in Epinga in 1976, most of the villagers fled for fear of reprisals. Stefanus Shimbodi took his entire family to Angola:

> In 1976, I went to Angola. Because of the SWAPO war I could no longer stay here. I fled with my family, my wife, children, and grandchildren. Some households stayed [in Epinga], some fled to Ondonga to settle there. We fled to Oluma [in Angola] leaving everything behind. All our homes were burned: we only took our cattle and left our goats. The soldiers kept coming back. One day the soldiers were at the dam washing their faces and SWAPO attacked and the villagers ran away. After this encounter the Boers burned the houses (interview, 16 December 2000).

Added Teresa Valombola: '[i]n 1976 the Boers burned down the school, clinic, and the church with everything in it (interview, 16 December 2000).' Marcus Paulus' words captures people's perception that they were caught between a rock and a hard place, i.e. between the security forces and the guerillas:

> In 1983, I fled from Omukukutu to Olukula because Koevoet was moving in from one side and SWAPO was coming from the other side. I lived here till 1987 when the war became worse. My neighbor was killed at the entrance of my cattle kraal. I fled to Kongolomuva near Okongo. All the other inhabitants of Olukula, five households in total, also fled (interview, 19 February 1993).

The violence not only undermined the livelihoods of the people who fled, however, but also of those who stayed. Most of the fighting took place during the rainy season, which corresponded with the agricultural season. In the dry season, much of the landscape in the floodplain resembled a open park landscape, characterized by large trees, dispersed bush and fenced homesteads with barren fields covering the higher ground, and dried out grass in the low-lying flood channels that offered good visibility. But, as the grain crops matured, the 8-9 foot long stalks of the staple, millet, greatly reduced visibility, providing excellent shelter to guerillas from the ground and the air. Moreover, in most of Ovamboland, millet fields surrounded the homesteads, and water sources were often located in the homesteads or the fields. The dense rainy season vegetation also facilitated guerilla ambushes because it allowed them to get very close to the Casspirs and Wolf Turbos that from close range offered little protection from armor-piercing RPG-7s and rifle grenades.

Security forces also feared the use of heavy anti-tank mines and anti-personnel mines on dirt roads and tracks. Patrols routinely drove through crop fields, especially in 'hot pursuit' and during gun fights. Handunge Henok Mukweni from the Okalongo area in the western floodplain had his crops repeatedly flattened by South African soldiers: 'the Boers on motor bikes always drove through my millet fields and those of my neighbors (interview, 13 December 2000).' The practice caused heavy crop losses and contributed further to a general climate of fear in which crop cultivation and food security were seriously compromised. Asked how the war affected food production, Djami Hifihambo explained:

> The most important factor was fear. If we heard cars we ran into our home and waited until the SADF came to interrogate us about SWAPO... The SADF would come and trample our fields and crops. They mostly did this with army trucks – they drove through the fields. There were also droughts. In sum, with fear reigning always you do not do such a good job of agriculture (interview, 13 December 2000).

Other vegetation was also negatively affected. For example, the fruit of the *oshipeke* (plural: *oipeke*) bush, which had helped Moses Mundjele's parents to survive a horrible famine in 1915-1916, was nearly wiped out during the liberation war:

Oipeke is simply a big bush with thorns. People eat *eemeke* [its fruit] anytime, even when there is not a drought. In Onengali you also have some *oipeke*. Before the war (which ended in 1989) there were many here. The army always ran over them and even over the millet. I do not know why. Nowadays there are but few *oipeke* left....*Oipeke* are so rare because trucks destroyed them during the war (interview, 17 May 1993).

The insecurity also inhibited hunting, directly leading to the early retirement of the few remaining professional Ovambo hunters. Moses Kakoto had hunted on horseback from his home in Okongo in the far east of Ovamboland during the 1950s and 1960s, and used a gun during the late 1960s. He abandoned his profession, however, 'because the war changed the situation and I became afraid to go into the bush. If they found you with a gun in the bush, Koevoet could kill you claiming you were a terrorist (interview, 17 February 1993).' In fact, an ex-SADF soldier from the former Gazankulu Homeland who served in Ovamboland in 1983-1984 recalled:

> I was based in Eenhana with Battalion 54 and before that at Ondangwa. I was with the infantry. We had been told that if we killed any civilians we were to place a stick that resembled a gun next to the body and say we thought that the victim had been carrying a gun. I patrolled on the border, on the Angolan side (interview, 16 June 2000).

Village headman Haikela Halwoodi, who lived close to the border summarized his perception of the war north of the cut-line as follows: '101 Batallion was introduced. It was notorious. When they entered Angola they ran over everything: houses, fields, etc. – this was the effect of the war (interview, 12 December 2000).' Although the Lutheran Church Pastor Stefanus Shimbodi had fled from the violence in Namibia to Oluma in Angola in 1976:

> [T]he war found us again in Angola. The Boers and the PLAN fighters came to Angola and Oluma also and beat people there too but there was not so much fighting then. I stayed in Oluma until peace returned to Namibia in 1989/1990. The beatings at Oluma were continuous. People tried to grow food but the Boers came and burned houses and this was not a situation conducive to hard work. You lived in fear. We grew just enough to take us to the next year. We did not see famine. Some households were affected by drought but others were not. PLAN fighters also helped needy households with maize flour. Not many other refugees settled at Oluma but young people who wanted to join SWAPO passed through the village. SWAPO had a base close by. The Boers attacked the Oluma base but it had been abandoned. By the time I arrived in Oluma the base had already been abandoned (interview, 16 December 2000).

Although South African incursions into Angola were destructive to those living in the vicinity of suspected SWAPO bases, incursions into the interior initially were intermittent. The situation changed during the early 1980s, however, when South Africa effectively occupied a large part of Cunene Province and attempted to establish a permanent UNITA presence in the area. Petrus Haunini had worked as a pastor for the Namibian-based Evangelical Lutheran Church (ELCIN) in Angola since the mid 1960s. In 1984, he and his wife Helena witnessed troops who claimed to be UNITA entering their area. The description he gave of how the 'UNITA' unit operated, however, suggests it may have been Batallion 32 soldiers impersonating UNITA. Batallion 32 used similar tactics and equipment as Koevoet, operated mainly in Angola and often passed itself off as UNITA. His wife helped the pastor to recount the war's events as the pastor explained that he was still easily overcome by his emotions:

> One day vehicles arrived at the mission. They dropped off soldiers and took up positions. They said they were UNITA. They started beating people (including the pastor) with sticks and batons until they bled. I asked 'why are you fighting' when a soldier aimed his gun at my brother. After this incident we moved from the mission to a simple hut in the middle of a field. UNITA returned a second time, burned the mission, took the church things and left again. They later found us hiding in the field where the hut was. UNITA interrogated me…and aimed a gun at me. I took my Bible and said: 'this is the only gun I know of.' A soldier said: 'shoot him' but the gun misfired three times and then another UNITA soldier said: 'he's innocent, leave him.' They dragged away another man who lived at the mission and killed him in the bushes nearby. We stayed there. UNITA later came back to burn our house. We were accommodated at another house. The people were afraid that the war was killing missionaries (interview, 15 December 2000).

The Hauninis emphasized that the mounting terror and violence involved an increasing number of villages, whose inhabitants either fled or hid in the bush, neglecting their crops. The MPLA government and the Namibian church initially provided supplies to help them over to the next harvest, but food was scarce:

> It was difficult to grow food – sometimes we hid for three days and could not go to the fields. You had to keep moving. We used to run away, we really had no time to properly take care of the crops. The same thing happened in many villages across Oukwanyama. UNITA was very disruptive. South African soldiers were also involved in this. The MPLA killed one of my relatives because they thought he was an UNITA spy. Later the SADF would kill and rob livestock and beat people and steal their things. The FNLA and MPLA moved out and then UNITA frequented the areas more often. The Boers joined UNITA in those areas. The war situation prevailed everywhere. Initially our mission had been a place of refuge. People fled into the very thick bush. Sometimes we dug trenches with paths. We put sticks and soil on top and lived inside with a torch. If soldiers entered on one side we left on the other side. We lived like mice. We only survived through the will of God. The trenches dug in the thick bush were zigzagged and covered with branches etc. The fighting usually took place in the morning. In the afternoon women cooked food outside the trenches. Men watched for the enemy from tree tops. If the enemy approached from the west we fled the trenches from the east. We kept the children in the trench next to the exit so that they had some fresh air but we did not allow them to leave the area so as not to leave footprints. When the war intensified with the coming of the PLAN fighters and the SADF,

interrogations and violence became even more prevalent. The 'war' taught us to dig trenches. We scavenged for food at abandoned homesteads. If we were lucky we might find some millet for the children. We boiled it in water – with salt if we had any, instead of pounding it. When we were walking, you could not raise your hand because the others would think you were signaling them and they would flee. We lived in the trenches with a group of over ten people. All people lived in such trenches, even when it rained. The homesteads were deserted and all people lived in trenches. During the rainy season people emerged from the trenches area and went to the fields near the mission (interview, 15 December 2000).

Maria Weyulu and her family similarly hid in the thick bush near their village Omulunga while Monika Hidengwa and her family moved farther into the Angolan interior to Ohaipeto village where they were hosted by another family until they could clear a plot to make their own farm (interviews, 16 July 1993).

Many of the terrorized inhabitants of Cunene Province, however, fled to Namibia. Handunge Henok Mukweni lived in Onambunga close to the Namibian border village Oikokola, and fled when he heard the tales of horror:

People from neighboring villages fled to our village and told us that people were killed and their homes burned. I did not pause to ask who did the burning. It was war, and we fled. I left my house as it was – we just ran away. I lost my livestock, granaries, huts, and most of my other possessions. We even left our hoes behind. We had no transport to take anything. We assembled at a dry seasonal watercourse across the border from where the South African army took us in trucks to a transit camp at Omugwelume village. After a while we were told that anyone with relatives in Ovamboland could leave the camp. The SADF fed us biscuits. Some of us slept in tents and others slept outside. We fled Angola in the dry season and we stayed at the camp during the rainy season....The Angolan war made me poor. (interview, 13 December 2000).

The first waves of refugees entered Ovamboland in 1977 and 1978. A large temporary refugee camp filled the wide flood channel at Okalongo in western Ovamboland. Some of the refugees were victims of UNITA violence. Others feared prosecution by the triumphant MPLA. South Africa recruited heavily among the young men for its military units, including Batallion 32. Some refugees later returned to Angola, but many refugees from this and later refugee waves settled in Oshakati. A number also settled in the Okalongo district (Julius Abraham, interview, 16 and 18 June 1993; Maria Weyulu, interview, 16 July 1993). The influx of refugees from Angola added to pressures on a social and physical environment that had already been stretched to the limit as a result of war-related destruction and dislocation.

Villagization, Killing Fields, and Terror on the 'Eastern Front'

While the Gazankulu Homeland in South Africa's Transvaal Province did not experience war-related violence during the late 1970s and 1980s, in contrast to both Namibia's Ovamboland and Angola's Cunene Province, it had, however, born the brunt of the violent forced removals of the late 1960s and 1970s (Unterhalter, 1987, 104-114; Surplus People Project, 1983; Murray, 1992, chapter 6; Harries, 1987). In addition, during the 1980s, Gazankulu's meager resources were further overburdened by the influx of large numbers of refugees from southern Mozambique (Piet Makhense Maluleke, interview, 13 June 2000; Nyanisi Mamaila Maswangane, interview, 17 June 2000; July Mathevula, interview, 20 June 2000; Khazamula Ben Maluleke, interview, 20 June 2000).

The inhabitants of Gaza Province, however, in many ways endured a war experience similar to that of the inhabitants of Cunene. After Mozambique's independence, its FRELIMO government allowed ZANU to establish guerilla bases inside its territory. These bases became targets of Rhodesian cross-border operations during the second half of the 1970s. After the fall of the Rhodesian Smith regime in 1980, however, the war in Gaza Province escalated. The *Resistencia Nacional de Moçambique* (RENAMO), also known the Mozambican National Resistance (MNR), introduced a war of terror in southern Mozambique that led to massive internal population dislocations and international refugee movements (Africa Watch, 1992, 7-8; Vines, 1991, 114-115; Isaacman, 1988; Hanlon, 1986, 145-146; Minter, 1994).

The Rhodesian cross-border raids did not trigger massive population dislocations or large scale destruction of homes, crops or domestic infrastructure. Rather, villagers hid in the bush when they heard the Rhodesian helicopters or vehicles approaching, and returned to their homes after the Rhodesians passed (Lusa Linyao Soyani, interview, 29 October 2000; Makaukane Manuel Nyamzane, interview, 29 October 2000; Jeremiah Mudzedzele Valoi, interview, 1 November 2000). As Johan Kondlwane Chauke, recalled, Rhodesian planes attacked Mozambican troops at his village, Mapanye: '[t]he planes attacked and we fled and hid in the bush. The planes attacked the soldiers. This was a short war. We could still live in our houses and cultivate and such things. The Smith soldiers asked for animals and we obliged (interview, 23 October 2000).'

As the Smith war ended in 1980 with the collapse of the white settler regime and Zimbabwe's first free elections, however, violence directed at the rural population in Gaza paradoxically increased. Although the fall of the Smith regime deprived RENAMO of its main support, South Africa stepped in and airlifted RENAMO's leadership and trainees to South Africa even before ZANU came to power in independent Zimbabwe (Davies, 1989, 104-105; Johnson and Martin, 1989, 1-18). In 1981, RENAMO forces crossed the Save River from central Mozambique and established bases in Zinave National Park and Banhine National Park in the far north of Inhambane and Gaza Provinces respectively. The main objective for establishing a RENAMO front in Gaza was to create a buffer zone against ANC guerilla infiltration through southern Mozambique (Cabrita, 2000, 194-197; Johnson and Martin, 1989, 17-20).

Whereas the Rhodesians had had little or no interest in the rural populations in Gaza, RENAMO forces lived entirely off the 'land' (i.e. the population and their livestock and food stores). Feeding RENAMO was a heavy drain on the food resources of affected households. In addition, RENAMO mutilated individuals to force locals to cooperation and to discourage them from betraying the RENAMO presence to government forces. Armando Baseketi Manganye, who lived in Tchai-Tchai close to the area where RENAMO first entered Gaza, stressed: '[a]fter the end of the Smith war appeared the *vangwaminomo*. Initially they did not kill but cut off lips – that's what the name comes from. In the beginning they did not kill but made people carry goods (interview, 19 October 2000).' Samuel Georgou Mbiza also lived in the northeast of Gaza, where RENAMO had its first bases:

> 'In the beginning they [RENAMO guerillas] were not so oppressive. They would ask for a goat to eat. The next day they would return and they would keep coming back until we had no animals left to give. In the next phase they would just rob all the remaining livestock, even taking them from the kraals. Next they commenced robbing the crop fields and subsequently they took the stored food from the houses. Then they took people to carry the goods they had robbed (interview, 21 October 2000).

Only interviewees from the northeastern and north of Gaza, the region around the Banhine and the Zinave National Parks where RENAMO initiated its operations in Gaza, recall a 'milder' initial phase of the war in Gaza (Fijao Ndlovu, interview, 26 June 2000, Julio Samuel Maziva, interview, 25 June 2000; Josia Khosa, interview, 25 June 2000). Throughout the remainder of Gaza, the memory of the RENAMO war is one of indiscriminate killing, maiming, looting, and burning, and even the interviewees from the northeast who recalled a first 'milder' phase, emphasized that a second 'killing' phase soon followed. The ruthless destruction that marked RENAMO's tactics in the second phase, which was partly a reaction to the FRELIMO government's counterinsurgency program in Gaza, set the pattern for RENAMO's *modus operandi* as it expanded its operations from the northeastern corner of Gaza into the rest of the province.

Some of the literature on the Mozambican civil war stresses that RENAMO entered southern Mozambique with the firm intention to totally destroy it. It argues that South Africa wanted to destabilize Mozambique by whatever means necessary to cause mayhem throughout the country, without concern for the civilian populations, and claims that RENAMO designated southern Mozambique as a 'destruction zone' because Gaza Province in particular was considered to be the heartland of rural support for FRELIMO (Anderson, 1992, 46-75; Vines, 1991, 114-115; Johnson and Martin, 1989, 17-28; Davies, 1989, 114).

This line of reasoning to some extent constitutes reading some of the war's history backwards. This is not to deny the magnitude of the destruction that RENAMO caused in southern Mozambique during the war, but rather to factor in that RENAMO escalated the violence against Gaza's inhabitants in response to FRELIMO's villagization campaign. FRELIMO concentrated the rural populations in villages, recruited, trained and armed local militias, and backed up the militias by regular army garrisons and 'reaction forces' stationed in district capitals

(Human Rights Watch, 1991, 27-28; Cabrita, 2000, 194-1998; Hall and Young, 1997, 129-130). Thus, the rural populations became not only the object and target of the war, but also the principal weapon of war, as farms, food and seed stocks, animals, crops, and fruit trees were pillaged and destroyed. In rural Gaza, crop fields were not located adjacent to the homesteads – as in Ovamboland and in Cunene Province - but were some distance away from them. In addition, while individual farms' fields often abutted in the Ovambo floodplain, in the interior of Gaza, homesteads were separated by bush vegetation, although neighbors not infrequently were within calling distance of one another. Moreover, water sources in Ovamboland and Cunene were concentrated at the location of settlement, whereas in Gaza, the dry season water sources were rivers, and homesteads were located on the higher ground, away from the rivers. As a result, in Gaza, daily life, crop cultivation, and fetching water took place in greater isolation from neighbors. Manuel Makapane Makuhane and Tsatsawane Marumbini Shithlangu explained that 'before the war the households were very isolated...Since the time of the Ngoni [the Nguni invasions of the 19th century] and the Portuguese [conquest in the 1890s] we had this dispersed settlement system (interview, 21 October 2000).' Tchiki Sefani Sumbane recalled that in the old days 'I could not see the next homestead from my house' while Dayina Mbondzo explained that people lived in dispersed homesteads but within walking distance of one another (interview, 24 October 2000). Thus, while individuals and households in distress in the Ovambo floodplain could warn their neighbors and call for help at home and on the fields, doing so proved much more difficult in the case of Gaza. As a result, the rural population of Gaza was even more vulnerable to intimidation, violence, and the commandeering of food, goods, livestock and people by both RENAMO and FRELIMO government soldiers.

FRELIMO initiated villagization programs throughout Mozambique in the late 1970s, but met with little success in most provinces, including Gaza. The threat of war, however, reversed this trend in Gaza Province. Albino Joao Tivane, the former head of the militia of the communal village of Mahungo and in 2000 the village headman, and Silvestre Ndevenene Xithlangu, his councillor, looked back favorably upon the early 1980s villagization drive: '[t]he war accelerated villagization. RENAMO could attack houses one by one in the dispersed settlement pattern and [RENAMO soldiers] killed many people. With the dispersed settlement it was also difficult to see who assisted RENAMO. With concentrated settlement the army could protect you (interview, 15 October 2000).' Ernesto Ringi Valoi recalled that in his area, preparations for the construction of a communal village began in 1980, before the RENAMO war affected his region: '[t]he government told us to create the village for better defense – it seems that there was war already.' Asked if the government supplied them with other reasons why communal villages were advantageous, he added: '[w]e were told that hospitals and shops would be constructed in the villages, that life would be easier there (interview, 2 November 2000).' Danyina Mbondzo, however, was more ambiguous about FRELIMO and villagization:

The *madeya* [communal villages, sing. lideya] started before the *matswanga* [RENAMO] commenced the killing. At the time they [RENAMO] were only asking for food, and were not killing yet. The killing by the *matswanga* started because the villagers were told to report the *matswanga* to FRELIMO. If they did not, FRELIMO killed them. When we reported the *matswanga*, FRELIMO would attack the *matswanga* and the *matswanga* started killing people because they reported them. We were staying in the communal villages. We moved...because we were afraid of the *matswanga*. FRELIMO ordered us to go the communal villages and they said that anybody who was found in the bush would be killed....The communal villages had no fence but soldiers planted land mines on trails leading to the villages. Some of the village's inhabitants were soldiers [militiamen] and received guns from FRELIMO (interview, 26 June).

People continued to use their old fields even after having moved to the communal villages (July Mapuvule Valoi, interview, 3 November 2000; Ernesto Ringi Valoi, interview, 2 November 2000; Jeremiah Mudzedzele Valoi, interview, 1 November 2000). The practice, however, was not without peril. As Danyina Mbondzo explained:

We continued to use our old fields at our abandoned former homesteads. But if you spent 2-3 days on your field they would take you back to the communal village.... FRELIMO killed my husband and RENAMO killed my daughter. One day when my husband had gone to the fields the *matswanga* visited him [her husband may have been staying at their old homestead while he was tending to the fields]. So FRELIMO thought he was collaborating with the *matswanga* and they killed him (interview, 26 June).

Moreover, the concentration of the population in the communal villages increased people's travel time to and from the fields, cutting into labor time available to prepare lands, seed, weed, and harvest. In addition, trips to the fields became increasingly dangerous, even though villagers traveled to and from fields and worked the land in groups with armed escorts. Mbhokota Chauke recalled that: '[w]e did not have time to cultivate because we were always fleeing. RENAMO was everywhere. You can not risk your life cultivating under such conditions: we hid in the bush. We suffered terribly (interview, 26 June 2000).' Magode Mukwatsyani Chauke explained: 'People were afraid. We did not work on our fields for long because we wanted to return to the village as quickly as possible (interview, 30 October 2000).' Even fetching water was dangerous: '[i]t was difficult to visit people and even to fetch water because of the ever-present danger of ambushes. The men had to provide armed escorts to the women who went to fetch water. We went in groups (Tchiki Sefani Sumbane interview, 24 October 2000).' Moreover, as Danyina Mbondzo stressed, staying on your crop field for more than a day – which had been common practice before the war – could not only arouse suspicions of RENAMO sympathies and result in punishment by the FRELIMO authorities, but also exposed a person to RENAMO violence.

Herding livestock also became increasingly perilous because livestock was a prime and easy target for RENAMO as well as a mobile store of food. In the dry season, cattle had to be grazed outside the village and the herds dispersed because of the shortage of grazing which made making guarding cattle difficult. Fineas Jack Ngonyama invested his earnings from eight migrant labor contracts to South Africa in cattle, goats, sheep and goods, but he lost everything during the war (interview, 1 November 2000; Alfred Hlahisi Chauke, interview, 28 October 2000 and Thomas Piet Chauke, interview, 28 October 2000).

The feeling of being caught between two fires is dramatically captured by Julio Samuel Maziva, whose story also demonstrates how RENAMO became increasingly ruthless:

> [T]hey started to look for FRELIMO leaders and kill them. Next they looted livestock and told us to leave the [communal] village and remain outside. When they found people outside of the village they would kill them. They killed my daughter-in-law. Many people were killed. RENAMO told us to leave our homes in the communal village and told us to go into the bush. But if we did they killed us so we did not understand what RENAMO wanted us to do. We had no place to live. We would hide in the dense bush. But when RENAMO found us they would kill us. I still do not know why RENAMO did this (interview, 25 June 2000).

Although people were often very reluctant to move to the communal villages, the threat of RENAMO made most eventually seek the relative safety of the FRELIMO villages or towns. Ngwenya Mhangeni lived at Mapungani and she recalled: 'when they [RENAMO] found people in a homestead they killed them, took their livestock and everything. When we heard gunshots we just ran. We did not take anything with us when we fled to Mapai, not even our blankets (interview, 25 June 2000).' In some cases, people had to be forced to move to the 'protected' villages. Tchiki Sefani Sumbane from Mukambeni in Massangena district explained that the inhabitants of the new village of Mukambeni in 1984 referred to those who refused to move to the village as the '*vanganonowa vangalavikuta lideyeni*, 'those who did not want to go the village.' They had to be brought into the village. They were told to come to the village until they understood (interview, 24 October 2000).'

Indeed, as RENAMO expanded its operations throughout Gaza, it employed pure terror and scorched earth tactics with the aim of forcing the rural population to abandon the FRELIMO communal villages. When this proved largely unsuccessful, RENAMO changed its tactics and attacked the communal villages themselves in order to destroy them. RENAMO attacks frequently took place at night and its soldiers indiscriminately shot people and torched homes (Mbhokota Chauke, interview, 26 June 2000; Fijao Ndlovu, interview, 26 June 2000; Magode Mukwatsyani Chauke, interview, 30 October 2000). The villagization campaign thus had multiple effects on land management and use, and food security in Gaza Province. For example, abandoning dispersed settlements in favor of communal villages meant that labor invested in laying the infrastructure for a productive local environment was lost. Moreover, even where people contrived to return to their old fields, the violence of war circumvented meaningful agricultural yield.

By the mid- to late 1980s, many communal villages were in turn abandoned after repeated attacks by RENAMO. The communal village of Shilemane in Chicualacuala district, however, was one of the few exceptions. Part of the reason may have been the presence of regular troops that supported its local militia. Still, although Shilemane's inhabitants successfully defended the village against RENAMO attacks, they nevertheless paid a heavy price. Papuseko Katini Ndlovu saw one of his sons killed and his wife and a second son abducted by RENAMO. He was immensely proud of his brother, who was one of the militiamen who defended the village (interview, 30 October 2000). Magode Mukwatsyani Chauke, another inhabitant of war-time Shilemane, condensed the village's victory and its suffering as follows: '[t]hey [RENAMO] attacked at night and we hid. Those who fled the village were killed. Those who stayed and defended the village survived (interview, 30 October 2000).'

The inhabitants of Mukambeni communal village in Massangena in the far north of Gaza also stubbornly held out against RENAMO. Although RENAMO had succeeded in destroying even the district capital of Massangena – itself a sanctuary for refugees from elsewhere – some of its inhabitants sought refuge in nearby Mukambeni and remained there until much later in the war, when the Mozambican army sent reinforcements from Mapai in central Gaza to expel RENAMO (Shivulani Maduhla Chauke, interview, 22 October 2000; Sanga Felipe Chauke, interview, 24 October 2000; Johan Kondlwane Chauke, interview, 23 October 2000; Manuel Makapane Makuhane and Tsatsawane Marumbini Shithlangu, interview, 21 October 2000). Sanga Felipe Chauke, who moved from his homestead in the countryside to the communal village of Mukambeni as the war progressed, became a member of the village militia, and never left (interview, 24 October 2000). Sara Kufamuni Manyike also stayed put: '[d]uring the RENAMO war we cultivated millet although we were always on the run...I did not leave because... I was mad that my son had been killed and I wanted to be killed also. I lost my firstborn in the war... Our big house was burned down (interview, 25 October 2000).'

Litlatla communal village was also repeatedly attacked. Some of its inhabitants hid in the bush and returned to the village as soon as the fighting died down. Thomas Piet Chauke returned to the village but lost all his livestock (interview, 28 October 2000). Alfred Hlahisi Chauke and his family found the trauma of two attacks to be more than they could bear, and they fled to the district capital while other Litlatla inhabitants fled to Zimbabwe and South Africa (interview, 28 October 2000).

Many other wartime communal villages in Gaza Province, however, were far less successful in withstanding RENAMO attacks. For example, Fineas Jack Ngonyama moved to Hassani-B communal village in 1983. The communal village was not yet completed when it suffered the first of many RENAMO attacks:

> We were attacked many times. The inhabitants fled and RENAMO camped there. We fled to Combumune-rio in 1984...We had much food in our homes and on the

fields at the time of this attack and RENAMO took it all....We could not take anything with us, there was no time (interview, 1 November 2000).

Jeremiah Mudzedzele Valoi recalled that RENAMO's favored time to attack communal villages was after the harvest:

> After we had moved to the communal village we continued to use our old fields. All people had fields below there so we all went. RENAMO attacked the communal village many times. Usually the attacks took place when we had harvested and they took our harvest and burned what they could not take with them...I fled to Combumune-rio. The entire village went there (interview, 1 November 2000).

After communal villages fell, small groups of its inhabitants occasionally sought refuge in inaccessible bush areas. For example, Armando Baseketi Manganye related that:

> [A]ll people fled to the village [Nwanyakatale]. The village militia fought RENAMO but RENAMO defeated them because it had bazookas and mortars. We fled to this low zone and lived here. Others fled away. My family lived in the bush and lived on a drink made from the palm tree... RENAMO did not follow us because we could flee deeper and deeper into it [the bush] when RENAMO came. We constructed very small shelters to protect us from the rain. We lived like this for two years. We were a group...of...13 families (interview, 19 October 2000).

The majority, however, would either flee to remoter district capitals, or the towns of the lower Limpopo valley, or Maputo, or they would seek refuge across the border in Zimbabwe and South Africa. The experience of the communal villages of Mahungo (Chibuto) and Dindiza (Chigubo), which were founded in 1982/1983, is illustrative. Although locally recruited militias armed with light weapons defended both villages against repeated attacks, they each succumbed to the RENAMO onslaught around 1987 and RENAMO subsequently established a base near Dindiza that became the headquarters for its southeastern Gaza front. The villagers lost loved ones, homes, livestock, and all their possessions as they scattered to such places as, for example, Chigubo's district capital (which had a military garrison) and Maputo (Olinda Gapasi Muhlanga, interview, 14 October 2000; Albino Joao Tivane and Silvestre Ndevenene Xithlangu, interview, 15 October 2000; Johani Nongoti Chauke, interview, 16 October 2000; Paulina Melione Muthlahisi, interview, 16 October 2000; Angelina Naife Mazive and Lucas Shivuti, interview, 17 October 2000; Francisco Johannes Manica, interview, 17 October 2000; District Administration of Chigubo, interview, 17 October 2000; Johani Nongoti Chauke, interview, 16 October 2000). According to the district administration of Chigubo, the war reduced the population of the district from 34,000 to 14-17,000 inhabitants. Most of the district's population fled to Mapai and Combumume and to the towns of the lower Limpopo valley, including Guija, Chokwe and the provincial capital Xai Xai (interview, 17 October 2000). A major safe haven for refugees from the interior of rural Gaza was South Africa's Gazankulu Homeland. By 1988, Josia Khosa no longer felt safe in Mozambique and decided to flee to South Africa, where he had worked as a contract laborer:

> Not all people can wait for death. Some people were brave enough to stay and they are still alive today. My first born son was killed by these people. He was still young. The *matswanga* [RENAMO] wanted the young ones to join.... We usually hid in different places because RENAMO would follow our tracks. One day I was tired of hiding and fled to South Africa (interview, 25 June 2000).

Conclusion

As refugees crowded into 'safe haven' villages, towns, cities and refugee camps in Mozambique, Zimbabwe and South Africa, stretching wood, water and other resources of their temporary new homes to the limit, bush overgrew their abandoned villages, homesteads, fields, dirt roads and footpaths on the eastern front of the Apartheid Wars. A particularly significant development, with potentially profound environmental consequences, is that while the Rhodesian authorities had rid the interior of Gaza of Tsetse fly infestation in the 1950s and 1960s, the bush encroachment of the 1980s may be facilitating its return. In addition, overgrown and mined roads, trails and sources of water continue to seriously inhibit post-war recovery of livelihoods in rural Gaza. As a result, many refugees and internally dislocated have not returned to their home areas, and tens of thousands of refugees from Gaza remain in South Africa. Moreover, the war and the population displacements that it caused in Gaza may have led to a dramatic and permanent change in settlement patterns in southern Mozambique because returnees chose to re-settle in the locations of the war-time communal villages. Relatively few people returned to pre-1980s dispersed settlement locations.

Bush vegetation also erased traces of dense human settlement and land use in the war-time killing zones on the western front of the Apartheid Wars. Some regions are heavily overgrown with thick, almost impenetrable thorn bush, although given the extreme dry season aridity of the region, *nagana* and sleeping sickness are not a threat in Cunene Province and north central Namibia. A decade after the end of the war in Namibia, however, the abandoned border villages have been re-populated. With the end of warfare in Angola, many areas in Cunene Province that have until now remained abandoned, may similarly be re-populated. The effects of the killing zones, and terror on the 'Western Front,' and of villagization, killing fields, and terror on the 'Eastern Front' consequently continue to impact local livelihoods and the environment, with considerable room for analysis of repercussions past, as well as trends both present and future.

Note

1 Fieldwork for this research project was made possible through the support of the US Institute for Peace (USIP) and Princeton University. The institutional sponsorship by the Center for African Studies and the History Department, Eduardo Mondlane University, the Arquivo de Patrimonio Cultural (ARPAC), Maputo, Mozambique, the University of Namibia, the Namibian National Archives, and the Giyani College of Education, Giyani, South Africa, is gratefully acknowledged. I also wish to express my appreciation for the comments and suggestions from the participants of the Davis Center for Historical Studies, Princeton University, where I presented an earlier version of the chapter.

References

Africa Watch (1992), *Conspicuous Destruction: War, Famine and the Reform Process in Mozambique.* New York: Human Rights Watch.

Africa Watch (1993), *Land Mines in Mozambique.* New York: Human Rights Watch.

Agricultural Officer, Travel Report 26-31 January (1972), OVA 40, f. 6/2/7-7. National Archives of Namibia.

Allen, T. and Morsink, H. (eds). (1994), *When Refugees go Home.* London & Trenton: Africa World Press.

Anderson, H. (1992), *Mozambique: A War Against the People.* New York: St. Martin's.

Birmingham, D. (1992), *Frontline Nationalism in Angola and Mozambique.* London: James Currey.

Cabrita, J. (2000), *Mozambique: The Tortuous Road to Democracy.* New York: Palgrave.

Cleaver, T. and Wallace, M. (1990), *Namibia: Women in War.* London: Zed Books.

Davies, R. (1989), 'The SADF's Covert War Against Mozambique.' In: Cock, J., Nathan, L. (eds.). *War and Society: The Militarisation of South Africa.* Johannesburg: David Philip.

De Kock, E. (1998), *A Long Night's Damage: Working for the Apartheid State.* Saxonwold: Contra Press.

Director Agriculture, 1 November (1968), Letter to Administrator. AGR 298, f. 45/1. Namibian National Archives.

Ellis, S. (1990), 'Of Elephants and Men: Politics and Nature Conservation in South Africa.' *Journal of Southern African Studies,* 20 (1), pp. 53-70.

Geldenhuys, J. (1995), *A General's Story from an Era of War and Peace.* Johannesburg: Jonathan Ball.

Grest, J. (1989), 'The South African Defense Force in Angola.' In: Cock, J., Nathan, L. (eds.), *War and Society: The Militarisation of South Africa.* Johannesburg: David Philip.

Hall, M. and Young, T. (1997), *Confronting Leviathan: Mozambique since Independence.* London: Hurst & Company.

Hanlon, J. (1986), *Beggar your Neighbours: Apartheid Power in Southern Africa.* London: Catholic Institute for International Relations.

Harries, P. (1987), 'A Forgotten Corner of the Transvaal: Reconstructing the History of a Relocated Community through Oral Testimony and Song.' In: Bozzoli, B. (ed.), *Class, Community and Conflict: South African Perspectives.* Johannesburg: Ravan Press.

Herbstein, D., Evenson, J. (1989), *The Devils are among Us: The War for Namibia.* London: Zed Books.

Holness, M. (1989), 'Angola: The Struggle Continues.' In: Johnson, P., Martin, D. (eds.), *Frontline Southern Africa.* Peterborough: Ryan.

Hooper, J. (1990), *Beneath the Visiting Moon: Images of Combat in Southern Africa.* Lexington, Massachusetts. & Toronto: Lexington Books.

Isaacman, A. (1988), 'Historical Introduction.' In: Magaia, L. Dumba Nengue: *Run for your Life.* Trenton: Africa World Press.

Isaacman, A., Isaacman, B. (1983), *Mozambique: From Colonialism to Revolution, 1900-1982.* Boulder: Westview Press and Hampshire: Gower.

Johnson, P. and Martin, D. (1989), 'Mozambique: Victims of Apartheid.' In: Johnson, P., D. Martin. (eds.). *Frontline Southern Africa.* Peterborough, Ryan.

Katjavivi, P. (1988), *A History of Resistance in Namibia.* London: James Currey.

Kreike, E. (1996), 'Recreating Eden: Agro-Ecological Change, Food Security, and Environmental Diversity in Southern Angola and Northern Namibia, 1890-1960.' Unpublished Ph.D. dissertation, Yale University.

Kreike, E. (Forthcoming), 'Hidden Fruits: A Social Ecology of Fruit Trees in Namibia and Angola, 1880s-1990s.' In: Beinart, W., McGregor (eds). *African Environments Past and Present.*

Leys, C., and Saul, J.S. (eds) (1995), *Namibia's Liberation Struggle: The Two-Edged Sword.* Athens, Ohio: Ohio University Press.

Marcum, J. (1978), *The Angolan Revolution. Volume 2: Exile Politics and Guerilla Warfare, 1962-1976.* Cambridge, Massachusetts: MIT Press.

Minter, W. (1994), *Apartheid's Contras: An Inquiry into the Roots of War in Angola and Mozambique.* Johannesburg: Witwatersrand University Press, London: Zed Books.

Moyo, S., O'Keefe, P., Sill, M. (1993), *The Southern African Environment: Profiles of the SADC Countries.* London: Earthscan Publications.

Murray, C. (2001 [1992]), *Black Mountain: Land, Class, and Power in the Eastern Orange Free State, 1880s-1980s.* Johannesburg: Witwatersrand University Press.

Nordstrom, C. (1997), *A Different Kind of War Story.* Philadelphia: University of Pennsylvania Press.

Potgieter, De Wet. (1995), *Contraband: South Africa and the International Trade in Ivory and Rhino Horn.* Cape Town: Queillerie.

Ranger, T. (1985), *Peasant Consciousness and Guerrilla War.* Berkeley: University of California Press.

Reid Daly, R. (1983 [1982]), *Selous Scouts Top Secret War.* Alberton: Galapo Publishing.

Secretary, Agriculture 13 April (1976), Letter to Secretary Bantu Administration and Development. OVA 57 f. 7/4/1-7. National Archives of Namibia.

Secretary, Agriculture, 22 June (1976), Letter to Chief Minister and Finance, Ondangwa. OVA 51 f. 6/13. National Archives of Namibia.

Stiff, P. (1999), *The Silent War: South African Recce Operations, 1969-1994.* Alberton: Galago.

Surplus People Project (1983), *Forced Removals in South Africa, Volume 5: The Transvaal.* Cape Town and Pietermaritzburg: Surplus People Project.

Vines, A. (1991), *RENAMO: Terrorism in Mozambique.* London: Centre for Southern African Studies, University of York & James Currey; Bloomington: Indiana Univ Press.

Unterhalter, E. (1987), *Forced Removal: The Division, Segregation and Control of the People of South Africa.* London: International Defense & Aid Fund for Southern Africa.

Urdang, S. (1989), *And Still they Dance: Women, War and the Struggle for Change in Mozambique.* New York: Monthly Review Press.

Chapter 6

Pesticides, Politics and Pest Management: Toward a Political Ecology of Cotton in Sub-Saharan Africa

Jim Bingen

A New Day for Cotton Farmers in Africa?

A series of recent political and economic events suggest that a new day may be dawning for Africa's cotton farmers. After an extraordinary boycott that slashed cotton production by 53 per cent during 2000-2001, Malian cotton farmers achieved significant and long-demanded price increases. In response, cotton production for 2001-2002 broke all previous records.

Equally important, it appears that the economic cold war between the World Bank and the French cotton industry is now over – with both sides claiming victory. In 2001 Mali joined Benin, Cameroun, Togo and Côte d'Ivoire in a major agreement to privatize important components of its vertically integrated parastatal cotton company, the *Compagnie Malienne pour le Développement des Textiles* (CMDT) and to reduce by two-thirds the government's share in the company.

Moreover, the French parastatal parent company, the *Compagnie Française pour le Dévelopement des Textiles* (CFDT), has re-invented itself from a classic colonial holding company to a more entrepreneurial, yet still largely public, company called *Dévelopement des Agro-Industries du Sud,* (DAGRIS). In principle the new name embodies a new strategy for operating more competitively in the new, more liberal economic world of cotton production, processing (ginning) and marketing.

Finally, in what may prove to be the most momentous change affecting Africa's cotton farmers, the French Cotton Association (*l'Association Française Cotonnière, Afcot*) has proposed the creation of an African contract regulatory body equivalent to those in Liverpool, Bremen and Le Havre. In the context of the emerging Organization for the Standardization of Business Law in Africa, this new body would replace the Liverpool Cotton Association and assume responsibility for setting and enforcing the trade rules for African cotton. Such a body would represent a historic step toward the de-colonization of African cotton marketing by shifting contract rules and enforcement to Africa.

Underlying these important institutional changes in the world of African cotton, however, the long-standing 'silver bullet' mentality, or a techno-centric paradigm, continues to dominate approaches to cotton production issues. Varietal development or improved cultivation practices are the preferred responses to declining productivity, just as new or more toxic chemicals such as endosulfan are re-introduced to deal with the resurgence of old pests and with increased pest resistance.

This chapter argues that a fundamental shift in thinking about cotton production – from a techno-centric to a more holo-centric paradigm – and to one embodying a concept of power will be required for African farmers to reap the benefits of recent institutional changes in the cotton industry. This involves nothing less than examining our underlying assumptions about the process of agricultural development in sub-Saharan Africa.

The topic of pesticides and pest management in cotton offers a useful tool for exploring how we might (re)introduce a concept of power into our thinking about the process and future of agricultural development in sub-Saharan Africa. It draws our attention to the mutually supportive set of governmental, economic, trade and science interests that promote and sustain sets of disempowering practices for African farmers. Moreover, the topic allows us to identify the ways in which African farmers might be able to use the power of knowledge, technology and capital to control the current, tightly coupled system of agricultural practices. Finally, the topic permits us to raise briefly the proposition that a broadening of democratic methods is a condition of African agricultural and rural development.[1]

This chapter begins with a general description of the conditions of small farmer cotton production in sub-Saharan Africa and an outline of two models of cotton processing and marketing. The following section raises some of the key issues arising from intensified production systems found throughout Francophone Africa that rely on chemical fertilizer and insecticides, as a preferred means to improve soil fertility and manage pests. These two brief discussions lay the groundwork for an examination of the three dimensions of power in what is called 'the pesticide treadmill.' These dimensions include: the policies and procedures encouraging pesticide use; the interests of organized science; and, pesticide regulatory and enforcement failure. The final part of this chapter reviews the power of alternative pest management practices. Experiences with, and issues raised by the use of farmer field schools are used to argue the need to connect knowledge, place and knowing in order to strengthen the contribution of democratic practices to agricultural development in Africa.

Cotton Production and Marketing in Africa

Two closely related characteristics of cotton production and marketing in sub-Saharan Africa set the stage for the political and policy issues discussed in this chapter. The first involves some key features of peasant farmer cotton production in sub-Saharan Africa, while the second involves the commercial requirements for marketing and processing cotton.

The largest numbers of cotton farmers in sub-Saharan Africa cultivate from one-half to two hectares of cotton under rainfed conditions and operate with very low levels of capital investment. They are subject to the uncertainty of the weather, but with fertilizer and pesticides their yields may hover around one metric ton per hectare.[2] Cotton is usually only one crop in an overall household production system that centers on food crops, and that relies on family members or customary village work groups to fulfill the labor requirements of production and harvesting. Most households, especially throughout West and Central Africa, employ animal-powered (oxen or horse) equipment for plowing, seeding and in some cases weeding.

In the world cotton market, or even for a domestic textile industry, commercial success depends upon the ability to assure a reliable and consistent supply of a specific type and quality of cotton (Gillham *et al.*, 1995). Given the African peasant farmer system of cotton production just described, this means that firms must achieve two objectives: reduce the variability in the quality of the cotton produced and collect a sufficient quantity of cotton for processing (ginning) from large numbers of peasant farmers working on separate plots over wide areas.[3] In sub-Saharan Africa, two models have evolved and continue to evolve in order to meet these objectives.

In most of Eastern and Southern Africa, private companies are authorized by a government board or agency to manage their own cotton production, collection, processing (ginning), and marketing for export and/or for the national textile industry. Each company develops its own approach to distributing supplies and equipment, providing production advice, and buying seed cotton from farmers. Some companies may try to organize groups of farmers in order to facilitate these activities, while others may work through individual distributors or buying agents who are free to devise their own methods for assuring the production and collection of a specified quota of cotton. In consultation with the companies, government usually sets producer prices and develops collaborative arrangements for cotton seed production and distribution. Since the companies must compete among themselves and sometimes with independent agents to buy cotton from individual farmers, the companies have little incentive to invest in the research and development of improved technological packages or in a production credit and input distribution program to encourage more intensive cultivation. Consequently, yields remain quite low (around 500 kilos per hectare), thereby leaving the companies to consider other options, such as early payment or premiums for quality, for gaining farmer loyalty.[4]

Since the early 1960s in West and Central Africa, DAGRIS (ex-CFDT) pioneered what is called an administered or managed monopoly model through national parastatal companies (The World Bank, 2000). With equity participation from, and technical assistance agreements with DAGRIS, each country established one national company to operate within a highly integrated global production and marketing system. Through this system, each national company acquires and distributes all production equipment and supplies to farmers. It also enjoys a monopoly to buy, collect and transport seed cotton for processing at company gins, and finally sell the baled cotton through an exclusive marketing agent (COPACO, *Compagnie Cotonnière*) that is an affiliate company of DAGRIS. Finally, each national company finances almost all the costs for research, equipment and infrastructure of the government national agricultural cotton research program, including arrangements for technical support from CIRAD (*Centre de Coopération Internationale en Recherche Agronomqiue pour le Dévelopement*). As a result the cotton technology package allows farmers to achieve yields in excess of 1 metric ton per hectare.

The machine-like operation of this model was largely responsible for the seven per cent per year increase in cotton from 1980 through 2000 in West and Central Africa.[5] Yields increased steadily from the early 1960s through the 1980s, while improved and expanded ginning facilities earned a high reputation for quality and on-time delivery for DAGRIS cotton from this region. Despite these overall accomplishments, producer prices were kept unnecessarily low and the management of the national companies suffered from the absence of adequate regulatory oversight and accountability. Reforms designed to introduce more competition into this model by improving national company management, increasing producer prices, and privatizing input distribution as well as ginning, are underway in several West and Central African countries. Presumably such reforms would improve further the competitive position of these countries and their cotton farmers in the world cotton market (Béroud, 2001).

In both models, the companies attempt to reduce the personnel and logistic costs of some field operations, such as consolidating the orders for, and distributing annual production supplies (including repayment for these supplies) and, assembling the cotton for pick-up from village collection points, with village-level organizations. Throughout West and Central Africa, this type of involvement by villagers in company operations over twenty-some years facilitated the emergence of cotton farmer unions that speak for cotton farmers' interests (see Bingen, 1998).[6]

Given the strength of some of these unions, the negotiations for reforming and liberalizing the managed monopoly model include consideration of an ownership share for the unions in the companies. Throughout East and Southern Africa, on the other hand, the competition among companies, the presence of independent buyers who purchase cotton for re-sale to these companies, and the absence of government regulations to enforce credit repayment from farmers to the companies that provided them with production inputs, has undermined similar efforts to establish and maintain cotton farmer organizations.

The structure and operation of the managed monopoly model since the early 1960s – and especially the emergence of political democracy since the late 1980s – has created the conditions for a voice for cotton farmers in cotton programs and policies. In contrast, the structure and operations of cotton companies operating under more competitive conditions has not encouraged the emergence of an independent voice for cotton farmers. Despite this important political difference between the models, most cotton farmers continue unquestioningly to welcome and actively seek to purchase any production technology improvements available through the companies, private suppliers or in local markets.[7]

Intensified Production

In order to produce what is marketed around the world as a 'softer side' commodity, cotton requires the widespread use of 'hard' chemicals, both inorganic fertilizers and pesticides, which raise serious environmental and human health issues for African farmers.

Inorganic Fertilizer and Soil Erosion

One of the central differences between cotton production in East and Southern Africa and West and Central Africa involves the widespread use (a production 'requirement' for working with a national company) of inorganic fertilizers by cotton farmers in the latter region. In the former region, the absence of fertilizer as part of the cotton technology package contributes significantly to low cotton yields and low farmer enthusiasm for cotton. While in part responsible for enhancing and maintaining the productivity of cotton, the continuing use of fertilizer has contributed to two worrisome soil problems.

The continuing use of fertilizer on the same fields – an increasingly common practice in the absence of fallowing land – increases soil acidity and depletes the soil of organic matter. This is the principal reason why yields continue to stagnate and in some cases decline in the older cotton regions throughout West and Central Africa. In addition, the availability of fertilizer engenders further environmental degradation that tends to be acknowledged usually by only those working at the grassroots. For years farmers have 'borrowed' from their supplied cotton fertilizer – shorted the required application – and used these captured quantities – however small – to enhance in some small way their food crop production. Consequently, in order to compensate for any shortfall in their expected cotton production these same farmers bring additional and commonly more marginal land under cotton cultivation. Such practices not only enhance the susceptibility of the already marginal lands to erosion, but also reduce the effectiveness of the fertilizer used on cotton.

The challenge under these conditions lies not in rejecting fertilizer use, but in finding ways to improve soil quality with organic fertilizers and to reduce soil erosion. The national company cotton programs have become increasingly sensitive to the natural resource management issues raised by the widespread and long-term use of fertilizer. The response by these companies, however, has been limited. Soil protection measures are commonly promoted in a project-like manner as an activity separate from and additional to regular production and harvesting practices. Furthermore, natural resource management (soil protection and health) concerns take a back seat to breeding and pest management in the cotton research programs supported by the companies. But even the passing nod to dealing with these issues risks being sacrificed as the companies attempt to 'liberalize' their activities by transferring responsibility for non-production activities, such as natural resource management, to other firms or government agencies.

Pesticides

Insects – not disease or fungi – are the main cause of crop damage and losses in cotton throughout sub-Saharan Africa. These insects include aphids, sucking and pricking insects as well as worms (bollworms) that attack the leaves and bolls and feed on the cotton plant at various stages in its life cycle. Insect damage varies widely by country, but in areas where damage is considered to be 'relatively moderate,' yield losses are about 30 per cent per year. For years, cotton pests have been controlled through program spraying, i.e., by a specified number and type of applications over specified intervals of time throughout the growing season. The current practice throughout West and Central Africa involves a 14-day program with the total number of applications ranging from four to six. Some undocumented evidence indicates that such program treatments reduce loses by about ten percent. The costs of pest management account for 25 to 30 per cent of the total costs of the inputs in cotton and represent 15 to 30 per cent of the gross margins.

The insecticides used are pyrethroid-organophosphate mixtures that are moderately toxic to mammals and usually quite toxic to birds, fish and beneficial insects, including bees.[8] However, few, if any, environmental studies have been completed. Anecdotal reports from farmers refer to the alarming disappearance of bees in the older cotton growing zones, while the few groundwater pollution studies have been carried out long after the growing season and the last pesticide application.

Pesticide resistance has become equally troubling. In 1995 cotton bollworm (*Helicoverpa armigera*) resistance to the relatively non-toxic pyrethroids became problematic and was compounded by additional damage from whiteflies (*Bemisia tabaci*). In response, the cotton companies in West and Central Africa decided to re-introduce endosulfan, a highly toxic chlorinated hydrocarbon for control and to fund research on the use of a more powerful pyrethroid insecticide. This is the classic 'pesticide treadmill' response in which increasingly more powerful formulations are regularly required to respond to the resistance developed by insects. As researchers address this problem, they have been able to reduce the volume of pesticides used by increasing the toxicity by weight. A recently completed study by the Sahel Institute in Mali illustrates this phenomenon. Researchers found that while the volume of pesticides used declined by 44 per cent, the proportion of active ingredient per volume has increased 40 per cent (Camara *et al.*, 2001).

The Pesticide Treadmill – Dimensions of Power

The technical understanding of the 'pesticide treadmill,' noted above, in which pesticide use begets more pesticide use in order to deal with insect's pesticide resistance is easily understood. But the less readily recognized political and policy dimensions that 'push pesticide use' are the subject of discussion in this section. In particular, this section examines three dimensions of policy and power behind pesticide use in terms of the following categories: policies and procedures that encourage pesticide use; the interests of organized science; and, inadequate regulations and controls.

Promoting Pesticide Use

There are three major sets of policies that encourage pesticide use. As part of their structural adjustment agreements, all governments in sub-Saharan Africa have eliminated their subsidies for agricultural inputs, including pesticides. Throughout West and Central Africa, however, all agricultural imports, including pesticides, are subject to preferential tariffs as 'agricultural goods.'[9] In short, the tariff structure does not discourage the promotion of program pesticide spraying as described above. Moreover, the lower tariff structure provides an incentive for both the national companies and private entrepreneurs to set prices on pesticides that would encourage farmers to realize their profits based on pesticide use.

In addition, through their affiliation in an integrated global production and marketing system, the national companies can pass on to farmers the savings that arise from the significant economies of scale in input purchasing. This same integrated system, however, as a function of its organizational efficiencies, pushes pesticide use in another way. As part of a global integrated organization, the national companies must order pesticides one year in advance of the next growing season. Given this kind of lead time, orders are placed on the basis of past practices and needs, and not in response to closer estimates of expected pest problems. Moreover, given the volatility of the world cotton market, this kind of advance bulk ordering – just the opposite of current 'just-in-time-inventory' builds in fixed costs that are passed on (perhaps unnecessarily) to farmers. Co-opting farmers in the ordering process – as some companies have started to do – does not resolve this problem. Moreover, in the name of farmer participation it cleverly evades any discussion of alternative pest management practices. Finally, since this type of ordering most always over-estimates actual need, it consistently leads to overstocking pesticides in village warehouses. As widely known through village-level discussions, this practice raises worrisome human health and safety issues. Inadequate storage facilities contribute to groundwater (village wells) pollution and to the easy availability of pesticides for inappropriate use on food crops.

A more 'liberalized' system of cotton production with multiple private suppliers of pesticides only obscures responsibility for village level cotton pesticide problems. It is more difficult, if not impossible, to regulate the type of pesticides available by private entrepreneurs in open and uncontrolled markets.

Under these conditions, stories of pesticide misuse and abuse make almost daily news. Furthermore, structural reform cutbacks in government services and the failure of reforms to agricultural extension have seriously impeded government regulatory services and supervision and monitoring of pesticide use at the village level.

Finally, in the name of sustainable agriculture and overcoming hunger, foreign assistance projects and programs provide significant sources of grant and loan funding for purchasing pesticides. Japan's International Cooperation Agency (JICA) has emerged as a major pesticide supplier for Africa and pesticides comprise one-half of this agency's Grant Aid for Increased Food Production (KR2) program. The 'Standard List' of pesticides available under this program includes 'highly hazardous' FAO/WHO Class Ib pesticides as well as 'moderately hazardous' Class II pesticides. Both classes of pesticides carry stringent use restrictions that are both difficult to apply and enforce in Africa (Tobin, 1996).

The World Bank is the other major international donor whose operational policies and activities can be seen to encourage pesticide use in its funded agricultural projects. The Bank's 1998 Operational Policy on Pest Management (OP 4.09) requires that all agricultural projects reduce reliance on pesticides and promote farmer-driven integrated pest management. A study by the Pesticide Action Network, however, found that over 70 per cent of the agricultural project documents failed to mention IPM. But two additional activities are perhaps of more concern: pesticide company personnel regularly participate in staff exchanges with the Bank, and Bank personnel have facilitated meetings and partnerships between pesticide companies and national extension services and others responsible for implementing agricultural projects in Africa (Tozum, 2001).

Organized Science

Integrated pest management (IPM) includes a range of practices from those involving more precisely calibrated spraying equipment to improve pesticide use to several types of bio-intensive practices that seek to limit pest pressure and to enhance beneficial insects (see Benbrook, 1996). The development of any type of IPM program, even those limited to the improved calibration of spray nozzles, requires solid 'bench science' that responds to farmer needs under different and specific agro-ecological conditions. Nevertheless, the development of practices geared to the population dynamics of pest insects, or the threshold of pest infestation that might include various cultivation practices, the use of resistant varieties and different types of chemical control requires a holistic and long-term research commitment to collaborate with farmers. With largely company-funded cotton research in most countries, however, most research focuses on responding to specific, immediate production interests at the expense of exploring a range of alternative and non-chemical pest management practices.

The threshold pest management program in Mali (LEC, *Lutte étagée ciblée)* illustrates the way in which a national cotton program seeks to implement an improved calendar spraying program without sacrificing its supervisory control of farmer practices. In 1988 the LEC program was tested in Cameroon and then developed in Burkina Faso. It was introduced in 1993 into the Mali cotton production program (see Michel and Togola, nd). The LEC strategy involves three stages. During a first stage, pesticides are applied following the standard application calendar (every two weeks), but at one-half the normal rate. In addition, scouting of key pests is encouraged to determine the need for any additional application. Scouting for natural enemies and understanding and analyzing trophic levels is not part of the LEC programs applied in the CMDT zone. In principle, as farmers become accustomed to these procedures, more sophisticated LEC program steps based first on threshold applications and finally more bio-intensive techniques are introduced.

It is estimated that the first step in LEC can cut pesticide use by almost 50 per cent and reduce pest management costs from 45-50 per cent. However, eight years after its introduction program in Mali, the program is not widely implemented. It is estimated that the program covers only four per cent of the total cotton zone. Farmer resistance or hesitation to adapt the practices does not appear to account for the low level of program application. On the contrary, the LEC procedures are designed for non-literate farmers, and during informal field surveys farmers express considerable interest in exploring ways to cut pesticide use and costs. Instead, the LEC procedures are designed to be closely supervised and it appears that the low adoption rate reflects considerable hesitancy on the part of the cotton company and of researchers to allow farmers more freedom in their pest management decisions. But even if a more adaptive or less controlling approach could be accepted in some countries, it is highly unlikely that the seriously constrained public extension services would have either the logistic means or the level of training required to advise farmers.

Regulatory Failure

The Rotterdam Convention on the Prior Informed Consent Procedure (PIC) is designed to reduce the risks associated with the use of pesticides through a series of procedures which limit the introduction of pesticides into countries that cannot safely manage them. Under the provisions of the legally binding PIC convention, governments can accept or refuse the importation of 22 stipulated pesticides, including several that could be used on cotton; each is banned or severely restricted for health or environmental reasons in at least two countries in different regions. Most countries with a governmental Designated National Authority responsible for implementing PIC have issued pesticide import decisions concerning this class of pesticides.[10]

As a 1994 study showed, however, most governments confront serious challenges in arriving at informed pesticide import decisions. Over 80 per cent of the countries surveyed lacked resources to manage the availability, distribution and use of pesticides and almost one quarter of the countries did not have approved legislative authority to regulate the distribution and use of pesticides. Most critical, over 60 per cent of the countries reported the absence of adequate internal systems to handle the processing of data on banned or severely restricted pesticides prior to import (Farah, 1994).

But even if these agencies were strengthened, they would find it difficult to control what amounts to the hidden global trade of pesticides. Since 1990 the Foundation for Advancements in Science and Education (FASE) has researched the export of banned and hazardous pesticides from the United States to developing countries. Based on a review of U.S. Customs records – the only source of data concerning pesticide exports – FASE found that of the 3.2 billion pounds of pesticides exported between 1997 and 2000, 65 million pounds were either banned or subject to restricted use in the United States. The most recent FASE research report suggests that international treaties such as PIC have contributed to recent sharp declines in the export of pesticides targeted by these treaties. But the continued inability to acquire adequate data raises serious questions about any government's ability to exercise adequate control over exports or imports. For example, in 1991 FASE could determine the specific compounds shipped for only 25 per cent of the shipments studied. There are serious limitations to information in the public record and strong tendencies to restrict public access to the little information that is on file. Shippers' names and addresses are commonly removed from the files – at the request of the shippers – and FASE has never been able to identify even 50 per cent of the specific compounds shipped. Under these conditions, even the strongest national authority would be challenged to control pesticide imports (Foundation for Advancements in Science and Education, 2001).[11]

A second major area of regulatory failure that works to continue pesticide use lies in the absence of government reporting on pesticide poisonings or incidents of misuse and abuse. Throughout sub-Saharan Africa – and in most industrialized countries, including the U.S. – voluntary and non-governmental organizations are the only watchdogs on pesticide use problems and poisonings.[12] Consequently, with the exception of the rare incidents in sub-Saharan that make international headlines, we are limited to accepting random reports and anecdotal evidence. This provides information about major acute problems, but only leaves us to speculate on the chronic effects of pesticide poisoning.

The most recent international incident involved endosulfan poisoning in Benin during 2000. Thirty seven people were killed and at least another 36 become seriously ill. This type of disastrous incident usually does not involve direct contamination from spraying, but from eating food – in this case maize – that becomes contaminated from sprays used on cotton, and drinking from re-used pesticide containers. In addition, as many observers have pointed out for several years, farmers do not wear protective clothing and practically nothing is known about the chronic poisoning that occurs from inhalation and dermal exposure, especially since low protein diets engender a higher susceptibility to pesticide poisoning (see Adjovi, 1998; also see OBEPAB, 2000).

The poisonings are not restricted to humans. There is anecdotal evidence as well of cattle deaths from eating treated stalks of cotton that have been left in the fields after harvest. Moreover, it is widely known, but not well-documented, that pesticides are frequently used for fishing and for 'hunting.' Finally, despite farmers' casual observations about the disappearance of bees in cotton production zones, there have been discussions of the possibility of cotton pesticide residues in honey.

Governments and cotton companies have permitted only very limited environmental impact studies of pesticides. But those undertaken found pesticides in over 25 per cent of the wells studied and at levels that exceeded the EU residue standards for drinking water. In addition to the human health risk, such residues in surface water also pose a risk for animals throughout cotton growing areas.[13]

Summary Observations

As the above discussion suggests, pesticide use is supported and encouraged through mutually supportive set of governmental, economic, trade and science interests. As with the 'green revolution technology' of an earlier era, these intertwined interests promote and sustain sets of energy and capital intensive practices that are required to maintain specific environmental conditions for production. These interests embody the power of knowledge, technology and capital to fashion a tightly coupled system of agricultural practices.

Economic liberalization or privatization programs do not touch these interests and in fact may exacerbate safety, health and environmental problems associated with pesticide use. Similarly, while research and implementation of IPM and Natural Resource Management programs help to address some of the environmental issues associated with pesticide use, they do not challenge the reductionist way in which most agricultural scientists see and practice in the world.

As long as this confluence of perspectives, influence and power remains unchallenged, there is little hope of being able to jump off the pesticide treadmill nor of being able to create the opportunities for farmer empowerment.

Localizing Power

The power of alternative pest management practices – either through IPM or through organic production practices – to challenge this confluence resides in the capacity to actualize the 'power of the local.' For both sets of practices this involves accepting the (scientific) legitimacy of local categories of thought and language about cultivation and pest management practices. From this point it is a short but difficult step to understanding all forms of scientific discourse as interpretative. Once this step is taken, then 'official' science or research loses its claim as superior knowledge and as the keystone in the tightly coupled system of knowledge, technology and capital (Fischer, 2000). The practice of farmer field schools offers one means for taking this step. These 'schools' are not an end in themselves. They are only a local starting point for development based on farmers becoming the instigators of, and implementing their own IPM activities.

Farmer Field Schools – A Means to Actualize Power[14]

The IPM Farmer Field Schools launched by the FAO in the late 1980s in the Philippines and in 1989 in Indonesia emerged out of efforts to address several production and pest management problems that were arising from the use of the 'green revolution' technology that had been introduced in the 1960s to improve rice production. Specifically, pest resurgence and resistance linked with the widespread use of insecticides threatened the gains achieved with the green revolution package. Moreover, researchers found that the management practices developed by some farmers were leading to yields that outperformed those on research stations; researchers also demonstrated the viability of biological, not chemical, controls of the major rice pests.

Based on these findings, the FAO Regional Program in Southeast Asia created the Farmers Field School approach as a way to combine farmers' knowledge with the ecological principles underlying their rice field agro-ecosystems.[15] Instead of using an approach to resolving farmers' production problems that was centrally uniform and technologically driven, the school approach was designed to be farmer driven and locally adaptive. The central idea was to allow farmers to become the 'experts' in managing the ecology of their fields for better yields, fewer pest problems, increased profits and less health and environmental risk.

In addition to building on four IPM principles,[16] the Farmer Field School approach embodies three critical 'learning domains' (see Dilts, 2001). The first involves a process through which farmers do not learn specific messages, but understand a process of learning that can applied continuously to their changing situations. The second is based on the assumption that farmers learn best among and from themselves through 'interaction and communicative action.' Finally, the school experience is seen as the starting point for empowerment and local institution building. In short, participants are encouraged to 'examine their internal or group constraints and options as they relate to a larger social, political, economic and ecological environment' (Dilts, 2001, p.18).

For the last ten years, the Farmer Field School approach has been slowly evolving into a Community IPM movement in which field school alumni have started to strengthen their own community institutions as well as become involved in local politics. In Indonesia, Dilts identifies an array of 'IPM farmer institutions,' including provincial-level congresses, in organizing political campaigns to elect IPM farmers to village level positions.

With guidance and support from the FAO Global IPM Facility, several farmer field school activities have been launched in West, East and Southern Africa. The programs differ significantly along several dimensions from the East and South Asian experiences. First, the schools respond to pest management in issues in both cash and food crops, but none of the pest problems addressed is as severe and immediate as the brown plant hopper crisis in rice. Related to this, none of the programs benefit directly from collateral research underway at an international research center. Third, while some of the preliminary assessments indicate that farmer field school alumni have established information exchange networks, the schools have not been operational long enough for a community IPM movement to begin to emerge. Due to their broader focus on production and pest management, African IPM programs are called 'Integrated Production and Pest Management Programs' (IPPM). Finally, the program only recently started receiving highly visible political support at the ministerial level. Consequently, whether field schools in sub-Saharan Africa can serve as 'forcing houses' to politicize African farmers into challenging the current structures of knowledge, technology and capital remains to be seen.

Summary Observations

Without question, the Farmer Field School approach offers a dramatically different learning and empowering opportunity from that offered through new pest management approaches such as the threshold management program (LEC), which is calendar spraying at half dosages – while calendar spraying remains the centerpiece of cotton pest management throughout West and Central Africa.

The learning principles of the Farmer Field School approach in themselves empower in two ways: through a reliance on building personal capacity, as well as reflective thinking and knowing; and in learning as a communal act that emerges through relationships between knowers and the known in a specific setting (see Palmer, 1993; Wheatley, 1994; Brown, 1997).

Power through Practice

The contribution that farmer field schools can make to farmer empowerment and development derives from the principle of practice based on farmers' spatialized social reality. They help farmers to realize and act upon an ethics of place that can subvert current instrumentalist approaches to development practice. As noted above, once farmers understand that scientific discourse is an interpretative enterprise, the established science of national agricultural research institutes loses its privileged claim as superior knowledge.

As in 'adaptive management,' the schools offer 'an approach to the management of complex systems based on incremental, experiential learning and decision making, buttressed by active monitoring of and feedback from the effects and outcomes of decisions' (Jiggins and Roling, 2000, p.29). The power of this process emerges as farmers begin to translate the awareness of themselves as scientists to their rights and responsibilities as citizens and thereby to make policy claims and become involved in public decision-making. As this occurs, farmers begin to appreciate that scientific discourse and political deliberation are two different, but mutually reinforcing, types of inquiry that can generate an important redistribution of power through socio-economic change and the eventual creation of new political interests.

If democracy is essential to African agricultural development, this chapter suggests that it is important to look at how to connect knowledge, knowing and democracy. In doing so, the new democratic processes can authorize the political space in particular settings for competing ways to look at the shape, future and contribution of agriculture to African development.

Notes

1   The discussion in this chapter draws heavily on material from Francophone Africa. This area, the Franc Zone, accounts for 15 per cent of the world cotton market and is the 4th largest world exporter. The political questions raised in this paper are equally relevant for farmers in both Anglophone and Francophone Africa.

2   This contrasts with yields under irrigated or flood recession conditions (for example, Egypt) that may exceed two metric tons per hectare.

3   Where agriculture is more highly mechanized, cotton farmers usually cooperate to gin their own cotton and sell fiber – not seed cotton – to brokers (buyers).

4   See Lele, U., *et al.* (1989). Cotton in Africa: An Analysis of Differences in Performance. Washington, DC, The World Bank. for one assessment of cotton performance in Anglophone Africa. Also see Food Security Research Project-Zambia (2000). Key Challenges and Options Confronting Smallholder, Agribusiness and Government Leaders in Zambia's Cotton Sector. Lusaka, Food Security Research Project..

5   On the other hand, some suggested the perceived quality of West Africa cotton on the world market was declining Estur, G. (1992). ' La Commercialisation du Coton: le Système CFDT-COPACO.' *Coton et Développement* 1(1ere Trimestre): 16-18.

6   See Sinaba, F. (2000). 'Après la Grève des Cotonniers Maliens.' *Grain de Sel* 16 (Novembre): 6.

7   Technology issues are rarely a priority for farmer organizations Bratton, M. and R. J. Bingen (1994). 'Farmers' Organizations and Agricultural Policy: Introduction.' *African Rural and Urban Studies* 1(1): 7-29.

8   These mixtures commonly include dimethoate (an organophosphate and a general use pesticide) as well as either cypermethrin or deltamethrin (synthetic pyrethroids, that are restricted use pesticides because of their toxicity to fish).

9   For a discussion of these tariffs in Côte d'Ivoire, see Ajayi, O. O. C. (2000). *Pesticide Use Practices, Productivity and Farmers' Health: The Case of Cotton-Rice Systems in Côte d'Ivoire, West Africa.* Hanover, University of Hanover.; in Mali, see Camara, M., *et al.* (2001). Etude Socio-économique de l'Utilisation des Pesticides au Mali. Bamako, Mali, Institut du Sahel, AGROSOC / Sécurité Alimentaire - Gestion des Ressources Naturelles Université de Hanovre, Institut des Sciences Economique - Projet Politique des Pesticides FAO, Projet Gestion des Pesticides au Sahel.

10 All the major cotton producing countries in Africa have a Designated National Authority, but Mali, Senegal and Côte d'Ivoire are the only countries that have not submitted pesticide import decisions.

11 Also see Foundation for Advancements in Science and Education (1996). Exporting Risk: Pesticide Exports from US Ports, 1992-1994. Los Angeles, FASE.

12 The U.S. ended its program of Pesticide Incident Monitoring in 1981. Now, *Beyond Pesticides,* a coalition of the National Coalition Against the Misuse of Pesticides and the Northwest Coalition for Alternatives to Pesticides, is the only group that compiles information on pesticide incidents Schubert, S., et al. (1996). Voices for Pesticide Reform: The Case for Safe Practices and Sound Policy. Washington, D.C., Beyond

Pesticides, National Coalition Against the Misuse of Pesticides, and Northwest Coalition for Alternatives to Pesticides.

13 J. Slaats, personal communication.

14 The discussion in this section draws heavily on Pontius, J., *et al.* (2000). *Ten Years of Building Community: From Farmer Field Schools to Community IPM.* Jakarta, FAO Community IPM Programme.; Braun, A. R., *et al.* (2000). Farmer Field Schools and Local Agricultural Research Committees: Complementary Platforms for Integrated Decision-Making in Sustainable Agriculture. London, Overseas Development Institute, Dilts, R. (2001). 'From Farmers' Field Schools to Community IPM. Scaling up the IPM Movement.' *LEISA Magazine* 17(3): 18-21.

15 The FAO program received significant political and policy support, especially in Indonesia, including a ban on almost 60 broad-spectrum insecticides being used on rice.

16 These include: growing a healthy crop; conserving natural enemies of insect pests; regular field monitoring; becoming IPM experts through participation in the Farmer Field Schools.

References

Adjovi, E. V. (1998), Quand l'Or Blanc Intoxique ses Producteurs. *SYFIA International.* http://www.syfia.com/presse.

Ajayi, O. O. C. (2000), *Pesticide Use Practices, Productivity and Farmers' Health: The Case of Cotton-Rice Systems in Côte d'Ivoire, West Africa.* Hanover, University of Hanover.

Benbrook, C. M. (1996), *Pest Management at the Crossroads.* Yonkers, NY, Consumers Union.

Béroud, F. (2001), 'Cotton Production in Francophone Africa.' *Cotton: Review of the World Situation* 54(4), pp. 11-14.

Bingen, R. J. (1998), 'Cotton, Democracy and Development in Mali.' *The Journal of Modern African Studies* 36(2), pp. 265-285.

Bratton, M. and Bingen, R. J. (1994), 'Farmers' Organizations and Agricultural Policy: Introduction.' *African Rural and Urban Studies* 1(1), pp. 7-29.

Braun, A. R., *et al.* (2000), Farmer Field Schools and Local Agricultural Research Committees: Complementary Platforms for Integrated Decision-Making in Sustainable Agriculture. London, Overseas Development Institute.

Brown, J. S. (1997), 'On Becoming a Learning Organization.' *About Campus* (January-February), pp. 5-10.

Camara, M., *et al.* (2001), Etude Socio-économique de l'Utilisation des Pesticides au Mali. Bamako, Mali, Institut du Sahel, AGROSOC / Sécurité Alimentaire - Gestion des Ressources Naturelles Université de Hanovre, Institut des Sciences Economique – Projet Politique des Pesticides FAO, Projet Gestion des Pesticides au Sahel.

Dilts, R. (2001), 'From Farmers' Field Schools to Community IPM. Scaling up the IPM Movement.' *LEISA Magazine* 17(3), pp. 18-21.

Estur, G. (1992), ' La Commercialisation du Coton: le Système CFDT-COPACO.' *Coton et Développement* 1(1ere Trimestre), pp. 16-18.

Farah, J. (1994), *Pesticide Policies in Developing Countries: Do They Encourage Excessive Use?* Washington, D.C., The World Bank.

Fischer, F. (2000), *Citizens, Experts, and the Environment.* Durham and London, Duke University Press.

Food Security Research Project-Zambia (2000), Key Challenges and Options Confronting Smallholder, Agribusiness and Government Leaders in Zambia's Cotton Sector. Lusaka, Food Security Research Project.

Foundation for Advancements in Science and Education (1996), Exporting Risk: Pesticide Exports from US Ports, 1992-1994. Los Angeles, FASE.

Foundation for Advancements in Science and Education (2001), 'Pesticide Exports from U.S. Ports, 1997-2000.' *International Journal of Occupational and Environmental Health* 7, pp. 266-274.

Gillham, F. E. M., *et al.* (1995), *Cotton Production Prospects for the Next Decade.* Washington, D.C., The World Bank.

Jiggins, J. and Roling, N. (2000), 'Adaptive Management: Potential and Limitations for Ecological Governance.' *International Journal of Agricultural Resources, Governance and Ecology* 1(1), pp. 28-42.

Lele, U., *et al.* (1989), *Cotton in Africa: An Analysis of Differences in Performance.* Washington, DC, The World Bank.

Michel, B. and Togola, M. (nd), Lutte Intégrée et Culture Cotonnière. Le Point sur la Situation au Mali. Sikasso, Mali.

OBEPAB (2000), Les Accidents Causés par les Pesticides Chimiques de Synthèse Utilisés dans la Production Cotonnière au Bénin. Cotonou, Bénin, Organisation Béninoise pour la Promotion de l'Agriculture Biologique.

Palmer, P. J. (1993), *To Know as We Are Known. Education as a Spiritual Journey.* San Francisco, Harper & Row.

Pontius, J., *et al.* (2000), *Ten Years of Building Community: From Farmer Field Schools to Community IPM.* Jakarta, FAO Community IPM Programme.

Schubert, S., *et al.* (1996), Voices for Pesticide Reform: The Case for Safe Practices and Sound Policy. Washington, D.C., Beyond Pesticides, National Coalition Against the Misuse of Pesticides, and Northwest Coalition for Alternatives to Pesticides.

Sinaba, F. (2000), 'Après la Grève des Cotonniers Maliens.' *Grain de Sel* 16 (Novembre), p. 6.

The World Bank (2000), *Cotton Policy Brief: The Administered Monopoly Model in the Era of Competition and Globalization.* Washington DC, The World Bank.

Tobin, R. J. (1996), 'Pest Management, the Environment, and Japanese Foreign Assistance.' *Food Policy* 21(2), pp. 211-228.

Tozum, N. (2001), 'New Policy, Old Patterns: A Survey of IPM in World Bank Projects.' *Global Pesticide Campaigner* 11(1).

Wheatley, M. J. (1994), *Leadership and the New Science. Learning About Organization from an Orderly Universe.* San Francisco, Berrett-Koehler Publishers.

Chapter 7

A Local Graft Takes Hold: The Political Ecology of Commercial Horticultural Production in Rural Mali

Stephen R. Wooten

Introduction[1]

A growing number of scholars studying development dynamics in low-income countries are now employing the 'livelihood' concept and identifying 'diversification' as a key livelihood strategy for contemporary rural people. According to Ellis, '(a) livelihood comprises the assets (natural, physical, human, financial and social capital), the activities, and the access to these (mediated by institutions and social relations) that together determine the living gained by the individual or household' (2000, p.10). Ellis defines livelihood diversification as 'the process by which rural households construct an increasingly diverse portfolio of activities and assets in order to survive or improve their standards of living.' (2000, p.27).

Researchers working within the livelihood diversification framework have identified three broad patterns by which rural producers typically seek to insure or enhance their lives: 1) agricultural intensification or extensification; 2) expansion of non-agricultural activities; and 3) migration (Ellis, 2000; Scoones, 1998). Adoption of any of these strategies depends on the co-occurrence of suitable 'assets' and a conducive 'institutional' environment.

In this paper I draw on the livelihood diversification framework in order to examine a case of specialized agricultural intensification in a Bamana-speaking community in rural Mali, West Africa. I examine a situation of agrarian change in which a sub-set of the population of the community is engaged in a horticultural production process geared toward meeting the demands of urban consumers in the Bamako, Mali's capital city. I use the plant propagation technique known as 'grafting' as a metaphor to help describe how a group of farmers have – apparently quite successfully – 'grafted' this specialized commercial agricultural activity, on to an existing agrarian system that is geared toward direct consumption. I begin with a brief introduction to the research setting and the 'base' food production system, and then turn to the particulars of market gardening in the community. I demonstrate the relative significance of this livelihood diversification strategy and identify a series of key factors that make this activity a viable strategy in this community. I conclude by exploring the wider significance of my case study. Specifically, I offer my thoughts on the role market gardening might play in other areas.

The Setting: Producing For Food and For Income in a Rural Malian Community

Located on the Mande Plateau in southwestern Mali, the community of Niamakoroni lies just below the Sahelian region in the Southern Sudanic zone. Annual rainfall in the area is approximately 900-1200 mm and occurs in the short span of 3-4 months, primarily from June through September. The nucleated settlement consists of a series of closely clustered adobe brick structures and associated shade trees. According to community elders, the settlement was founded at the close of the 19th century when a lineage segment from a nearby community settled there in order to gain access to new farmland. Contemporary residents of Niamakoroni, like their ancestors before them, assert a Bamana (Bambara) ethnic identity. In 1993-1994, the community had a total resident population of 184.

As is the case in most Bamana communities (Becker, 1990; 1996; Grosz-Ngate, 1986; Konate, 1994; Lewis, 1979; Paques, 1954; Toulmin, 1992), the people of Niamakoroni live in a tight-knit, rural community in which men, particularly senior men, occupy central positions. In the community, descent is traced patrilineally and control over productive resources is generally corporate in nature. Age and gender are important characteristics in social, political, and economic contexts with elders dominating juniors and men typically holding more power than women. Becker (1990, p.315) refers to this situation as 'a patrilineal gerontocracy.' The dominant residence pattern is patrilocal, and marriages are frequently polygynous. In the community, the primary residential and food production and consumption unit is called a *du* (*duw*, plural), in the Bamana language (*Bamanankan*).

Niamakoroni's *duw* are multi-generational, joint families in which junior agnates live and work under the authority of the group's eldest male agnate, the *dutigi* (leader of the domestic group). As senior members of their lineage groups, *dutigiw* have access to land and the authority to direct the labor of those who live with them in order to produce sufficient harvests to sustain local consumption patterns. The community consists of five domestic groups. In 1993-94, these *duw* ranged in size from eighteen to fifty-four individuals. The members of each *du* live in close proximity to one another and typically eat their meals together from a common hearth. A clear gender division of labor exists within the domestic arena in the community. Women are responsible for food processing and cooking, as well as all household maintenance tasks, including sweeping, hauling watering and washing. Men typically have few household obligations, aside from building and maintaining houses (see also Creevey, 1986; Thiam, 1986).

Like their counterparts in Bamana communities throughout Mali (Becker, 1996; 2000; Grisby, 1996; Lewis, 1979; Konate, 1994; Thiam, 1986; Toulmin, 1992) and in many of the farming villages across the West African savanna (Hart, 1982; Meillassoux, 1981; Norman et al., 1981), the people of Niamakoroni strive to meet the bulk of their food needs through farming activities managed at the household-level by the *dutigi* and attempt to satisfy other needs with income generated through production activities organized at the individual or small group-level (Wooten, 1997). Here, I provide only a brief overview of the household-level, domestic consumption aspect of this agrarian economy before turning to an analysis of the market gardening domain. In the language of the grafting process, the local food production system is the 'base stock' onto which rural farmers append the market gardening 'scion.'

Producing for Life: The Household Economy

During the short-lived rainy season, the vast majority of able bodied, working-age (roughly 12-45 years of age) community members focus their productive energies on the cultivation of food crops, a process community members referred to as *ka balo* (for life). Working under the direction of their *dutigi*, members of each household labor diligently to insure that their food coffers are filled at harvest time. Very clear gender relations of production mark this production process. The men in each *du* work collectively in their group's main field (*foroba*) to produce staple crops (millet, sorghum, cowpeas), while the married women in each group work individually in fields assigned to them by the *dutigiw* to produce the sauce crops (*nafenw*), such as okra and peanuts – items that complement the grains to complete the daily meals. Aside from assisting their mothers or sisters-in-law, unmarried girls are rarely involved in agricultural activities. Instead, they devote most of their time to household tasks such as hauling water, childcare, and sweeping domestic areas. Likewise, senior men and women do not participate directly in the household economy. They are retired from direct productive roles in the domestic economy and spend most of their time tending small private plots during the rainy season. Those men and women who are active in their household economies spend the vast majority of daylight hours during the rainy season tending to the food crops.

At the end of each rainy season, a village-wide work team composed of all the active men in the community harvest in rotation each *du*'s main cereal field. Each group's harvest is stored in its own granary for use throughout the year. For the most part, each woman harvests her own sauce field. In some cases individual women recruit assistance from the other women in their *du*. Women's crops are typically bagged and stored in their respective houses for use when they prepare meals in their *du*. Throughout the year, consumption is strictly a *du*-level activity with meals prepared in turn by the married women in each household and composed of products resulting from the men and women's distinct food production processes.

Producing for the Market: Opportunities for Income Generation

In addition to laboring within the context of their respective *duw* for domestic consumption, individuals of all ages in Niamakoroni have the option to engage in independent commodity production activities that will earn them personal incomes. People typically classify income-generating activities as *ka wari nyini* (for cash/money) activities. Due to the seasonal nature of labor demands in the rain-fed farming cycle, most people do not devote time to such personal activities until the close of the year's farming season. However, once their obligations to the food economy are met, most people – young and old, male and female – devote at least some amount of time to producing or collecting products that are sold in nearby markets. For example, some people produce charcoal, while others craft mats and brooms. However, despite considerable diversity, people are quite uniform in viewing market gardening as the premier avenue available for income generation and potential accumulation (Wooten, 1997).

The Development of Commercial Horticulture in the Community

Based on accounts I solicited from older members of the community, commercially oriented fruit and vegetable production began in Niamakoroni several decades ago. Nene and Shimbon Jara, two of the community's male elders, told me that in the 1950s during the dry seasons, their fathers began clearing lowland areas around the village, where sufficient water for irrigation existed, in order to cultivate fruits and vegetables – crops that urban dwellers in the capital city were purchasing with increasing frequency (Villien-Rossi, 1966). They undertook this activity in order to gain access to personal incomes, which could be used to buy consumer items. In short, they pursued this activity as a means to enhance their livelihoods.

Nene and Shimbon were young men at the time and apparently aided their fathers in this process. They said that the lowland areas were covered with dense vegetation and that clearing them proved to be a very demanding task. Once cleared, they fenced their areas and planted crops such as bananas, tomatoes and papaya. Each subsequent dry season the pioneers cleared more area and each year, seeing how well they were faring, a few more enterprising men joined their ranks – clearing, fencing and cultivating more dry season gardens.

In the intervening years, market gardening has become an increasingly more important part of the local economy – it is now a central component of the local livelihood portfolio. By the mid-1990s I was able to identify and follow the activities of 22 separate garden production units (GPUs), each led by a particular garden leader or *nakotigi*. The vast majority (19/22; 86 per cent in 1993-94) of the garden leaders in Niamakoroni are married men. Most garden leaders are assisted in the production process by younger brothers or sons and daughters and in some cases wives. The garden leaders establish cropping patterns, organize labor, make the important decisions regarding harvest and marketing. They sell the produce and distribute the proceeds as they see fit. In short, with support from their helpers, garden leaders manage the day-to-day production operations of a vibrant and expanding, commercially oriented agricultural activity.

In 1993-1994, Niamakoroni's 22 garden leaders operated a total of 34 distinct plots, ranging in size from 378 to 9720 m^2 with an average of 3212 m^2. These gardens are always clearly marked and well-protected from livestock damage. They are typically fenced with a combination of logs, brush, and living thicket. The market gardeners of Niamakoroni grow two basic types of crops in their plots: fruits and vegetables – items that are in high demand in the capital city (see also Becker, 2000; Konate, 1994). The most common types of vegetables grown are tomatoes, bitter eggplant, beans, hot pepper, and cabbage. Of these, tomatoes and bitter eggplant are the most popular, typically occurring in all gardens. Fruit crops also play a major role in the gardens. Often these plantings occupy a large percentage of an enclosed garden area, sometimes as pure orchards, while in other cases they were inter-cropped throughout the garden. The vast majority of gardens held at least some mature (productive) fruit plantings including banana, papaya, mango, and various citrus species. When fruit crops were present, bananas were the most abundant crop grown. Papaya was the next most common fruit crop. The majority of plots also had mango trees. Most gardens included citrus stock as well. This category included lemons, oranges, mandarins, tangelos and grapefruits with lemons being the most common type. The gardens were clearly geared toward items that gardeners knew their urban counterparts were eager to consume: crops that have a ready market and thus could generate income.

As a commercial production process focusing largely on exotic crops requiring significant inputs, gardeners typically need to purchase many items in Bamako. They buy French vegetable seed in small, specialized boutiques and fertilizer and pesticides from dealers throughout the city. They also make use of locally available manure and domestic sweepings. Gardeners also purchase orchard stock in the capital and obtain grafting materials there as well. The market gardeners maintain relationships with the providers of these inputs and some take them on credit. Once the needed inputs are secured the production process can begin.

The garden heads organize their helpers to clean and prepare the soil, often beginning during the limited free time at the end of the cereal production process. Some gardeners make use of village labor teams to weed gardens prior to the main gardening season or to mend fences.

Whereas cereal agriculture depends on rainfall, market gardening depends on consistent irrigation. In Niamakoroni this ranges from watering by hand from shallow hand-dug wells to irrigation by diesel pump and high-density plastic line. Depending on the operation, a gardener might have any where from one locally produced *juruflen* or gourd bucket to two or three machine pumps (each worth about 400 US dollars). There is a great variety among these market gardeners and in some cases a considerable degree of capitalization.

As the dry season progresses watering of the garden becomes increasingly more important. This means that as the streambeds begin to dry up – beginning in

February or March – gardeners must begin to dig or make more use of existing wells. There are some gardens in which there are multiple, deep and wide wells and others where there are many shallow wells. By April or May only those gardens with dependable wells are able to continue production at a reasonable scale.

Each gardening group spends the better part of every day in the garden attending to the various tasks at hand – even in the hot, dry season. Overall, people say that the time after the harvest and before the next planting of the cereal crop is no longer a relaxed period. My observations on activity levels throughout the agricultural calendar support this claim. In the gardens they undertake such operations as sowing, transplanting, weeding, pruning, fertilizing, applying insecticides, watering and harvesting. The harvest leads directly to the marketing domain.

The bulk of the produce from Niamakoroni's gardens is transported to Bamako's markets by bicycle. Whatever the item in season, it is loaded into a locally made basket and attached to an inexpensive, single speed bicycle and delivered to a suburban market. The journey from the village to the market is an arduous one that necessitates the negotiation of a very steep and unstable dirt path leading off of the Plateau and then a ride of about an hour and a half to the selling point. The loads typically weigh around 40 kilos and present a considerable challenge for the rider.

The produce is brought to a site where urban market traders – mostly young women – purchase whatever they can find. There is always a stable cohort of buyers at these suburban markets. Most of Niamakoroni's gardeners sell their produce at either Sebenikoro or Djikoroni, both suburban communities of Bamako. Some buyers will also venture out toward the village in order to get an edge on other perspective buyers. Unfortunately, this kind of competition has not translated to increased prices for the producers who are always complaining that the market women are getting all the money.

As I stated at the outset, the main objective in the garden production process is income generation. *Nakotigiw* manage their resources with the goal of earning as much as they can. Garden crops are extremely rare in the local diet and when they do appear they are typically damaged or partially spoiled. Through garden crops, they seek to translate their own labor and the labor of their assistants into disposable personal income. Clearly, however, different garden operations have different resource endowments and thus different potentials in this regard. For example, the three women garden leaders having the smallest, least complex operations have relatively limited income potential. However, comparatively speaking, this sector of the economy has the most potential to generate significant cash flows.

Relative to other commodity production activities in the community, market gardening has the most income generating potential. Small scale marketing of bush resources (e.g. shea butter, charcoal), crafts (e.g. mats, brooms, beds) and the sale of the limited produce from elders' and women's fields (e.g. peanuts, sorghum) all pale in comparison with the dynamic garden sector (Wooten, 1997).

In order to get a sense of the potential income levels from market gardening I did two things. First, I simply asked *nakotigiw* to offer an estimate of how much they could make from their gardening activities. Knowing full well the limitations of this approach I also made several straightforward income projections based on existing crops and my knowledge of the sale prices of various goods.

In the course of my standard *nakotigi* interviews I asked each respondent how much money his garden could generate. While I was aware that the figures would not be dependable or accurate, I felt that important comparative and relative insights could be gained. The range of their speculations is quite interesting. One respondent stated that he could earn up to 750,000 FCFA ($2,500), while another stated that he could earn only 20,000 CFA ($67). Most people (n=8) said they could make about 100,000 CFA ($333). (Note: These figures reflect pre-devaluation rates, 300 FCFA/$1.)

I also made independent income estimates based on firmer established data. In my physical survey of the active gardens I made a systematic count of the number and reproductive status of fruit plantings in each plot. Knowing how many productive plantings there were, how much fruit a tree could give in a year, and average sale prices, I was able to estimate the value of particular crops.

As I mentioned above in the context of cropping strategies, bananas were universally voted the best garden crop. Gardeners firmly believed in the value of bananas. Mature fruit-yielding banana plantings were present in all garden plots, except those controlled by the three women. As noted above, these women had yet to plant any fruit trees in their plots.

In making the calculations I relied on my survey data, estimates of crop size and on sale price records. The number of plantings was firm and accurate. The potential production (in kilos) per planting per year was a conservative estimate. Rehm and Espig (1991) state that under well-managed conditions an individual mature banana planting can yield a crop, in the form of a bunch of fruit, every 4-6 months. They estimate that these bunches can weigh between 35-40 kilos. Considering that conditions in Niamakoroni are not necessarily optimal for banana cultivation (i.e., there is restricted understanding of issues of ecophysiology and fertilization strategies, as well as a myriad of production constraints), I estimated only one harvest per planting per year and a conservative bunch weight of 20 kilos. (Based on my own direct observations, some individuals in the community did harvest more than once a year and some did obtain heavier bunches. For example, producers often told me that their banana bunches weighed between 35-40 kilos upon sale in Bamako. Likewise, Becker (pers. comm. 1996) found bunch weights of 35 kilos at Namasadankan.) As far as the price used in the calculations, over the year I recorded sale prices for all crops whenever possible. The range for a kilo of bananas was 80-100 FCFA. In making my projections I used the mean sale price, 90 FCFA/kilo.

Based on my calculations, the value of the banana crop alone in Niamakoroni during the 1993-1994 period was $35,064. The individual with the largest number of banana plantings (n=736), Shimbon Jara, could have made up to $4,416 from this one crop alone. In this light, Shimbon's own estimate of a total possible garden income of $2,500 appears quite conservative. The individual with the fewest banana plantings (n=36), Baje Jara, could have made $216. His income projection was $133. Clearly, the garden heads were conservative estimators of their gross incomes.

Having similar data for the papaya crop, I was able to make parallel projections. In making these calculations I used an estimated crop size of 40 fruits per tree per year and an average price of 4,000 FCFA per basket of 25 fruits. The projected value of Niamakoroni's papaya crop for the year was $9,668. The individual with the most mature plantings (n=76), Dansoni, could have earned $1,621 from this crop. The individual with the fewest mature plantings (n=4), Sunje, could have made $85.

These few examples clearly indicate that the potential incomes from market gardening are considerable, especially for Mali, which has a very low per capita income (i.e., $260, Imperato 1996). Based on proceeds from these two crops alone the gross per capita income for the 183 residents of Niamakoroni would be approximately $244 – almost the national average! And this figure is based on conservative estimates for only two crops. However, I should caution the reader that we know that such income is not metered out equally across the population. As I discuss elsewhere (Wooten, 1997; 2003a.) income generated through gardening is most definitely not distributed uniformly in the community. Most significantly, as I mentioned above, the vast majority (19/22; 86 per cent) of the garden leaders were married men and these individuals are the primary benefactors of this relatively lucrative livelihood diversification strategy. However, despite an unequal pattern of participation, the production of specialized fruits and vegetables in this community is certainly an activity in which relatively large amounts of cash can be generated. As such, it represents a valuable addition to the livelihood portfolios of at least a sub-set of Niamakoroni's population. Market gardeners in this community are clearly involved in a rewarding agricultural intensification process, a process that enhances their livelihoods with an in the inflow of cash.

Market Gardening as a Viable Livelihood Diversification Strategy in Niamakoroni

Why has this livelihood diversification strategy worked? What assets and/or institutions (Ellis, 2000) have contributed to the success of the market gardening graft in Niamakoroni? I suggest that there are three central factors that make this activity possible: 1) changes in regional political economy, 2) the suitability of the local agro-ecological environment, and 3) the strength of the base food system – the rootstock in this grafting operation.

Bamako's population has expanded steadily and dramatically since the French set up their administrative center there at the end of the 19th century. In 1994, it was estimated to be home to more than 800,000 people (Diarra et al., 1994, p.230) and more recent estimates place the number at just over 1 million.

Furthermore, according to Diarra and colleagues (1994, p.239), only 7 per cent of the population of Bamako is now engaged in agriculture and/or livestock production. Clearly, urbanization in Bamako, as in other contexts around the world, has been associated with a major shift in production and consumption patterns. This shift has come in the form of increased dependence on rural areas for cereal staples (Staatz, Dione, and Dembele, 1989), as well as for new, more specialized agricultural products as well.

Over the decades since French colonial troops began consuming locally grown fresh produce, a significant group of Bamako's residents have become increasingly more interested in acquiring and consuming fruits and vegetables (Development Alternatives, Inc., 1990; Pale, 1955; République du Mali, 1992). Changes in diet due to such factors as governmental nutritional campaigns and consumption shifts in an emerging middle class and the presence of a large number of foreign aid workers mean that there are increasing numbers of consumers for specialized horticultural items in the capital. For communities such as Niamakoroni that are within bicycle or 'market distance' of the capital, location within the regional market is a key asset that can be used in livelihood diversification.

Because market gardening is primarily a dry season activity it is restricted to very distinct locations, areas with adequate water resources for irrigation. Areas that fit this requirement are limited to lowlands with high-water tables or streambeds. The people of Niamakoroni refer to such areas as *falayorow* (lowlands) or *koyorow* (stream-lands). At any point throughout the year these areas stand in relative contrast to the rest of the village landscape. While most of the area around the village is hilly, open savanna with trees and shrubs appearing only intermittently, these areas are relatively low, closed environments with almost continuous tree cover. In the midst of the dry season, when the vast majority of the area around the community shifts to the various shades of yellow and brown so much associated with the West African savanna, these areas remained verdant, a constant reminder of the humidity of the rainy season.

The relatively lush character of Niamakoroni's lowlands and stream areas stems from the dynamics of the area's watershed and specifically from the presence of small streams (*kow*), as well as a high water table (PIRL, 1988). Although the stream that runs through the village's main lowland rarely exceeds two meters in breadth and a meter in depth, residents claim that it carries water throughout the year. Thus, the gardeners of Niamakoroni have a fairly rare natural resource at their disposal. Their dry season streams are a real local asset.

The expansion of market gardening in Niamakoroni is supported by a relatively strong 'base' food system. As I noted above, household members work together during the rainy season to produce food stocks that will keep them fed throughout the year. If all goes well, this food system provides a stable and dependable foundation for forays into the commercial realm. As I mentioned, all people have the right to pursue independent activities to earn incomes. They are able to do so because they have a firm subsistence base. The gardeners and the charcoal producers in the community carry out their activities with energy and subsistence security provided through their participation in a collective food economy. Should a tomato crop fail or a charcoal endeavor go awry, individuals will still have a meal. Moreover, gardening occurs at a time when there are very few household labor demands. While the food system depends on timely collective input during the rainy season, it does not require devoted labor during the dry season. In this sense, the gardeners are making use of local institutional structures and processes organized at the household level in order to enhance their personal livelihoods.

A Prospect for Other Rural Malian Communities?

The market gardeners of Niamakoroni individuals are pursuing a livelihood diversification strategy in which they can take advantage of their site-specific position within the regional political economic environment and their local agro-ecological endowment. And, they are doing so from a firm subsistence 'base' foundation. Simply put, the conditions are right for a successful market gardening graft in this community.

However, this constellation of factors does not occur uniformly in Mali. For those in farming communities without access to water for dry season horticultural activities or those in communities far removed from urban food markets or trading centers, fresh produce production is not an option. People in such communities can and do try to generate income in other ways (Brock and Coulibaly, 2000). Many migrate in order to obtain cash. Some produce charcoal or gather fuelwood. If environmental conditions are right, some devote part of their rainy season labors toward the production of crops such as cotton or peanuts which can be stored and/ or transported more easily and sold on the domestic or international market.

In short, market gardening will not be a suitable livelihood diversification strategy for most rural Malians or for many of their counterparts in other rural African settings. However, for some well-positioned people who have access to key assets and the support of a healthy food economy, commercial horticultural production does present an opportunity for enhancement. Moreover, it is a strategy that is rurally based, that does not compete with food production processes, and that offers a relatively significant return to labor. For these reasons, it might be more sustainable than other alternatives. For example, migration can leave communities with a labor shortage at key moments in the production cycle. Cash crop production during the rainy season can compete for critical land and labor resources. Even small-scale charcoal industries can threaten local plant communities and overall environmental stability (for example Wooten, 2003b). Moreover, because it is a viable rurally based production process, market gardening offers a way for young men to stay in the community. Their continued presence can facilitate the maintenance of healthy intergenerational relations and transfers of knowledge. In this regard, it is worth noting that Niamakoroni is one of the few places in contemporary rural Mali where we have good evidence for the continued significance of hallmark Bamana expressive culture such as the famous *ciwara* performance tradition. (Wooten, 2000)

Wider Implications: The Importance of Local Initiatives and Local Constraints

Like their counterparts in low-income countries across the African continent and around the globe (Carney, 1998; Ellis, 2000; and Scoones, 1998), scores of rural people in Mali are actively seeking to diversify their livelihoods – in some cases, for basic survival and in others as a way of enhancing their life conditions (Brock and Coulibaly, 2000). What general lessons can be learned about rural livelihoods and their diversification from this case study?

While it is unlikely that the specific livelihood diversification strategy discussed here will be appropriate for large numbers of poor rural farmers, the case offers an important general lesson for those concerned with poverty reduction in low-income countries. It is important to bear in mind that no outside assistance has been rendered to the aspiring market gardeners of Niamakoroni. No non-governmental organization (NGO) executives or planners have developed 'projects' to serve them, no state extension agents have 'advised' the local population on new techniques. Rather, enterprising individuals have read their situation, have identified their assets and have drawn on their institutional security to respond forcefully to an emerging market opportunity for specialized goods.

Universal strategies for poverty reduction have proven largely ineffective over time. By contrast, the livelihood diversification approach to improvement of quality of life rural areas stresses the effectiveness of locally tailored developments, developments in which local people identify and mobilize site specific the assets and institutions. This case supports the notion that local people, living in rural settings, working with keen knowledge of local resources and local constraints are sensitive to, interested in, and able to diversifying in order to enhance their livelihoods. If conditions are right and risks are limited, rural people will pursue novel livelihood diversification strategies. The nature of the strategies they adopt or pursue will, of course, depend on the suite of assets and institutions present.

In recent years, the Governments of Mali and other low-income African countries have announced their firm commitment to poverty reduction campaigns in rural areas. Apparently, the African state is increasingly more eager to support sustainable rural livelihood diversification processes. This case suggests that the visions and actions of rural people may offer some of the best insights into effective ways forward in this process.

Note

1 My research in Mali has been funded by a variety of sponsors over the years: Fulbright, NSF, the US Department of Education, the Department of Anthropology at UIUC, the African Studies Center at UIUC, the James S. Coleman African Studies Center at UCLA and the College of Arts and Sciences at the University of Oregon. I am truly grateful for the support provided by all these entities. Larry Becker and Tom Bassett have offered valuable input along the way. The people of Niamakoroni have been truly amazing in their hospitality and patience. Aw nice! Thank you all! Finally, I thank Bill Moseley for drawing me into the African Studies Association 2001 panels that gave rise to this publication project and for his diligent efforts in editing this volume. Bill and I first met in Mali in 1987 and it is wonderful to know that our Mali paths continue to cross to this day. I ni ce!

References

Becker, L. (1990), 'The Collapse of the Family Farm in West Africa? Evidence from Mali.' *Geographical Journal* 156(3), pp. 313-322.'

Becker, L. (1996), 'Access to Labor in Rural Mali.' *Human Organization* 55(3), pp. 279-288.

Becker, L. (2000), 'Garden Money Buys Grain: Food Procurement Patterns in a Malian Village.' *Human Ecology* 28(2), pp. 219-250.

Brock, K. and Coulibaly, N. (2000), 'Sustainable Rural Livelihoods in Mali.' *IDS Research Report 35.* Brighton: IDS.

Carney, D. (1998), 'Implementing the Sustainable Rural Livelihood Approach.' In Carney, D. (ed.) *Sustainable Rural Livelihoods: What Contribution Can We Make?* London: Department for International Development, pp. 3-23.

Creevey, L. (1986), 'The Role of Women in Agriculture in Mali.' In L. Creever (ed.) *WomenFarmers in Africa: A Study of Rural Development in Mali and the Sahel.* Syracuse: Syracuse University Press.

Development Alternatives, Inc. (1990), *A Pre-Feasibility Study of Malian Horticultural Export Crops.* (A paper prepared for USAID/Mali).

Diarra, S. *et al.* (1994), *Mali. In Urbanization in Africa: A Handbook.* Tarver, J. (ed.). Greenwood Press, pp. 230-245.

Ellis, F. (2000), *Rural Livelihoods and Diversity in Developing Countries.* Oxford: Oxford University Press.

Grisby, W. (1996), 'Women, Descent, and Tenure Succession among the Bambara of West Africa: A Changing Landscape.' *Human Organization* 55(1), pp. 93-98.

Grosz-Ngaté, M. (1986), *Bambara Men and Women and the Reproduction of Social Life in Sana Province, Mali.* Ph.D. dissertation, Michigan State University.

Hart, K. (1982), The *Political Economy of West African Agriculture.* Cambridge: Cambridge University Press.

Imperato, P. (1996), *Historical Dictionary of Mali.* Scarecrow Press.

Konate, Y. (1994), *Household Income and Agricultural Strategies in the Peri-Urban Zone of Bamako, Mali.* Ph.D. dissertation, State University of New York, Binghamton.

Lewis, J. (1979), *Descendants and Crops: Two Poles of Production in a Malian Peasant Village.* Ph.D. dissertation, Yale University.

Meillassoux, C. (1981), *Maidens, Meal and Money: Capitalism and the Domestic Community.* Cambridge: Cambridge University Press. (French orig. 1975).

Norman, D., Newman, M. and Ouedraogo, I. (1981), 'Farm and Village Production Systems in the Semi-Arid Tropics of West Africa.' *Research Bulletin No. 4.* Hyderbad, India: ICRISAT.

Pales, L. (1955), *L'alimentation en A.O.F.* Dakar: ORANA.

Paques, V. (1956), *Les Bambara.* Paris: Presses Universitaires de France.

Projet Inventaire des Ressources Ligneuses et Occupation Agricole des Terres au Mali (PIRL). (1988), *Notice de Cercle, Cercle de Kati, Région de Koulikoro.* Bamako, Ministère de l'Environnement et de l'Élevage, Direction Nationale des Eaux et Forêts.

Rehm, S. and Espig, G. (1991), *The Cultivated Plants of the Tropics and Subtropics.* Weikersheim, West Germany: Verlag Josef Margraf.

République du Mali. (1992), *Rapport National sur la Nutrition.*

Scoones, I. (1998), 'Sustainable Rural Livelihoods: A Framework for Analysis.' *IDS Working Paper 72.*

Staatz, J., Dione, J. and Dembele, N. (1989), 'Cereals Market Liberation in Mali.' *World Development* 17(5), pp. 703-718.

Thiam, M. (1986), 'The Role of Women in Rural Development in Segou Region of Mali.' In Creevey, L. (ed.) *Women Farmers in Africa.* Syracuse: Syracuse University Press.

Toulmin, C. (1992), *Cattle, Women and Wells: Managing Household Survival in the Sahel.* Oxford: Oxford University Press.

Villien-Rossi, M.L. (1966), 'Bamako, Capitale du Mali.' *Bulletin d'IFAN*, sér. B, 28 (1-2), pp. 249-380.

Wooten, S. (1997), *Gardens Are For Cash, Grain Is For Life: The Social Organization of Parallel Production Processes In A Rural Bamana Community (Mali).* Ph.D. dissertation, University of Illinois.

Wooten, S. (2000), 'Antelope Headdresses and Champion Farmers: Negotiating Meaning and Identity Through the Bamana Ciwara Complex.' *African Arts* 33(2), 18-33, pp. 89-90.

Wooten, S. (2003a), 'Women, Men and Market Gardens: Gender Relations and Income Generation in Rural Mali.' Human Organization 62(2), pp. 166-177.

Wooten, S. (2003b), 'Losing Ground: Gender Relations, Commercial Horticulture and Threats to Local Plant Diversity in Rural Mali.' In Howard Borjas, P. (ed.) *Women and Plants: Gender Relations in Biodiversity Management and Conservation.* London: Zed.

Chapter 8

Risk Positions and Local Politics in a Sahelian Society: The Fulbe of the Hayre in Central Mali

Mirjam de Bruijn and Han van Dijk

Introduction

Ecological variability poses enormous challenges for people inhabiting semi-arid regions all over the world, and for Sahelian pastoralists and cultivators in particular. The ensuing insecurity about ecological conditions for crops and pastures is the main problem with which Sahelian populations have to contend to ensure their survival.

Normally, ecological risks are treated either as an individual matter or as a stochastic phenomenon striking individuals or groups of people at random. People's individual strategies tend to be geared towards the aversion or minimization of risks by diversification of income sources and low-input production strategies, such as extensive cultivation and livestock keeping. Others have pointed to the necessity of developing collective strategies to counter risks and to the fact that societies have been deeply influenced by the extreme variability in ecological conditions. The French geographer Gallais (1975) coined the term *la condition sahélienne* to refer to a number of innate tendencies that react in a specific way to collective and individual risks in Sahelian societies. In earlier work we have argued that the strategies and cultural understandings people develop may be understood as being structured around the single most important problem, namely ecological variability (De Bruijn and Van Dijk, 1995).

In this chapter, we want to take the discussion further and argue that ecological risks are highly politicized phenomena. Historical analyses over the years have demonstrated that risks in the Sahel were not evenly distributed over the population (see Cissoko, 1968; Tymowsky, 1978; Iliffe, 1987; Gado 1993). Indeed political hierarchies and rules of access to productive resources acted to divert the consequences of ecological calamities onto other more vulnerable groups (see De Bruijn and Van Dijk, 1993, 2001; Van Dijk, 1999). In short, individuals and groups occupied structurally different 'risk positions' (Beck, 1992) with respect to their exposure and vulnerability to ecological and other risks, and were differentially excluded or included in networks mediating access to productive resources and sources of capital necessary to mitigate the consequences of risk.

This chapter focuses on the changing risk positions of social groups since the beginning of the 20th century in the Hayre, a Sahelian region in central Mali where Fulbe pastoralists vested their power in the 17th and 18th centuries. It shows how a combination of changes in the political context, an ecologically unstable environment and internal politics have led to a new division of risk positions in society and to the exclusion of specific groups from certain environmental resources and amenities. The discussion is organized as follows: a short description of socio-political conditions in central Mali at the end of the 19th century (placed in the context of the ecology of the Sahel and of the influence of French policies on local social and political relations); an analysis of changes after Mali's independence (trends after the political transition of 1991 and the impact of administrative decentralization on communities); and an assessment of the link between regulation of resource and changes in risk positions. A case study of the situation in Dalla, the capital village of the Fulbe chiefdom in the Hayre, highlights the changes in risk positions between the various social groups. In the final section we discuss the idea of collective action. It seems that individual differences in risk positions preclude the formation of political alliances to counter political, economic and ecological marginalization.

The Sahel

The Ecological Situation

The area known as the Sahel is a semi-arid region stretching in an easterly direction from the Atlantic Coast as far as Sudan and beyond. Located just south of the Sahara, the climate is characterized by high temperatures, high evaporation, and a rainy season of 3-4 months with an annual rainfall of between 200 and 600 mm. The amount of precipitation is highly variable in time and space. Annual rainfall in any given year may deviate by as much as 40% below or above the long-term average (Put and De Vos, 1999). Even higher deviations in biomass production have, therefore, been observed (De Leeuw *et al.*, 1993). Combined with variations in the physical environment such as soil characteristics, slope and topography, a large variety of production conditions can be observed in any single year.

Most inhabitants of the Sahel subsist on cereal cultivation, livestock keeping, gathering, or any combination of these activities. Other characteristics such as population density, main cropping system, type of livestock production system, and integration in the market vary from one Sahelian area to another (Raynaut, 1997). More recently, temporary or permanent migration to better-endowed areas in the Sudanic, Guinean and even to the humid forest zone on the coast has increased in importance. In order to make the best use of the variability in rainfall and physical conditions, migration is used by each group or individual as a risk mitigation mechanism. However, the degree and the direction of this mobility may vary from one year to another and from one group to another. Even within one group, a large variety of strategies may exist depending on family situation, resource endowments, personal history and social position.

The Political Ecology of Risk in the Nineteenth-Century Sahel

At the end of the 19th century when the colonization of the Sahel by the French was a reality, Sahelian societies were hierarchically organized. The social strata were politically defined. A similar structure could be found in other West African regions: in the Futanke Empire of Bandiagara, Segou and Kaarta, Fulbe empires in the Adamawa and Sokoto areas in northern Cameroon and Nigeria and in the Futa Jallo in Guinea. Polities of the Tamacheck and the Sonrai, though not empires at the turn of the century, were also structured in this vein due to the influence of earlier empires. At the apex of the hierarchy was a political elite alongside a religious elite (Islamic or animistic), then a large group of vassals among whom herders and cultivators were to be found. At the bottom of the hierarchy were the slaves who formed the class of non-free people as opposed to the other strata who were regarded as nobles. Between these groups were intermediary groups of ill-defined status such as merchants, bards and artisans.

These empires were built on the exploitation of a high-risk ecological environment through control over people. Land was available in abundance but according to historical sources (Cissoko, 1968; Gado, 1993; Webb, 1995), the ecological environment was, even throughout the 17th to 20th centuries, characterized by recurrent droughts and by irregular rainfall. The wealth of the empires had to be organized around the exploitation of the environment and of the people. The latter was done through organized labor in the form of slavery and the trade in people, the accumulation of livestock and people by raiding neighboring societies and the control over trans-Saharan and regional trade systems. This system of government can be explained as an organization to deal with the risks inherent in the ecology of the Sahel. Thus a specific political organization developed in which the raiding of other people, enslavement and the denial of their rights to own their own means of production were the most basic elements of control (cf. Reyna, 1990).

People were assigned a specific position in this political framework and were differentially exposed to risk. By the very fact that slaves had no control over the fruits of their own labor, and frequently not even over their own land, they were coerced into handing over most of the commodities they produced. In situations of scarcity they were the first to face hardship. Vassals, by the nature of their status, occupied an ambiguous position. In principle they had an independent position *vis-à-vis* the political apex. However, they were often forced to give in to claims by the political class and to hand over part of their production.

Risk was not evenly distributed within these groups. People varied in their vulnerability to risk depending on the number of livestock and the amount of land they owned, the size of their family, and social and political relations. Mere chance, for example in the case of livestock disease, the incidence of pests, illness of family members or the localized nature of rainfall, could make the difference between poverty and a position of relative wealth.

Risk in the Sahel was also closely connected to mobility, which has always been the principal risk- mitigation mechanism in the region. Slaves were, in general, immobilized in villages to control their productive activities, whereas nobles and vassals were allowed to travel and move with their animals to look for better pastures and opportunities to ensure survival. Vassals, who were cattle herdsmen, moved regularly with their herds to find the best pastures and water resources. Religious clerics traveled to administer religious services and organize instruction. With increasing control from the political center, the regulation of access to resources was centralized and the movements of herdsmen became regulated (Van Dijk, 1999; De Bruijn and Van Dijk, 2001).

Over time, with French colonization, followed by the independence of African states, this configuration of risk positions changed fundamentally and led to transformations in the exploitation of natural resources. The two processes of changing risk positions and changing exploitation of the environment are closely linked and resulted in a situation in which new forms of coexistence, marginality and mobility developed.

Nineteenth-Century Fulbe Society in the Hayre

The Hayre is a region in central Mali that has always been on the margin of the Inland Delta of the Niger, a resource-rich region that has frequently been the object of contestation. The Hayre is located in the middle of the Niger Bend in central Mali, south of the mountains connecting the Bandiagara Plateau with Mount Hombori. The area can be subdivided into a zone covered with forest on clayey soils with laterite in the subsoil, and a zone of sand dunes covered mainly with annual and perennial grasses, herbs and sparse trees. Most of the cultivators and groups of sedentary Fulbe pastoralists can be found in permanent villages at the foot of the mountains in the north of the area, where the water table is closer to the surface. Towards the sand dunes, camps of mobile Fulbe pastoralists are to be found as well as hamlets of cultivators who moved into this area because of lack of space in their home villages near the mountains and on the Bandiagara Escarpment and Plateau. A more elaborate description of the area and its position in the regional political ecology can be found in De Bruijn and Van Dijk (1995, 2001).

At the beginning of the 19th century, the Fulbe gained control over much of central Mali and built the Maasina Empire. The Diina as it came to be known, was led by a pious Muslim, Sheeku Aamadu, who tried to turn it into a strictly organized theocracy. However, the influence of the rules and reorganization did not extend to the periphery. In the Hayre where another Fulbe group had gained power in the 17th-18th century (De Bruijn and Van Dijk, 2001) the Maasina influence was significant and contributed to the basic social organization of the communities.

Different population groups lived in the Hayre. Cultivators and herdsmen made use of the area but both livelihoods were clearly separate. The herdsmen were organized in loosely structured bands that also undertook mutual raids to accumulate cattle and people. The herders were Fulbe and Tamacheck. Why the Fulbe gained dominance in the area is not clear. It might have been due to the support they received from the larger Fulbe empires or to their need to ensure access to pastureland and to defend their herds against other invading or raiding Fulbe or Tamacheck groups. The fact is that they became the dominant political force in the region, and established Maasina with Dalla as the main village. Fulbe political leadership went hand in hand with the Islamization of the region (see Angenent *et al.*, 2002).

As to be expected, the cultivators in the region were sedentary. They lived in organized settlements with a high degree of central political control to minimize the risk of plunder from neighboring tribes. Most of the cultivators belonged to the Sonrai, Dogon, Kurminkoobe and Bambara ethnic groups.

The Distribution of Ecological Risk

A number of divisions in social and political terms can be discerned at the end of the 19th century based on ethnic affiliation, modes of subsistence, religion (Muslims versus animistic groups), and raiding or non-raiding groups. Internally these societies were also divided into social categories based on power differences and on the notion of nobility that was linked to being a free person. Within Fulbe society this hierarchy followed the scheme outlined above including the political elite (the *weheebe*), the religious elite (the *moodibaabe*), noble vassal groups who herded cattle (the *jallube*), nobel merchants and courtesans (the *diawaambe*), artisans (the *nyeeybe*) who are linked to the noble people, and slaves (the *maccube*) who are considered non-noble, non-free and of minor status at the bottom of the social order.

The slaves were the labor reservoir. Among them, a division was made between various categories of slaves depending on the status of their master and the slaves' internal organization or hierarchy. Within these social layers, further divisions were made in a hierarchical way between being more noble or more slave than the other. There were many former free cultivators among the slave population who were simply incorporated by the noble people to work for them. After all, all the land in the Hayre belonged to the noble Fulbe and the political and religious elite had most of the land under its control.

For the *Jallube* herders land had a different significance. They depended on access to pastureland and not to small cultivable plots. The herdsmen also possessed house slaves, but did not own slaves or estates as the elite did. In fact it was the political and religious elite who owned all the land and who decided who could have access to it. Being a slave may have been preferable to being a poor wandering herder because a slave at least had access to land through his master, who in turn wanted his part of the harvest.

During times of drought however, access to the produce of the land was reserved for the noblemen who sent their slaves away if times became too hard. These slaves migrated temporarily or simply died. Many herdsmen lost their cattle and became poor people and potential slave labor for the elite, or they migrated to see if they could find a niche elsewhere. In the political circumstances of the time, it seems highly probable that they then became slaves in another political constellation (see Iliffe, 1987).

Free cultivators were always prey to the warring Fulbe in need of labor for their estates and their houses and probably also for trade in order to generate revenue. To protect themselves against the Fulbe these cultivators built their villages on the escarpment and developed a warning system against raiding bands. The Dogon system is extensively described in this way (Gallais, 1965, 1975; Van Beek and Banga, 1992).

The assignment of risk positions was orchestrated by the political elites who favored the Islamic clergy because of their spiritual qualities, and some groups of artisans. The pastoral groups were largely left to their own devices as long as they handed in tribute and participated in raids and wars (but were exploited in the sense that they were the guardians of the herds of the noble elite). The elites defended the grazing lands of the pastoralists, but this service was of limited value in drought years. The slaves carried the largest burden during drought times. They often died, were sent away, or had to work hard in order to produce food for their masters.

On the other hand the social hierarchy worked as a safety valve for people who had lost their basic source of subsistence, for example a herder who had lost his cattle. A poor herder could be incorporated into the social system as a slave or in another lower group and thus survive difficult times. Nevertheless most poor would have opted to leave and become a slave elsewhere.

Thus the division of risk positions was in the hands of the political elite who were supported in this by the Islamic clergy. Herders as well as slaves had to live according to the whims of the elite who controlled all social relations and access to land and other resources.

Changes in the Twentieth Century

French colonization brought fundamental changes to Fulbe livelihood structure. In the course of twenty years they established an effective monopoly on organized violence throughout the Sahel. This had a tremendous impact on the organization of the management of natural resources and the economy. The position of cultivators, who were contained within well-defined areas where they enjoyed relative safety and protection from raiding, altered fundamentally. Now protected by the French colonial administration, they were able to expand their area of cultivation and within forty years they had occupied most of the area of sand dunes south of the Hayre (See Gallais, 1975). Villages of Sonray and Dogon descended from the cliffs to the plains.

For some time the Fulbe were able to prevent occupation of their pastureland because of the difficult water situation but in the end were unable to stop further encroachment on their land. The territorial control they exercised was based on military prowess, which acquired no legal recognition of the colonial state since it declared all the vacant and unoccupied land to be the private property of the state. Pastureland and forest were both regarded as vacant and unoccupied. This process continues today and gradually all the remaining open areas of the plains are being put under cultivation.

Though the French officially abolished slavery, it took much longer for the *maccube* to acquire some degree of independence. The liberation of slaves was not a top priority for the French administration and their span of control in remote areas such as the Hayre was so limited that they were not able to exercise daily control there. In fact they gave the political elite a free hand in maintaining control over the court slaves who were simply registered as family members of the noblemen. The name of the former slave group changed to *riimaybe*, which means 'liberated slaves'. Today the *riimaybe* group consists of all groups who had servile status (bondage) in pre-colonial times.

A major change in this field was triggered by the famine of 1913-14. In the absence of modern inventions such as food aid and labor migration, this famine, recorded as the worst of the 20th century, ravaged the Hayre. Whole quarters of villages were wiped out (see also Suret-Canale, 1964; Marchal, 1974). Slaves died in their scores or were sent away to more fertile areas around the lakes northwest of the Hayre, the available food having been seized by the nobles. Since slavery had officially been abolished, nothing obliged the slaves who went away ever to return to their masters and a large number seem to have broken with their masters during this period.

After the Second World War, French colonial policy took a new turn. Elections were organized and could only be held if all citizens were free and equal in the eyes of the law. This in effect dealt the final blow to the institution of slavery. Relations of dependence expressed in exchange of labor and resources continued to exist between noblemen and their former slaves but officially power could no longer be exercised.

The vassal herdsmen were gradually freed from their overlords. They were no longer needed as the basis of military power and they no longer had access to labor and cattle in the form of booty from raids. Unlike the slaves of the political elite, these slaves took their independence and their former masters lost a source of manual labor. They continued to herd their cattle and, compelled by lack of labor, had to undertake cereal cultivation themselves thus becoming semi-settled transhumant livestock keepers.

Their overlords, the *weheebe* chiefs, had to adjust to the new power. They became part of the colonial administrative system that intervened actively in their affairs and deposed traditional authorities when they were not performing their tasks according to their standards. The overlords were made responsible for the collection of taxes and became complicit in the colonial administration, since they were allowed to keep some of the taxes for themselves. As a result they were no longer accountable to their subjects but instead to the colonial administration. Having lost their military function, they tried to maintain an image of importance by participating in the colonial administration's festivities, showing up with all their former military pomp (see Angenent *et al.*, 2002). In short, the extraversion of Fulbe society in the Hayre became a fact.

After independence many more things began to change and new players entered the field. Under the First Republic, headed by Modibo Keita, attempts were made to break the last vestiges of power of the traditional authorities regarding control over labor and over natural resources. State-run enterprises were made responsible for agricultural production, collectivization of land was promoted, and new government services were given the task of exercising control over all aspects of life, such as forest resources, land tenure, the development of livestock and cereal production.

After 1968 the pendulum swung back when the Second Republic was established. The socialist experiments were discontinued but attempts to modernize agricultural production were intensified. The reason for this was the beginning of a period of devastating drought, which lasted from 1968 until the mid-1990s. Aid money poured into the country to help reform the agricultural sector that was regarded as backward, unsustainable and ultimately responsible for the bad ecological situation and the desertification of the Sahel.

These efforts proved as futile and ineffective as the attempts at collectivization and modernization had in the early 1960s (see Van Dijk and De Bruijn, 1995; De Bruijn and Van Dijk, 1999a, 1999b) and only contributed to a further erosion of the socio-economic position of important sectors of the population. At the beginning of the 1990s, these policies were abandoned after the fall of the Second Republic. The Third Republic embarked upon an ambitious scheme of administrative and political decentralization with the aim of restoring local accountability for the welfare of the population (see Van Dijk and Hesseling, 2002).

This process of administrative decentralization could be potentially beneficial for local population groups because it brings politics closer to marginalized groups. On the other hand it is feared that the potential for conflict will increase since there is no longer a central power to quash these conflicts, and that processes leading to exclusion and decentralization will just be re-enacted at this lower administrative level (Van Dijk and Hesseling, 2002). Further research is warranted since these decentralized administrative structures only started to function recently.

The Depastoralization of Natural Resource Management in Dalla

In this section the focus is on the specific changes that have occurred in the division of access to natural resources. It is the story of the gradual marginalization of the pastoral groups in the area over the 20th century. Their risk position has become worse than the risk position of the former slave groups. We turn our attention to the situation in and around Dalla, the oldest capital of the chieftaincy of the Fulbe in the Hayre.

Changing Risk Positions in the Chiefdom of Dalla

Although the elite of Dalla lost all its administrative powers and was deprived of its former slave labor, it has kept a firm grip on politics and natural resource management around the village. Contrary to the situation amongst the Dogon, the *riimaybe* were not helped to acquire land, although their weak position *vis-à-vis* the Weheebe was noticed by the French colonial government. A French lieutenant wrote to his superiors: '*J'ai appris que les Bérébés* (Weheebe: authors) *empechaient les Riimaybe et Habe d'étendre leurs lougans, dans le but évident d'empêcher les malheureux se pouvour jamais rachêter*'.[1] The *riimaybe* did not have the right to acquire land if they were directly put to work in their master's house. If a Dalla noble wanted to sell his land to a *diimaajo* (pl. *riimaybe*), the Chief of Dalla prohibited it and bought the plot for himself. This continued to be so in Dalla even after the *riimaybe* were completely liberated in 1946. The chief was also given the authority to patrol the bush to enforce the French Forestry Code and to exploit it with local labor for his own profit.[2] He could thus also prevent the clearing of fields in the bush.

The 1968-73 drought was bad in the Hayre but did not have a disastrous effect on the local economy. The harvests were poor and livestock perished but the population disposed of sufficient reserves to survive the dry spell. At least this is how the population remembers that period of drought today. What was new, however, was the aid in food and money from the international community, which made the situation easier even though part of this aid was siphoned off by corruption at the level of the administration. The drought of the 1980s had a much more profound impact. Livelihoods were severely affected by these droughts and a large proportion of the population was forced to seek refuge in more fertile regions, having lost their livelihood in the Hayre.

In the post-drought years, the problems have not decreased. Conflicts over natural resources have risen, and it is easy to see that, with the advancement of time and an increase in drought and poverty, the pastoral groups around Dalla have lost out to their competitors, the Dogon, *diawaambe*, *weheebe* and *riimaybe*. Cultivators from Dogon villages have started to clear fields in pasture areas and the *riimaybe* of Dalla have sought new opportunities to occupy the land. The *diawaambe*, some of whom grew rich during the droughts, have laid claims to both pasture and agricultural land.

Competition between the Dogon and the Fulbe The following case illustrates the process of changing positions in local politics. In 1964, even before the droughts, the Chief of the Dogon of Diamweli, Kansa Ongoiba, asked the Chief of Dalla for permission to clear fields on the Seeno-Manngo at Petil Camil. Yerowal Nuhum, the Chief of Dalla refused. But after Nuhum's death and after the 1968-73 drought, the Dogon of Diamweli began to clear land on the Seeno-Manngo at this site and established a cultivation hamlet, i.e. a hamlet only used during the cultivation season. They felt they were in a strong position because one of Kansa's sons had become *attaché de cabinet* in the Ministry of Interior. Bukary Yerowal Dikko, who was chief at that moment united his most important Fulbe deputy chiefs from Karena, Nani and Sigiri and went to the *chef d'arrondissement*, who sided with the Dogon. The Fulbe attacked the administrator and were put in prison. A brother of the Chief of Dalla, who worked in Segou as teacher, was called to intervene on their behalf with the *Commandant de Cercle*, one administrative level higher. He agreed to arrange matters on condition that the Fulbe would not claim the tax money they were entitled to from the administration (as the American government compensated the Malian government for lost tax revenues provided they agreed not to levy taxes on livestock during the drought). The Fulbe agreed, the money was left with the administration and the Dogon were removed from the Seeno-Manngo. In 1976 the conflict flared up again. The district administrator, a Pullo (pl. Fulbe) this time, called all the parties together and decided in favor of the Fulbe. A covenant was signed agreeing that from then onwards no new cultivation sites would be allowed on the Seeno-Manngo and that the area would be reserved as pasture. However, in 1984 the Dogon of Boumban, just south of Dalla, bribed the *Commandant de Cercle* and obtained permission to cultivate on the Seeno-Manngo near Daajem.³

Changing   positions within Fulbe society Another conflict over land, between Dalla and Karena and between various groups in Dalla, shows that the Fulbe were also divided internally. In the early 1980s the *riimaybe* of Dalla started clearing land on various occasions in the bush between Dalla and Karena. The Fulbe of Karena and three other pastoral settlements protested because the fields were located near a number of small ponds that provided water for livestock in the rainy season. Not only did the fields hinder access to the ponds but the Fulbe would also run the risk of having to pay compensation money if their livestock accidentally damaged crops in nearby fields. The *riimaybe*, on the other hand, appealed to ancestral rights to these fields. In the distant past there had been Kourminkoobe villages in this area and one can still find the remnants of blast furnaces. The *riimaybe* consider themselves, having become free, the rightful heirs of the Kourminkoobe who were captured by the Fulbe. The Chief of Dalla, Bukary Yerowal, backed them. However, under pressure from the pastoralists he turned down the claim by the *riimaybe*.

Later, after the drought of 1985 the Chief of Karena visited the Chief of Dalla, with a request to reconsider the occupation of these fields. After all, the Fulbe had lost their cattle and were eager to cultivate the more fertile land in depressions where water was available. At that moment the bard of Dalla and some Diawaambe, who cleared the land without anyone knowing about it, had already occupied the best parts of the area. The Fulbe of Bankassi, the settlement nearest to the fields, still regard this land as having been stolen from them. They considered the area as pastureland that should remain so, and given the provisions of the Land Tenure Code they were correct. Their ancestral claims were not recognized under the provisions of the Land Tenure Code with respect to the clearing of land because all land that has been vacant for more than ten years automatically becomes the (private) property of the state. Fields in this area would restrict other activities and were too close to water resources. Permission to clear fields here would have to be refused given the regulations in force. The administration did not change this situation because the agricultural officer responsible was bribed. So, this encroachment on pastoral land was made in silence.[4]

In the end the Fulbe lost because they were deprived of their source of political power, cattle that had perished in the drought. They were also no longer necessary as political and military support for the *weheebe* because the Fulbe armies had ceased to exist. In the past the conflict of interest between pastoralism and cultivation, which is equally a conflict between flexibility and the centralized political organization of the Maasina Empire, was regulated by the management scheme of the Diina. Now even the Diina rules are left for what they are and the management of natural resources is being taken over by the Malian state, which represents sedentary and anti-pastoral interests.

Changing positions in the village of Dalla The last conflict to be discussed here is even closer to the heart of power of the chiefdom. It was a severe threat to social cohesion in the village of Dalla and concerned areas set aside as pasture way back in the 19th century: the *harima* and *burti*. The *harima* is reserved pastureland next to the village meant for small ruminants and *burti* are strips of land acting as passageways for animals during times of cultivation.

The *harima* is one of the most fertile pieces of land in Dalla. Animals have dropped their dung on the soil for ages and though in the past most was transported to the surrounding fields, a lot of nutrients have remained in the soil. With declining numbers of cattle and growing pressure on land around Dalla, as testified by the accounts of conflicts above, pressure on the chief to open the *harima* for cultivation also mounted, although this would militate against Diina rules and even modern legislation since customary rights were recognized in this body of law. The Chief of Dalla, Bukary Yerowal, and later on Hamidou Yerowal gave in to pressure but decided that it would be better to take advantage of the *harima*, and thus were among to first to occupy a field as near as possible to the village and a cotton garden where they could plant mango trees. As a result the whole village rushed to snatch their share of the available land. At the moment only the market place and degraded parts have escaped occupation.

Apart from the conflicts between villagers about the boundaries dividing their newly established fields, a major conflict arose in 1991 over the pastoral vocation of the *harima* and the *burti*. When the rush on land occurred around 1985 there were hardly any people with livestock but by 1991 some *diawaambe* had been able to reconstitute considerable herds and were confronted with the problem of where to leave their animals at night. All the land around the village is under millet cultivation and fields block all road access. They asked the chief to remove occupation of this land. The chief gave in and had his brother and nephew lay out the *burti*. The *Riimaybe* occupying this land responded by threatening to chase the animals. The *diawaambe* then put more pressure on the chief, declaring that they would complain to the administration if he did not force the *Riimaybe* off the *burti*. This would mean the chief would be removed from office.[5] The chief consulted the former Imam, his father-in-law, as to what to do. The well-respected old man, who is regarded as a saint in Dalla, took the side of the *diawaambe* because it was closer to the Islamic doctrine of the Hayre. He called the *Riimaybe's* spokesmen and told them to stop the conflict and abandon the fields on the *burti, harima* and some of the ponds that were in contested territory. Now the hierarchy has been turned completely on its head. The former subjects of the pastoralists, the *diawaambe* and the *Riimaybe*, are contesting hegemony over natural resources in Dalla. Nor is the chief any longer in control as he has to resort to the moral authority of the Islamic clergy.

From these conflicts it becomes clear that the influence of the *jallube* pastoralists in Dalla has become insignificant. In the first conflicts in the 1960s the *weheebe* defended their interests. Later on they supported the *riimaybe* who were looking for land to cultivate because of the declining harvests *vis-à-vis* pastoral interests. In the conflicts following the droughts there seems to be a return of pastoral power in Dalla but this power is not represented by the *jallube* pastoralists. Instead *diawaambe* entrepreneurs, who manage commercial herds, have become the champions of the pastoral way of life, and *moodibaabe*, defending what they believe to be Islamic orthodoxy.

Another important change in comparison with the past is the reference that is made to the modern state as the ultimate authority to appeal to in case of serious conflict. The extent to which people are able to win conflicts is closely related to their bargaining power in relation to the administration. In the first conflict, the chief was able to turn down the appeal without recourse to the state. After the drought in 1973, the administration had to be bribed, just as in the second conflict bribery resolved the conflict. In the third conflict, the threat of appeal to the state against the chief was sufficient to force a (temporary) solution. In this game of power the *Jallube* no longer play a role. In Dalla itself there are no *Jallube* families left. In the surrounding areas there are three small hamlets of *Jallube*, Boussouma about 2.5 km away with seven families, Hoggo Loro 1.5 km away consisting of one family, and Bankassi with four families. The rest have migrated to other parts of Mali or sought refuge on the Seeno-Manngo.

The parties in all these conflicts agree on nothing except for the fact that the power of the *Jallube* is at present negligible. With the droughts and the loss of their cattle they have lost their only source of power. Their political power has disappeared although they have often got their way by bribing the administration. In the absence of cattle they have no bargaining power left. This weak position is the result of a long historical process. However, the position of the *riimaybe* as a group of cultivators is developing in reverse. They are profiting from state policy and agrarian developments in the region. Although in ideology they are still regarded as the lowest stratum of society in economic terms and also in social reality, they have a much better position than the pastoralists.

The Encroachment of 'Outsiders' on the Seeno-Manngo

To complete the history of the relations between the Inner Delta and the Hayre we will briefly recount the events concerning the pastures of the Seeno-Manngo. This history sketches the impact of policy with regard to natural resource use on a regional scale on the risk positions of the various groups in the Hayre. In regional politics, the influence of the Fulbe elites is negligible. So even if they wanted to defend the rights of their pastoral vassals they do not have the means to do so.

Until fairly recently this vast area of high-quality range[6] was only used during the rainy season and a short period afterwards by local herds from the Hayre in the north and from the Seeno-Gonndo and the Mondoro area in the south. The use of the area was dictated by the seasonal availability of water. After a period of deterioration at the end of the 19th century, herds prospered once again in the colonial period and the French saw the danger of overexploiting the delta. At the same time they also wanted to develop the livestock sector. They appreciated the potential of the Seeno-Manngo, not only for pasturing animals in the growing season but also in the dry season. Their reasoning was that pressure on the pastures in the Inner Delta could be relieved (which they considered overexploited or converted to rice cultivation). The development of watering points on the Seeno-Manngo could primarily serve to keep the herds on the drylands for a longer period of time (Doutresoulle, 1952).

This policy was based on the assumption that all the herdsmen from the drylands would direct their herds to the Inner Delta of the Niger after the rains had stopped. This is, however, only true of the Fulbe herdsmen who have lost most of their pastures to the colonization of their territory by Dogon cultivators who descended from the Bandiagara Escarpment after the French conquest of central Mali in 1893 (see Gallais, 1975). For the Hayre, Seeno-Manngo and the area around Mondoro this is not the case. The herds in these zones remain as far as possible in their home region. Herdsmen and cultivators alike practice the cultivation of millet on permanent fields. This is only possible because of the manure that is produced by the cattle and goats that remain in these zones during the dry season. The watering points that they developed by themselves over the course of the 20th century were the basis for this shift to agro-pastoral land use (Van Dijk, 1995). The external policy to open up the Seeno-Manngo disturbed this system.

During the colonial period attempts were already being made to draw the Seeno-Manngo into the orbit of the delta herds. Between 1956 and 1958 seven boreholes were drilled and equipped with windmills to draw water. The exploitation of the pastures and agricultural land around these boreholes caused considerable strife among the region's inhabitants. As there were no provisions for the maintenance of the windmills, they were soon out of order again (around 1960) (Gallais and Boudet, 1979). After the 1969-73 droughts, another attempt was made to develop the Seeno-Manngo. The livestock service, with loans from the World Bank, started a well-digging program (see Gallais 1984) to make more permanent exploitation of the Seeno-Manngo possible. However, according to the pastoralists, this also attracted cultivators to the area (ODEM, 1978). In addition there were more grandiose plans to drill a number of boreholes in the middle of the dune area and equip them with solar pumps that supposedly demand minimal maintenance. From this scheme only one borehole is still functioning (see Van Dijk and De Bruijn, 1995).

With the drought of 1983-85, the effects of the government wells became clearer. Enormous herds from the north and even from Burkina Faso were attracted to the Seeno-Manngo, one of the few areas where water and some range were still available. This led to enormous overstocking and, as a result, 75% of the local livestock perished. The herdsmen of the Seeno-Manngo were not able to ward off the outsiders because they had no say over the modern wells.[7]

Since then, every rainy season sees the arrival in the Seeno-Manngo of numerous herds owned by urban traders and civil servants from the Inner Delta, conducted by salaried herdsmen. They cause damage to the fields of the local inhabitants and use up the range. They try to stay in the area as long as possible because the pastures of the waiting areas near the Inner Delta are also overexploited. The pastures in the inland delta also have decreased enormously. The livestock service tried to promote this tendency by deepening the ponds, creating new wells and improving the old wells but when pastoralists wanted help to improve or repair their own wells their requests were turned down. Officials refused to discuss the issue of land tenure around the government wells. The local pastoralists want this issue to be settled before any new initiatives are taken. Specifically they are worried about their position *vis-à-vis* newcomers.[8]

Decentralization in Mali

Since the political transition in 1991, the Mali government has embarked on a project of political decentralization. In 1999 the final stage was realized with elections for mayors and the establishment of rural communities. The idea of this process is to bring governance closer to the ordinary people so that they themselves may make decisions about their lives.

Dalla has become a small rural commune consisting of 18 villages. The constellation of this commune reflects power relations. In fact it consists of a large village of noble people: *weheebe, moodibaabe* and *diawaambe* and their *riimaybe*, separate *riimaybe* villages and some temporary hamlets of herdsmen. The *beweejo* mayor of this commune found his support among *riimaybe* and *weheebe*. He is a brother of the present chief of Dalla. The *jallube* pastoralists are invisible, living in camps on Dalla territory but having no say in this political game. It is clear that they were hardly involved in the election campaigns. For them the chief is another *beweejo* who is not prepared to represent them when necessary.

The *weheebe* retain a firm grip on all matters concerning land use and politics. Though the *riimaybe* are nominally free, they are entirely dependent on the *weheebe* for access to land since the land around Dalla remains in the hands of the latter. In return the *weheebe* rely on their votes in local municipal-council elections.

In another place inhabited predominantly by pastoralists, the pastoralists have claimed a commune of their own, having obtained permission from the government to establish it and to elect their own mayor and community council. This independent stance has its historical roots in pre-colonial times when this village claimed independence from the Fulbe chiefdoms in the region. However, over the past decades numerous Dogon agriculturalists have settled in hamlets on their pastureland and turned thousands of hectares into cropland. To secure their claim to this cropland they are trying to develop water resources with the help of outside agencies. The pastoralists have no way either of preventing these people settling on their village land or of forcing them to abandon their pastureland. Thus the ability to regulate access to territory, pastureland and cropland is dependent on the specific context and political organization of each community and the status of its inhabitants within their own society.

Finally the different groups in the Hayre have changed places in the hierarchy of risk positions: the *diawaambe* and *riimaybe* have become better off, while the *jallube* pastoralists have become worse off.

Individual Differences and Collective Action

One wonders whether there is not a basis for collective action that may counter this kind of process. It is clear that the traditional socio-political hierarchy does not provide a basis for this and only when it comes to imposing state policies on local pastoral groups do these hierarchical relations serve a purpose. However, as was shown in the preceding section, the way these relations are operated only serves to deepen the marginalization of the pastoral groups. The rise in the political position of the groups surrounding the traditional political elite in Dalla (*diawaambe, riimaybe, moodibaabe, nyeeybe*) is not the consequence of their collective efforts and concerted action. They are carried on the stream of political developments in the region that favors their interests: the favorable policy for sedentary agriculture and the decentralization process, and their influence as electorate in the elections. The reverse is true for the pastoral *jallube*.

Of course these groups are not an undivided whole and not all members have the same risk position. In this chapter we have chosen to present the social categories as collectivities because, as social history shows, they have functioned and today still operate as such in local politics. People have a sense of belonging to a social category. It is part of their ideology.

However, this does not mean that these social categories are the basis for collective action as a number of structural factors inhibit the development of institutions or movements for collective action. In the past, collective action could only be set in motion by the political center through the vertical ties with subordinate social categories The first is the fragmented nature of Fulbe political organization. Society is not only subdivided in status categories but, at the level of these groups, organization is highly segmentary in nature. Between the vassal pastoralists, the only group with sufficient people and status to challenge the authority of local leadership and the administration, all kind of opposition exists amongst the various lineages composing this group, making it difficult to organize or even to envisage a unified group. For political leaders it is easy to play a game of divide and rule.

Another major factor inhibiting collective action is the covariance of risk, meaning that people in the same risk position have to face the same risks at the same time. For them it is more profitable to invest in their own enterprise than in collective devices for risk mitigation (Platteau 1991). This is clear when one analyzes collective mechanisms for the redistribution of productive resources such as land and livestock. These are all geared to the transfer of property to a restricted group of kin and do not involve a kind of solidarity or general reciprocity towards members of the community (Van Dijk, 1994; De Bruijn, 1999).

The third point follows on from this. Though groups of people may be attributed similar characteristics within a structural political framework this demonstrates little about a specific individual's particular situation or risk position. Differences between individuals and families in wealth and vulnerability to risk are so vast that they preclude the formulation of any common interest in relation not only to risk mitigation strategies but also to outside intervention and contextual changes. The image of an egalitarian pastoral society is a myth (Sobania, 1990).

Conclusion

We have tried to show some aspects of the relation between a high degree of risk and the political ecology of pastoral societies in the Sahel. The concept of risk position was introduced to pinpoint the position of groups and individuals in relation to their exposure to risk and vulnerability. With the help of this framework we have shown how the structural position of the former vassals of Fulbe chiefdoms, leading a pastoral way of life, has eroded to such an extent that they have become the most marginalized group in Fulbe society. On the other hand developments have enabled the former slave groups to climb up the risk hierarchy.

During the colonial period the Fulbe political elite became detached from their following, the vassals. Today they are no longer accountable to their former vassals but rather to their former slaves who form the basis of their political power in the sedentary villages and are far more accessible for community council elections. The mobile pastoralists have lost their claims to land and, given their mobile existence, have moved out of the political centers to marginal areas beyond the reach of election campaigns to areas where no or only limited cultivation takes place.

A more detailed analysis of recent political change with respect to administrative decentralization reveals that this process is continuing unabated. However, the scope for collective action to counter these transformations is limited given a number of structural factors in the organization of Fulbe society, and the group of former vassals in particular.

Notes

1 National Archives file 2E-4: Politique indigène: Correspondances cercle de Bandiagara: 1899-1907, Le Lieutenant Gateau à cercle de Macina, 18 April 1903.
2 National Archives file 3R-6: Foresterie au Soudan, Le Gouverneur des Colonies et le Gouverneur du Soudan Français à M.M. les Administrateurs Commandants des Cercles de la Colonie, 15 December 1927. National Archives file 3R-39: Eaux et Forêts: 1916-1918, L'Administrateur en chef de 1-er Classe à Ms. Les Administrateurs des Cercles et le Commandant de la Région de Tombouctou 15 April 1916.
3 This story was told by Moussa Yerowal Dikko, then a teacher in Segou, who intervened on behalf of his family members with the *Commandant de Cercle*. The other leading persons in this conflict, Kansa Ongoiba, Yerowal Nuhum Dikko and Bukary Yerowal Dikko, have all died. The administrators retired and moved out of the region.
4 This conflict was related to us by several informants, among whom the late bard, himself one of the people involved, Allay Jangiina, the former aid of chief Yerowal Nuhum, and several Fulbe from settlements around Dalla, Nu Saidu Jallo from Hoggo Loro and Hamma Ngarya Jallo of Bankassi.
5 Many more incidents occurred in the past that would have justified his removal. This last grave incident would tilt the balance.
6 Doutresoulle (1952: 66) estimates the potential area of the Seeno-Manngo, Seeno-Gonndo and Seeno Mondoro at 5,000,000 ha.
7 In addition a Tuareg chief got permission to equip one of the boreholes drilled in the 1950s with a motor pump and watered his own cattle and those of his dependents in this way for as long as he deemed necessary.
8 In our presence, a senior official at the Ministry of Natural Resources and Livestock Keeping asked local herdsmen to cooperate with the Delta herdsmen in order to manage the Seeno-Manngo. The local herdsmen were very shocked. They felt they had lost their customary rights to the Seeno-Manngo.

References

Angenent, C., Breedveld, A., De Bruijn, M. and Van Dijk, H. (2002), *'Le Hayre de Alu Maane, Récit sur un petit royaume peul'*, Leiden: Brill.
Beck, Ulrich (1992), *Risk society. Towards a new modernity*, London: Sage.
Cissoko, S-M. (1968), Famines et épidémies à Tombouctou et dans la Boucle du Niger du XVI-e au XVIII-e siècle. *Bulletin de l'IFAN*, XXX, série B (3), pp. 806-821.
De Bruijn, M. (1999), 'The pastoral poor: hazard, crisis and insecurity in Fulbe society Central Mali.' In Azarya, V., Breedveld, A., De Bruijn, M. and Van Dijk, H. (eds) *Pastoralism under pressure, Fulbe societies confronting change in West Africa*, Leiden: Brill, pp. 285-312.
De Bruijn, M. and Van Dijk, H. (1993), 'State Formation and the Decline of Pastoralism: Fulani Pastoralists in Central Mali.' In Markakis, J. (ed). *The Decline of Pastoralism in the Horn of Africa*. Den Haag: Institute of Social Studies. London: The Macmillan Press Ltd, pp. 22-142.
De Bruijn, M. and Van Dijk, H. (1995), *Arid Ways. Cultural Understandings of Insecurity in Fulbe Society, Central Mali*. Amsterdam: Thela Publishers.
De Bruijn, M. and Van Dijk, H. (1999a), 'Insecurity and Pastoral Development in the Sahel', *Development and Change*, 30(1), pp. 115-139.

De Bruijn, M. and Van Dijk, H. (1999b), 'Ressources vivrières de base ou élevage ? Deux projets de développement chez les Fulbe éleveurs du Mali central.' In Botte, R. Boutrais, J. and Schmitz, J. (eds.), *Figures Peules*, Paris: Karthal, pp. 445-462.

De Bruijn, M. and Van Dijk, H. (2001), 'Ecology and Power in the Periphery of Maasina: The Case of the Hayre in the Nineteenth Century.' *Journal of African History*, 42 (2001), pp. 217-238.

de Leeuw, P., Diarra, L. and Hiernaux, P. (1993), 'An Analysis of Feed Demand and Supply for Pastoral Livestock: The Gourma Region of Mali.' In Behnke, R., Scoones, I. and Kerven, C. (eds). *Range Ecology at Disequilibrium: New Models of Natural Variability and Pastoral Adaptation in African Savannas*. London: ODI, IIED, Commonwealth Secretariat, pp. 136-152.

Doutresoulle, G. (1952), *L'élevage au Soudan Français*. Alger, E. Imbert éditeur.

Gado, B. (1993), *Une histoire des famines au Sahel: Étude des grandes crises alimentaire (XIXe-XXe siècles)*. Paris: l'Harmattan.

Gallais, J. (1965), 'Le paysan dogon.' *Les cahiers d'Outre-Mer*, VIII, pp. 123-143.

Gallais, J. (1975), *Pasteurs et paysannes du Gourma: la condition sahellienne*. Paris: Centre National de la Recherche Scientifique.

Gallais, J. (1984), *Hommes du Sahel, espaces-temps et pouvoir. Le delta intérieur du Niger 1960-1980*. Paris: Flammarion.

Gallais, J. and Boudet, G. (1979), *Étude d'un avant projet de code pastoral, concernant plus spécialement la région du Delta Central du Niger au Mali*. Maison Alfort, IEMVT.

Iliffe, J. (1987), *The African Poor: A History*. Cambridge, Cambridge University Press.

Marchal, J.-Y. (1974), *Récoltes et disettes en zone soudanienne: chronique des saisons agricoles au Yatenga (Haute Volta) 1907-1973*. ORSTOM, section de géographie.

ODEM (1978), *Évaluation d'une enquête d'opinion auprès des populations sédentaires du Séno-Mango*, Mopti, Opération de Développement de l'Élevage dans la région de Mopti.

Platteau, Jean-Phillipe (1991), 'Traditional Systems of Social Security and Hunger Insurance: Past Achievements and Modern Challenges', in Ahmad, E., Drèze, J. Hills, J. and Sen, A. (eds), *Social Security in Developing Countries*, Oxford: Clarendon Press, pp. 112-171.

Put, M. and Sjoerd De Vos (1999), 'Klimaatonderzoek in West Afrika.' In Rooilijn, Raynaut, Claude (dir.) (1997), *Sahels. Diversité et dynamiques des relations sociétés-nature*. Paris: Karthala.

Reyna, S. (1990), *Wars without end: The political economy of a precolonial African state*. Hanover: University Press of New England.

Sobania, N. (1990), 'Social Relationships as an Aspect of Property Rights, Northern Kenya in the pre-Colonial and Colonial Periods.' In Paul, W., Baxter, T. and Hogg, R. (eds.) *Property and People: Changing Rights in Property and Problems of Pastoral Development*. Manchester, Dept. of Social Anthropology and International Development Center, University of Manchester, pp. 1-20.

Suret-Canale, J. (1964), *Afrique noire, occidentale et centrale, tome 2, l'ère coloniale 1900-1945*. Paris, Éditions Sociales.

Tymowsky, M. (1978), 'Famines et épidémies à Oualata et à Tichit XIXième siècle.' *Africana Bulletin* 27, pp. 35-53.

Van Beek, W. and Banga, P. (1992), 'The Dogon and their Trees.' In Croll, E. and Parkin, D. (eds). *Bush Base: Forest Farm, Culture, Environment and Development*. London: Routledge, pp. 57-75.

Van Dijk, H. (1994), 'Livestock transfers and Social Security in Fulbe Society in the Hayre, Central Mali.' *Focaal*, 22/23, pp. 97-112 [Special issue Franz Von Benda-

Beckmann, Keebet Von Benda-Beckmann, Hans Marks (eds), Coping with insecurity: an 'Underall' Perspective on Social Security in the Third World].

Van Dijk, H. (1995), 'Farming and Herding after the drought: Fulbe agro-pastoralists in dryland central Mali.' *Nomadic Peoples* 36/37, pp. 65-84.

Van Dijk, H. (1999), 'Ecological Insecurity and Fulbe Pastoral Society in the Niger Bend.' In Azarya, V., Breedveld, A., de Bruijn, M. and van Dijk, H. (eds.) *Pastoralists under Pressure? Fulbe Societies Confronting Change in West Africa.* Leiden: Brill, pp. 237-265.

Van Dijk, H. and Mirjam de Bruijn. (1995), 'Pastoralists, Chiefs and Bureaucrats: A Grazing Scheme in Dryland Central Mali', in J.P.M. van den Breemer, C.A. Drijver and L.B. Venema (eds) *Local Resource Management in Africa*, pp. 77-96, Chicester: John Wiley & Sons.

Van Dijk, Han and Gerti Hesseling. (2002), 'Mali. de gevaren van decentralisatie', in Jan Abbink and Rijk Van Dijk (eds), *Grenzen en ethniciteit*, Assen, van Gorcum (in Dutch).

Webb, J. Jr. (1995), *Desert frontier: ecological and economic change along the Western Sahel, 1600-1850.* Madison WI: University of Wisconsin Press.

PART III
GLOBAL ENVIRONMENTAL
POLITICS AND CONSERVATION
IN AFRICA

Chapter 9

Buying (into) and Selling Conservation Among Maasai in Southern Kenya

Jennifer E. Coffman

[Then newly appointed KWS Director David Western's] goal is to help Kenyan pastoralists grab a direct share of the $436 million in tourism-related revenues that flowed into the country last year. If landowners find wildlife more valuable than crops or cattle, Western hopes, they will start to protect it themselves.

> Yvonne Baskin (1994) 'There's a New Wildlife Policy in Kenya: Use It or Lose It'

Kenyans are practical thinkers, not reflectors of imported ideologies.

> Former Kenyan President Daniel arap Moi (1986) *Kenya African Nationalism: Nyayo Philosophy and Principles*

Introduction[1]

The importance of wildlife to former and present-day Kenya is undeniable. Nearly all of Kenya's pre-colonial communities hunted as part of their subsistence strategies; animal products were exchanged within and between different African communities as parts of tribute and bartering systems; ivory and other animal products were central to centuries of trans- and intercontinental trade; and meat from wild animals and ivory supported early European explorers and colonial troops, as well as comprised a significant portion of the household budget for colonial administrators and early settlers (Gibson, 1999:4; see also Western, 1994; Bonner, 1993; Yeager and Miller, 1986; Collett, 1987; Saitoti, 1978). Today, especially in Maasailand, where rural Kenyans live and on what they base their livelihoods inextricably connects them to wildlife-related policies and businesses, as well as wildlife[2] itself. But, the industries and interests surrounding Kenya's wildlife extend far beyond the country's borders, as representatives from governments, businesses, conservation groups, and nongovernmental organizations (NGOs) all around the world claim a stake in Kenya's wildlife policies and use rights (Gibson, 1999; Bonner, 1993). Community-based wildlife resource management programs attempt to address some of these competing demands, while also ensuring livelihoods for growing populations of humans and functioning habitats for variable populations of other species.

Community-based wildlife resource management within Kenya's Maasailand[3] operates within a much larger trans-cultural logic steeped in conservation ideals. Conservation ideology in Kenya began in earnest during the colonial era, and it prescribes techno-managerial practices that target not only wildlife, but also land, livestock, and people. This approach can include what is called community conservation. Usually funded from development budgets, community conservation has proliferated since the 1980s along with the expansion of NGOs' activities in Africa (see Barrow, Gichohi, and Infield, 2001; Berger, 1993).

In this chapter, I use ethnographic detail from one localized conservation effort, called *Maendeleo kwa Uhifadhi* (MKU),[4] to provide both a case study of how locally-incarnated practices exist within global discourses that inform national and international wildlife conservation policies. By examining the relations between the organization MKU and the community of Maasai who are involved with it, we can address the following questions: how do we (as researchers, planners, and participants) make sense of community conservation? How might small-scale projects encourage diversification of economic activities, while still enabling the preservation of wild animals, given that economic diversification appears to be the most likely means for survival for focal communities? Following that, isn't it good enough for community-based conservation efforts to enable members of the community to stay *where* they are, in a geographic sense, even if not exactly *how* they were, in regards to intra-community relations and livelihoods?

Analytic Framework

Anthropology can play a crucial role in exploring wildlife conservation because the discipline is dedicated to the study of human beings in all times and places, and thus provides various tools and frameworks to understand how humans inhabit, construct, represent, impact, claim, and compete over their environments (see Hodgson, 2001; Escobar, 1999b; Brosius, 1999). Importantly, anthropology embraces the notion of change over time – that human societies are not fixed and bounded, but rather always engaged in process, in change. Socio-cultural anthropology approaches studying process by being critical and self-reflective. It can guide studies of environmental issues, such as wildlife conservation, by exploring how to write in multi-sited contexts; how to 'discern articulations between the local and the global'; how to comprehend emergent forms of political agency; how to identify and analyze the ways in which knowledge is produced; how to describe and understand phenomena of resistance, attempts to theorize nature, and discourses of development (Brosius, 1999: pp.278-79; see also Escobar, 1999a and 1995; Hodgson, 1999, 2001; Rocheleau *et al.*, 1995; O'Connor, 1998; Descola and Palsson, 1996; Leff, 1995).

While remaining firmly rooted in anthropology, I have adopted the general and complementary framework proposed by political ecology. This approach proposes that environment serves as locus and resource-base for the ways in which power relations have enacted and perpetuated patterns of inequality within variably defined analytical levels, from 'local' to 'overarching world system' (see, for example, Brosius, 1999; Escobar, 1999a, 1999b, and 1995; Biersack, 1999; Ingold, 1998 and 1993; O'Connor, 1998; Bates and Lees, 1996; Peet and Watts, 1996; Rocheleau, Jama, and Wamalwa-Moragori, 1995; Rocheleau, Steinberg, and Benjamin,1995; Martinez-Alier, n.d.). Accordingly, the manipulation and implementation of wildlife conservation policy should be viewed as historically-situated and culturally-informed manifestations of broad political negotiations.

Through both anthropology and political ecology, I recognize that 'discourse matters' (Brosius, 1999). As will be seen below, concretized discourse – that which has been set down in writing through government policies, legal land surveys, and contracts – matters tremendously in relation to conservation ideology and pastoral livelihoods. This recognition is crucial to understanding the avenues and constraints of operation experienced by contemporary conservation projects, like MKU.

Maendeleo Kwa Uhifadhi (MKU)

Within Kenya, wildlife tourism generates more than one-third of the nation's foreign exchange revenue, and NGO-sponsored conservation projects that focus on community-based wildlife resource management continue to grow and attract more international donor funds than ever before (Gibson, 1999; see also Bonner, 1993; Miller and Yeager, 1994). Since Kenya's two most heavily trafficked wildlife viewing areas, Maasai Mara Reserve and Amboseli National Park,[5] are located within Maasailand, this emphasis on internationally sponsored wildlife conservation has had a significant impact on Maasai peoples. Former Kenya Wildlife Service director (1994-1998) David Western described the natural transition to policy-regulated, community-based conservation among Maasai: 'Maasai had traditionally hunted wildlife during droughts and regarded them as second cattle... [m]onetary and other benefits from wildlife, in other words, could be seen as a Maasai tradition in disguise' (1994: p.34).[6] Ethnography can help us to explore what it means to and for Maasai when the management of 'second cattle' becomes the primary source of their livelihoods – despite ongoing 'wildlife/human conflicts.'

Kenya Wildlife Service's working definition of wildlife/human conflict is 'any and all disagreements or contentions relating to destruction, loss of life or property and interference with rights of individuals or groups that are attributable directly or indirectly to wild animals' (KWS, 1994: p.23). Contemporary revenue-sharing programs, in which gate fees for national parks and reserves are shared with communities residing along the peripheries, have attempted to mitigate wildlife/human conflict in Kenya and encourage support for state policies regarding wildlife, thus promoting a favorable environment for tourism. Many Maasai argue, however, that the lands appropriated for parks and reserves, ineffective revenue-sharing projects, restrictive government laws regarding wildlife, and even the order of words in the very term 'wildlife/human conflict'[7] all underscore how state-level systems of governance have historically privileged wildlife over rural people. *Maendeleo kwa Uhifadhi* (MKU) was established with these tensions in mind and proposed to serve as a bottom-up responsive alternative to the aforementioned policies.

Not associated with a park system or dispersal area, Maasai involved with MKU do not benefit from revenue-sharing projects linked to the national parks and reserves, although they do tend to share in the grievances mentioned above. MKU is overseen by two directors, both of whom are men, elders, and Maa-speakers – characteristics which provide essential cultural capital in rural, patrilineal Maasailand. MKU is described by its directors as a grassroots conservation project guided by ideals of long-term, conservation-based development. MKU stems from both directors' desire to provide economic incentives for local Kajiado Maasai to maintain their land and support their herds in concert with wildlife populations, despite increasing trends of individuation of land titles, restriction of access to decent grazing lands, boundary disputes, population growth, and non-sustainable resource extraction, such as marble and gemstone mining, and charcoal production. MKU intended to use its property and the properties of its participating neighbors to protect local wildlife and attract an eco-tourism clientele. The eco-tourists, in turn, provided the necessary income to pay dividends to participating Maasai, and as such, literally support the directors' assertions that 'conservation pays'. More recently – and in light of a general decline in Kenya's tourism sector – MKU has itself had to refocus its means to support its overall goals, as will be discussed below.

The general approach to community-based wildlife conservation stems from a variety of discourses that have worked together, and occasionally against one another, to create and enforce the need for the conservation of what are called 'natural resources,' which include wildlife. As such, community-based wildlife conservation appeals to the selective preservation of certain species through conservation, for example, expert managerial techniques (Brulle, 1996; Brosius, 1999). Most, if not all, community-based conservation programs rely on the ability to delineate and enforce boundaries, including those between gazetted and privately owned lands, as well as between and among private landholdings. This may seem obvious and even necessary. There are several important corollaries, however, that are worth mentioning, and they include: active monitoring of land boundaries and household membership for the purposes of evaluating participation and providing remuneration; the explicit provision of fiscal incentives and compensation for participation; and reliance on and validation of agreements to particular conditions through paper contracts, land surveys, and other forms of written documentation. It is worth reiterating that concretized discourse, that which has been set down in writing, matters tremendously as a means to enforce behaviors agreed upon in contracts and to access particular resources.

The dominant conservation narratives in Kenya have been perpetuated by donor experts, expatriate advisors, leisure-time conservationists (many of whom are not Kenyan nationals), media coverage of environmental crises and impending species extinctions, particular academic agendas, certain brands of international assistance, and domestic constituencies (see Adams and Hulme, 1998; Brockington, 2001). That latter group is of keen interest for the simply stated observation that some of the imported agendas and discourses have indeed become inextricably integrated into local ideologies prior to the conception of MKU. Thus, MKU evolved from idea to organization while negotiating 1) then-new trends in community-based wildlife conservation inspired in part by Zimbabwe's CAMPFIRE;[8] 2) the extant cultural logic of discrete boundaries of land ownership at the level of homestead, and, in some cases, household; and, 3) serious drought coupled with increasing human population size and, thus, competition over basic resources.

All Maasai who participate in MKU's conservation programs belong to homesteads situated on properties that are held through individual land titles; none belong to any current incarnation of group ranches.[9] To participate in MKU's wildlife conservation programs, landowners[10] agree in writing to accommodate and even encourage the expansion of wildlife populations by 1) not allowing hunting, charcoaling, gemstone or marble mining on the portions of their property committed to the MKU program, 2) maintaining a 'grassbank', a portion of their land reserved for drought use only (the rest of the land is then grazed rotationally), 3) prohibiting anyone else's livestock from grazing on their land, and 4) allowing wildlife counts to occur on their properties so that wildlife populations, as well as participants' adherence to supporting those wildlife populations, can be monitored. The directors of MKU see these criteria as a means of improving pastoral production by increasing livestock health through good grazing land management, as well as supplementing livestock-derived wealth by receiving dividends for helping to conserve wildlife. MKU land is subject to these same practices, and also serves as a grassbank for neighbors during times of drought.

The local pastoral stakeholders can also become stockholders in a fiscal sense, as they invest money in a landowners' association (discussed below) that, along with its attendant bank account, has been designed and overseen by MKU leadership, a board of trustees, and a consensus decision-making process. The stockholders' generate some profits from their abilities to attract eco-tourists to their combined properties. This model of investing in conservation has been actively seized and promoted by those self-identifying Maasai who comprise the community-base of MKU. One participant succinctly stated, 'My family is benefiting.' To abide by the conditions of joining MKU, participants must be aware of their property boundaries, and, ultimately, restrict the use of their properties to members of their own homesteads, all of whom, in effect, are then working in conjunction with MKU standards. As of 2001 (my most recent visit), this accounted for approximately 260 people across two dozen homesteads and nearly 10,000 acres.

Situating MKU

'The key to natural resource management and conservation is knowing where your land is. Otherwise, there is no security if people can dispute it.' So explained Nicholas, MKU's primary director. The events that allowed MKU to become the owner of 250 acres of former Maasai-held land, the ensuing challenges to that ownership, and the ways in which MKU participants subsequently managed MKU and neighboring lands emphasize the recondite issues of ownership and management of land in this region of Kajiado, as well as throughout much of Kenya. Stories of shifting boundaries, land-grabbing, violence, and protests over land rights pervade the Kenyan daily papers and radio news and the popular imagination. These stories and issues of ownership serve both as manifestations of and strong influences on the complex, and occasionally rocky, relationships that existed between MKU directors, staff, and the surrounding community. The colonial history that led to the selling of the land – of that land being sellable at all – provides a necessary context to understanding current struggles between rapidly fading communal ideals and governmentally-sanctioned notions of discrete ownership and measurability of commodified land.

Situating Maasai in Kenya

Neither Maasai peoples nor the state of Kenya in which they are partially situated can be described as a 'discrete functional unit', and yet both are readily identified as groups between which relations are mediated for politico-economic purposes (Haugerud 1995, p.11). Prior to British colonial conquest in the late 19th century, Maasailand encompassed a territory spreading from the east near Lake Victoria toward the coastal plains, and from the highlands north of Nairobi southward, east and west, to the Tanzanian steppe. Within this territory lived a dozen independent groups that did not comprise a singular political system, but nonetheless collectively were Maasai (Fratkin, 2001; Spear and Waller, 1993).

The creation of Kenya, the politico-colonial entity, marked the beginning of an era promoting and enforcing individuated titled land ownership within what had before included less-rigidly defined territories regulated by ownership of many different kinds. By the early 1900s, after having experienced inter-sectional conflict, cattle and human diseases, and European colonial penetration, the Maa-speaking communities in East Africa halted an era of expansion (Waller, 1993). Colonial agreements sanctioned by British and German governments drew a line on a map and thus formally divided Maasai peoples between two colonial administrations, one occupying present-day Kenya, the other Tanzania. Each administration implemented treaties that confined Maasai peoples to reserves and disrupted what had previously been permeable boundaries between pastoralists, cultivators, and foragers. Within Kenya, the 1904 and 1911-12 Agreements, isolating the highlands for colonial settler use, forced Maasai peoples into two reserves, the populations of which were subsequently combined into a 35,000 square kilometer reserve, which has become today's Kajiado and Narok Districts.

Despite restrictions imposed by the Agreements, Maasai pastoralists continued to move their herds irrespective of the boundaries of the Maasai Reserve, where grass or watering points were often not ample. Pastoral praxis included a system of land tenure through which territorial rights to water and pasture were conferred to a particular section or locality (*olosho*) and recognized by other Maasai sections (*iloshon*). Even as such, those territories were neither exclusive nor excluding, as especially evidenced during times of drought. Further, the pastoralists of so-called Maasai territories often welcomed 'acceptees' from non-Maasai communities to live among them, thus challenging the 'legally defined and ethnically exclusive Reserves' designed by colonial administrators (see Waller, 1993, p.227 and *passim*).

Through the establishment of the Kenya Land Commission in the 1930s, the National Parks Ordinance of 1945, the African Land Development individual grazing and stock improvement program in the 1950s, and Group Ranches in the late 1960s, among other efforts, Maasai pastoralists have found their territories usurped and transformed by multiple interests. Development efforts adopted during the colonial and post-colonial administrations targeting Maasai have primarily focused on increased livestock production for the meat industry. Meanwhile, these initiatives have diminished shared access to land either by imposing 'unnatural' collectives (for example, group ranches) or, conversely, by sub-dividing communal localities into private parcels of land. Although some entrepreneurial Maasai, and a number of non-Maasai, have been able to accumulate land for themselves or profit by selling it off, others have been marginalized and become unable to subsist as pastoralists. In the post-colonial era, many of these marginalized Maasai have become at least part-time wage-earners because they have been forced from their lands or as a means to help them maintain those lands.

Owning and Managing the Land

Kenya's rural populations struggle for security within arenas of money-based markets and individual ownership of land. With individuated land titles to marginal lands, many Maasai families in Kajiado and Narok Districts have found themselves without ample grassland and with no water-bearing sites on their properties (Berger, 1993; Western, 1994). MKU was able to set up its operation because one such struggling family, the Olkipaarets, had little choice but to sell a portion of their land.

To briefly summarize, Reverend Olkipaaret,[11] a Maasai, had prospered under the 1950s African Land Development Scheme. As both a local Christian leader and businessman, he was considered a 'progressive' in an area of mostly 'unimproved' pastoralists. He held a title deed to approximately 2,000 acres. He also believed that livestock, especially cattle, should remain at the heart of Maasai community and saw his effort in conjunction with the ALD program as a means to make that possible in the changing political and socio-economic climate of late colonialism.

By the time of the Reverend's death in the mid-1980s, his adult children had begun to raise children of their own, thus sub-dividing the family's property among a growing population. Due to a variety of factors, the family fell into debt, and by 1990 his sons agreed to mortgage a large portion of the family land through the Agricultural Finance Corporation (AFC). Within the next year or so, the Olkipaaret family was in default of their loan, and the AFC threatened to foreclose on their property. Nicholas heard about this from a friend of his who had been an age-mate of Reverend Olkipaaret.

Rural development banks foreclosed on similar properties within Maasailand regularly, and close associates of the bankers benefited by purchasing very cheap land and houses which they could then rent to others (perhaps including the very families which had previously owned them) and/or use the land for altogether different purposes than herding. Nicholas had been searching for land on which to locate permanently. MKU's other director, Olmeut, agreed with Nicholas to purchase a section of the land for an amount that would prevent foreclosure. Nicholas and Joshua, one of the late reverend's sons, served as the primary negotiators, and agreed that the Olkipaaret family would sell to MKU 250 acres of land for the balance of the loan (slightly higher than the going rate per acre at the time). Nicholas was especially pleased; he envisioned the area as an ideal place to start a wildlife conservation project. He was also hopeful that the price he paid for the land, as well as the accommodations he and MKU staff literally built for the Olkipaaret family, would establish the beginnings of a neighborly relationship.

MKU, the conservation organization, became the official, legal owner of 250 acres of land. Nicholas, Olmeut, and MKU staff moved into the area and set up their tents. MKU camp workers, most of whom were Maa-speakers and half of whom were hired from local families, assisted in building new houses for some members of the Olkipaaret family. Although MKU's land purchase was arguably the reason that the Olkipaaret family would be able to retain on most of their land, certain members of the family claimed it was a travesty that they had lost any of their land at all.

In the mid-1990s, a bitter land dispute erupted between the MKU directors and certain members of the Olkipaaret family. By that point, MKU had been operating from that site for two years. Nicholas had received his copy of a new, government map officially demarcating the boundaries between his and surrounding properties. He noticed an error. MKU was missing fifty acres.

The new government map arrived around the same time that rumors of Nicholas's alliance with Safina began to circulate. Safina,[12] a then-unregistered oppositional political party under the partial leadership of Richard Leakey,[13] was not well-received in this region of Kajiado, which had a strong history of support for KANU, the ruling party of then-President Daniel T. arap Moi and Vice-President George Saitoti, the latter of whom claimed Maasai heritage. Further, with Richard Leakey as the most obvious figurehead of Safina, claims of Nicholas supporting Safina fueled local conspiracy theories. In the midst of this charged political atmosphere, Nicholas calculated that the map delivered to him was erroneous. After noting the error, Nicholas said that he walked the perimeter of the property and discovered that some of the beacons marking the property boundary had been moved; not only were they not where he remembered them, but he found evidence that the holes to sink the beacons had been recently dug and the old ones filled in.

Nicholas, along with fellow directors of MKU, had scheduled a meeting with the surveyor, the men of the Olkipaaret family, and local elders, including the Paramount Chief himself. The Paramount Chief called for a new survey, and, not surprisingly, the missing 50 acres were found and returned, on paper, to MKU (this is a highly abridged version of what was an incredibly intriguing survey). The beacons, on the ground, were also replaced.

Tensions eventually subsided. Through ongoing visits and conversations, MKU staff and their neighbors came to know one another better. Meanwhile, several of the Maasai households in the area continued to be mired in debt. They had neither sufficient livestock from which to draw, nor the funds to repay other debts, repair or run any vehicles, cover school fees, or in some cases even meet costs for domestic consumption. As suspicions about MKU began to fade, even initially resistant neighbors began to join the MKU conservation program as a way to generate much-needed revenue consistently, as well as to educate themselves further on the new order of community-based conservation.

In 2000, MKU built upon the conservation program and launched a landowners' association. All participating landowners already involved in the other aspects of community-based wildlife conservation (as discussed above), were invited to join the landowners' association by investing a one-time fee of KSh 2000/ (about US $35 at the time) and then purchasing shares at KSh 100/ each (about US $1.75). The maximum amount of shares a landowner could buy was limited by the amount of land owned. None of the families who purchased shares could afford to buy more than a fraction of their maximum at the time of joining. Returns on shares derived from eco-tourists who visited MKU camp paid a daily rate into the landowners' association's bank account. The shareholders, then, met quarterly, and in conjunction with MKU leaders and a board of directors, decided how to split, reinvest, or otherwise invest the dividends. They also adjusted the cost of new shares. By the end of the first year, the cost of a single share jumped from KSh 100 to 450 (about US $7.90 at that time).

The bigger issue of the almost aggressive acceptance of the association by local Maasai is the increased reliance on and internalization of the power of paper. Land surveys, contractual agreements, bank notes, meeting minutes, and other examples of concretized discourse had become essential to the livelihoods of even rural Maasai. Prior to the arrival of MKU, many had watched former neighbors lose by not learning the rules of precise documentation.

By having clearly delineated and documented property boundaries, approved by and on file with the district surveyor, a landowner could legally protect his – and it was usually but *not* exclusively 'his' – land from being grabbed or encroached upon by an unwelcome outsider. The landowner could use the land title to secure a loan from the bank, as the Olkipaaret family did from the AFC. Of course, the landowner could also default on the loan, as the Olkipaaret family did with the AFC, and possibly lose the land. Now, the landowner can use the land as a measure of investment potential in the landowner's association described above.

Nicholas had described the guiding principle for MKU's conservation projects as encouraging the local community to protect and 'invest' in wildlife resources as a source of wealth. Through MKU, local Maasai receive monetary compensation for maintaining their land according to certain criteria and allowing wildlife to graze upon it. People who maintained their land according to project guidelines received more money than those participants who violated any guideline. Thus, the rules by which local Maasai participated in these conservation efforts reified the boundaries between them and non-participants, as well as among themselves, as a means to provide security over what all participants recognized as scarce resources.

Conservation as Development

How can we now approach what development or donor organizations mean by 'community-based wildlife resource management', a conceptual offspring of the larger category of 'community-based conservation'? I argue that the phrase succinctly includes taken-for-granted notions of certain animals being 'wildlife', with 'wildlife' meaning a 'resource', commodity, thing-to-be-managed; 'management' being designed and/or done by a particular body of experts; and, people of a given 'community' being invited by those experts to participate in a project designed to teach them how to manage the resources of their local area as part of global enterprise. All of this, of course, presupposes the necessity of some version of 'development'.

'Development' is, at best, a highly ambiguous concept, but is often tied to increasing economic growth and expanding engagement in national and international economies supposedly in an attempt to make poor people better off. Critiques of development are now ubiquitous, and they include recognition that development experts have generated programs based on prototypes of generalized environments (for example, semi-arid rangeland, tropical forest, coastal swamp), which are then imposed upon areas roughly similar to a given prototype, where they often fail to meet their stated objectives (see Sachs, 1992; Esteva, 1992; Green, 1993; Danaher, 1994; Korten, 1995; Mander and Goldsmith, 1996; O'Connor, 1998). Often such development-as-economic-growth schemes neglect to contextualize the targeted environment in terms of historical patterns of land use by humans and non-humans. Further, critics charge that development projects seem to operate as an 'anti-politics machine' (Ferguson, 1990; see also Fisher, 1997; Igoe, 2001), overlooking the personalities, contestations, and local-level politics which inevitably impact the likelihood of any project's 'success,' short-term and long-term, while simultaneously expanding bureaucratic power. And, although many development projects propose an 'injection of capital' to activate the project – which is then supposed to somehow take on a self-supporting life of its own – the project is often propped up throughout its duration by outside donor monies and other support (staff, equipment, other goods).

In terms of what they expect 'development' to provide for them, local, rural Maasai people tended to equate development with better meeting basic needs – having access to clean water, fuel, schools, and health clinics. These basic needs are clearly tied into larger logics, and the question remains how best to meet them.

Still promoting sustainable development but pitched as a possible alternative to being 'carried' by the national government and foreign donors, projects focusing on community-based wildlife resource management have been implemented in Kenya, as well as in many other countries. Despite some changes in the ways in which the development apparatus operates through such programs, these projects have yet to prove 'wholly indigenous' or 'self-sustaining' (see Hulme and Murphree, 2001). They may, however, offer some hope for an overhaul in the ways in which government agents and bi- and multilateral donors think about development, as well as about community.

Logan and Moseley (2002, p.7) list the three chief criteria for delineating 'community' in community-based conservation programs as geographic contiguity, social homogeneity, and self-definition. These may seem to be intuitively reasonable policy guidelines, but they are by no means unproblematic. As Logan and Moseley (2002, p.7) state, 'the first two are fraught with conceptual and practical impediments to the third, that is, to coherent local self-definition and resource sovereignty' (see also Agrawal and Gibson, 2001). In a lesson not lost on those who criticized the implementation of group ranches within Kenya, geographic proximity is not necessarily an indicator of social affinity, nor do ascribed boundaries necessarily correlate to local understandings of and access to various resources (i.e., grazing land, watering holes, etc.). Any group of people bounded together under the rubric of community can only bear the appearance of *being fixed* (or fixable) in space or time to someone intent on managing them in a particular sort of way.

Challenging that version of community, and for our purposes here regarding MKU, community should be seen not as some organic, homogeneous whole, but rather as an ad hoc group of neighboring landholders who have agreed to participate in a particular conservation program. This version of community is more closely aligned with the processes of change and movement – even at household levels – that we see on the ground. For MKU, self-identifying Maasai participants, MKU directors, and even certain among MKU staff comprise the community base. They live in close proximity to one another (and as a totality occupy contiguous parcels of land), abide by a particular set of rules, and acknowledge and interact with one another as members of this same 'community-based' program. And, occasionally new members join and others may leave, indicating a change in the constituency over time and therefore better reflecting rural realities.

Theorizing Community-based Conservation

Community-based wildlife resource management can be described as steeped in a tense mixture of preservation and conservation ideologies. Preservationism and its conceptual younger cousin, deep ecology, suggest that nature should be viewed as an intact whole, irreducible to the sum of its parts, and that 'the richness and diversity of all life on earth have intrinsic value' (Brulle, 1996: pp.65-66). Preservationists claim that wilderness is essential to the well-being of humanity and human values, and that the preservation of wilderness should supercede economic concerns (Brulle, 1996, p.65). Conservation, as a theoretical orientation, has its roots in the idea that humanity must develop a stewardship of natural resources; otherwise, we operate as a destabilizing environmental force and thus impair our future (Brulle, 1996, p.68). The discourse of conservation invites a technical/managerial approach to 'nature', which can in this vein also be called 'natural resources',[14] and the result has been a professional, technically managed economy which 'rationally develop[s] natural resources to meet long term human needs' – the greatest good for the greatest number (Brulle, 1996, p.64, p.68; see also Sachs, 1996; O'Connor, 1998). Conservationists, then, see nature as a collection of parts, and they also see ways in which those parts are quantifiable, commodifiable, and usable.

In the 20th century, national parks and game reserves in Kenya were borne out of the overlapping ideologies of 'wildlife conservation' and rational economics. Throughout pre-Industrial history, as one argument goes (see Western and Wright, 1994; Western, 1994), conservation referred to processes by which food supplies and/or cultural symbols were sustained in order to satisfy human needs. Although we can assume that conservation by this simple definition included ongoing negotiations of social relations (certainly of a different demographic scale than during the colonial era or today), the forms of those social relations and the motivations for and implications of particular types of conservationist behavior remain an open question. With the onset of intense capital production, the notion of conservation became both more abstract and more definitive. As O'Connor (1998) describes, nature, while being something beyond or separate from the everydayness of humans, became a discrete entity on and through which capital production worked.[15]

Within Kenya, parks and reserves, and the wildlife in and around them, had been deemed worth saving by international capitalists interested in refuges for hunting or photographic safaris, as well as by preservationists interested in protecting something which seemed threatened by industrial expansion and rapid population growth. As O'Connor suggests, involvement in the capitalist mode of production produced a view of pristine nature or wilderness as poised in opposition to industrialized, commoditized, civilized culture, or, as translated into place by Rocheleau (n.d.), 'ecologies worth saving' versus 'landscapes to live and work in'.[16] O'Connor moves to deflate this dichotomy by showing how 'social labor' mediates between these categories which, upon close scrutiny, can best be described as heuristic divisions (see also Rigby, 1985, 1992; Ingold, 1998). Likewise, with regard to the creation of Kenya's parks and reserves and recent related efforts at community-based wildlife resource management, there is ample evidence of the inability to make a clear distinction between nature/culture, leisure/work, or conservation/utilization.

Still, one man came to believe not only that such splits were possible, but also crucial to the survival of Kenya's wildlife. He is Richard Leakey,[17] and he was tapped by Kenya's former President Daniel arap Moi in 1989 to oversee the transition of the Wildlife Conservation and Management Department (WCMD) to Kenya Wildlife Service (KWS), of which Leakey would then be the director from 1990-94 and again from 1998-99. Because KWS began with Leakey and remains heavily influenced by his vision, his take on the ways in which *conservation* can be posited as a means by which to accomplish at least selective *preservation* is instructive. The following quote is one example of Leakey's highly publicized disagreements with David Western during Western's stint as KWS Director (1994-98) over the conditions of wildlife utilization and community-based wildlife management:

> The only way to win this battle is to avoid the price tag.... I am not personally opposed to wildlife utilization. But restricting it to private reserves run largely by Caucasians is like sitting on a time bomb that will go bang. Biodiversity must not be regarded as the preserve of the foreigner. We mustn't make the mistake of excluding people from their land. One way to soften the inside/outside divide is to get into community involvement. This has become fashionable. But, having been a champion of sharing revenue with communities, I am now opposed to it. Poor people cannot be expected to make the right judgments about the protection of species. Communities must share resources...but it's not a question of asking them to get involved in managing national parks. Boundaries [of national parks and reserves] must be kept intact and protected. We need to recognize that national parks are sacrosanct; they are not larders to be plundered...and exploited by later corrupt governments. We must get our priorities right: nature is invaluable. Biodiversity cannot be given a price. We must stop messing about with it from a sense of guilt. It is unrealistic to think we will go forward by saying that species must pay to stay, given Africa's present constructs. It is Homo sapiens who must pay. The point is that species must stay, so we must pay. (quoted in Macleod, 1997)

In this passage, Leakey draws on ideas of both preservation and conservation and thus hints at a tension which still plagues KWS and wildlife policy more generally. While Leakey calls for the protection of 'nature' and the inviolable, invaluable importance of wildlife (thus invoking ideals of preservation), he also demands ongoing expertise for monitoring and managing parks and wildlife, as well as fundraising to make it all possible (thus invoking conservation practices). In other words, 'biodiversity cannot be given a price', but there are real costs to its maintenance and protection. Outside of the parks and reserves should be the domain of the locals and could include certain forms of wildlife utilization from which they can generate their own projects and revenue. That which is *within* the parks and reserves, he insists, should indeed be preserved and managed separately from community-based projects, with all revenues generated by park and reserves being invested back into the parks and reserves, and not the local communities. He recommends hardening 'the inside/outside divide' by enforcing and protecting park boundaries and by ensuring that locals make their livings beyond the gates. These suggestions presuppose an inflow of outside capital to support the international cause of wildlife conservation, and also necessitate a group of managerial experts and fundraisers who share Leakey's vision. In spite of (or, as some argue, because of) David Western's four year stint as KWS director (1994-1998) before the return of Leakey (for 1998-1999), Leakey's vision continues to inform KWS practice.[18]

As seen above, issues of wildlife management have emerged and been informed by shifting socio-political dialectics among multiple, intersecting levels of social relations. Wildlife conservation seems to stem from the idea that people destroy nature (i.e., wildlife and their habitat in this case) because economic activity is incompatible with conservation goals (see Collett, 1987), and yet people are by default the stewards of nature and work to save 'it' by making it economically productive. How, then, might we endeavor 'to capture the interplay of structural constraint and situational contingency' (Comaroff and Comaroff, 1991, p.313) in decisions regarding wildlife resource management?

Who Supports Community-Based Wildlife Resource Management

Western challenged Leakey's vision by trying to appease multiple stakeholders while addressing the aforementioned 'structural constraint and situational contingency.' Drawing from his years of experience around Amboseli, Western started a pilot phase of an extension service, called Community Wildlife Service (CWS), to 'establish modalities for partnership and management of wildlife by communities' (KWS, 1994, p.22).[19] CWS offered such incentives as wildlife-related revenue sharing, consumptive utilization, and assistance to tourist enterprises to those landowners who not only allowed wildlife to inhabit their land, but also accepted training and 'certain responsibilities delegated by KWS' (KWS 1994, p.22). In line with CWS, Western and then-chair of the KWS Board of Trustees, Hilary Ng'weno, commissioned a 5-Person Review Group 'to independently look into the views of landowners and local communities on the prevailing wildlife/human conflicts' (KWS, 1994, p.21):

> The Review Group included persons from a cross-section of communities with a stake in wildlife including ranchers (both individual and group), tourism industry, conservation NGOs, women and environment. In addition the group was given a rapporteur and resource persons from KWS. The mission of the Review Group was to consult with interested parties and visit exemplary conflict areas soliciting views and solutions from people involved in activities at the ground level. Special attention was to be given to wildlife control.

In July and August of 1994, the Review Group visited pre-announced locations throughout Kenya. At each location, area representatives, as well as all interested individuals, participated in public hearings in which people were encouraged to speak openly.[20] Such area representatives as the secretary of a group ranch, a clerk from a town council, chief executives of farmers' unions, business leaders, tour operators, NGO representatives, and others were asked to submit memoranda outlining their primary concerns about 'wildlife/human conflict'. These memoranda were to delineate the stakeholders and their concerns about the costs and benefits of co-existing with wildlife.

Examples the Review Group provided of wildlife/human conflict included 'killing people and livestock, destroying crops and infrastructure, spread disease to livestock, competition with livestock for grazing and water developed at great costs and efforts by private landowners' (KWS, 1994, p.23). Interestingly, the Review Group also included a distinction between

> true wildlife/human conflicts, and clashes of interest which may be called human/wildlife/human conflicts to distinguish them from the true ones. The true wildlife/human conflicts which are caused by interactions between animals and people directly are obvious preoccupations of KWS. The other category includes person-to-person conflicts between stake holders with polarised group or self interests intersecting at the socio-economic or political level. (KWS, 1994, p.4)

Such an emphasis on contestation has become 'increasingly formulaic, routinized and naturalized', and the term 'stakeholders' serves as the bureaucratized version of the idea of contestation, 'a dominant motif in a large number of contemporary analyses and interventions' (Brosius, 1999, p.280). The common trend of including words like 'stakeholders' in such position papers presupposes contestation over rights of access and use, but usually cannot follow through with resolutions. Indeed, the Review Group composed a list of stakeholders, and then posed the question of which ones should get priority and which ones will likely go with needs/demands unmet.

The public hearings themselves, and many of the memoranda, followed a particular order: first, locals stated their problems relating to various categories of conflict and compensation; second, locals stated their views on current and potential solutions and compromises; third, locals suggested ways to maintain a dialogue 'with particular reference to forms of organization and representation and communication channels preferred' (KWS 1994, p.27). Based on the hearings, memoranda, and discussion among themselves and their resource personnel, the Review Group summarized their findings and produced a report, which they submitted to KWS on 4 October 1994. The memoranda listed multiple issues, dealing with a range of topics and requests, for example, compensation for deaths, KWS uniforms, revenue-sharing, assistance in starting tented camps, culling during holidays so meat could be used for celebrations, competition over grazing resources between wildlife and livestock, consumptive utilization, assistance to prevent defaulting on loans with the Agricultural Finance Commission (AFC), and much more (KWS, 1994, Appendices).

During the public hearings, dozens of people demanded higher compensation for the wildlife-caused deaths and injuries of humans, but the report stated that KWS would not assume responsibility for compensations, as that fell to the National Treasury. The report also suggested that KWS officials continue to assist in the development of wildlife enterprises, and also implement provisions in policy to include utilization in the forms of private game reserves, game farms, orphanages, and domestication. At the moment, all of the pilot projects related to these efforts were officially 'illegal' because of government laws restricting use of wildlife. One of the most controversial suggestions of the report was to lift the bans on sporthunting – Presidential Ban on Hunting (Legal Notice No. 120, 20 May 1977) – and reverse Act No. 5 (1978) and Legal Notice No. 181 (21 August 1979), which prohibited the sale and trade of wildlife and wildlife products. By removing these 'obstacles' to consumptive wildlife utilization, the report argued, those living near parks and reserves would be invested in wildlife conservation. The overall orientation of the report was the popular catch phrase heard throughout Kenya: 'Wildlife must pay its way,'[21] a direct contradiction to Leakey's vision.

Popular tourist destinations for wildlife viewing, Amboseli National Park, Maasai Mara Reserve, and Nairobi National Park, as well as the vast expanses of Tsavo East and Tsavo West National Parks, are all located in or around Maasailand. Because of this, domestic and international conservationists have linked the fate of wildlife to the will (and fate) of Maasai peoples. Maasai populations continue to grow while simultaneously becoming increasingly sedentarized due to land restrictions, titles, and fences. With these factors in mind, the memorandum from Kajiado Central to the Review Group is of particular note. The memorandum makes explicit that 'both wildlife and livestock are valuable national resources' (KWS, 1994, Appendices) and then states the following:

> The wildlife graze and water in direct competition with domestic livestock... (Please note that all ranchers have taken AFC [Agricultural Finance Corporation] loans to purchase improved stock, develop water resources among other development activities and loans money must be repaid regardless of any circumstances.) The effect of this become frustrating to the ranchers affected in that, while wildlife is migratory livestock keeping has become more and more sedentralised [sic].

This specific memorandum sets out three major recommendations, including better compensation to stockowners 'for direct competition on resources utilized by game' (the author suggested a formula for doing so); permission, guidance, and economic assistance for ostrich farming; and better and more quickly dispersed compensations for wildlife-caused injuries and deaths of humans and livestock. It makes no mention of sporthunting or 'consumptive utilization of wildlife', with the exception of ostrich farming. The memorandum also asks that KWS distribute these benefits not just to those Maasai living on the peripheries of the parks and reserves, as previous revenue-sharing programs did, but to all pastoralists in the area. These latter points all resonate deeply with the concerns and demands of Maasai with whom I worked and who lived not on the peripheries of the parks and reserves, but beyond or between them. And, as suggested in the memorandum, these Maasai continued to see no direct benefit coming to them from KWS throughout Western's tenure and despite his attempts. What they found instead were incentives to participate in the conservation program run by MKU. Although the government owns all wildlife, it does not own all industries promoting wildlife resource management with community participation. There are other 'stakeholders'.

Western's directorship ended when he was eventually pushed out of an economically troubled KWS in 1998.[22] Leakey was re-appointed and began to re-invigorate what distinguished his style of conservation from Western's, including his ability to attract international donor funds. Even though revenue-sharing continued, Leakey still pushed his model of parks and reserves management. Not surprisingly, when Leakey left KWS again in 1999, his stress on expert management and capital injections from foreign sources continued, as evidenced by the recent (2001) government approval to have a portion of the Maasai Mara Reserve called the Mara Triangle managed by the private firm Mara Conservancy. Letters to Kenyan daily newspapers (for example, Bennett, 2001) broached the subject of multiple stakeholders in areas targeted for wildlife conservation, but also served as meta-commentary on the highly public debate about conservation, and its profitability, in general.

Leakey's approach to wildlife conservation, hardening the inside/outside divide, and the conservation of the parks and reserves themselves did not directly impact MKU's own project. To the Maasai who participated in MKU's projects, and received cash for doing so, Leakey's proposal posed no threat; they lived just far enough away from the parks and reserves that they received none of the revenue-sharing monies from gate fees. MKU was located in an area where most Maasai professed to be opposed to sporthunting, unless the targets were hyenas, and they were by no means inundated with tourists. But the implications of Leakey's words – upholding notions of land as bounded, discrete, and separable areas on and through which to preserve (or produce) 'nature'/'wildlife', perpetuating the conditions of governance or management by a distanced body of experts, and dismissing (though perhaps sympathetically) the ability of 'the poor' to make 'the right' decisions about 'resource management' – raise many more questions that Western seemed to be trying to answer.

The category of 'wildlife' and its concurrent, shifting discourses are 'manifestly constitutive of reality (or, rather, of a multiplicity of realities)...and define various forms of agency, administer certain silences, and prescribe various forms of intervention' (Brosius, 1999, p.278; see also Escobar, 1999a and 1999b, Ingold, 1998 and 1993). That wildlife conservation through community-based wildlife resource management should be considered a self-evident, rational solution to a self-evident environmental problem of 'wildlife/human conflict' warrants serious examination and has clearly been contested. As exemplified in the MKU case above, the emergence and resolution of a dispute over land boundaries between the directors of a conservation project and local Maasai landowners cannot be understood without broaching such questions as who owns land? At what price? How is land ownership documented and regulated? For what purpose is land being demarcated and used? Toward selective responses to those questions is perhaps how best to direct this tale that otherwise has no clear-cut origin or foreseeable end.

Conclusions

Formulating a wildlife resource management project or any other sort of development plan is to engage in a model, an abstraction that will not unfold predictably on the ground. For most Maasai in southern Kenya, the promise of any given development project is tempered, though never fully foretold, by Kenyan history's reports of exploitation and/or unintended consequences, acts and events which have emerged through the implementation of treaties,[23] policies,[24] and other development initiatives. In and around MKU, debate among MKU's directors, neighbors, and others involved, about the goals and deployment of MKU conservation programs came from and led to ongoing negotiations as ideals clashed, models were re-worked, and various unpredictables (good and bad) intruded during the process of establishing MKU and implementing MKU's specific projects. That MKU has survived and attracted new membership is testimony to the importance of ongoing dialogues, flexibility in design, and, very likely, scale. But, we might want to ask whether Leakey's vision of wildlife conservation is sustainable over the long-term, and how his vision is likely to impact Maasai around national parks and reserves, as well as those, like MKU, which are betwixt and between them.

I would argue that the promise of long-term sustainability for community-based wildlife conservation, as currently and most typically practiced in Maasailand, is illusory for two key reasons. One is that the community will continue to adopt and be transformed by various incarnations of capitalist praxis so that it is no longer the pastoral community that tourists want to have conserved along with the wildlife. The second reason, which is indeed a grim complement to the first, is that the lands on which all of various contractual agreements have been based will eventually be re-surveyed with the precision of new equipment and tied to fixed, geodetic points or monuments. Then, the results of this imminent survey will not agree with the numbers of acres that people think they own, and on which some of them have mortgages based.

With the various incarnations of 'community-based' conservation in the post-colonial era, pastoral people have become more reliant on their landholdings in terms of acres and accountability for what they are *not* doing on that land than for what they formerly did through subsistence production. For instance, mining, charcoaling, and agricultural production are not considered commensurate with attracting wildlife. Over time, people have begun to depend more heavily on the representation of their land – what the paper in the records office claims to be the number of acres held by an individual and that which can serve as the basis of bank loans or land sales – rather than on the physical land that once supported their main wealth of livestock. When that number of acres on paper is then disputed by another more 'technologically accurate' representation of land holdings, these systems of wealth generation will likely be shaken, to say the very least. Land disputes underscore the disconnect between the popularization and power of an ideology that privileges precise boundaries, technically accurate maps, and written documentation and the recent history among Maasai of negotiable and contested boundaries, inaccurate maps, and the fading but still socially meaningful import of oral agreements.

NGOs promoting an ideal of community-based resource management have often enforced their own contradictions by claiming to protect an idealized pastoral livelihood for Maasai, while at the same time requiring measures which work against the realization of pastoral life. The 'community' targeted for development is, by necessity of the program, transformed into something else. The directors of MKU managed to avoid this contradiction by never pretending to preserve Maasai *pastoralism* as if it were a static system of production. Rather, they instead undertook a project designed to conserve the ability for participating Maasai to stay on their land while also maintaining that land for wildlife populations. In this sense, and as stated above, MKU as a project has thus far succeeded in promoting 'community conservation' by enabling members of their community to stay *where* they are, in a geographic sense, although not exactly *how* they were, in regards to intra-community relations and livelihoods. They now endeavor to protect that 'where' by guaranteeing shareholders the right to retain their shares, even if a new land survey should prove that the shareholders' land holdings are less than the shares represent.

MKU's vision of land, wildlife, livestock, and people management has derived from ecological estimates of productive resource use, all of which flow logically from conservation discourse. Conservation planning and policy in general continue to draw heavily from systems theory and cybernetic models, as reflected in current computer programs which enable trained users to map out biotic communities or ecosystems, variably defined depending on the scale of analysis. This process relies on the collection of discrete bits of data, which are then used as 'inputs' in a computer program that provides an interactive model of a given ecosystem. The ecosystem, then, is arbitrarily bounded for purposes of such mapping. Operating within Kenya and Tanzania's Maasailand, as well as the western United States, one such ecosystem model is SAVANNA developed by Coughenour, Reid, and Thornton (2000) in conjunction with the International Livestock Research Institute (ILRI), Future Harvest, and Colorado State University.[25] Altogether more complex and of far greater spatial resolution[26] than previous models employed in these regions, SAVANNA has been developed to forecast possible outcomes for various decisions on land use. In the words of one of its creators, SAVANNA is '…a decision-making planning tool that is helping us to develop management practices that are more equitable for both wildlife and people' (Higgins, 2000). SAVANNA, thus, upholds the conservation ideal of viewing nature as a collection of parts that function together and which can be successfully managed. SAVANNA has been heralded as the 'new ecological model' which will help in 'restoring harmony between wildlife and humanity' (World Bank, 2000).

Whether one subscribes to a cybernetics approach to human-wildlife-land policy as a zero-sum game, to a deep ecologist's view that wilderness areas must be dramatically increased out of respect for the innate worth of all life, or some position in between these, it is difficult to disagree with the claim that there have been grave ecological *and thus* managerial problems in and around Maasailand throughout much of the past century. Like a high-tech *Farmers' Almanac*, computer modeling such as SAVANNA's is used to quantify those ecological problems and predict possible outcomes. What such a model cannot predict is the ways in which targeted human populations, such as Maasai in Kajiado, might make sense of the dramatic changes that they continue to experience. SAVANNA cannot '*restor[e]* harmony between wildlife and humanity' (emphasis mine), as claimed within the World Bank newsletter (2000), because the form and substance of relations between wildlife and humanity have been irrevocably transformed over the past century, and they continue to be transformed before our very eyes. The developers of SAVANNA, however, have worked with locals as they consider a variety of options. To do this successfully is to recognize that 'community-based' models *should* convey that even global impacts on communities are still manifest in highly specific ways. Thus, a community-based conservation project should be culturally compatible with its participants, should respond to locally perceived needs, should involve men and women in planning and carrying out the changes that affect them, should respect the existing social organizations, and should be flexible (Kottak, 1999).

One last note about Leakey's vision of wildlife conservation: it is only possible with ongoing international attention and investment. This means that tourism will remain absolutely crucial in and around Maasailand. But, how do we, as political ecologists, conservationists, and/or Maasai, reconcile the possibility that tourists in southern Kenya want to see 'authenticity' as embodied in warriors, herders, ornate Maasai weddings, and mud-dung huts, not techno-savvy Kenyans living in cinder block homes with televisions? An immediate area of interest, then, is how to orient tourist experiences to being more attuned to the multiple realities of those upon whom they gaze, while also alerting tourists to the ecological impacts and economic consequences of their own activities. Again, it seems we cannot escape the political consequences of historically situated practice. And again, it seems as though contradictions generated from within historically situated practice generate future actions, actions made reasonable by over a century of struggle between nature and capital, and attempts to conserve both. Recognizing this opens up new discussions for how we can potentially reinvigorate and reclaim the concept of *community* conservation.

Notes

1   I am grateful to Fletcher Linder, Laura Lewis, and Clark Gibson for feedback on an earlier version of this manuscript, as well as to William Moseley for his comments and encouragement. I am indebted to those in Kenya who assisted me with their keen insights and graciousness in handling my numerous questions. This work was supported by the James Madison University Program of Grants for Faculty Assistance.

2   I employ the term 'wildlife' in keeping with popular, contemporary international usage that privileges certain animals over others. For example, the booklet *Tuhifadhi Wanyama Wetu wa Porini* [*Let's Conserve Our Wildlife*] and a complementary teacher's guide were produced through the WCMD in 1989 to explain to Kenyans 'what conservation is, state the importance of conserving wildlife and explain how governments, non-governmental agencies and individuals work to do this' (written by Richard Leakey in foreword of book; Gachuhi, 1989a and 1989b). The guide includes a three-page section entitled 'Wildlife Pictures'. Though this may not be a comprehensive list of 'wildlife', it does include the following animals, in order of appearance: lion, leopard, cheetah, hyena, hunting dog, buffalo, hippopotamus, giraffe, zebra, elephant, crocodile, ostrich, Thomson's gazelle, dikdik, topi, waterbuck, Grant's gazelle, hartebeest, impala, bushbuck, wildebeest, oryx, eland (Gachuhi, 1989b: pp.36-38). These tend to be the ones most important for tourism.

3   Most people typically identify Maasai as pastoralists, given the importance that the ideals of a pastoral lifestyle still hold for most self-identifying Maasai.   Ideally, pastoralists' livelihoods depend upon their livestock (cattle, goats, sheep, camels, and/or donkeys), from which they derive milk, meat, and hides, as well as other goods for trade, and on which they occasionally rely for transport.   Today, pastoralist ideals do not preclude agricultural activities (and many rural Maasai do maintain small gardens) or wage labor, although most of the 300,000 Maasai in southern Kenya inhabit semi-arid, savanna areas where an exclusively agricultural (or, for that matter, pastoral) lifestyle is not viable.

4   Kiswahili for 'development through conservation.'   This name and the names of MKU participants are pseudonyms; identities have been masked at the request of research participants.

5   Maasai Mara Reserve encompasses 1,800 square kilometers, Amboseli 380 square kilometers.

6   Pastoralist studies have proliferated in the years since Kenya's independence, and Rigby (1992, pp.6-8) suggests that they tend to follow two general paths.   The first subscribes to a belief that pastoral Maasai can be integrated into a market-based (read: capitalistic) national economy while still remaining 'Maasai' *because* pastoralism is really nascent or rudimentary capitalism (see Schneider, 1979; Spencer, 1988, 1993; and less explicitly Reader 1997).   All they need, the argument continues, is some guidance and assistance by a team of interdisciplinary experts.   The second path, which Rigby (1992, p.7) describes as appealing to 'the anthropological refugee from the fields of conflict between ethnocide and ethnogenesis,' leads back to 'a relativist, isolationist, functionalist, and hence out-dated anthropology' that seeks to 'save' a particular picture of a discrete, organic, and thus 'different' (i.e., non-Western) culture or society.   Rigby's description of these two predominant paths for pastoral studies may appear extreme, but he deploys them as frameworks for understanding the bases for the majority of recent efforts at developing – or preserving – Maasai.   Either way, 'the Maasai' appear to some experts to remain in need of help, and numerous top-down development interventions,

generated by national and international authorities and experts, have been deployed to that general end.

7   In more common parlance in Kenya, one would hear 'human/wildlife conflict'.

8   See for example Metcalfe, 1994; Gibson, 1999; Hulme and Murphree (eds), 2001 (see especially chapters by Ivan Bomd and James Murombedzi); Logan and Moseley, 2002.

9   In the mid-1960s, foreign 'development experts', most of whom were British and American (including USAID), proposed developing a group ranch scheme. The Lawrence Report of 1966 advocated land tenure as a means to provide security for smallholders throughout Kenya, and approved of the group ranches as a way to provide Maasai with legal land title and security over grazing lands without further dividing their districts into individual ranches (Holland, 1987, p. 17). The government agreed to the details set forth in the Lawrence Report and implemented the Land (Group Representatives) Act of 1968, which divided trust land, in this case Maasailand, into group ranches and set forth certain regulations and guidelines to 'manage' the ranches (Berger, 1993, p. 20; see also Campbell, 1993). According to this scheme, elders would hold land under communal title, all group ranch members would be led by representatives in an elected group ranch committee, and no individual could sell the property in part or whole without consent from fellow group ranch members (Berger, 1993, p. 20; Bentsen, 1989, p. 99). The ranches would vary in size and, depending on 'resources' within a given ranch, could include anywhere from sixty to three thousand members (Bentsen, 1989, p. 98). After the first group ranches were established, it became evident that the 'sociological groupings' formulated by ranch policies did not correspond to the basic social units which Maasai themselves recognized as politically, territorially, or economically important (Holland, 1987; Galaty, 1980; Fratkin *et al.*, 1994; Rigby, 1985 and 1992; Bentsen, 1989).

10   In some cases, one or more of the sons would also sign the contracts to acknowledge shared authority/decision-making over the property, as well as to recognize what was in effect an informal distribution of the land among adult sons who were now raising their own children.

11   This is a pseudonym to protect the family's privacy.

12   The party's name 'Safina' is Kiswahili for 'ark', which holds interesting connotations about all members of the party (and perhaps Kenyans in general) being in the same boat, about a search for deliverance, and also about Leakey's own role as former KWS director – steward of wildlife. Thanks to Dr. Robert E. Daniels for bringing these connections to my attention.

13   Whereas souring relations between neighbors may have resulted in the past in accusations of witchcraft or vampirism (see Rigby, 1985, 1992), current slander was at its most injurious in terms of political associations poorly received within a given area.

14   It is beyond the scope of this chapter to deal with the concepts of 'nature' and 'resources', particularly as others have done so in great detail (see, for example, Sachs, 1992; Shiva, 1992; O'Connor, 1998; Escobar, 1999; Ingold, 1998; Merchant, 1980).

15   Our (western) fascination with the nature/culture split has not been reserved to studies of European or American phenomena alone. According to Beidelman (1968, pp.80-81, cited in Rigby 1985, p. 59), Maa-speakers perpetuated a number of such popular dichotomies (strikingly similar to our own), as well: spheres of God and creation; Maasai and outsiders; society (*enkang*) and nature (bush); men and women. Beidelman and Rigby both noted the importance of structural oppositions within the three major types of social units from which society is formed: clans, polygynous families, and age-sets. Roles for Maasai, though described in opposition to one another, clash and blend,

emerge out of and merge into one another over time.   In other words, they are simultaneously inseparable and mutually constitutive.

16 At the same time, the concept of leisure grew increasingly important in the lives of many in western, industrialized societies, and leisure, too, was defined in opposition to work (France, 1997, p. 3). The burgeoning tourism industry capitalizes on these distinctions by promoting a need for leisure. Kenyan tourism insists that leisure should be spent visiting Kenya's (well-managed) nature – wildlife, parks, etc.

17 Leakey, son of paleontologists Louis and Mary Leakey, had gained international regard himself for his work with fossils and also as longstanding head of National Museums of Kenya. Because of his work and public persona, he was highly regarded among international conservationists. Leakey said that he found out about his appointment as Moi announced it on the radio (Dickey, 1990, p. 110). Leakey had publicly accused WCMD (then under Perez Olindo) and the ministries of corruption and gross inefficiency. That Leakey was chosen instead of Perez Olindo (for Olindo's career path, connections, and speculation on his displacement, see Bonner, 1993; and Mbugua, 1995) to serve as director of KWS led to notable grumbling among other bureaucrats.

18 When considering the controversy of wildlife management practices, as well as how KWS has arguably been prone to a cult of personality, a simple review of the KWS directorship roll proves to be instructive. It includes Richard Leakey (appointed by President Moi in 1989 to oversee the transformation of the Wildlife Conservation and Management Department (WCMD) into KWS; resigned in 1994; re-appointed in 1998; re-assigned from KWS to the Head of Public Service and Secretary to the Cabinet in 1999), David Western (appointed by Moi in 1994; fired in 1998 and then immediately reinstated only to resign a week later), Nehemiah Rotich (assumed directorship in 1999 and suspended in December 2001), interim director Joseph Kioko, and Michael Wamithi (appointed in December 2002).

19 A Maasai elder living by Maasai Mara told a World Bank representative if the World Bank would fund killing all of the elephants and lions, the rest of the animals could stay (Kiss, 1995, personal communication).

20 The Review Group avoided using the phrase *baraza*, as their intentions were posed somewhat differently from those of most Kenyan *barazas* (see Haugerud, 1995).

21 And some officials at the World Bank agree. In an interview with Agnes Kiss (1995), she told me, 'We don't need to save every single lion.' She also dismissed the argument that pastoralists are innate conservationists, or that 'indigenous people' always participate in maintaining wildlife and environments, as complete bunk. She offered deforestation around Tana River and the history of poaching as support. Almost as a compromise between Leakey and Western's positions, Kiss suggested that there are hard and soft boundaries for gazetted areas: Tana River has hard boundaries, Maasai Mara has soft and thus may have to be altered. Regarding the issue of aggregating and then dividing benefits so that people from all areas around the reserves and parks share the money that all of the areas combine to generate, Kiss explained that people living in those areas which generate more money also put up with greater tourist traffic, including wear and tear on the environment and constant invasions/disruptions. She asserted that it was unfair to have people living around heavily-trafficked areas like Maasai Mara supporting those people who live in less-trafficked areas like Tsavo. Kiss suggested, therefore, that some areas, like Tsavo, must be sacrificed and de-gazetted.

22 Many argue that Western was also pushed out for political reasons, including a refusal to allow mining and hotel construction in certain gazetted areas.

23 For example, colonial Kenya's 1904 and 1911 Agreements restricting Maasai to reserves in southern Kenya to open up territory for white settlement.

24 For example, Act No. 5 of 1978 and Legal Notice No. 181 of 1979, which restricted capture and sales and expressly banned exports of wildlife and wildlife products, as well as led to further complaints by Kenyans that the government cared more about wildlife than it did people.

25 ILRI is one of 16 international research centers funded by CGIAR, which is the Consultative Group on International Agricultural Research. CGIAR is co-sponsored by the World Bank, the United Nations Food and Agriculture Organization (FAO), the United Nations Development Program (UNDP), and the United Nations Environment Program (UNEP).   Future Harvest is supported by CGIAR, including direct contributions from ILRI (see http://www.futureharvest.org/news/savannarelease.shtml). The collaboration between ILRI and Colorado State to develop SAVANNA is funded in part by the United States Agency for International Development's (USAID's) Global Livestock Collaborative Research Support Program and is part of a larger effort to produce an Integrated Modeling and Assessment System (IMAS) to monitor and predict interactions of drought, human nutrition, and wildlife-livestock conflicts in East Africa (Coughenour, Reid, and Thornton, 2000, p. 17).

26 Resolution here refers to the ability to model small areas to provide greater detail than previous models. For example, the developers of SAVANNA describe their model as capable of predicting the future of an area as small as a fifty-yard wide water hole (World Bank, 2000; see also Coughenour, Reid, and Thornton, 2000, p. 6).

References

Adams, W. and d. Hulme. (1998), 'Conservation and Communities: Hanging Narratives, Policies and Practices in African Conservation.' Working Paper 4. Manchester: Institute for Development Policy and Management.

Agrawal A. and C.C.Gibson. (eds). (2001), *Communities and the Environment: Ethnicity, Gender, and the State in Community-Based Conservation.* New Brunswick, N.J.: Rutgers University Press.

Barrow, E., H. Gichohi and M. Infield. (2001), 'The Evolution of Community Conservation Policy & Practice in East Africa' in Hulme, David, and Murphree, Marshall (eds). *African Wildlife & Livelihoods: The Promise & Performance of Community Conservation.* Oxford: James Currey Ltd.

Bates, D. and S. Lees. (1996), 'Introduction.' In Bates, Daniel and Lees, Susan (eds), *Case Studies in Human Ecology.* New York: Plenum Press.

Biersack, A. (1999), 'Introduction: From the 'New Ecology' to the 'New Ecologies'.' *American Anthropologist* 101(1), pp. 23-35.

Bonner, R. (1993), At the Hand of Man: Peril and Hope for Africa's Wildlife. New York: Knopf.

Brockington, D. (2001), 'Outlines of a Political Economy of Environmentalism in Tanzania.' Presented at the African Studies Association's Annual Meeting.

Brosius, J.P. (1999), 'Analyses and Interventions: Anthropological Engagements with Environmentalism.' *Current Anthropology* 40(3), pp. 277-309.

Brulle, R.J. (1996), 'Environmental Discourse and Social Movement Organizations: A Historical and Rhetorical Perspective on the Development of U.S. Environmental Organizations' in *Sociological Inquiry* 66(1), pp. 58-83.

Coffman, J. (2000), *'Without Money, There Is No Life': Global Forces and the Invention of Wildlife in Southern Kenya.* The University of North Carolina at Chapel Hill: Doctoral dissertation.

Collett, D. (1987), 'Pastoralists and Wildlife: Image and Reality in Kenya Maasailand.' In Homewood, K.M. and W.A. Rogers (eds), *Conservation in Africa.* Cambridge: Cambridge University Press.

Comaroff, J. and J.L. Comaroff. (1991), ' 'How Beasts Lost Their Legs': Cattle in Tswana Economy and Society.' In Galaty, John. G., and Bonte, Pierre (eds), *Herders, Traders and Warriors: Pastoralism in Africa.* Boulder: Westview Press.

Comaroff, J.L., and J. Comaroff. (1991), *Of Revelation and Revolution: Christianity, Colonialism and Consciousness in South Africa.* Chicago: The University of Chicago Press.

Comaroff, J.L., and S. Roberts. (1981), *Rules and Processes: The Cultural Logic of Dispute in an African Context.* Chicago: The University of Chicago Press.

Coughenour, M., R. Reid and P. Thornton. (2000), *The SAVANNA Model: Providing Solutions for Wildlife Preservation and Human Development in East Africa and the Western United States.* Washington, DC: Future Harvest. Report available online via: http://www.futureharvest.org/news/savannarelease.shtml.

Escobar, A. (1992), 'Grassroots approaches and alternative politics in the Third World,' *Futures* 24(5), pp. 411-436.

Escobar, A. (1995), *Encountering Development: The Making and Unmaking of the Third World.* Princeton: Princeton University Press.

Escobar, A. (1999a), Whose Knowledge, Whose Nature? Biodiversity Conservation and Social Movements Political Ecology.' *Journal of Political Ecology.*

Escobar, A. (1999b), 'An Ecology of Difference: Equality and Conflict in a Glocalized World.' In Arizpe, Lourdes (ed), *World Culture Report 2.* Paris: UNESCO.

Esteva, G. (1992), 'Development.' In Sachs, Wolfgang (ed), *The Development Dictionary: A Guide to Knowledge as Power.* London: Zed Books Ltd.

Featherstone, M., S. Lash and R. Robertson. (1995), *Global Modernities.* Thousand Oaks, California: Sage Publishers.

Ferguson, J. (1990), *The Anti-Politics Machine: 'Development,' Depoliticization, and Bureaucratic Power in Lesotho.* New York: Cambridge University Press.

Fisher, W. (1997), 'Doing Good? The Politics and Antipolitics of NGO Practices' in *Annual Review of Anthropology* (26), pp. 64, 439.

France, L. (1997), *The Earthscan Reader in Sustainable Tourism.* London: Earthscan Publications, Ltd.

Fratkin, E. (2001), 'East African Pastoralism in Transition: Maasai, Boran, and Rendille Cases' in *African Studies Review,* 44(3), pp. 1-25.

Fratkin, E., K.A. Galvin and E.A. Roth (eds.). (1994), *African Pastoralist Systems: An Integrated Approach.* Boulder: Lynne Rienner Publishers.

Gachuhi, D. (ed). (1989a), *Tuhifadhi Wanyama Wetu wa Porini.* Nairobi, Kenya: Department of Adult Education and Wildlife Conservation and Management Department.

Gachuhi, D. (ed). (1989b), *Tuhifadhi Wanyama Wetu wa Porini: The Teacher's Guide.* Nairobi, Kenya: Department of Adult Education and Wildlife Conservation and Management Department.

Galaty, J.G. (1980), 'The Maasai Group Ranch: Politics and Development in an African Pastoral Society.' In Salzman, Phillip Carl (ed), *When Nomads Settle: Processes of Sedentarization as Adaptation and Response.* New York: Praeger.

Galaty, J.G. (1993a), 'Maasai Expansion and the New East African Pastoralism.' In Spear, Thomas, and Waller, Richard (eds), *Being Maasai: Ethnicity and Identity in East Africa*. Athens, Ohio University Press.

Galaty, J.G. (1993b), '"The Eye that Wants a Person, Where can It Not See?": Inclusion, Exclusion, and Boundary Shifters in Maasai Identity.' In Spear, Thomas, and Waller, Richard (eds), *Being Maasai: Ethnicity and Identity in East Africa*. Athens, Ohio University Press.

Galaty, J.G., D. Aronson, and P.C. Salzman (eds) (1981), *The Future of Pastoral Peoples: Proceedings of a Conference Held in Nairobi, Kenya, 4-8 August 1980*. Ottawa, Canada: International Development Research Center.

Galaty, J.G., and P. Bonte. (eds.) (1991), *Herders, Traders and Warriors: Pastoralism in Africa*. Boulder: Westview Press.

Galaty, J.G., and D.L. Johnson. (1990), 'Introduction: Pastoral Systems in Global Perspective.' In Galaty, J.G., and D.L. Johnson (eds), *The World of Pastoralism*. New York: The Guilford Press.

Galaty, J.G., and D.L. Johnson (eds). (1990), *The World of Pastoralism*. New York: The Guilford Press.

Gibson, C. (1999), *Politicians and Poachers: The Political Economy of Wildlife Policy in Africa*. New York: Cambridge University Press.

Gitonga, E. and M. Pickford. (1995), *Richard E. Leakey: Master of Deceit*. Nairobi: White Elephant Publishers.

Higgins, M. (14 February 2000), 'Savanna model tracks delicate balance in Africa' on Environmental News Network, available at http://www.enn.com/news/enn-stories/2000/02/02122000/savanna_9943.asp.

Hodgson, D. (1999), 'Images and Interventions: The Problems of Pastoral Development.' In Anderson, David and Broch-Due, Vigdis (eds), *The Poor Are Not Us: Poverty and Pastoralism*. Oxford: James Currey.

Hodgson, D. (2001), *Once Intrepid Warriors: Gender, Ethnicity, and Cultural Politics of Maasai Development*. Bloomington: Indiana University Press.

Hulme, D. and M. Murphree (eds). (2001), *African Wildlife & Livelihoods: The Promise & Performance of Community Conservation*. Oxford: James Currey Ltd.

Igoe, J. (2001), 'Scaling up civil society: Donor money, NGOs, and Tanzania's pastoral land tenure movement.' Presented at the African Studies Association's Annual Meeting. Houston, TX.

Ingold, T. (1993), 'The temporality of the landscape.' *World Archaeology* 25(2), pp. 152-174.

Ingold, T. (1998), 'Culture, nature, environment: steps to an ecology of life.' In Cartledge, B. (ed), *Mind, Brain and the Environment*. Oxford: Oxford University Press.

Kottak, C. (1999), 'The New Ecological Anthropology.' *American Anthropologist* 101(1), pp. 23-35.

Leakey, R. and V. Morell. (2001), *Wildlife Wars: My Fight to Save Africa's Natural Treasures*. New York: St. Martin's Press.

Leff, E. (1995), *Green Production: Toward an Environmental Rationality*. New York: Guilford Press.

Logan, B.I. and W.G. Moseley. (2002), 'The Political Ecology of Poverty Alleviation in Zimbabwe's Communal Areas Management Programme for Indigenous Resources (CAMPFIRE).' *Geoforum*. 33(1), pp. 1-14.

Macleod, F. (1997), 'Africa Must Pay for Its Wildlife.' *The Mail and Guardian*, 26 September.

Mander, J. and E. Goldsmith. (1996), *The Case Against the Global Economy: And for a Turn Toward the Local*. San Francisco: Sierra Club Books.

Martinez-Alier, J. (n.d.), 'Ecological Distribution Conflicts, Sustainability and Valuation.'

Marsh, G.P. (1864), *Man and Nature: Earth as Modified by Human Action*. Cambridge: Harvard University Press.

Mbugua, N.W. (1995), 'When Poachers Called the Shots and Govt Stood Back Helplessly.' *Sunday Nation*, 14 May. Nairobi, Kenya.

Merchant, C. (1980), *The Death of Nature: Women, Ecology and the Scientific Revolution*. New York: Harper and Rowe.

Metcalfe, S. (1994), 'The Zimbabwe Communal Areas Management Porgramme for Indigenous Resources (CAMPFIRE).' In David Western and R. Michael Wright (eds), *Natural Connections: Perspectives in Community-based Conservation*. pp. 161-191

Neumann, R. (1998), *Imposing Wilderness: Struggles over Livelihood and Nature Preservation in Africa*. Berkeley: University of California Press.

O'Connor, J. (1998), *Natural Causes: Essays in Ecological Marxism*. New York: Guilford Press.

Peet, R. and M. Watts. (eds) (1995), *Liberation Ecologies: Environment, Development, Social Movements*. London: Routledge.

Piot, C. (1999), *Remotely Global: Village Modernity in West Africa*. Chicago: The University of Chicago Press.

Reader, J. (1997), *Africa: A Biography of the Continent*. New York: Alfred A. Knopf.

Rigby, P. (1985), *Persistent Pastoralists*. London: Zed Books, Ltd.

Rigby, P. (1989), 'Ideology, Religion and Ilparakuyo-Maasai Resistance to Capitalist Penetration.' *Canadian Journal of African Studies* 23(3), pp. 416-441.

Rigby, P. (1992), *Cattle, Capitalism and Class*. Philadelphia: Temple University Press.

Rocheleau, D., M. Jama, and B. Wamalwa-Muragori. (1995), 'Gender, Ecology, and Agroforestry: Science and Survival in Kathama.' In Thomas-Slayter, B., and D. Rocheleau (eds), *Gender, Environment, and Development in Kenya: Perspectives from the Grassroots*. Boulder: Lynn Reinner.

Rocheleau, D., P. Steinberg and P. Benjamin. (1995), 'Environment, Development, Crisis, and Crusade: Ukambani, Kenya, 1890-1990.' *World Development* 23(6), pp. 1037-1051.

Ruttan, L.M. and M.B. Mulder. (1999), 'Are East African Pastoralists Truly Conservationists?' *Current Anthropology* 40(5), pp. 621-653.

Sachs, W. (ed). (1992), *The Development Dictionary: A Guide to Knowledge as Power*. London: Zed Books Ltd.

Sachs, W. (1996), 'Neo-Development: "Global Ecological Management"' in Mander, Jerry, and Goldsmith, Edward (eds). *The Case Against the Global Economy: And for a Turn Toward the Local*. San Francisco: Sierra Club Books. pp. 239-252.

Schneider, H.K. (1979), *Livestock and Equality in East Africa*. Bloomington: Indiana University Press.

Scott, J.C. (1976), *The Moral Economy of the Peasant: Rebellion and Subsistence in Southeast Asia*. New Haven: Yale University Press.

Shiva, V. (1992), 'Resources.' In Sachs, Wolfgang (ed), *The Development Dictionary: A Guide to Knowledge as Power*. London: Zed Books Ltd.

Spear, T. and R. Waller (eds). (1993), *Being Maasai: Ethnicity and Identity in East Africa*. Athens: Ohio University Press.

Spencer, P. (1988), *The Maasai of Matapato: A Study of Rituals and Rebellion*. Bloomington: Indiana University Press for International African Institute.

Spencer, P. (1993), 'Becoming Maasai, Being in Time.' In Spear, T. and R. Waller (eds), *Being Maasai: Ethnicity and Identity in East Africa*. Athens: Ohio University Press.

Talle, A. (1988), *Women at a Loss: Changes in Maasai Pastoralism and Their Effects on Gender Relations*. Stockholm: Studies in Social Anthropology.

The Economic Review. (1995a), 'Making Waves: Leakey's presence in proposed party sends shivers through KANU and opposition.' Issue 134: pp. 4-7.

The Economic Review. (1995b), 'Master of Deceit?' Issue 134: pp. 8.

The Economic Review. (1995c), 'Olindo's Return.' Issue 134: pp. 9.

The Economist. (2001), 'A New Game Plan'. 28 June.

The Weekly Review. (1990), 'The Struggle Continues.' 7 September, pp. 27-32.

Waller, R. (1990), 'Tsetse fly in western Narok, Kenya.' *Journal of African History* 31, pp. 81-101.

Waller, R. (1993), 'Acceptees and Aliens: Kikuyu Settlement in Massailand.' In Spear, T. and R. Waller (eds), *Being Massai*. Athens: Ohio University Press.

Western, D. (1982), 'Amboseli National Park: Enlisting Land Owners to Conserve Migratory Wildlife.' *Ambio* 11(5), pp. 302-308.

Western, D. (1994), 'Ecosystem Conservation and Rural Development: The Case of Amboseli.' In Western, D. and R.M. Wright (eds), *Natural Connections: Perspectives in Community-based Conservation*. Washington, DC: Island Press.

Western, D. and T. Dunne. (1979), 'Environmental Aspect of Settlement Site Decisions among Pastoral Maasai.' *Human Ecology* 7(1), pp. 75-98.

Western, D. and P. Thresher. (1973), *Development Plans for Amboseli*. World Bank Report. Nairobi, Kenya: World Bank.

Western, D. and R.M. Wright. (1994), 'The Background to Community-based Conservation.' In Western, D. and R.M. Wright (eds), *Natural Connections: Perspectives in Community-based Conservation*. Washington, DC: Island Press.

Widner, J. (1992), *The Rise of a Party-State in Kenya: From Harambee to Nyayo*. Berkeley: University of California Press.

Wolf, E. (1972), 'Ownership and Political Ecology.' *Anthropological Quarterly* 45, pp. 201-205.

World Bank. (7 August 2000), 'New Ecological Model Helps Predict the Future' in *Development News – The World Bank's Daily Webzine*. Available at http://www.worldbank.org/developmentnews/archives/html/aug7-11-00.htm (accessed 5 February 2002).

Yeager, R. and N. Miller. (1986), *Wildlife, Wild Death*. Albany: State University of New York Press.

Chapter 10

Placing the Local in the Transnational: Communities and Conservation Across Borders in Southern Africa

Rachel B. DeMotts

Introduction[1]

The proliferation of transfrontier conservation initiatives reaches across the globe and includes as many as 117 different regions that cross state borders.[2] These initiatives seek to integrate environmental and wildlife management across political boundaries in the hopes that a larger, more holistic approach to ecosystem management will yield not only positive environmental outcomes but also increased revenue from ecotourism and benefits for local communities. Environmental, economic, and political reasons for establishing these initiatives range widely, including consideration of the cross-border nature of ecosystems and the alleviation of the tragedy of the commons, a desire to increase tourism revenues, regional integration, and peace and security (Katerere et al., 2001). Consequently, the potential issues to be addressed by these initiatives range from the reestablishment of wildlife migration and watershed management to interaction with local residents and governance over new international parks.

This intersection of community-based conservation and transfrontier conservation initiatives raises important questions about roles for local communities, which will be the focus of this chapter. Emphasis on community level involvement is important not only for economic reasons, but as a possible way to right the wrongs of past conservation policies that included forced resettlement, loss of access to natural resources, and interference in traditional cultural practices in rural communities. Nowhere is the emphasis on transfrontier conservation initiatives more prominent than southern Africa, where at least 8 separate initiatives are in different stages of negotiation, implementation, and establishment.

Conservation across borders presents definitional as well as practical implementation problems. In this chapter I will use 'transfrontier conservation initiatives' to refer to any cross-border efforts to link conservation and environmental management. There are many terms for this integration, however, and their usage is not consistent. Projects in the region refer to wildlife corridors, which may or may not cross state boundaries but are part of a number of proposals for larger conservation areas. Other terms range from peace parks to transfrontier conservation areas, transfrontier parks, internationally adjoining protected areas, protected area complexes, and transboundary natural resource management areas. Even the difference between transborder and transfrontier is contested, as 'transborder' could represent borders within states (such as national parks) rather than across a frontier with another state. The difference between 'area' and 'park' also suggests different conceptions of boundaries, with parks having the potential to reify lines on the map in ways that conjure up political memories of exclusion and forced resettlement for those who live in the path of conservation projects.

Both the ways in which transfrontier conservation is envisioned or named and policy approaches to it in southern Africa vary. The World Conservation Union's (IUCN) use of the term 'peace parks' dates to the early 1980s, when transfrontier conservation was seen as tool for addressing both environmental issues and political tensions in historically contested regions (Ellis, 1994; Koch, 1998; de Villiers, 1999). Yet the politicized nature of the term 'peace parks' has raised disagreement about its applicability by putting too much emphasis on past conflicts and not enough on conservation, and discussions of conflict resolution are often reduced or removed in current project plans that refer to peace parks.[3]   In particular, what is often not directly addressed is the role of local communities in these new conservation areas. While community-based conservation has gained currency in the region, with examples such as conservancies in Namibia, community trusts in Botswana, and the CAMPFIRE program in Zimbabwe, it is as yet unclear how (or if) local communities will be included in international conservation.

This chapter will trace the evolution of community-based conservation policies in Namibia as a case that is widely considered to be a model for the inclusion of local communities in conservation initiatives. Namibia's head start on community-based conservation provides a lens through which to examine ways to integrate conservation in local contexts, and provides a contrast with current approaches to transfrontier conservation in South Africa. Under colonial rule, the two countries shared a similar approach to the creation of protected areas, which forced the removal of local people from their land, implemented policies that restricted natural resource use, and excluded local residents from national parks. The post-colonial period, however, witnessed a divergence in conservation policies. The early development of community-based natural resource management in Namibia, or CBNRM, contrasts with a late-blooming environmental movement in South Africa. Both countries are now pursuing transfrontier conservation initiatives, but differ significantly in their approaches to the involvement and role of local communities in such programs. While Namibian approaches are focused on the creation and extension of conservancies managed by local communities, South Africa's focus is on finding ways to connect local communities to larger protected areas through means such as contractual national parks. The result is that while Namibia appears to be trying to use community-level projects as a basis for the creation of international conservation areas, South Africa's approach extends existing national parks into larger, mixed land use areas and tries to create minor roles for local communities around these international parks. In addition, recent problems have emerged in South Africa around the lack of consultation with communities living in proposed park areas. This is not to argue that one approach is intrinsically better than the other, but rather to problematize the idea of community-based conservation in international boundary areas and suggest that the inclusion of local communities in transfrontier conservation may be more complex than is indicated by planning for these initiatives. Moreover, projects that claim to be community-based and have local interests at heart often fail to treat communities as stakeholders, and not all transfrontier conservation initiatives in the region have the same approach to local participation.

Namibia: Conservation into Communities

As an extremely arid country, most of Namibia's 1.7 million people live in the far north where most of its arable land is located. Colonial conservation strategies were much the same as in other countries in Africa, focused on the creation of national parks and protected areas that created fenced, policed wildlife habitat and excluded local communities from traditional land use practices.[4] General trends in wildlife populations in the past 30 years have seen an increase in numbers on privately held land and a decline in numbers on communal land.[5] Community-based natural resource management (CBNRM) is the primary strategy in Namibia for addressing this decline, and many CBNRM initiatives are based in the northern part of the country.

Integrated Rural Development and Nature Conservation (IRDNC), a grassroots Namibian organization, established the earliest community-based conservation initiatives in Namibia.[6] Founded in 1983 by an anthropologist, Margaret Jacobsohn, and an environmental activist and forester, Garth Owen-Smith, IRDNC's first project was to create a community level natural resource management initiative in Purros in northwestern Namibia. As early as 1982 Owen-Smith had been working with local communities in northwestern Namibia to train community game guards, local residents who monitor wildlife in the area despite their lack of ownership. Seeing that colonialism had robbed local people of natural resource control and that they no longer had an incentive to care for wildlife, IRDNC wanted to find a way to generate community benefits from growing tourism in the area, and tie development efforts to a sustained program of conservation (Owen-Smith, 1997). While national policy at this time was based on state ownership of all wildlife, these grassroots projects helped set the stage for a post-independence shift in state willingness to devolve resource control to the local level.

In addition, the experiences of the Herero and Himba people in the area belied a greater conflict between government conservation policies and local communities' livelihoods. A drought in 1979-1982 killed many cattle in the region, but by 1987 populations had bounced back and growing numbers of elephants were impinging upon grazing lands outside of parks. A Herero elder summed up this tension neatly: 'When my cattle were starving Nature Conservation chased them out of the Skeleton Coast Park – the last place where there was still food. They [park officials] said that area was for wild animals and they would shoot cattle that came in. I had to put my cattle inside a kraal and watch them die, knowing that just downriver, inside this park, there was fodder. So why doesn't Nature Conservation keep its elephants away from our food?' (Jacobsohn, 1991, p.210).

The project consisted of three key elements. First, a per person tourist levy was paid to the Purros community by the Endangered Wildlife Trust, a tour-organizing group in the area. The distribution of these funds required the creation of the Purros Conservation Committee, which consisted of a representative of each of the six lineage heads of the community. Second, a craft market was set up in order to sell Himba- and Herero-made items to tourists. Third, a labor pool for conservation-related work was created. This allowed not only for such endeavors as tree counts and rhino monitoring but it also served as a source of income for local people. The guiding principles of this project – returning control of wildlife to local communities and keeping a portion of benefits from tourism at the local level – became central in national conservation strategies that emerged after 1990. 'At a 1990 post-independence workshop to restructure the Directorate of Nature Conservation, Namibian conservationists selected the principles of involving local communities and returning benefits to them as one of their top five priorities' (Jacobsohn, 1991, p.222). How, then, was this shift reflected in national environmental policy after independence? What follows is an examination of the process of restructuring conservation in Namibia after independence and the roles played by government, NGOs, and donors in making it happen.

Post-Independence Environmental Policy

Even though it was the first country in the world to make conservation a constitutional principle, Namibia was faced with a long list of unaddressed environmental challenges at its independence in 1990. According to the Ministry of Environment and Tourism (MET), a new agency established in 1991, these challenges included the following:

- Slow and uneven economic growth and continued subsistence living
- Population pressure on resources
- Loss of productivity of rangelands, or 'desertification'
- Lack of planning and coordination in natural resources management
- Residents of communal areas alienated from resources such as wildlife
- Weak controls on private sector exploitation of resources (overfishing, pollution)

- Lack of information, awareness, education and popular participation (Brown, 1997)

This list of difficulties was too much for a newly independent government to handle on its own, and some of the burden fell on a growing local NGOs community, which included environmental organizations such as the Namibian Nature Foundation (NNF), Save the Rhino Trust, the Cheetah Conservation Fund, and the Namibian Community Based Tourism Association (NACOBTA), (Bauer, 1999). Independence also witnessed the arrival of international NGOs, particularly the World Wildlife Fund (WWF) and the World Conservation Union (IUCN). This international attention was also reflected in the establishment of government-to-government donor assistance initiatives as the US Agency for International Development (USAID) and numerous European development agencies arrived on the scene.

With so many emerging actors, cooperative arrangements were required for an effective environmental agenda and partnerships between government agencies and NGOs developed quickly.[7] A combination of factors encouraged this mutual relationship: the need for field expertise such as that gained by IRDNC, limited government resources and capacity after independence, and close personal relationships between officials of the ruling party, the South West African People's Liberation Organization (SWAPO) and Namibians interested in establishing environmental NGOs. New government agencies had the ability to develop and advocate legislation, but lacked technical expertise or sufficient funds to implement projects. NGOs established a presence in the field and attracted qualified experts to their staffs, but they lacked authority and funds. International donors, especially USAID, had the money to give without the local presence to apply it in the most effective manner. It seemed that collaboration of resources, knowledge, and authority had the most potential to engender significant benefits towards the cause of environmental conservation.

The first major cooperative project to emerge from this convergence of objectives was the Living in a Finite Environment Program (known as LIFE), designed largely by the MET, funded by USAID, and implemented by WWF with technical assistance and lessons learned from IRDNC. The stated goal of the LIFE program is the 'Improved quality of life for rural Namibians through sustainable natural resource management' (Jones, 1999b, p.60). Its complementary statement of purpose is that 'communities derive increased benefits in an equitable manner by gaining control over and sustainably managing and utilizing natural resources in target areas' (Jones, 1999b, p.60).

The project has gone through two major incarnations: first, it sought to prepare local communities for wildlife management through the training of game guards as begun by IRDNC. The LIFE program was, thus, at first an extension of IRDNC-type projects to the Caprivi, the northeastern-most region of Namibia. This geographic shift was based on several factors, including the basic desire to expand the use of the IRDNC model, the existence of variable wildlife populations in the Caprivi, community willingness to participate in the program, and the perceived ability of LIFE to have a quick, positive impact on the region. The project established a Steering Committee that made small grants to communities to assist in the creation of tourism projects. The committee consisted of representatives of a number of local NGOs, but was chaired by the MET. Decision-making was by consensus, but the MET and USAID retained veto power over 'any activity which is contrary to their respective policies or regulations' (Brown, 1999b, p.60). Currently, in its second version, the project is being reworked for two purposes. The Steering Committee was replaced with a new umbrella organization called The Namibian Association of CBNRM Support Organisations (NACSO)[8] in the hopes of having a grant making process that is more Namibian and less USAID-driven.[9]   Second, this restructuring was undertaken with an eye towards USAID's decision to phase out its funding for LIFE by 2004 due to the fact that the average income of Namibians now places the country above the ceiling to qualify for aid. USAID will continue to fund other projects, however, that are more regional and less bilateral in nature. Under these circumstances, the main focus of community-based conservation in Namibia is to prepare local communities to take over wildlife management, and to establish local tourism businesses that will become self-sustaining.

The Growth of Conservancies as CBNRM

While CBNRM policies at the national level in Namibia have taken various forms, one of the most prominent is the creation of conservancies. Conservancies began as areas in which private landowners were given the authority to manage and use shared wildlife populations. Extending back into the 1960s, conservancies were allowed on commercial lands so that farmers could jointly manage wildlife populations among their properties (Barnes *et al.*, 2002). They were also allowed to 'farm' wildlife, the profitability of which increased with increased property size. The drive behind conservancies initially was, thus, primarily for financial gain.

In 1992, as community-based conservation initiatives grew in national prominence, the Ministry of Wildlife, Conservation, and Tourism (MWCT) began to make legal provisions for the creation of conservancies on communal lands. While this was more of a debate about possibilities than realities – residents of communal areas still had no legal claim to wildlife – it nonetheless opened the debate on the issue of wildlife tenure (if avoiding the issue of land tenure). A policy document issued by the MWCT defined conservancies as '...a group of farms and/or area of communal land on which neighbouring landowners/members have pooled their resources for the purpose of conserving and utilizing wildlife on their combined properties and/or area of communal land' (Jones, 1999a, p.5).

The fact that this initiative was being considered at all was seen to be a major step toward sustained wildlife management. In practice, however, communities were already being prepared for conservancy status through a variety of activities sponsored by LIFE, for example, game guard training, the establishment of locally representative wildlife management committees, and the creation of locally-run tourism businesses. Consequently, as the national government created a process for giving conservancies legal status, communities were already undertaking activities that would fall under conservancy management. By 1995 legislation was in place to support this move and conservancies in communal areas essentially became group-owned businesses based on wildlife management and tourism income.

As of April 2003, Namibia had 19 registered conservancies in communal areas. Fourteen of these are located in either the Caprivi or Kunene, the two regions that received the initial training and project assistance from LIFE and IRDNC, respectively. There are at least 31 other potential conservancies at various stages in the gazetting process.[10] Local members of each conservancy select a representative management committee, which in concert with IRDNC and the LIFE Program develops a sustainable management plan for the community and makes decisions about how benefits from tourism will be distributed. Some conservancies opt for payments to individual members, while others channel income directly into community projects such as schools or health centers (USAID, 2002). Conservancies are generally reliant on grant funding at their inception, but this too is beginning to change. Salambala Conservancy, for example, was established in June of 1998 with grant funding through the LIFE program, and in October 2002 agreed on its first budget that was independent of grant funding. Its revenues are largely from a hunting concession, which allows the conservancy to contract with a private hunter for a set number of elephants, buffalo, and several smaller trophy animals on an annual basis. In 2001 and 2002 the Salambala Conservancy Committee made payments to each of the 19 villages in the conservancy; in 2001 the payments were N$2000 per village and in 2002 the committee agreed to distribute N$2500 per village.[11] These funds were used in a variety of ways, with several villages building houses for teachers but the majority saving the money for use in future projects[12] such as grinding mills or other projects. Accountability for the funds and their use, however, are still issues to be addressed, as some funds were being kept by individuals in the village rather than deposited in the bank, while in one case local indunas gave each smaller area N$100 and did not know how it was used.

Despite the appeal of this form of management for returning resource control to local communities, conservancies on communal land face a series of difficulties in their establishment that those in commercial areas do not. These include:

- The definition of community and of conservancy boundaries
- Competing interest groups within communities
- Competition between new conservancy institutions and established institutions
- Differences in scale between appropriate social units and resource management units
- Uncertain land tenure

- Unequal levels of support available to assist all the communities wishing to form conservancies (Jones, 1999a, p.1).

The first four conservancies have been registered since 1998, and some are just beginning the process of becoming financially self-sustaining (Barnes *et al.*, 2002). Jones (1999a) cites four important factors that conservancies must handle effectively in order to be sustainable: evolution over time and their ability to adjust to change, good facilitation by NGOs in meeting accountability standards, shared objectives among the participants, and community choices in favor of continued participation and balancing the needs of the conservancy with other lifestyle considerations (e.g. cattle farming). Though unmentioned in the previous list, a key factor in the future will be the issue of financial support and whether the conservancies will eventually be able to reach self-sustainability, the unstated but implicit goal behind their businesslike focus. Nonetheless, these conservancies have been developed at the community level with the involvement of local people and are designed to integrate local social and economic interests with conservation objectives.

Transfrontier Conservation Initiatives

Like most countries in southern Africa, Namibia is developing transfrontier conservation initiatives. In particular, the Caprivi region, a fingerlike extension of land that is in some places only 40 kilometers wide, is a key location both of community-based conservation projects and transfrontier initiatives. Efforts to integrate conservation across borders in this region reflect the need to connect this small area to its surrounding environment and the shared culture of communities in this part of Namibia that borders Zambia, Zimbabwe, Botswana, and Angola.

Advocacy for regional environmental initiatives comes partly from USAID, which articulates a new vision of grant making beyond its traditional bilateral assistance programs. USAID has also shifted away from bilateral grants and prefers to fund NGOs and civil society rather than work through government agencies. The USAID Regional Centre for Southern Africa (RCSA) was established in 1995 for the purpose of implementing USAID's Initiative for Southern Africa (ISA). The ISA contains three strategic objectives and two special objectives, as follows:

Strategic Objectives:
- Increased Capacity to Influence Democratic Performance;
- A More Integrated Regional Market;
- Accelerated Regional Adoption of Sustainable Agriculture and Natural Resource Management.

Special Objectives:
- *Increased Regional Capacity to Manage Transboundary Natural Resources* [emphasis added];

- Create Capacity for More Informed Regional Decision Making. (IUCN-ROSA, 1997, p.xi)

To implement this objective, USAID began seeking organizations with experience in the region to implement transfrontier conservation initiatives.[13]

In a recent effort to advance transboundary management, RCSA issued a Request for Funding Proposals (RFP) in July of 2000 specifically soliciting NGOs interested in the construction of transborder conservation projects beginning late in 2000 and running until the fall of 2003. The RFP defined its target as follows:

> The activity solicited in the document will address economic development and sustainable utilization and management of natural resources within a proposed transboundary natural resources management area (TBNRMA). *A transboundary natural resources management area is a relatively large area, which straddles a frontier between two or more countries and covers a large-scale natural system (ecosystem). The area requires a process of cooperation across boundaries to maximize conservation and sustainable natural resources management to the benefit of the stakeholders.* [emphasis original] A TBNRMA can encompass a variety of land tenure arrangements, and may include protected areas or parks, communal areas, privately owned areas, state lands and/or international river basins. (RCSA, 2000)

The focus of this project is located in the 'Four Corners TBNRMA,' the area in which the borders of Botswana, Namibia, Zambia, and Zimbabwe are in close proximity.[14] In many respects, these projects reflect simply an expansion of ecological scale in the hopes of conserving larger pieces of land, addressing the needs of migratory species, providing better structures for managing shared water resources, and so on. In the case of Caprivi, the focus is to help make a very small strip of land ecologically viable by connecting it to surrounding territory. The Caprivi is also in the path of the Okavango River as it flows south into the Okavango Delta, Botswana's largest tourist attraction that boasts one of the single greatest concentrations of biodiversity in the world. Insuring proper management of water and rivers in the area is key to the future of the Delta, while connecting the Caprivi to the Delta is likely bring tourist revenue to the Strip. Moreover, significant numbers of elephants move from the Chobe National Park in Botswana up through the Caprivi and into Zambia, and as the main tourist attraction in the park, cooperative management is a pressing issue as the herds continue to grow in size.

By 1998, transborder initiatives were surfacing in government documents as well. The MET circulated a document in June of 1998 seeking the input of NGOs and other potential partners on its plan 'A Conservation and Tourism Development Plan for Caprivi,' a portion of which included advocacy for connecting game parks and conservancies in Caprivi to protected areas in Botswana, Angola, and Zambia. While the initial plan for Caprivi was primarily a domestic one – improvement of park infrastructure, increased opportunities for tourism-related employment, fostering sustainable trophy-hunting in the area, and building partnerships with local communities and NGOs – it also acknowledged a commitment to 'pursuing the ultimate goal of transboundary natural resource management within SADC [Southern African Development Community]' (Tarr, 1998, p.5).

Projects in the Caprivi were interrupted by a late 1999 secessionist uprising in which a small number of poorly armed, untrained Caprivians attacked the Namibian Broadcasting Corporation's offices and other key buildings in Katima Mulilo, the regional capital city. The secessionists, calling themselves the Caprivi Liberation Army (CLA), demanded the reunification of Caprivi with the Lozi Kingdom, a pre-colonial kingdom in south-central Africa, which has a titular king in Zambia and members in Namibia, Botswana, Zambia and Zimbabwe. The Caprivi constitutes a slice of what was once this kingdom. This uprising, while put down by the Namibian military in less than a day, nonetheless contributed to subsequent killings of some Namibians and three French tourists in the area. It is suspected that Uniao Nacional para a Independencia Total de Angola (UNITA), the Angolan rebel group led by Jonas Savimbi until his death in February 2002, is responsible for these killings and that it assisted the Caprivian rebels out of a desire to retaliate for Namibian government support of the Angolan government forces (MPLA) in its civil war against UNITA.

The interruption of the environmental program by the civil conflict, however, was brief. LIFE, in coordination with the Ministry of Environment and Tourism and IRDNC, is currently engaged in transfrontier conservation initiatives with Botswana, Zambia, and Zimbabwe. The object of this project is not to create a giant protected area with reified borders, but rather to build on the success of conservancies at the local level in a border area where communities, despite their location on different sides of a political boundary, share common cultural and historical ties that make the border more relevant for national politics than for daily life. It is hoped that strengthening conservation ties across borders will lead to increased tourism, the re-establishment of wildlife migration patterns, and equitable water use in the area. From a grassroots perspective, however, transfrontier conservation is nothing new. IRDNC has been involved in cross-border exchange visits and efforts to bring communities on the shared boundaries of the Caprivi together for nearly as long as it has been working in the Caprivi.[15] Small-scale initiatives, such as the staff members of the Kwando Conservancy in East Caprivi visiting villages across the border in Zambia to discuss fire prevention, are now becoming an even more prominent part of IRDNC's projects in the region. This view sees TBNRM as 'transboundary CBNRM,' a connection that makes clear the importance of working with communities locally before they come together internationally.[16]

Yet, even with a history of locally based conservation in the Caprivi, roles for local communities are complex. Current land use in the area includes five protected areas, conservancies in various stages of development, a state forest, agricultural projects, and communal land not currently under conservation (Mendelson and Roberts, 1997). Yet even with the dominance of a community-based approach in the Caprivi, top-down agendas are not completely absent. The aforementioned 'Four Corners TBNRMA' project grant funded by USAID was awarded to the African Wildlife Foundation (AWF) in late 2000; the grant consists of US$ four million over a three-year period and covers a 25,000 square kilometer area in four countries along the Zambezi River. Lacking a presence on the ground in Namibia prior to the receipt of this grant, AWF has encountered difficulties working effectively with the existing organizations and structures in Namibia. AWF's focus is fourfold: improved landscape management, the development of sustainable conservation business ventures, the facilitation of stakeholder processes in TBNRM, and the development of information systems to track and document the TBNRMA process.[17]   The emphasis on creating local enterprises is seen by some Namibian and Botswanan organizations as making an end run around existing partnerships because AWF has, in some cases, offered funds directly to community-based organizations rather than going through the NGOs that help communities manage funds and support project implementation.[18] AWF is seen as lacking experience in and knowledge of the area, and some local conservationists have complained that AWF spent the first year and a half of its three-year grant buying vehicles and setting up office without building local partnerships. Most fundamental, however, is the concern that communities' roles as primary stakeholders in TBNRM are being affected by AWF's 'incompetent' approach, resulting in the relegation of communities to secondary or tertiary stakeholders.[19] This comment reflects a theme in comments made about AWF made by many local activists, in that AWF is seen as having failed to consult with local communities about their needs and focusing instead on the collection of data on wildlife that conservancies have already been recording, or trying to bring in private enterprises that will bring limited if any benefits to communities.

What is clear in the Namibia case, however, is that most TBRNM projects, especially in the Caprivi, reflect a connection to the past establishment of community-based conservation initiatives. This history of Namibian conservation projects at the local level is, therefore, serving as a mechanism to create a framework for community involvement in larger conservation projects. TBRNM in the Caprivi reflects the desire to enable local communities to manage resources across borders even when land tenure varies, rather than to create large international protected areas. This approach contrasts with the South African focus on protected areas along its borders, which will be discussed in the next section.

South Africa: Communities into Conservation

South Africa lacks a strong history of community-based conservation initiatives and environmental issues have taken somewhat longer to appear on its national agenda than in Namibia (Cock, 1991; Steyn and Wessels, 2000). While a number of NGOs are engaged in community-level conservation projects, these initiatives are more recent and the strategy is not as prevalent as in Namibia. The South Africa case also demonstrates a discursive contradiction between a stated desire to ensure roles for local communities and a parks-based, rather than community-based, approach to transfrontier conservation initiatives.

Prior to 1988, environmental discourse in South Africa reflected what Cock (1991) calls an 'authoritarian conservation perspective.' This began to change with the emergence of environmental NGOs that linked issues such as nuclear waste, air pollution, and overpopulation to the liberation struggle against apartheid (Steyn and Wessels, 2000). More recently, South African National Parks (SANP) has begun to implement policies to include local communities by attempting to 'link the protection of biodiversity to human needs' (Cock and Fig, 2000). Cock and Fig question whether this shift constitutes 'fundamental change or a shallow restructuring,' and list the changes in park policies around land restitution, improving accessibility to the parks for area residents, increasing tourism and revenues, eliminating racism and sexism in management and employment, and developing cultural resources and assisting with heritage management. The establishment of a Social Ecology Unit at Kruger National Park in 1996, for example, was hailed as an important step in connecting Kruger to its neighbors in a more positive way, but the Social Ecology Unit is often heavily criticized for its failures and the park is still regarded as being inattentive to the concerns of local residents along its border, to the point of 'Krugerisation' coming to stand for community- insensitive management (Refugee Research Programme, 2002). What is important to note about these initiatives is that they remain park-centered and may actually expand the role of the SANP in the areas surrounding national parks. This is a different approach to community conservation, in that peripheral roles for local residents are being grafted onto existing parks in a way that does not fundamentally alter control over wildlife or natural resources. Even land restitution, which is discussed below, is not as clear-cut as might be expected.

Transfrontier Conservation Initiatives

Of all the countries in the region, South Africa has the most clearly articulated and strongly advocated approach to transfrontier conservation. It is widely perceived that the South African government's pursuit of 'peace parks' is one of the driving forces behind transfrontier conservation in the region more generally. South Africa is currently pursuing at least five major transfrontier conservation initiatives which are based in its existing national parks with minimal or no additions of other kinds of land. This is in clear contrast with its partner countries, who often first must establish extensive infrastructure and create national parks or environmental management frameworks prior to being considered 'ready' to participate in a transfrontier conservation initiative.

The Peace Parks Foundation (PPF), a South African NGO founded by Dr. Anton Rupert, also the founder of WWF-South Africa, is currently engaged in the development of seven transfrontier conservation areas (TFCAs) in southern Africa. They include territory in Botswana, Lesotho, Malawi, Mozambique, Namibia, South Africa, Swaziland, Tanzania, Zambia and Zimbabwe. The organization's first major success story was the establishment of the Kgalagadi Transfrontier Park on the border of South Africa and Botswana on 12 May 2000. This agreement committed South Africa and Botswana to manage their pre-existing national parks, the Kalahari Gemsbok National Park in South Africa and the Gemsbok National Park in Botswana, as an integrated ecological unit. There remain functional policies to be worked out involving border crossings, tourist infrastructure upgrade, implementation of research projects and integration of conservation strategies; but the fences have been removed and wildlife is free to roam. Other proposed projects in the region are in varying stages of development. Some have clearly drawn borders while others are still being negotiated. What is consistent, however, is an emphasis on delineated territories, rather than broader integration of environmental management strategies or wildlife use policies, which might be less politically contested than the creation of international parks.

The largest current emphasis is on the Greater Limpopo Transfrontier Park (GLTP), the core area of what was formerly called the Gaza-Kruger-Gonarezhou Transfrontier Conservation Area (GKG TFCA). PPF plans indicate that there will be a 35,000 square kilometer park as the first step towards a larger TFCA, having scaled back its original emphasis on the entire TFCA to first focus on the park area within it. Covering 100,000 square kilometers,[20] the Greater Limpopo Transfrontier Conservation Area will constitute an area roughly the size of Portugal once completed, enclosing parts of five national parks, private game reserves, communal land, and contractual national parks.[21] South Africa, Mozambique, and Zimbabwe signed a formal agreement committing to the creation of the GKG TFCA on 10 November 2000. This document provides for the initial establishment of a park that would be smaller than the eventual target area, with the goal of developing more detailed agreements to establish a larger park over time. The preamble of the trilateral agreement displays the priorities of the three governments as follows:

> The Government of the Republic of Mozambique, the Government of the Republic of South Africa, and the Government of the Republic of Zimbabwe:
> *Recognising* the principle of sovereign equality and territorial sovereignty of their states;
> *Conscious* of the benefits to be derived from close co-operation and the maintenance of friendly relations with each other;
> *Acknowledging* the necessity to conserve the environment for the benefit of all the people of Southern Africa;
> *Desiring* to promote ecosystem integrity, biodiversity conservation and sustainable socio-economic development across international boundaries...
> (emphasis original)[22]

The agreement also ties conservation to human development and puts economic considerations on par with conservation policy itself. This emphasis on economic benefits, however, does not specify who is to benefit, but rather proclaims the need for 'all of the people' of southern Africa to benefit – without indicating what kind of benefits everyone is to receive. This reflects tensions over who will gain from increased tourism revenues to the park and what kinds of jobs will be available and for whom.

The history of this area presents a number of challenges to the creation of a fully integrated environmental management zone. Kruger Park has a history of use by South African Defence Force (SADF) to provide military support for Resistencia Nacional Mocambicana (RENAMO) bases across the border in Mozambique (Ellis, 1994; Koch, 1998). Military operations in the area also tracked Mozambican refugees as they fled through Kruger Park, and suspicions of illegal ivory and rhino horn smuggling conducted by military units in the park still abound (Ellis, 1994). The ecology and wildlife on the Mozambican side of the border also has past trauma to overcome; in addition to the drought of 1991-92, many animals have been poached over the years for the survival of those fleeing the civil war. Even more generally, 'Protected areas and wildlife in southern Africa have thus suffered considerable damage because of social conflicts stemming from past colonial styles of conservation management as well as from the negative impacts of warfare and militarisation that affected most of the region in the post-colonial period (Koch, 1998, p.60).' The civil war in Mozambique also turned many residents of southern Mozambique into refugees who fled into Zimbabwe, Swaziland, and South Africa. The question of future repatriation of these refugees remains unaddressed; at least some of the communal land areas in Mozambique slated for inclusion in the GLTP are the sites of abandoned villages decimated by civil war. The Refugee Research Programme (RRP) of the University of the Witwatersrand, for example, stopped its voluntary repatriation efforts when it learned of the transfrontier park out of concern that those Mozambicans they were assisting to return home from South Africa might be shortly be moved again.[23] What might happen if refugees now living in South Africa, Zimbabwe or Swaziland decide to try to return home after the establishment of the park is an example of the potential tensions between local residents and the GLTP.

Beyond repatriation, however, there is concern regarding the significant amounts of communal land slated for inclusion in the park that is still currently occupied by local communities. There are approximately 30,000 Mozambicans living in what has been declared the Limpopo National Park (LNP), the area formerly known as Coutada 16 which constitutes Mozambique's contribution to the GLTP. The majority of these people live along the Limpopo River along the eastern border of the LNP, while some 6,000 live along the Shingwedzi and Olifants Rivers closer to the KNP and the South African border. The Sengwe Corridor, which is needed to connect the northernmost part of the Kruger National Park to Gonharezhou National Park (GNP) in Zimbabwe, is also populated. Officials are currently pursuing the creation of a contractual national park-type arrangement in the Sengwe corridor, in which the land would be retained by the community but managed as part of the larger park.[24] The current controversy and instability around land tenure and redistribution in Zimbabwe, however, do not bode well for its participation in the park. In addition to communities in the corridor area, some Zimbabweans have moved into the GNP itself and while the government claims to have spoken out against this, it is not clear how the issue of the new park residents will be addressed.

Consequently, each country is faced with both common and different issues in establishing the park. Beyond extensive issues around local communities, for example, the preparedness of the territory to support ecotourism varies greatly. Table 10.1 presents my synthesis of some of the main differences that will have to be addressed if plans are to proceed.[25] Land with different legal status and ownership, lack of preparation for tourists, standardization of legal environmental management policies, conflict resolution mechanisms, and considerations of local communities are just a few of the possible sticking points for the GLTP. The PPF has identified priority issues to be addressed as wildlife restocking, infrastructure establishment, ranger training and staffing expansion, poaching control, and deforestation.[26]

Table 10.1 Country Comparison: Greater Limpopo Transfrontier Park

	South Africa	*Mozambique*	*Zimbabwe*
Proposed land area	Kruger National Park (KNP) and the Makuleke area, managed jointly	The Limpopo National Park (LNP), formerly Coutada 16 area	Gonarezhou National Park (GNP) and Sengwe Corridor (connects GNP to the KNP)
Infrastructure development	Extensive infrastructure for tourism already in place	Extremely limited tourism facilities and poor infrastructure	Some tourism facilities, but negative affects of political instability
Biodiversity status and issues	Numerous species and heavy concentration of wildlife, esp. big game	Need for wildlife repopulation – very limited at present	Similar biodiversity to Kruger, but massive problem of poaching due to drought and starvation
Potential local community interactions	No communities within Kruger, but dense settlement to the south and west	Communities within the LNP, especially along the Limpopo and Shingwedzi Rivers	Communities along the park border and in the park itself due to resettlement; also in corridor area

These differences also include varying levels of economic benefits that each state may be able to glean from the new park. In meetings as early as 1990 between Dr. Anton Rupert and President Chissano of Mozambique, the potential economic benefits to Mozambique from transborder initiatives were established as a topic of emphasis.[27]   Poverty reduction is a stated goal of the GLTP project in Mozambique.[28] Despite the potential for major political problems in establishing this park, much of the focus of the emerging project plans is on sustaining the environment as a source of economic gain.

While community participation and benefits remain part of the discourse around the GLTP, they are often treated as something for the three countries to deal with individually rather than as a whole – in direct contrast with the conservation issues that dominate the planning process. At a July 2001 Ministerial Meeting of environment Ministers Francis F. Nhema of Zimbabwe, Valli Moosa of South Africa, and Fernando Sumbana of Mozambique, Minister Moosa expressed his view that community representation or participation was an internal issue for the individual countries and must be dealt with as each country saw fit. Moreover, he was opposed to raising the expectations of local communities by agreeing to hold a meeting of community representatives concurrently with a Ministerial meeting.[29] These objections fly in the face of the public commitments to make conservation participatory and centered around community participation and benefits.

Roles for Local Communities?

While project plans and officials make general promises about benefits to and roles for local communities, the projects are clearly framed in terms of parks with delineated borders with wildlife conservation and tourism the major goals. The PPF Project Profile for the area lists among its concerns the 'problems of increasing human encroachment into the area [Mozambique]' but also states its commitment not to force relocation of existing settlements.[30] At the same time, even if they are not a priority, local economic benefits have been given some attention in the plans. A community-based natural resources management project funded by the PPF in Zinave National Park (Mozambique), which has been discontinued, stressed that 'The program is designed to ensure that the people who live in and around the Park derive maximum benefit from any future development of tourist facilities.'[31] Besides the questions of just what constitutes 'maximum benefit,' communities do not appear to have been consulted prior to the establishment of these projects, which might have brought to light not only local environmental knowledge and communities' concerns about tourism projects and living in or near new parks.

Moreover, a discursive contradiction exists between the PPF and the South African Department of Environmental Affairs and Tourism about the relative importance of local communities and wildlife in the broad national conservation agenda. While the PPF is vague about roles for local communities, the government is clearer in its position about local communities in defining a transfrontier park, the label applied to the GLTP:

> What is a transfrontier park? Definitions vary, but essentially all a transfrontier park means is that the authorities responsible for areas in which the primary focus

is wildlife conservation, and which border each other across international boundaries, formally agree to manage those areas as one integrated unit according to a streamlined management plan. *The authorities also undertake to remove all human barriers within the transfrontier park so that animals can roam freely* [emphasis added].[32]

A transfrontier park is contrasted with a transfrontier conservation area (TFCA):

Slightly different than a transfrontier park, a transfrontier conservation area usually refers to a cross-border region where the different component areas have different forms of conservation status, such as private game reserves, communal natural-resource management areas, and even hunting concession areas. Fences, major highways, railway lines or other barriers may separate the various parts. Nevertheless, they border each other and they are managed for long-term sustainable use of natural resources, although free movement of animals between the different parts is not possible.[33]

This second definition could have been written for the GLTP as it is today, with its variation in land use, environmental management policies, parks and communal land. The use of language such as the 'encroachment' of humans into wildlife habitat and the authorization to 'remove all human barriers' within the new park hardly suggest a community-friendly approach.

Plans for the GLTP called for at least one section of the fence between the KNP and the LNP to be lifted in April 2002. A barrage of criticism of the park expansion and concerns about the impact of wildlife on the communities in the area, however, apparently derailed this plan and pushed back fence removal to December 2002, when several small, symbolic sections of the fence were cut down. Thirty elephants were moved from Kruger to Coutada 16 in October 2001, but this was done without informing the roughly 30,000 Mozambicans living in the area.[34] Since then wildlife translocation has continued, though the animals that have been moved are, for the time being, confined to a fenced area close to the South African border but not far from the communities in the Shingwedzi River area. A consultation with local residents held in Maputo during the last week of April 2002 was brimming with hostility towards the park, indicated by the assertion by one local leader that residents would rather wage war on wildlife than move from their ancestral lands.[35]

Moreover, a study by the Refugee Research Programme (RRP) in March 2002 indicated that 40 percent of local LNP residents interviewed had never even heard of the new park, and that more than 80 percent would refuse to move regardless of what they were offered in return.[36] The German Development Bank (KfW) has also warned park officials that its financial support of the project will be reconsidered if community consultation is not improved. KfW divisional chief for southern Africa Kurt Hildebrand stated that, 'We are completely opposed to forced removals. Even a hint of this would destroy the philosophy of the entire project, and would destroy its viability.'[37] The notion of just what constitutes forced removal, however, remains a somewhat nebulous one. The community priorities for the Project Implementation Unit of the LNP for 2003 focus on two central issues. First, communities will be consulted about the realignment of the park border along the Limpopo River, which currently constitutes the eastern border of the LNP. Second, communities along the Shingwedzi River, deeper in the park, will be given the option to move with compensation or to stay and 'adapt' to living in the park.[38] What remains unclear is just how communities will be compensated, where they will go, and what living in the park might look like or if it is even truly feasible. Besides their general opposition to moving, communities in the LNP area have expressed concerns about access to water (as most of them are dependent on the nearest river), possible dangers to themselves and their livestock from wildlife, and loss of their ability to live on land that has cultural and historical significance or visit the graves of their ancestors (Refugee Research Programme, 2002).

While some nods are made towards community involvement, then, the lack of clear planning for it, the unresolved issues of local communities within the park, and the language of both the PPF and the South African Department of Environmental Affairs and Tourism suggest that the parks and wildlife-centered approach to conservation is alive and well in the region. What appears to be happening is that rather than developing conservation initiatives around communities, there are efforts being made to graft small symbolic roles for communities onto larger park-based projects. The best example of this is the creation of a contractual national park in the Pafuri triangle, the northernmost region of Kruger National Park that borders both Mozambique and Zimbabwe. The Makuleke people were removed from this land in 1969 so that it could be incorporated into the KNP, and the Makuleke filed a land claim for its return in 1995. Through a lengthy negotiation process, SANP and the Makuleke agreed to the creation of a contractual national park in the area (deVilliers, 1999; Steenkamp & Uhr, 2000; Steenkamp *et al.*, 2001). The Department of Land Affairs found the claim valid, but the land was returned to the Makuleke under strict conditions: the land must be used for conservation purposes only for 99 years (no prospecting, mining, residence, or agriculture), no development will be allowed without a positive environmental impact assessment, and if the land is ever put up for sale SANP retains the right of first refusal (Reid, 2001). SANP now manages the land for the Makuleke based on a 50-year lease, and the Makuleke have contracted with a private business to establish and operate a small tourist lodge in the park. While this is widely considered to be a successful case for communities, it did not come without a high degree of ongoing SANP control.[39] Nor does this agreement indicate what might have happened if the petitioning community had not been amenable to keeping the land in question under conservation and instead wanted to reoccupy and/or use it for other purposes such as agriculture or mining. Within the Makuleke community, however, concerns exist that if the borders are opened under the GLTP that their interests in tourism may be negatively impacted if they are not included in the planning process, or that they may be affected by the now-rampant poaching in southwestern Zimbabwe.[40]

What is important to note about contractual national parks is that despite their billing as a way to include local communities in conservation and provide them with economic benefits, 'The contractual national park model was initially developed...as a way to meet conservation objectives and extend South Africa's protected area network without heavy investment in land purchase' (Reid, 2001). This frames the strategy not as a means to land restitution but a way to 'grow' national parks on the cheap. Any benefit to local communities is thus secondary at best, and reflects the park-oriented focus of this approach.

Concluding Thoughts

In this chapter, I have argued that transfrontier conservation initiatives in southern Africa vary in their approaches to the participation of local communities. In the case of Namibia, the community-based approach to transfrontier conservation can be traced to two important factors. Both its head start on conservation at the grassroots level and its subsequent national policy commitment to community-based conservation projects and conservancies reflect efforts to decentralize natural resource control. This emphasis on community involvement is reflected most clearly in its transfrontier conservation initiatives in the Caprivi. In this way, existing community-based conservation initiatives form the basis for their extension into larger areas.

South Africa's late-emerging emphasis on community involvement in conservation is taking place alongside its transfrontier conservation initiatives rather than forming the basis for them, and focuses on ways to provide benefits for communities from existing national parks rather than creating locally-driven projects independent of the imperatives of national parks. Moreover, while explicit commitments have been made to include local communities in transfrontier conservation, there are contradictions within project plans and ambiguity remains about appropriate (and inappropriate) roles for local communities. While communities are said to be an important part of these projects, they have not been treated as equal stakeholders in the negotiation and implementation processes. As is becoming apparent, this lack of consultation in the South African case may have negative consequences for the willingness of donors and NGOs to support the GLTP, as well as for the communities in its path.

List of Acronyms

AWF	African Wildlife Foundation
CBNRM	Community-based natural resource management
CLA	Caprivi Liberation Army
GLTP	Greater Limpopo Transfrontier Park
IRDNC	Integrated Rural Development and Nature Conservation
IUCN	World Conservation Union
KfW	German Development Bank
KNP	Kruger National Park (South Africa)

LIFE   Living in a Finite Environment
LNP   Limpopo National Park (Mozambique)
MET   Ministry of Environment and Tourism (Namibia)
MPLA   Movimento Popular da Libertacao de Angola
MWCT   Ministry of Wildlife, Conservation, and Tourism (Namibia)
NACSO   Namibian Association of CBNRM Support Organisations
PPF   Peace Parks Foundation
RENAMO   Resistencia Nacional Mocambicana
RRP   Refugee Research Programme (University of Witwatersrand)
SADC   Southern African Development Community
SADF   South African Defence Force
SANP   South African National Parks
SWAPO   South West African People's Liberation Organization
TBNRM   Transboundary natural resource management
TBNRMA   Transboundary natural resource management area
TFCA   Transfrontier conservation area
UNITA   Uniao Nacional para a Independencia Total de Angola
USAID   United States Agency for International Development
WWF   World Wildlife Fund

Notes

1   Thanks to Lawrence Markowitz for his ongoing counsel in the development of this project and to the MacArthur Dissertators Group at the University of Wisconsin-Madison for their comments on an earlier draft of this chapter. I am also grateful to my host organizations, Integrated Rural Development and Nature Conservation/World Wildlife Fund in Namibia, and the Refugee Research Programme in South Africa. Funding for the fieldwork that contributed to this chapter was provided by the University of Wisconsin-Madison's Scott Kloeck-Jenson Travel and International Internship Grant programs, the University of Wisconsin's MacArthur Consortium Scholars program, and a Fulbright-Hays Doctoral Dissertation Research Abroad Program Grant from the U.S. Department of Education.

2   Presentation by Karl Zimmerer, Conference on Globalization and Geographies of Conservation, University of Wisconsin-Madison, April 19, 2002; see also Zbicz and Green, 1997.

3   For example, the central statement of purpose of the Peace Parks Foundation [see www.peaceparks.org] reads as follows: 'The primary objective of the Peace Parks Foundation is to promote Transfrontier Conservation Areas in Southern Africa. Through these proposed 'peace parks' the Foundation is working with governments, the private sector and local communities to protect our environment and unlock the huge economic potential of the region's tourist industry. The peace parks will help to bind together Southern Africa's nations in a vast network of sustainable and environmental partnerships, protecting their unique natural inheritance for generations, and promoting a culture of peace and cooperation.'

4   For the example of the development and creation of Etosha National Park, see Berry, 1997.

5   One notable exception to the trends on communal land is found in Kunene, home of the former Damaraland and Kaokoland homelands. The Kunene region was the home to the first community-based conservation initiatives in Namibia beginning in the early 1980s (to be discussed later), which is generally regarded to be a key part of its success in monitoring and maintaining wildlife populations more successfully than most other regions. There is also some indication that wildlife in Caprivi, another locus of more recent community based conservation projects, is experiencing improvements as well. For more on these projects see Jacobsohn, 1991; Owen-Smith, 1997; and Jones, 1999a.

6   IRDNC continues to play a key role in the establishment of community-based natural resource management projects in Namibia as well as in transfrontier conservation, especially in the Caprivi region.

7   Personal interview, Peter Tarr, head of the Office of the Directorate of Environmental Affairs, Ministry of Environment and Tourism, 13 July 2000, Windhoek, Namibia.

8   Members of NACSO include: MET, WWF/LIFE Program, IRDNC, NACOBTA, the Rossing Foundation, the Legal Assistance Center (LAC), NNF, the Nyae Nyae Development Foundation of Namibia (NNDF), the Namibian NGO Forum (NANGOF), Namibian Development Trust (NDF), the University of Namibia, the Desert Research Foundation of Namibia (DRFN), RISE, and CRIAA SA-DC.

9   Personal interview, Anna Davis, former field staff at IRDNC and current head of the CBNRM Unit of the Namibia Nature Foundation, 12 July 2000, Windhoek, Namibia. The primary function of the CBNRM Unit at the NNF is to set up monitoring and evaluation systems for local conservancies in order to demonstrate to USAID that its grant money is being effectively used. NNF is also responsible for the financial administration of these conservancy grants, as local communities generally have little or no way to administer funds.

10 Personal communication, Anna Davis, head of the CBNRM Unit of the Namibia Nature Foundation, 1 April 2003; see also Barnes *et al*, 2002 for background.

11 Salambala Conservancy Financial Planning/Budget Meeting, Bukalo Agricultural Center, Caprivi Region, Namibia, 15-16 October 2002.

12 Discussion of use of funds at the Salambala Conservancy Committee Workshop on Benefits Distribution, Bukalo Agricultural Center, Caprivi Region, Namibia; 22 October 2002.

13 Personal interview, Chris Weaver, WWF/LIFE Program Chief of Party, 5 July 2000, Windhoek, Namibia.

14 Originally, this project would also have included Angola and the western portions of Caprivi, but due to Namibia involvement in the Angolan civil war and the unstable nature of that immediate area, projects that consider an even wider reaching territory have been put on hold. The recent cessation of hostilities may enable consideration of expanding conservation initiatives into southeastern Angola as well, but progress is likely to be slow.

15 Personal interview, Margaret Jacobsen and Garth Owen-Smith; Co-Directors/Founders, IRDNC; 24 November 2002; Katima Mulilo, Namibia.

16 Personal interview, Richard Diggle, Regional Director of IRDNC in Caprivi, 28 November 2002; Katima Mulilo, Namibia.

17 Presentation of AWF's Four Corners Initiative by Daudi Sumba, AWF Staff, at the Four Corners Regional TBNRM Forum, Victoria Falls, Zimbabwe, October 29-November 1, 2002.

18 Personal interviews, October-December 2002, staff members of WWF, IRDNC, NNF and the Chobe Wildlife Trust.

19 Personal communication, prominent Namibian conservationist, Windhoek, Namibia, December 2002.

20 The vast majority of land identified for the TFCA is in Mozambique, with South Africa's contribution consisting of Kruger National Park and some privately held game reserves on its western border, followed by the Sengwe Corridor, the Gonharezhou National Park, and some small bordering game reserves in Zimbabwe. See www.peaceparks.org for updated maps.

21 http://www.peaceparks.org/profiles.kruger.html.

22 Peace Parks News, 'New Transfrontier Animal Kingdom,' Edition #2, November 2000, Cape Town.

23 Personal communication, Hernan del Valle, Head of the Refugee Research Programme, January 2003.

24 Personal interview, Lamson Maluleke, AWF Community Development Officer, White River, South Africa, 20 March 2003. See also the discussion of the Makuleke land claim to follow, which has been cited as a model example for the pending agreement in the Sengwe area.

25 For more details on the physical characteristics of each proposed areas and capacity building grants, see http://www.peaceparks.org/profiles/kruger.html.

26 http://www.peaceparks.org/profiles/kruger.html.

27 http://www/peaceparks.org/story/beginnings.html.

28 Ibid.

29 Minutes of Meeting, Tri-Nation Ministerial Committee, Gaza-Kruger-Gonharezhou Transfrontier Park; Sheraton Hotel, Harare, Zimbabwe; 11 July 2001.

30 http://www.peaceparks.org/profiles/kruger.html.

31 http://www.peaceparks.org/profiles/projects/12.html.

32 Definition taken from the SA Department of Environmental Affairs and Tourism's website, http://www.environment.gov.za/, section on Transfrontier Conservation.

33 Ibid.

34 J. Arenstein, 'Political Grandstanding Threatens World's Biggest Reserve,' Mail & Guardian, 25 April 2002.

35 Ibid.

36 The full report is available on line: See 'A Park for the People? Greater Limpopo Transfrontier Park – Community Consultation in Coutada 16, Mozambique' at www.wits.ac.za/rrp.

37 J. Arenstein, 'Political Grandstanding Threatens World's Biggest Reserve,' Mail & Guardian, 25 April 2002.

38 Personal communication, Arrie VanWyk, Head of the Project Implementation Unit of the LNP, 3 March 2003. See also the Peace Parks Foundation's Quarterly Progress Report October-December 2002, available at www.peaceparks.org.

39 For another case of contractual national parks in South Africa, see Glavovic 1996. 'Resolving People-Park Conflicts through Negotiation: Reflections on the Richtersveld Experience,' *Journal of Environmental Planning and Management*, 39 (4), pp. 483-507.

40 Personal interview, Lamson Maluleke, AWF Community Development Officer, White River, South Africa, 20 March 2003.

References

Barnes, J, MacGregor, J. and Weaver, L.C. (2002), 'Economic Efficiency and Incentives for Change within Namibia's Community Wildlife Use Initiatives,' *World Development*, 20 (4), pp. 667-681.

Bauer, G. (1999), 'Challenges to Democratic Consolidation in Namibia,' in Joseph, R. (ed.), *State Conflict, and Democracy in Africa*. Boulder: Lynne Rienner.

Berry, H. (1997), 'Historical review of the Etosha Region and its subsequent administration as a National Park,' *Madoqua*, 20 (1), pp. 3-12.

Cock, J. (1991), 'Going Green at the Grassroots: The Environment as a Political Issue,' in Cock and Koch, eds., *Going Green: People, Politics and the Environment in South Africa*. Oxford: Oxford University Press.

Cock, J. and Fig, D. (2000), 'From Colonial to Community-Based Conservation: Environmental Justice and the National Parks of South Africa,' *Society in Transition*, 31 (1), pp. 22-36.

Ellis, S. (1994), 'Of Elephants and Men: Politics and Nature Conservation in South Africa,' *Journal of Southern African Studies*, 20 (1), pp. 53-69.

Glavovic, B. (1996), 'Resolving People-Park Conflicts through Negotiation: Reflections on the Richtersveld Experience,' *Journal of Environmental Planning and Management*, 39 (4), pp. 483-507.

IUCN-ROSA [World Conservation Union-Regional Office for Southern Africa]. (1997), *Profiles of Donors: Supporting Environment and Development Initiatives in Southern Africa*. Harare: IUCN-ROSA.

Jacobsohn, M. (1991), 'The Crucial Link: Conservation and Development,' in Cock, J. and Koch, E. (eds.), *Going Green: People, Politics and the Environment in South Africa*. Oxford: Oxford University Press.

Jones, B. (1999a), *Rights, Revenues, and Resources: The problems and potential of conservancies as community wildlife management institutions in Namibia*. Evaluating Eden Programme, Paper No. 2. IIED: London.

_____ (1999b), *Community-based Natural Resource Management in Botswana and Namibia: an inventory and preliminary analysis of progress*. Evaluating Eden Programme, Paper No. 6. IIED: London.

Katerere, Y., Hill, R. and Moyo, S. (2001), 'A Critique of Transboundary Natural Resource Management in Southern Africa,' IUCN-ROSA Series on Transboundary Natural Resources Management – Paper 1. Harare: IUCN-ROSA.

Koch, E. (1998), 'Nature has the Power to Heal Old Wounds: War, Peace, and Changing Patterns of Conservation in Southern Africa,' in Simon, D. (ed.), *South Africa in Southern Africa: Reconfiguring the Region*. Oxford: James Currey.

Mendelson, J. and Roberts, C. (1997), *An environmental profile and atlas of Caprivi*. Windhoek: Gamsberg Macmillan Publishers,

Owen-Smith, G. (1997), 'The Kaokoveld: Southern Africa's Last Wilderness,' in Tarr, P. (ed.), *Namibia Environment*. Windhoek: MET.

RCSA (USAID Regional Center for Southern Africa). (2000), 'Program Description: Request for Concept Papers, Initiative for Transboundary Management of the Okavango/Chobe/Hwange/Caprivi/Mosi-Oa-Tunya/Kafue Area.'

Refugee Research Programme (2002), 'A Park for the People? Greater Limpopo Transfrontier Park – Community Consultation in Coutada 16, Mozambique,' Report available online at www.wits.ac.za/rrp.

Reid, H. (2001), 'Contractual national parks and the Makuleke community,' *Human Ecology*, 29 (2), pp. 135-155.

Schoeman, A. (1997), 'Conservation in Namibia: Laying the Foundation,' in Tarr, P. (ed.), *Namibia Environment*. Windhoek: MET.

Steenkamp, C. and Uhr, J. 2000. 'The Makuleke Land Claim: Power relations and CBNRM in a South African case study,' IIED Evaluating Eden Programme, Occasional Paper No. 18. IIED: London.

Steenkamp, C., Grossman, D., Koch, E. & Massyn, P-J. (2001), 'Private Sector Investment and Safari Hunting in a Co-Managed Conservation Area: A Case Study of the Makuleke Region of the Kruger National Park,' Safari Club International Foundation Wildlife Conservation Issues – Technical Series no 003. SCI: Washington.

Steyn, P. and Wessels, A. (2000), 'The Emergence of New Environmentalism in South Africa, 1988-1992,' *South African Historical Journal*, 42, pp. 210-232.

Tarr, P. (1998), 'A Conservation and Tourism Development Plan for Caprivi,' MET vision statement/concept paper. Windhoek, Namibia: MET.

USAID: Namibia FY (2002), Congressional Budget Justification, Namibia Activity Data Sheet, available at http://www.usaid.gov/country/afr/na/673-003.html.

Zbicz, D. and Green, M. (1997), 'Status of the world's transfrontier protected areas,' *Parks* 7(3), pp. 5-10.

Chapter 11

'(S)hell in Nigeria': The Environmental Impact of Oil Politics in Ogoniland on Shell International

Phia Steyn

Introduction

In the past decade the interface between environmental and human rights on the one hand, and economic development on the other, has become a major focus of attention. The emergence of international interest in and concern over the environmental and social costs of economic development is a direct consequence of the establishment of a new international political order in the post-Cold War era. In the absence of Cold War tensions, the international political community in the 1990s increasingly started to pay constructive attention to the state and the future of planet Earth and its inhabitants, and to global human rights abuses.

This state of affairs prompted many ethnic minority groups living in oil-producing regions in the developing world, with the support of international human rights and environmental organizations, to publicize the environmental and social impact of oil production on their people and their traditional lands. The internationalization of their struggles ensured support on an international scale for these ethnic minority groups as they began to make demands to multinational oil companies and national governments in the course of the 1990s. These demands included the elimination of environmental damage and contamination, environmental rehabilitation, respect for the life, health and culture of the inhabitants of the regions, and the implementation of sustainable systems of oil production. In some struggles more extensive political rights and a share in the wealth generated by oil production have also been central to the demands made to national governments.

Accusations of environmental and human rights abuses by the oil industry have cast doubts on the relationships between multinational oil companies and their host governments, and the environmental and social management practices of these oil companies in developing countries (see Frynas, 1998; Frynas, 2002; Detheridge and Pepple, 1998). While the oil industry has always been inextricably bound to the struggle for human wealth and power, the darker side of the industry, such as massive corruption, the fomentation of political upheavals in particular countries and the total disregard for the environmental and social impact of production, has in recent years made headlines across the globe. National governments of developing countries have also had to face much criticism for the way they manage their oil resources, place the interests of multinational oil companies above the interests of ethnic minority groups in their countries, and for the political, economic, social and environmental marginalisation of these minority groups.

This chapter aims at exploring the environmental impact of oil politics in Ogoniland, Nigeria, on the multinational oil company Royal Dutch/Shell (hereafter Shell International). In terms of oil-related environmental and human rights conflicts, the struggle of Ken Saro-Wiwa and the Ogoni people against the Nigerian Federal government and Shell Nigeria in the course of the 1990s, emerged as a landmark in the oil-related political processes in both Nigeria, on a national level, and more generally in oil-producing developing countries on an international level, for a number of reasons. Firstly, it highlighted internationally the political and economic injustices associated with the oil industry in Nigeria in particular, which in turn have contributed to similar investigations being launched in other parts of the developing world. Secondly, the campaign and strategies of the Movement for the Survival of the Ogoni People (MOSOP) presented other oil affected minority groups, with similar grievances, with a 'blueprint' on how to articulate their grievances to both their national governments and the oil companies operating in their territories (Osaghae, 1995; Human Rights Watch, 1999a, 1999b).

Thirdly, the activities of MOSOP directly resulted in a decision by Shell Nigeria in 1993 to suspend all oil production in Ogoniland. The company has since then repeatedly stated that it will only resume oil production in the area at the invitation of the Ogoni people (Shell Nigeria, 1996). Lastly, the Ogoni struggle, together with the Brent Spar incident in the United Kingdom in 1995, have directly impacted on the way in which Shell International views human rights and sustainable development within oil producing communities in which the Group operates across the globe. This has led to far-reaching changes within the Group in terms of both human rights and the environment (Sykes, 2001).

In this chapter, attention will be directed at three main aspects, namely the development of the oil industry in Nigeria and environmental problems associated with oil production in the country in general and in Ogoniland in particular; the environmental and human rights struggle of Ken Saro-Wiwa and the Ogoni in the 1990s, and the environment-related political impact of the struggle on Shell International.

The Nigerian Oil Industry

Oil, Environment and Ethnic Minority Groups

Until the end of the Biafran Civil War in 1970, the Nigerian economy was dominated by the agricultural sector. From 1970 onwards the focus shifted towards oil and the production thereof, which contributed to the stagnation and decline of both the agricultural and industrial sectors in the country (Filani and Onyemelukwe, 1981). The development of the Nigerian oil industry dates back to January 1906 when the Colonial government issued a number of prospecting licenses to the British Colonial Petroleum Corporation covering an area of 100 square miles on the Rofutoro and Lafagbo Rivers in the Benin district.[1] Concessions were also granted in 1907 to the better-known Nigerian Bitumen Corporation who drilled thirteen wells in the area near Lekki Lagoon between 1907 and 1914. Though some of the wells yielded bitumen-deposits and petroleum, the Corporation never succeeded in exploiting its finds profitably and was liquidated in 1914.[2]

With the passing of the Mineral Oil Ordinance no 17 of 1914 further oil exploration and exploitation in Nigeria were limited to British and British colonial companies. After the First World War two British companies, namely the D'Arcy Exploration Company and the Whitehall Petroleum Corporation, briefly explored for oil between 1919 and 1922. Both companies were unsuccessful in finding any oil in commercially viable quantities, which led to a suspension of all serious investigations into the petroleum potential of Nigeria in the 1920s.[3]

Despite the negative reports of the 1920s, interest in the petroleum prospects of the country was revived in the 1930s with the joint application of Royal Dutch/Shell and British Petroleum (BP) to explore for oil in the colony. A concession covering the whole of Nigeria was granted to Shell-BP in 1937. Their first real break-through come only in 1951, but the source was limited and commercially exploitable oil was first discovered in 1956 at Oloibiri in the Niger Delta, and at Ebubu and Bomu in the Ogoni section of the Delta in 1958. Production at Oloibiri started in 1958 with 6,000 barrels per day (b p/d)[4] (Adebayo and Falola, 1987).

Between 1958 and 1961 the oil industry was completely dominated by Shell-BP. The Nigerian federal government opened up the oil industry to more role-players from 1961 onwards and important newcomers included Mobil, Gulf and Safrap (now ELF). Important developments in the initial phase of the Nigerian oil industry include the passing of the Petroleum Profits Tax Ordinance in 1959, in terms of which the Nigerian government obtained 50 per cent of the profits of the oil companies, and the opening of the first oil refinery at Alese Eleme (in Ogoniland) close to Port Harcourt in 1966. This refinery was managed by the Nigerian Petroleum Refinery Company which was a joint venture between the Nigerian government (55 per cent), Shell (22.5 per cent) and BP (22.5 per cent) (Ikein, 1990; Central Office of Information, 1960; Kirk-Greene and Rimmer, 1981; Tims, 1974).

The Nigerian oil industry remained small until 1970, after which its rapid development coupled with a corresponding increase in the daily production as well as the importance of oil world-wide, contributed to the emergence of the oil industry as the dominant sector within the Nigerian economy. The income the federal government derived from oil sales and taxes consequently became the main source of income and since the 1970s oil revenue has accounted for more than 90 per cent of Nigeria's total foreign export earnings (Anon, 1990; Frank, 1984).

Following the general trend among members of the Organization of Petroleum Exporting Countries (OPEC), of which Nigeria became a member in 1971, the Nigerian government set out to increase its participation in the oil industry from 1970 onwards. This was to be achieved through a systematic process of nationalization and the government created the Nigerian National Oil Corporation (NNOC) in May 1971 to facilitate the nationalization of oil companies operating in the country (Tims, 1974; Sampson, 1988; Panter-Brick, 1978). The nationalization of Shell-BP began in June 1973 when the government obtained a 35 per cent equity stake in the company. In June 1974 this percentage was raised to 55 per cent and in 1979 to 60 per cent (Tims, 1974; Arnold, 1977; Kirk-Greene and Rimmer, 1981). The government's equity stake in Shell-BP reached an all-time high of 80 per cent in 1979 when it nationalized BP's remaining 20 per cent share as retribution for the latter's provision of oil to South Africa. From 1979 on the federal government, through the Nigerian National Petroleum Council (NNPC),[5] controlled 80 per cent of the Shell Petroleum Development Company of Nigeria Limited (SPDC – commonly referred to as Shell Nigeria) while Royal Dutch/Shell was left with only a 20 per cent stake in this joint venture. In 1988 the NNPC reduced its equity stake in Shell Nigeria to 60 per cent and sold ten per cent of the shares to Royal Dutch/Shell and five per cent each to ELF and Agip. In the 1990s the NNPC sold an additional five per cent of its shares to ELF (Shell Nigeria 1996a). At present Shell Nigeria is thus a joint venture composed of the NNPC (55 per cent), Royal Dutch/Shell (30 per cent), ELF (ten per cent) and Agip (five per cent). Since 1960, the market share of Shell Nigeria has continued to decline from almost 90 per cent, to 74.47 per cent in 1970, 51.37 per cent in 1981, and 42.17 per cent in 1997. The company still remains the biggest oil producer in the country (Human Rights Watch, 1999c; Frynas, 2000; Detheridge and Pepple, 1998).

As in many other parts of the world oil exploration and production in Nigeria have over time affected and disturbed the ecological balance in the oil producing areas. Despite the existence of environment related regulations for the oil industry (for example the Mineral Oils Regulations of 1963 and article 25 of the Petroleum Act no 51 of 1969), oil companies neglected to ensure that their activities were environmentally sound, while the federal government neglected to enforce the legislation in place. This state of affairs can be attributed to two reasons: firstly, the federal government, as the majority equity shareholder in all the major oil companies that operate in Nigeria, shares in the responsibility to ensure that the oil industry does not harm the natural and human environment. However, acknowledging and acting upon this responsibility involves a lot of capital, which the federal government either cannot or will not spend. Secondly, the federal government's dependence on oil for more than 80 per cent of its revenue and more than 90 per cent of its total foreign export earnings, in turn has meant that it became extremely important for the government to keep Nigeria's daily oil production as high as possible at all costs. The official government policy further dictates that in the case of commercial oil discovery, all other economic activities within the affected area have to make way for oil production. In the process oil production has led to widespread environmental destruction, while the polluting of agricultural land and river networks has impacted negatively on communities in oil producing areas (Frynas, 1998; Ikein, 1990; Human Rights Watch, 1999d).

While the federal government acknowledges a whole range of environmental problems in Nigeria (see Areola, 1998), its attitude towards the pollution and environmental damage caused by the oil industry remains negative. In one of the number of publications issues by the federal government in its defense at the height of the Ogoni crisis, the government proclaims that 'in progress, something just have to give...There are hundreds of oil communities scattered throughout the delta region. It is not that they are suffering in silence. Rather, their leaders are prepared to accept the fact that there is a price to be paid for all modern development' (Institute for the Promotion of Unity and Understanding, no date, p.32).

A factor that has contributed to the oil industry's disregard for the environment is the fact that the oil producing areas are mostly inhabited by ethnic minority groups that have traditionally played a limited role in federal and, at times, regional politics. Many other ethnic minority groups in the Niger Delta, such as the Ijaw and the Ogbia therefore share the grievances of the Ogoni. In general, oil producing communities have not reaped the benefits that oil production has brought to the Nigerian federal state. Before 1990 the federal government received approximately 90 per cent of the net profits of the oil industry through taxes, royalties and its majority share in the major oil companies. Oil producing areas, by contrast, received only 1.5 per cent of the net profits until 1992 and thereafter firstly three per cent and later 13 per cent. This 13 per cent is not paid directly to the oil producing communities but is channeled through the Oil Mineral Producing Areas Development Commission, which was created in 1992 (Ikein, 1990; Human Rights Watch, 1999b; Shell Nigeria, no date; Sygne, 1993).

Oil Production in Ogoniland

The Ogoni people are one of approximately 250 ethnic minority groups in Nigeria and have some 500,000 members.[6] Their traditional territory is in the Rivers State in south-east Nigeria where they occupy an area of about 650 km^2. The population density in Ogoniland is approximately 770 people per km^2 which is considerably higher than the national average of 95.8 people per km^2.[7] Ogoni territory stretches over the local authorities of Gokana, Khana and Tai-Eleme. Different theories exist regarding the origin of the Ogoni, but it is generally agreed that they settled in their current territory in Nigeria before the fifteenth century. The Ogoni are divided into six clans, namely the Nyo-Khana, Ken-Khana, Babbe, Gokana, Tai and Eleme, each of which is headed by a *Gbenemene* (king). The six clans control 111 villages in Ogoniland (Leton, 1992; Saro-Wiwa, 1992; Osaghae, 1995).

As a minority group within the majority dominated political system in Nigeria, the Ogoni have played a limited role in political processes on a federal level since the country's independence in 1960, the result being that their claims in the 1990s that their political needs and aspirations are not met within the Nigerian political framework, became an important part of the Ogoni struggle. The Ogoni's political marginalization is closely linked with their economic marginalization in the independence era. Their traditional territory is situated in the oil-rich Niger Delta, with oil production in Ogoniland and in the neighboring territories, inhabited mostly by ethnic minority groups, constituting the cornerstone of on-shore oil production in the country.

Commercially viable quantities of oil were first discovered at Dere in Ogoniland in 1958, and Shell-BP started with oil production in that area (the Bomu oil field) in the same year. In 1965 Nigeria's first oil refinery was built at Alesa Eleme which falls within Ogoni territory. Oil production also expanded in Ogoniland, and by the 1990s Shell Nigeria was producing oil in this area at 96 oil wells situated on five oil fields. The maximum daily capacity of Shell Nigeria's oil production in Ogoniland was 28,000 barrels per day (b p/d). Another multinational oil company, Chevron (operating as Chevron Nigeria Limited in a joint venture with the NNPC) also received concessions from the federal government to operate in Ogoniland and began oil production in this region in 1980. Shell Nigeria, however, remained the biggest oil producer in the area until its withdrawal from Ogoniland in 1993. Contrary to claims laid by the Ogoni and environmental interest groups, oil production in Ogoniland does not account for the majority of Shell Nigeria's daily production (Shell Nigeria manages 94 oil fields in the country and produces about one million b p/d). Ogoniland, as the fifth largest oil-producing region in the Rivers State, contributed only three per cent to Shell Nigeria's total daily production until 1993 (Saro-Wiwa, 1992; MOSOP Canada, no date; Human Rights Watch, 1999c; Osaghae, 1995; Shell Nigeria, no date; Institute for the Promotion of Unity and Understanding, no date; Shell Nigeria, 1996b).

The exploration for and the production of oil in Ogoniland have, since 1958, led to radical changes in the economic activities of this ethnic group. The polluting of their agricultural land and water networks by the oil industry gradually denied the Ogoni access to their traditional economic modes of production. The situation is exacerbated by the fact that the Ogoni did not reap the benefits of oil production in their territory over time. Since the federal government nationalized all land and mineral rights in 1978, no oil producing community has had the right to claim part of the profits from oil production in its territory (Osaghae, 1995; Saro-Wiwa, 1992).

Their political, economic and environmental marginalization prompted the Ogoni in 1990 to launch a struggle against the Nigerian federal government and Shell Nigeria. One of the main objectives of this struggle was to convince Shell Nigeria to pay constructive attention to the environmental problems of Ogoniland that resulted from oil production in their territory. Particular emphasis was placed on the polluting of their land and water resources through oil spills, and the air and noise pollution resulting from the practice of gas flaring. The Ogoni further accused Shell Nigeria of not initiating enough development programs despite the fact that Shell Nigeria and not the federal government had launched most of the developments in Ogoniland, including a hospital, two clinics and school buildings (see Human Rights Watch, 1999b; Saro-Wiwa, 1992; MOSOP Canada, no date).

An Overview of the Ogoni Struggle, 1990-2001

Though the Ogoni began to voice their grievances against Shell Nigeria and the federal government well before 1990, their struggle against these two parties in effect only started with the founding of the Movement for the Survival of the Ogoni People (MOSOP) in 1990. Garrick Leton (president) and Edward Kobani (vice-president) headed MOSOP.[8] Contrary to the commonly held belief, Ken Saro-Wiwa was not a founding member of this organization. Shortly after its founding he applied to MOSOP's executive council to appoint him as spokesperson and public relations officer (Hattingh, 1997; Saro-Wiwa, 1992).

The peaceful resistance campaign MOSOP initially conducted centered round environmental, economic and social issues in that the organization attempted to persuade Shell Nigeria and the federal government to pay constructive attention to the Ogoni's environmental, economic and social problems. MOSOP also launched a media campaign to inform the general public in Nigeria of the problems of oil producing communities in general, and of the Ogoni in particular. With the adoption of the Ogoni Bill of Rights on 26 August 1990 the Ogoni entered the political sphere. This Bill of Rights was drawn up and signed by the executive committee of MOSOP and the traditional leaders of five Ogoni clans, and demanded greater social, economic, environmental and political rights for the Ogoni (Institute for Unity and Understanding, no date; Saro-Wiwa, 1992; 'Ogoni Bill of Rights,' 1990).[9]

The Nigerian government's failure to react to the Ogoni Bill of Rights prompted the Ogoni leaders to adopt an addendum to this document on 26 August 1991. The Addendum to the Ogoni Bill of Rights requested MOSOP to bring the problems of the Ogoni to the attention of, *inter alia*, the United Nations Commission on Human Rights, the Commonwealth Secretariat and the African Commission on Human and Peoples Rights. MOSOP was specifically requested to focus on the environmental and economic problems that the Ogoni faced due to Shell Nigeria's oil production in their territory, and the political and social problems of ethnic minority groups within the Nigerian federation. The Ogoni struggle was thereafter internationalized mainly because of the actions of Saro-Wiwa who presented the case of the Ogoni to the United Nations and the Unrepresented Nations and Peoples Organization. Support from human rights and environmental organizations also found expression in investigations by

Greenpeace (*Shell-shocked*, 1995) and Human Rights Watch (*The Ogoni crisis*, 1995) (Osaghae, 1995; Rowell, 1994; *The New York Times*, 1995a).

Between 1990 and 1994 the activities of MOSOP led to a direct confrontation between the federal government and the Ogoni people. E.E. Osaghae (1995) provides two reasons why the Ogoni took the law into their own hands: firstly, the inability of the federal government to react positively to the demands of the Ogoni encouraged MOSOP to force its demands for political autonomy onto the Nigerian government, and secondly, the radicalization of MOSOP after Saro-Wiwa took over the presidency from Leton in 1993.[10]

The most important immediate outcome of the confrontations in this period was the permanent withdrawal of Shell Nigeria from Ogoniland in January 1993 following an attack on Shell employees. The confrontations also led to conflict within the leadership cadre of MOSOP, which polarized this movement into two factions by May 1993. The one faction consisted of the more moderate members, including its president, Leton, and the vice-president, Kobani. The other faction was more radically orientated and was led by Saro-Wiwa, Goodluck Diigbo and Ledum Mitee. The conflict centered round four issues, namely what the balance should be between confrontation and reconciliation in the Ogoni's struggle against Shell Nigeria and the federal government; whether the Ogoni should participate in the presidential elections (planned for 12 June 1993); the tactics that should be employed in the handling of conflict between the Ogoni and neighboring ethnic groups, and the political structure of MOSOP. The final break within the executive council in June 1993 left Saro-Wiwa and Mitee in control of MOSOP as President and Vice-President respectively (Birnbaum, 1995; Institute for the Promotion of Unity and Understanding, no date).

The violent activities of the Ogoni youth organization, the National Youth Council of Ogoni People (NYCOP), during the failed national presidential elections of June 1993, gave the federal military government the necessary excuses to intervene in Ogoniland after the elections were annulled. The government launched *Operation Restore Order in Ogoniland* which was characterized by numerous human rights abuses, including murder, by federal troops. The main target of this military operation was MOSOP which was branded a radical and secessionist movement. Saro-Wiwa consequently became a victim of military harassment and was arrested four times in the course of 1993 (*Weekly Mail & Guardian*, 1995; Osaghae, 1995; Human Rights Watch, 1999b; Saro-Wiwa, 1995).

In the meantime, conflict between the Ogoni leaders increased after a committee of 13 Ogoni traditional leaders distanced themselves in December 1993, in an open letter in the press to the Nigerian head of state, the notorious Gen. Sani Abacha, from the lawless and violent activities of MOSOP and NYCOP. In reaction to this letter, NYCOP branded the 13 Ogoni leader as 'vultures' and accused them of working against the interests of the Ogoni people. By May 1994, the conflict within the Ogoni prompted the Gokana *gbenemene* (king) to call a meeting of all interested parties. This meeting was perceived by MOSOP and NYCOP to be anti-Saro-Wiwa and was therefore strongly opposed by both organizations. A warning was subsequently issued by the two organizations that the leaders would be attacked if the meeting went ahead as planned. The military governor of the Rivers State, Lt.-Col. Duada Komo, was informed of these threats and he undertook to provide the necessary protection for those traditional leaders who wanted to attend the meeting (Orage, no date; Institute for the Promotion of Unity and Understanding, no date).

The planned meeting was held in Goikoo at the palace of the Gokana *gbenemene* on 21 May 1994 and was attended by a large number of Ogoni leaders. Events, however, went terribly wrong when a large crowd attacked the Gokana palace. In the chaos that ensued Chiefs Albert Badey, Edward Kobani, Samuel Orage and Theophilus Orage were murdered. At the time of the meeting Saro-Wiwa was campaigning in the Goikoo district. At the Kpopie-junction, about one km from Goikoo, he was stopped at a military roadblock and prohibited from entering the area. The order not to allow Saro-Wiwa near Goikoo at the time of the meeting was given by Komo, and the Nigerian police escorted him back to Port Harcourt (Birnbaum, 1995).

After these murders the federal government sent in the Rivers State Internal Security Task Force to suppress the riots in Ogoniland that followed this event. A number of people were arrested – including Saro-Wiwa on 22 May 1994 - – in connection with the murders, and held without charge or access to legal representation for months (eight months in the case of Saro-Wiwa). In November 1994 Abacha appointed the Civil Disturbances Special Tribunal (CDST)[11] to try cases arising from the events at Goikoo. The CDST consisted of two federal High Court Judges, I.N. Auta (chairperson) and E.E. Arikpo, and a high ranking military officer, Lt.-Col. H.I. Ali (Birnbaum, 1995; Anon, no date).

On 28 January 1995 formal charges were laid against Saro-Wiwa, Mitee, Barinem Kiobel, John Kpuinen and Baribor Bera. Saro-Wiwa, Mitee and Kiobel were charged with planning and procuring the Goikoo murders, while Kpuinen and Bera were charged with participating in the actual murders. All five individuals were tried as a group and the trial commenced on 6 February 1995. On 10 February 1995 an additional ten people[12] were charged for directly participating in the Goikoo murders. Their trial lasted approximately eight months and attracted a great deal of attention from the international media and interest groups. The impartiality of the Tribunal was called in question and some studies have concluded that the trial was unfair and in breach of both the Nigerian Constitution of 1979 and numerous human rights conventions to which Nigeria is a party (Birbaum, 1995; Human Rights Watch, 1999e).

In a controversial judgement in October 1995 the CDST found Saro-Wiwa, Barinem Kiobel, John Kpuinen, Baribor Bera, Saturday Dobee, Felix Nuate, Nordu Eawo, Paul Levura and Daniel Gbokoo guilty of murder. The other six defendants were acquitted. On 30 and 31 October 1995, Saro-Wiwa and the eight other Ogoni convicted were sentenced to death. Despite international appeals for clemency, the Provisional Ruling Council confirmed the sentences on 8 November 1995. Ken Saro-Wiwa and the eight other Ogoni were hanged in the Port Harcourt Prison at 11:30 on 10 November 1995 (Anon, no date; Orage, no date).

Saro-Wiwa's execution was a turning point in the struggle of the Ogoni against the Nigerian federal government and Shell Nigeria. Internally, his death robbed MOSOP of his dynamic leadership and the organisation initially struggled to regain its former initiative and strength. However, through the leadership of Ledum Mitee MOSOP has since 1996 once again focused attention on the fundamental issues that sparked-off the struggle in 1990, namely the economic and environmental marginalization of the Ogoni due to oil production in their homeland (Mitee, 2001).

The Ogoni position on the return of Shell Nigeria to Ogoniland has also hardened, and they hold the view that the oil company can return to their traditional territory if it meets all their demands. These demands include *inter alia* that Shell Nigeria must carry out a thorough environmental impact assessment to ascertain how much damage oil production has done to the environment in the area between 1958 and 1993; that Shell Nigeria must undertake extensive clean-up operations to rehabilitate the environmental damage, and that the company must pay the Ogoni US $80 billion in compensation and past royalties (*Weekly Trust,* 2001).

The Ogoni's continued refusal to allow Shell Nigeria to resume oil production in Ogoniland on the company's terms have in turn encouraged other oil producing minority groups to began directing demands at the oil companies and the federal government. The most notable of these struggles is that of the Ijaw, who in terms of numbers and geographical distribution, have the potential to disrupt oil production in the Niger Delta in a way that the Ogoni would never be able to do (Osaghae, 1995; Human Rights Watch, 1999a; Human Rights Watch, 1999b).

The Environmental Impact of Oil politics in Ogoniland on Shell International

As mentioned in the introduction, the end of the Cold War ushered in a period of unprecedented attention being paid, on international and national political levels, to the state and the future of the environment, and to human rights abuses around the globe. This concern, however, was countered in the energy sector by the Gulf War (1990-1991) which in essence amounted to a struggle over the oil resources of the Persian Gulf (Yergin, 1992). According to Joseph Stanislaw (1991), the Gulf crisis created what he calls the 'new world oil order' in which energy security was placed back onto international and national political agendas in an effort to ensure oil supplies to governments, their citizens and their industries.

This new world oil order created an environment in which it became perfectly acceptable for oil companies to continue with business as usual whilst at the same time greenwashing their images to show greater sensitivity towards the demands for sustainable environmental management that emerged strongly after the Earth Summit in 1992. Oil companies in general continued to view their main role as meeting the energy needs of society, to a large extent regardless of the human and environmental costs of oil production, while governments continued to urge oil companies to ensure uninterrupted production and the expansion of proven reserves to meet the energy needs of the not so distant future (see Beers and Capellaro, 1991).

Prior to 1995, environmental thinking in Shell International did not differ much from the prevailing views of the industry at large. Earlier statements from the company on sustainable development, voiced in 1991 (see Hubert van Engelshoven, 1991), lacked formal articulation in any formal company documents, which in turn meant that it received almost no attention in the way the company conducted its business around the globe. However, two events in 1995 changed this position of Shell International with regard to both the environment and its social corporate responsibility (Sykes, 2001).

Shell International first made world headlines in 1995 when it announced that it was decommissioning its Brent Spar storage and loading buoy, that had been operating in the North Sea oil fields, and that it would dispose of the Brent Spar in deep-water. This announcement met strong resistance from Greenpeace who argued that the toxic materials remaining in the installation would cause widespread environmental destruction in the North Sea. Greenpeace successfully mobilized public support in Europe that Shell International was left with no alternative but to back down on its original plans and to announce that they would re-evaluate their options. The Brent Spar incident turned into a public relations nightmare for the company even despite the fact that Greenpeace had to apologize publicly to Shell International for using the wrong technical data which invalidated all their claims that deep-water disposal would be more harmful to the environment than on-shore disposal (Dickson and McCulloch, 1996).

The negative publicity created by the Brent Spar incident ensured that the media would quickly pick up on events that were taking place in Nigeria in the same year. At the time of the Brent Spar conflict, Ken Saro-Wiwa and his fourteen co-accused were on trial for the Giokoo murders. MOSOP and their allies in the international environment and human rights communities were very successful in publicizing the role Shell International played in environmental and human rights abuses in the Niger Delta in general, and in Ogoniland in particular. This publicity directly led to serious questions being asked about Shell International's conduct in Nigeria and the company soon found itself being placed 'on trial' in the international media. Shell International's obvious reluctance to intervene on behalf of the fifteen Ogoni, especially after Saro-Wiwa and eight other Ogoni were sentenced to death and subsequently executed, tarnished the image of the company even further and by the end of 1995 the name Shell became synonymous with bad environmental practices and with human rights abuses (see Pyke, 1996; Anon, 1995a; *The Star*, 1995; *The New York Times*, 1995).

The events of 1995 led to a major internal investigation in Shell International which lasted about one year. The company concluded that while they believed at the time that they were doing the right things, society at large did not agree and that the environment was much higher on society's priority list than what the company formerly believed. They also found that the notion of sustainable development was very pertinent to society, as was the concept of publicly reporting on its activities in order to open up the company to outside scrutiny (Sykes, 2001; Sharp Paine, 1999).

The review in 1996 resulted in fundamental changes within Shell International: in 1997 the company revised its Business Principles and included for the first time principles on sustainable development and corporate social responsibility. This signaled an acknowledgement from the company that they have environmental and human rights responsibilities towards society in addition to a responsibility to shareholders, customers, employees and those with whom it does its business. Shell International outlined its responsibility to society in the new Business Principles as 'to conduct business as responsible corporate members of society, to observe the laws of the countries in which we operate, to express support for fundamental human rights in line with the legitimate role of business and to give proper regard to health, safety and the environment consistent with our commitment to contribute to sustainable development' (Royal Dutch/Shell, 1997; Human Rights Watch, 1999a).

Since 1997 the company has gradually started to move in a 'greener' and a more open direction. It now publishes an annual report on non-financial matters to the public and shareholders in an effort to be more open and transparent in its management. The first report, published in 1998, was entitled *Profits and Principles – Does There Have to be a Choice?*, and examined the company's performance during 1997-1998 in terms of its new business principles (Human Rights Watch 1999a). Active dialogue has also been established with a number of well-respected environmental non-governmental organizations and the company has committed itself to making a contribution to sustainable development (Sykes, 2001).

This commitment to contribute to sustainable development has found expression in a number of environment-related activities. Shell International was the first oil company to address the issue of climate change and its role in producing gases that negatively impact on world climate. The company has come up with its own climate change strategy that includes the acknowledgement that it will continue to produce oil and gas to fuel for the next 20-30 years, to provide more natural gas, to develop its business in gas-fired power generation which produces less than half the CO_2, to develop renewable energy sources, to reduce the emissions of greenhouse gases in its own operations and to fund programs to help improve our understanding of climate change (Greenpeace USA, 1997; Royal Dutch/Shell, no date).

Shell International has also invested in developing new technologies to facilitate the move from oil to gas as the main energy source of the future, to facilitate the expansion of gas to liquids production, and it has increased its investment in renewable energy. Between 1997 and 1998 the company set up Shell International Renewables with an initial budget of US $500 million. A further US $50-100 million was committed to renewables in the second half of 2001. As part of its renewable energy strategy, the company bought out Siemens Solar and now ranks second in world market share, while it has also stepped up activities in the wind energy market (Sykes, 2001).

Concluding Remarks

Shell International has come a long way since its shock discovery in 1996 that environmental and human rights issues do matter in the post Cold-War political environment. By 2000 the company's annual *People, Planet and Profits* (Royal Dutch/Shell, 2001) report voiced clear positions on a diversity of issues including biodiversity, bio-fuel, bribery and corruption, child labor, climate change, eco-efficiency, health and safety, and global warming to name but a few. Its position within Nigeria, however, remains problematic and claims that their operations have become more environment and community friendly have met resistance amongst oil-producing ethnic minority groups (Mitee, 2001). An internal review of Shell Nigeria's community projects in 2001 further highlighted the discrepancies between the actual performance of the community projects and the claims made by Shell Nigeria with only 31 per cent of projects evaluated found to be successful (Shell Nigeria, 2001).

The challenge in the twenty-first century for Shell International specifically, but also for all oil companies operating in African countries, will be to balance the demands of the oil-producing communities with their vested business and political interests in the countries they operate. Only then will Shell International be able to claim success for their new environment and socially sensitive approach to oil and gas production. However, whether or not Stanislaw's new world oil order will allow for such a radical departure from traditional oil practices in Africa, and whether or not African governments will start to recognize the legitimacy of claims made by oil-producing communities remains to be seen.

Notes

1   Nigerian National Archives, Enugu Branch (NNAE), CSE 8/4/59-CSO 368/09: Mr Crewe – Governor of Nigeria, 30.08.1909 (letter). The British Colonial Petroleum Corporation had limited success in Nigeria and from 1916 until the company went into liquidation in 1924, it focused all its attention on its interests in Romania. Public Record Office (PRO, London), BT 31/17953/91326: British Colonial Petroleum Corporation.

2   BP Archives (BPA, Coventry, England), BP 44063, Letter from the Petroleum Department, 12.11.1936.

3   BPA, BP 44063, Letter from the Petroleum Department, 12.11.1936; NNAE, CSE 3/13/6-B706/1921: Letter from the Crown Agents for the Colonies (no Nigeria 830), 8.6.1920; NNAE, ABADIST 13/5/87-114/21: Secretary, Southern Provinces – Resident, Owerri Province (no B. 706/1921), 19.10.1921 (memorandum).

4   PRO, CO 852/34/7: E. Melville – Secretary of State for the Colonies, 15.12.1936 (minute).

5   In 1977 the NNOC merged with the Nigerian Ministry of Petroleum Resources to form the Nigerian National Petroleum Corporation (NNPC).

6   Ten groups account for 80 per cent of the total Nigerian population, while three groups, namely the Yoruba, the Hausa-Fulani and the Igbo dominate politics in the country.

7   The national average is based on the 1991 census.

8 There seems to be uncertainty regarding the founding date of MOSOP with various sources citing 1988, 1990, 1991 and 1992 respectively. Since MOSOP uses 1990 in its own publications, for the purpose of this chapter 1990 is taken as the year in which MOSOP was founded.

9 The traditional leaders of the Eleme clan had no part in the Ogoni Bill of Rights. The signatories included Saro-Wiwa, as well as two leaders who were murdered at Goikoo in May 1994, namely Edward Kobani and Samuel Orage.

10 There was a significant increase in the number of confrontations between MOSOP and the federal government after Saro-Wiwa took over as president in 1993. After he was arrested in May 1994 in connection with the Goikoo murders, the levels of confrontation dropped considerably (See Anon 1995B).

11 The CDST was convened in accordance with the Civil Disturbance Decree No 2 of 1987. Babangida originally issued the decree in 1987 and it was used during his period as head of state whenever civil disturbances broke out. According to the Decree all people that can either directly or indirectly be connected to an act, directly share in the guilt of the act. Both the person who committed a murder and the persons indirectly involved in it, are therefore guilty of murder, which crime had to carry the death penalty (Anon *no date*; Birbaum 1995).

12 Pogbara Afa, Saturday Dobee, Monday Danwin, Felix Nuate, Nordu Eawo, Paul Levura, Joseph Kpante, Michael Vizor, Daniel Gbokoo and Albert Kagbara.

References

Adebayo, A.G. and T. Falola. (1987), 'Production for the Metropolis: The Extractive Industries' in T. Falola (ed.). *Britain and Nigeria: Exploitation or Development?* London: Zed Books.

Anon. (1990), 'Oil to the Rescue: Don't throw it Away Again.' *The Economist* 317 (7679, 3 November), p. 56.

Anon. (1995a), 'Multinationals and their Morals.' *The Economist* 337(7943, 2 December), p. 18.

Anon. (1995b), 'The Ogoni Crisis: Nigeria's Shame.' *LH Rights* 2 (December), pp. 14-15, 17.

Anon. (no date), 'On the Sentences of Ogoni Civil Disturbances Tribunal' (Information provided by the Nigerian High Commission in Pretoria, South Africa).

Areola, O. (1998), 'Comparative Environmental Issues and Policies in Nigeria' in U. Desai (ed.). *Ecological Policy and Politics in Developing Countries.* Albany: State University of New York Press.

Arnold, G. (1977), *Modern Nigeria.* London: Longman.

Beers, D. and C. Capellaro. (1991), 'Greenwash!' *Mother Jones* 16 (2, March/April), pp. 38-42.

Birnbaum, M. (1995), *Nigeria: Fundamental Rights Denied. Report of the Trial of Ken Saro-Wiwa and Others.* London: Article 99.

Central Office of Information. (1960), *Nigeria: The Making of a Nation.* London: Foreign Office.

Detheridge, A. and N. Pepple. (1998), 'A Response to Frynas.' *Third World Quarterly* 19 (3), pp. 479-486.

Dickson, L. and A. McCulloch. (1996), 'Shell, the Brent Spar and Greenpeace: A Doomed Tryst?' *Environmental Politics* 5(1, Spring), pp. 122-129.

Filani, M.O. and J.O.C Onyemelukwe. (1981), 'Nigeria' in H. De Blj and E. Martins (eds). *African Perspectives: An Exchange of Essays on the Economic Geography of Nine African States*. New York: Methuen.

Frank, L.P. (1984), 'Two Responses to the Oil Boom: Iranian and Nigerian Politics after 1973.' *Comparative Politics* 16 (April), pp. 295-314.

Frynas, J.G. (1998), 'Political Instability and Business: Focus on Shell in Nigeria.' *Third World Quarterly* 19 (3), pp. 457-478.

Frynas, J.G. (2000), 'Author's Reply. Shell in Nigeria: A Further Contribution.' *Third World Quarterly* 21 (1), pp. 157-164.

Greenpeace USA. (1997), *Industry and the Climate Change Debate: Membership and Positions of International Lobby Groups*. Washington: Greenpeace USA.

Hattingh, J. (1997), 'Shell International and the Ogoni People of the Rivers Province in Nigeria: Towards a Better Understanding of Environmental Justice in Africa.' Unpublished paper presented at the conference 'Environmental Justice: Global Ethics for the 21st Century.' Melbourne (1-3 Oct).

Hubert van Engelshoven, J.M. (1991). 'Corporate Environmental Policy in Shell.' *Long Range Planning* 24(6), pp. 17-24.

Human Rights Watch. (1999a), 'The Price of Oil: The Role of the International Community.' <http://www.hrw.org/hrw/report/1999/nigeria/Nigew991-12.htm>.

Human Rights Watch. (1999b), 'The Price of Oil: Protest and Repression in the Niger Delta.' <http://www.hrw.org/hrw/report/1999/ nigeria/Nigew991-08.htm>.

Human Rights Watch. (1999c), 'The Price of Oil: Oil and Natural Gas in Nigeria.' <http://www.hrw.org/hrw/ reports/1999/nigeria/Nigew991-03.htm>.

Human Rights Watch. (1999d), 'The Price of Oil: The Environment.' <http://www.hrw.org/hrw/reports/1999/nigeria/Nigew991-05.htm>.

Human Rights Watch. (1999e), 'The Price of Oil: International Law.' <http://www.hrw.org/ hrw/reports/1999/nigeria/Nigew991-11.htm>.

Ikein, A.A. (1990), *The Impact of Oil on a Developing Country: The Case of Nigeria*. New York: Praeger.

Institute for the Promotion of Unity and Understanding. (no date), *Ogoni: Facts of the Matter*. Gwagwalada: IPUU.

Kirk-Greene, A. and Rimmer, D. (1981), *Nigeria Since 1970: A Political and Economic Outline*. London: Hodder and Stoughton.

Leton, G.B. (1992), 'Statement' in MOSOP, 'Ogoni Bill of Rights', <http://www. mosopcanada.org/info/mosop0370.html>. (This is the electronic version of the original document published in Port Harcourt in 1992.)

Mitee, L (President of MOSOP). (2001), Personal interview with Phia Steyn. Port Harcourt. 22 June.

MOSOP Canada. (No date), 'The Story of Shell and their Involvement in Ogoni.' <http://www.mosopcanada.org/shell.html>.

Orage, L.S. (No date), 'Justice Prevailed: The Case of the Republic of Nigeria vs Kenule B. Saro-Wiwa, *et al*,' (Information provided by the Nigerian High Commission in Pretoria, South Africa).

'Ogoni Bill of Rights' (Information provided by the Nigerian High Commission in Pretoria, South Africa). (1990).

Osaghae, E.E. (1995), 'The Ogoni Uprising: Oil Politics, Minority Agitation and the Future of the Nigerian State.' *African Affairs* 94, pp. 325-344.

Panter-Brick, K. (ed.). (1978), *Soldiers and Oil: The Political Transformation of Nigeria*. London: Frank Cass.

Pypke, D. (1996), 'Partners in Crime?' *World Press Review* 43 (16 Jan), p. 16.

Rowell, A. (1994), 'Shell-Shocked: References' (footnote 25). <http://www. greenpeace.org/~comms/ken/refer.html#5>5</a> (Jul).

Royal Dutch/Shell. (no date), *Climate Change: What does Shell Think and Do About it?* London: Shell International.

Royal Dutch/Shell. (1997), *Statement of General Business Principles*. London: Shell International.

Sampson, A. (1988), *The Seven Sisters: The Great Oil Companies and the World they Made*. London: Coronet Books.

Saro-Wiwa, K. (1992), *Genocide in Nigeria: The Ogoni Tragedy*. Port Harcourt: Saros.

Saro-Wiwa, K. (1995), *A Month and a Day: A Detention Diary*. London: Penguin Books.

Sharpe Paine, L. (1999), 'Royal Dutch/Shell in Transition (B).' Harvard Business School Publication no N9-300-040 (25 Oct). Boston: Harvard Business School.

Shell Nigeria. (1996a), 'The Environment.' <http://www.shellnigeria.com/factfile/ environ.html#delta>.

Shell Nigeria. (1996b), 'Shell Nigeria offers plan for Ogoni.' <http://www.shellnigeria. com/news/ prlis.html> (8 May).

Shell Nigeria. (no date), 'Shell in Nigeria: Factfile Summary.' <http://www.shellnigeria. com/factfile/ facsum.html>.

Shell Nigeria. (2001), *Report of the Stakeholder Review of SPDC Community Development Projects Completed in the Year 2000*. Lagos: SPDC.

Stanislaw, J. (1991), *The New World Oil Order: Strategies for the 1990s*. Cambridge, Mass: Cambridge Energy Research Associates.

Sygne, R. (1993), *Nigeria: The Way Forward*. London: Euromoney Books.

Sykes, R. (Group Environmental Advisor for Shell International) (2001), Personal interview with Phia Steyn. London. 15 September.

The New York Times (*Late New York Edition*) (1995a), 28 March, p. A12.

The New York Time (*Late New York Edition*) (1995b), 3 December, p. 14.

Tims, W. (1974), *Nigeria: Options for Long-Term Development*. Baltimore: Johns Hopkins University Press.

The Star (South Africa) (1995), 22 November, p. 21.

Weekly Mail & Guardian (South Africa) (1995), 13-19 January, p. 14.

Weekly Trust (Nigeria) (2001), 16-22 February, p. 17.

Yergin, D. (1992), *The Prize: The Epic Quest for Oil, Money and Power*. New York: Simon & Schuster.

Chapter 12

Whither African Environment and Development?

William G. Moseley

Introduction[1]

This volume is essentially about the connections between African rural livelihoods and emerging environmental narratives, regional political economies, and environmental programs. As the case studies in the book suggest, global and local actors have spawned a complex array of environment and development programs and policies in Africa over the past two decades, including community based wildlife management, fire suppression, decentralization, community based natural resources management, transnational parks, and ecotourism. Driving these programs and policies at the international level are powerful discourses regarding sustainable development, poverty-induced environmental degradation, desertification, deforestation and NGO efficaciousness. Regional political economy also has a strong influence on local resource management strategies, including regional conflict, the economic and political interests of states, corporate interests and, in some instances, emerging economic opportunities. Local actors react to, interpret and engage these discourses and political economic conditions to produce the contemporary African landscape of environment and development initiatives. This chapter reviews conclusions related to the book's major themes and then attempts to distill future policy and program directions that emanate from the volume's case studies. The book's major themes include (i) the influence of certain global environmental narratives on African environmental policy and practice; (ii) the interplay between regional political economy and rural livelihoods; and (iii) environmental management as a result of global environmental politics and local agency.

Rhetoric(al) Questions: Environmental Narratives and African Realities

The connection between global environmental narratives and African environmental policy and practice has been a strong element of political ecology research in Africa since the mid-1990s and a central theme of this book. While significant work has been done on deforestation, desertification and range management for example, this volume interrogates a new set of orthodoxies (sustainable development, poverty-induced environmental degradation and anti-burning thinking) that, like the aforementioned, also appear to have stronger moorings in global political economy than African empirical realities. The studies by Logan, Moseley and Laris not only add to the growing list of environmental paradigms whose application in Africa must be viewed with skepticism, but they further enrich the debate about narrative formation, persistence and influence.

Narrative Formation

Logan's critique of the meta-narrative of sustainable development clearly shows how this concept, the progenitor of the modern field of environment and development, has been enveloped by the global neo-liberal agenda. Ironically, the creation and proliferation of the sustainable development concept was, in part, facilitated by pressure from the developing world (as witnessed at the 1992 Rio Earth Summit) to give equal or greater consideration to development in environment-development programming. However, in conceptually reconciling environment and development as facilitating rather than competing objectives, the dominant, Northern donor-backed, version of sustainable development privileges a narrowly conceived vision of development (as laissez-faire economic growth) that many African national governments find problematic. Furthermore, the empirical reality in Africa suggests that development defined as laissez-faire economic growth, contrary to the rhetoric, is largely incompatible with environmental sustainability.

Narrative Persistence and Influence

Moseley's work on poverty induced environmental degradation illuminates the role of national level elites (in conjunction with donors and international capital) in promoting environmental narratives that further their own political economic interests. In other words, environment-development narratives not only circulate amongst policymakers because they make intuitive sense at an abstract and un-interrogated level, but because they support the status quo. In the case of Mali, this means a continued expansion of cotton production that allows the government to pay its employees and meet its debt obligations. Furthermore, the narrative of poverty induced environmental degradation may have gained wide spread appeal at the international level because it is consistent with a body of neo-classical economic theory (the major theoretical framework of the multilateral lending institutions) regarding the time preference behavior of the poor. Unraveling the grass roots level reality in Mali entails a recognition of significant wealth differences between households at the village level, the connections between this wealth and cotton production, and the tendency of wealthy cotton farmers to inflict as much or more environmental damage than their less affluent neighbors.

Laris' study makes an important contribution to environment-development scholarship by describing how environmental narratives may have little ground level impact if those implementing policy have limited operational reach. In this particular case, the Malian Forestry Service had long sought to implement an anti-burning policy (inspired by widely held beliefs within the agency regarding desertification and environmental degradation) but was largely ineffectual until the 1980s when they received increased support from international donors in aftermath of the Sahelian drought. Here, support from donors and a fining system that fed into the agency's annual budget, provided a set of perverse incentives to increasingly ruthless field agents that drove ecologically legitimate burning underground and poisoned relations between communities and the forest service.

The volume's case studies suggest that the most influential and durable narratives are those that are supported by institutional power, are in harmony with the interests of power brokers at multiple scales, and are consistent with broader disciplinary systems of knowledge. Narratives that meet all three of the aforementioned requirements either are left untested (i.e., no one bothers to test their veracity) or persist in face of contrary empirical evidence that is labeled exceptional, outlying or particularistic.

In conclusion, these findings build on Leach and Mearns' (1996, p.6) 'theorizing [of] received wisdom in development policy' in many ways. First, they show how local level policy makers and development agents (as opposed to outside consultants, donors and supra-national policy makers) opportunistically deploy environmental narratives. Second, they suggest that time preference theory be added to the existing list of problematic scientific paradigms (for example, climax vegetation theory, tragedy of the commons) that buttress environmental orthodoxies in Africa. Third, they demonstrate that successful narratives not only attract institutional support, but in the process of being promoted by large institutions, may actually be transformed to become conceptually more consistent with the ideological orientation of the organization in question (the case of sustainable development and many of its donor proponents). Finally, they show how environmental narratives may have little to no grass roots level impact in some instances if implementing agencies have limited operational reach.

Embedded Realities: Political Economy, Rural Livelihoods and the Environment

The volume's second section explores the interplay between regional political economy and rural livelihoods. It examines a timely set of regional phenomena that represent an interesting cross section of broader scale issues impacting local African livelihoods today. These issues, including war, interactions with the global agro-industrial complex, decentralization, and emerging regional markets, have influenced local livelihoods in profound ways.

Embedding African Livelihoods in a Multi-Scaler Reality

Understanding the impact on local livelihoods of political economic processes operating at multiple scales was a key thematic thrust of this section. The notion of isolated, subsistence-based African livelihood systems is now largely a myth or an anachronism. The case studies in this section explored the local level influence of power dynamics operating at global, regional, national, sub-national and local scales.

The South African border wars described by Kreike are perhaps the most extreme example of regional and national political economy ravaging local livelihoods. As Kreike noted 'population dislocations and the terror of war turned cultural landscapes of farms and villages into deserted bush-encroached "wilderness"…[that]…not only caused a regional crisis in food security in the 1980s, but also severely handicaps post-war agro-ecological recovery.' While conflict clearly disrupts livelihoods in the short term, Kreike very interestingly elaborates on the longer term, repercussions for a working landscape that is depopulated by civil conflict. Given that civil war has erupted in several areas of the continent over the past ten years (for example, Sierra Leone, Liberia, Côte d'Ivoire, Sudan, Somalia, Congo-Kinshasa and Rwanda), the environment-development dimensions of these conflicts are likely to receive increasing attention.

Although Bingen's case study dealt with cotton production in Africa, the real focus was an investigation of the links between farm level pesticide use, national policies, organized science and the global pesticide industry leading to a problem known as the pesticide treadmill. In shedding light on the vertically integrated systems of cotton production in West and Central Africa that encourage (if not require) farmers to overuse pesticides (leading to pesticide resistance among cotton pests and the poisoning of wildlife), Bingen suggests that a fundamental problem is that decision-making power has been taken away from the local level.

An important exception to the notion that political economy (largely at the sub-national scale in this instance) is generally detrimental to local livelihoods is Wooten's discussion of Malian market gardeners (perhaps the clearest example of a success story in this volume). Here local people effectively exploit regional political economy to their benefit. While the economic success of this engagement is documented clearly by Wooten, the environmental impacts, if any, of this new activity are left unexplored. This raises the possibility that livelihood strategies could flourish over one time span, and be less successful over a longer period. For example, gardeners' use of pesticides (which Wooten mentions) could conceivably create problems which affect the longer term viability of the livelihood system.[2] Nonetheless, these market gardeners (arguably) appear to be more successful than their compatriots who farm cotton as a cash crop (as discussed by Moseley and Bingen).

The case that Wooten presents is somewhat exceptional in the literature because, as opposed to the usual story of problematic engagement with the market, local people are relatively successful at exploiting the regional political economy.

A key distinction, however, is that these gardeners are exploiting a relatively local change in political economy, the growth of the Bamako fruit and vegetable market (a market with fewer connections to the global economy). Competition among retailers and wholesalers in this market is more intense than many international markets because it is composed of a variety of actors operating at the local and regional scales. This contrasts with many international commodity markets wherein the African producer only has one potential buyer for his or her crop and has limited information about producer prices offered in others areas (although information exchange amongst cotton producer unions, for example, is beginning to change this situation). The high number of traders and more manageable scale of the Bamako fruit and vegetable market allows local people to engage it with a relatively high level of information and the freedom to choose between input suppliers and produce buyers (although market gardeners still complain of being exploited by market women from Bamako).

De Bruijn and van Djik examine the impacts on Fulbe pastoralists' livelihoods in central Mali of changes in regional political economy, national level policy and local power struggles. Their analysis covers a much longer time span than that of the other authors in this volume. Their central point is that 'ecological risks are highly politicized phenomena.' They chart how pastoralists became increasingly marginalized over the 20th century, with their risk position becoming worse than that of their former slaves, *riimaybe* cultivators. The current policy of decentralization in Mali further exacerbates the declining risk position of pastoralists.

Tensions Between National Economies and Local Livelihoods

Related to the interaction between different scales of political-economic influence is the recurring issue of tension between national and local economic interests. This cross cutting issue not only emerges from the case studies in this section, but several others in the book. The chapters reveal these tensions, for example, in the cotton, oil and wildlife industries in Africa. In all three instances, national governments have colluded with international capital to exploit local resources: oil in Ogoniland, soil resources in African cotton growing regions, and wildlife habitat in East and southern Africa. In many cases, it appears that local livelihoods are subordinate to national development objectives. A quote in Steyn's study by a Nigerian official aptly captured central government sentiments in this regard. '[I]n progress, something just have to give...There are hundreds of oil communities scattered throughout the delta region. It is not that they are suffering in silence. Rather, their leaders are prepared to accept the fact that there is a price to be paid for all modern development.' A similar perspective was expressed by a Malian official in Moseley's chapter: '...the national interest must override the local. "Mali cannot feed itself . . . The Priority is development. One cannot stop development, even to save the country's heritage."'

The tension between the national and the local levels often exists, in part, because of differences in how community members and outsiders conceptualize and exploit natural resources. Locals typically engage with the environment in support of their own livelihoods (for example, use of wildlife as a source of food). In contrast, national governments generally exploit natural resources to the benefit of national or global economies (for example, use of wildlife for nature tourism and sport hunting). In some instances, local and extra-local uses of the environment may be incompatible. This incompatibility is enhanced when neither side benefits from the other's use of the resource. Local uses of a resource may generate little to no tax revenue for the national government. External exploitation of the environment may involve limited revenue sharing or, worse yet, be exclusionary.

Why do African governments often side with, or allow themselves to co-opted by, international capital in their exploitation of local resources when local development should, seemingly, be a priority of the state? This may have something to do with a lack of diversified economies in many African countries, and therefore a lack of a broad base of economic activities that may be taxed to support government activity. Under such circumstances, governments may collude with international capital to increase their share of the returns from a particular industry and become overly dependent on a small number of export sectors. For example, oil was 90 per cent of government revenues in Nigeria, cotton approximately 50 per cent of government revenues in Mali, and wildlife tourism the leading source of foreign exchange for Kenya. In such situations, national governments become extremely reluctant to undertake measures that may compromise revenue streams, regardless of the ecological or social consequences.

Not only do national and international actors seek to exploit natural resources differently from locals, they often have a relative monopoly on factors (knowledge, contacts, technology) that allow them to connect successfully with the international market for a particular good. For example, the Kenyan Government and tourism operators are able to cater to affluent tourists because they have the contacts and infrastructure that local people do not possess.

A vexing question is how to resolve the tensions between local and national economic interests. It must admitted that those at the national and global levels wouldn't really care about resolving these tensions if it were not for the fact that local people have not fully cooperated with the attempts of broader scale (i.e., national, regional and global scale) political and economic interests to exploit local level resources. Local people encroach on national parks, shoot marauding wildlife, protest against pollution from oil exploitation, or go on strike when revenues from cotton production are too low. Local people have been able to garner the support of international environmental organizations in some instances (for example, Ogoniland). In other situations, they have received mixed support or outright opposition (for example, many environmental organizations oppose local encroachment on national parks).

In conclusion, a muliti-scaler understanding of contemporary rural African livelihoods is essential if we are to have a comprehensive understanding of local level realities. This conclusion essentially reinforces a fundamental tenet of regional political ecology (and a key reason for the development of the regional political ecology approach in the early 1980s).[3] The tension between national political economies and rural livelihoods is interesting because it resembles a phenomenon in the early post-colonial period wherein many African governments extracted resources from their hinterlands to subsidize urban and industrial development (Gillis *et al.*, 1987). While the tension between the local and national levels over rural resource control continues in the present, very often we now find that national governments are simply resource expropriation conduits for global capital (a much older and tenacious process on the African continent (Amin, 1977)).

Programmatic Outcomes: Global Environmental Politics and Conservation in Africa

The volume's third section examines the links between African environmental management, global environmental politics and local agency. The studies in this section suggest that rural Africa's ability to acquire support from international environmental organizations is mixed. Local communities ability to garner support is influenced by environmental narratives which they may or may not be able to manipulate in their favor.

According to Coffman, global environmental politics and narratives tend to be problematic for rural communities in Kenya. She notes that 7.6 per cent of Kenya's land was gazetted into 54 parks and reserves by the late 1980s, and that tourism revenue account for over a third of foreign exchange earnings. The importance of wildlife tourism to the economy led then Kenyan President Moi to appoint Richard Leakey, a firm believer in the park-based approach, as head of the Kenya Wildlife Service for two tenures in the 1990s. Moi deftly employed the connections of Richard Leakey to bolster international support for wildlife preservation and polish the image of the Kenyan ecotourism industry, a multi-million dollar enterprise and Kenya's largest source of foreign exchange. While recognizing the needs of local people, Leakey's policies often compromised local livelihoods. Coffman's conclusions are consistent with the findings of Laris, earlier in this volume, who describes how the administration of Moussa Traore in Mali tapped into the international discourse on desertification in the 1980s to support its campaign to fight fire (lucrative in terms of international dollars and fines collected from rural communities). The campaign to fight fire not only led to the indiscriminate fining of rural communities, but adversely affected savanna ecology and led to the decay of indigenous knowledge and institutions of traditional hunters that internally policed local burning practices.

Broader scale political and economic interests respond to the local level with initiatives like community-based natural resources management (CBNRM). While the rise of CBNRM may, in part, be related to a genuine concern to improve the welfare of local people, it also exists because local people are interfering with the old park model. In other words, this approach reflects a process of negotiation that is occurring between different scales of economic interest. In the cases examined in this volume, national governments have an interest in controlling wildlife and associated habitats for the global market, only giving back to community as much as is necessary to make the system work. While CBNRM may be more genuine in Namibia, we also get superficial attempts at applying the approach. According to DeMotts, South Africa still has a park-based approach in which 'peripheral roles for local residents are being grafted onto existing parks in a way that does not fundamentally alter control of wildlife or natural resources.' Furthermore, a history of regional wars has often left local residents highly suspicious of South African led transborder conservation initiatives. For example, former residents in an area slated to be a national park near the South African border in Mozambique feel that transborder conservation initiatives are being used to encroach on land that they were forced to abandon during the war years.

Of course it is not entirely new to assert that there has been a problematic history in Africa associated with the actions of international environmental organizations (for example, Schroeder, 1997; Neumann, 2000). Previous studies, and many of the cases in this book, may lead to the conclusion that environmental organizations and discourses are categorically bad for rural livelihoods in Africa. An interesting contradiction to this generalization is the case of Shell Oil in Ogoniland outlined by Steyn. Here the people of Ogoniland are able to garner the support of the international environmental movement in their fight against the government of Nigeria and Shell Nigeria. Furthermore, Ogoni connections with international environmental organizations, and more a general concern among First World consumers for the environment, has led Shell International to reform its practices in Nigeria (at least superficially).

In conclusion, rural communities are not entirely powerless in the face of global environmental concerns as they, at least in theory, have the ability to engage and employ related discurses in their favor. An important element of the Ogoni struggle was the charismatic leader, Ken Saro-wiwa, who played a key role in attracting international support for the cause. Saro-wiwa's role in the Ogoni struggle is somewhat analogous to the role played by Chico Mendes for rubber tappers in Brazil (Mendes garnered the support of international environmental organizations for rubber tappers in their struggle against ranching interests) (Revkin, 1990). Perhaps the lesson here is that local people may leverage global environmental narratives to their advantage if they can portray themselves as environmental 'good guys' and have the *savoir-faire* to relate to international environmental organizations and the media. Such barriers are difficult to overcome as: 1) poor, disenfranchised people may not always have an international public relations expert at their disposal; and 2) local people often encounter environmental discourses that are biased against them (such as notions that the poor are environmental degraders or that local people are a threat to wildlife).

The Way Forward: Whither African Environment and Development?

The case studies in this book lead us to the conclusion that local people in Africa must play a key role in securing their livelihoods and meeting resource challenges. This is not a surprising inference and it is a position long advocated by cultural ecologists, ecological anthropologist, environmental historians and indigenous knowledge advocates, among others. The book's case studies further suggest, however, that local input often is not enough, that policies and programs are needed to facilitate this input, and counter-balance other knowledge and power structures, at multiple scales. This second conclusion is derived in large part by use of political ecology as a framework of analysis. While the political ecology framework, with its emphasis on multi-scaler analysis of the connections between local resource systems and internal and external power dynamics, is useful for highlighting problems, it is less suggestive about future directions. To this end, ideas and approaches for future directions that emanate from the authors in this volume are discussed in the following, concluding paragraphs..

Logan suggests that environmental security (ES) might be one solution to the resource-based tensions that exist between the global, national and local levels. ES may be thought of as (a) an evaluative instrument and (b) an approach to avoid resource conflict. Logan quite deliberately chose to emphasize the forward looking, conflict avoidance aspect of the environmental security framework. According to Logan , 'ES may be seen as a framework for improving resource availability at several geographic scales (local, national, regional) and at establishing legal and institutional frameworks for resource adjudication and conflict prevention/resolution at several political levels.' As an approach to resource conflict avoidance, environmental security holds a certain amount in common with CBNRM, *gestion de terroir* and, more generally, decentralization, because all seek to have local resources managed by local level institutions. The difference is that ES entails addressing resource tension at multiple scales (rather than solely at the local scale) and hence is more consistent with political ecology analysis that examines local resource degradation problems in the broader political economy context. ES is therefore a potential solution, or framework, for addressing the very problems we have been discussing and seems particularly appropriate given its attention to scale.

As an evaluative instrument (rather than a framework for improving resource availability), it must be acknowledged that ES has been employed by some commentators and scholars to produce Malthusian leaning analyses (for example, Kaplan, 1994, Homer-Dixon, 1995) linking population growth, to resource scarcity, to conflict. This contrasts with work by Logan (1999) or the Southern African Regional Institute for Policy Studies (SARIPS, 2002) that attributes resource scarcity to power distribution rather than population growth.

One nagging question when applying ES as a forward looking solution is whether the inherent power inequities between local, national and global levels will unduly influence the process of negotiated distribution. On the agricultural front, Bingen's notion of farmer field schools might creatively be combined with the ES framework to promote empowerment at the local level and challenge broader knowledge systems and western science. According to Bingen, the farmer field school approach entails 'a process through which farmers do not learn specific messages, but understand a process of learning that can be applied continuously to their changing situations . . . that farmers learn best among and from themselves . . . [and that] . . . the school experience is seen as the starting point for empowerment and local institution building.' Bingen's emphasis on recognizing the potential value of indigenous knowledge is reflected in several other studies in this volume (especially Laris, Wooten and Moseley).

ES might also be combined creatively with the notion sustainable livelihoods, a concept that connotes both the short and long term, social and ecological viability of local level, economic activities. Chambers and Conway (1992, p.7) have defined a sustainable livelihood as one 'which can cope with and recover from stress and shocks, maintain or enhance its capabilities and assets, and ... provide opportunities for the next generation.' Sneddon (2000) notes that sustainability cast at the scale of the livelihood, or household, is less convoluted than the sustainable development discourse directed at the national level. Sneddon's assessment is consistent with our own critical analysis of the sustainable development approach in Africa as well as this volume's attention to livelihoods.

In sum, the case studies in this volume underscore the value of local agro-ecological understanding in an increasingly interconnected, multi-scaler world in which local people and outsiders may not conceptualize and use natural resources in the same manner. Political economic power is used by groups operating at multiple scales (local, national, international) to dominate the discourse regarding the environment and ensure that their resource needs are given priority. While the notion of sustainable development has been subsumed by the dominate neo-liberal agenda, and thereby discredited, the long term viability of rural African livelihoods is still incumbent upon a notion of sustainability that is in tune with the environment and the needs of local people. This will only happen when rural Africans themselves are empowered and given voice at the local level as well as at other scales in the global decision making hierarchy.. If and when local people, or their representatives, are given an equal seat at the negotiation table at other levels (provincial, national, regional, international), we will begin to see a change in the discourse regarding African environment and development. This does not mean that the local will always dominate the national or international, but it may occasionally ensure more equitable decision making.

Notes

1   The author wishes to thank B. Ikubolajeh Logan and one anonymous reviewer for feedback on this chapter.
2   While Wooten's case looks promising as a success story, it remains to be seen whether this engagement with regional political economy is environmentally sustainable. Other potential cases of rural African livelihoods successfully engaging regional political

economy (yet where the environmental dimension of this economic success is under-explored) include cotton farmers in northern Côte d'Ivoire (for example, Bassett, 2001) and maize farmers in Zimbabwe (for example, see discussion of this case in Obia, 1997).

3   Political ecology grew out of cultural ecology and radical development studies in the 1980s (Bryant and Bailey, 1997; Stott and Sullivan, 2000; Watts, 2000). While cultural ecology is renown for the study of human-environment interactions at the local level, some scholars became disenchanted with the traditional form of this approach that did not adequately consider the local level impact of, and interaction with, political and economic processes operating outside the area of study (for example, Watts, 1983; Blaikie, 1985). I deliberately refer to the more traditional cultural ecology approach in this instance because some self-described cultural ecologists increasingly take account of non-local political economic factors in their analysis.

References

Amin, S. (1977), *Capitalism and Unequal Development*. New York: Monthly Review Press.

Bassett, T.J. (2001), *The Peasant Cotton Revolution in West Africa. Côte d'Ivoire, 1880-1995*. London: Cambridge University Press.

Blaikie, P.M. (1985), *The Political Economy of Soil Erosion in Developing Countries*. London: Longman.

Bryant, R.L. and S. Bailey. (1997), *Third World Political Ecology*. New York: Routledge.

Chambers, R. and G.R. Conway. (1992), 'Sustainable Rural Livelihoods: Practical Concepts for the 21st Century.' *Institute of Development Studies Discussion Paper 296*. London: Institute of Development Studies.

Gillis, M., D.H. Perkins, M. Roemer and D.R. Snodgrass. (1987), *Economics of Development*. New York: W.W. Norton & Company.

Homer-Dixon, T. (1995), 'The Ingenuity Gap: Can Poor Countries Adapt to Resource Scarcity?= *Population and Development Review* 21 (3), September, pp. 587-612.

Kaplan, R. (1994), 'The Coming Anarchy: How Scarcity, Crime, Overpopulation, Tribalism, and Disease are Rapidly Destroying the Social Fabric of our Planet.' *The Atlantic Monthly*. 273(2), pp. 44-65..

Leach, M. and R. Mearns. (1996), Environmental Change and Policy: Challenging Received Wisdom in Africa. In In Leach, M. and R. Mearns (eds.). *The Lie of the Land*. Oxford: James Curry.

Logan, B.I. (1999), 'Environmental Security, Sustainable Development and Resource Management in Africa: Some Conceptual Considerations.' Paper presented at the *Methodology Workshop, Southern African Political Economy Series Trust*, Harare, Zimbabwe, July.

Neumann, R. (2000), 'Primitive Ideas: Protected Area Buffer Zones and the Politics of Land in Africa.' In: Broch-Due,V. and Schroeder, R. (eds.) *Producing Poverty and Nature in Africa*. Stockholm: Nordiska Afrikainstitutet.

Obia, G.C. (1997), 'Agircultural Development in Sub-Saharan Africa.' In: Aryeetey-Attoh, S. (ed.) *Geography of Sub-Saharan Africa*. Upper Saddle River, New Jersey: Prentice Hall.

Revkin, A. (1990), *The Burning Season*. Boston: Houghton Mifflin.

SARIPS. (2002), 'The Southern African Regional Institute for Policy Studies Annual Workshop Proceedings.' Harare, Zimbabwe: SARIPS.

Schroeder, R. (1997), 'Reclaiming Land in the Gambia: Gendered Property Rights and Environmental Intervention.' *Annals of the Association of American Geographers.* 87(3), pp. 487-508.

Sneddon, C. (2000), ' "Sustainability" in ecological economics, ecology and livelihoods: a review.' *Progress in Human Geography* 24(4), pp. 521-549.

Stott, P. and S. Sullivan. (2000), *Political Ecology: Science, Myth and Power.* London: Arnold.

Watts, M. (1983), *Silent Violence: Food, Famine and Peasantry in Northern Nigeria.* Berkeley: University of California Press.

Watts, M. (2000), 'Political Ecology.' In *The Dictionary of Human Geography, 4th Edition.* Malden, MA: Blackwell Publishers Ltd., pp. 590-592.

Index